COLONISTS IN BONDAGE

Colonists in Bondage

WHITE SERVITUDE

AND CONVICT LABOR IN AMERICA

1607-1776

By

Abbot Emerson Smith

The Norton Library

W · W · NORTON & COMPANY · INC ·
NEW YORK

First published in the Norton Library 1971
by arrangement with The University of North Carolina Press

Books That Live
The Norton imprint on a book means that in the publisher's
estimation it is a book not for a single season but for the years.
W. W. Norton & Company, Inc.

PUBLISHED SIMULTANEOUSLY IN
CANADA BY GEORGE J. MCLEOD LIMITED, TORONTO

SBN   393   00592   5

PRINTED IN THE UNITED STATES OF AMERICA

1 2 3 4 5 6 7 8 9 0

PREFACE

I T IS more than five years since this book was completed, and nearly four years since the author entered the armed forces. A visit home on leave has given opportunity to review but not to revise the manuscript, and to hand it over for publication to Dr. Carl Bridenbaugh and Dr. Lester J. Cappon of the Institute of Early American History and Culture. Their undertaking to see it through the press while the author returns to overseas duty is acknowledged with the utmost gratitude.

Three grants of funds have aided in the researches which went into the preparation of this book. Work was begun at Oxford University in 1930 during the last year of a Rhodes Scholarship, and continued during the following year with the assistance of a Beit Senior Research Scholarship, which made possible a journey to the British West Indies. The resulting thesis was accepted for the degree of Doctor of Philosophy at Oxford. In 1939 a grant from the Social Science Research Council gave opportunity to finish work in England on eighteenth-century aspects of the subject.

The appearance of Dr. Richard B. Morris's *Government and Labor in Early America,* with its valuable and painstaking use of evidences from colonial court records, was of course much too late to permit its consultation in the preparation of this work. Dr. Morris provides an ampler survey of the legal basis of indentured servitude, which is outlined in the last chapters of this book, but a reading of his work does not indicate a necessity of revising the conclusions independently arrived at here. One point, however, is perhaps worth mention: in discussing "servants" in the New England colonies Dr. Morris is able quite properly to use a great deal of evidence without the necessity of distinguishing always between that which refers to indentured and that which refers to free servants. Such a distinction was necessary for this book, and was very difficult to make. The conclusion was reached, I hope not mistakenly, that most of the "servants" mentioned in New England records were free, and it followed that they did not come within the scope of this investigation.

Among the many scholars, librarians, and archivists who have helped in the preparation of this study I should like to make more special acknowledgment of my debt to Professor V. T. Harlow, now of the University of London, who first suggested the subject to me; to Professor V. H. Galbraith, of Oxford University; and to Professor S. E. Morison of Harvard University. The manuscript was read by the late Professor Charles M. Andrews shortly before his death; it must be one of the last of the multitude of historical projects to which he gave so generously of his advice and sympathy.

A. E. S.

CONTENTS

CONTENTS

PART III

THE SERVANT IN THE PLANTATIONS

PART ONE

The Trade In Servants

CHAPTER I

INDENTURED SERVANTS
AND REDEMPTIONERS

THIS BOOK is about those white people who went to the
British colonies in North America and who, because they
were unwilling or unable to pay the cost of their own passage,
became bond servants for a period of years to some colonial
master who paid it for them. They were variously known as
indentured servants, redemptioners, or, in order to distinguish
them from the Negroes, as Christian or white servants. Many
of them were convicts from the jails, transported instead of
being hanged; a few were political and military prisoners taken
in war or rebellion. There were rogues, vagabonds, whores,
cheats, and rabble of all descriptions, raked from the gutter and
kicked out of the country. There were unfortunate French,
German, and Swiss Protestants fleeing from religious persecution, starving and unhappy Irish, rack-rented Scottish farmers,
poverty-stricken German peasants and artisans, brash adventurers of all sorts. People of every age and kind were decoyed,
deceived, seduced, inveigled, or forcibly kidnapped and carried
as servants to the plantations. There were many ordinary individuals of decent substance, and a few even who were entitled
by the custom of the time to be called gentlemen.

More than half of all persons who came to the colonies

south of New England were servants. The Puritan communities, scanty in their agriculture, chary of favors, hostile to newcomers as they were, received few. Farther south, on the contrary, they were hailed with delight by planters and farmers who wanted cheap labor, by speculators who needed more settlers to validate their grants of land, by colonial proprietors who wished to build up the population. It was universally agreed, said a committee of the Council of Foreign Plantations about 1664, that people were the foundation for the improvement of all Plantations, "and that people are encreased principally by sending of Servants."[1] In they poured, the good, bad, and indifferent together. They formed the principal labor supply of the earlier settlements. Not until the eighteenth century were they superseded in this respect by Negroes, and not until the nineteenth did an influx of free white workers wholly remove the need for indentured labor. In the West Indies, though their value as workers declined more rapidly before the competition of Negroes than it did in the continental colonies, they yet continued in demand simply as white men, to bolster up the inadequate numbers of the militia and give some feeling of security against the blacks. Seldom did the supply of good white servants equal the demand.

From the complex pattern of forces producing emigration to the American colonies one stands out clearly as most powerful in causing the movement of servants. This was the pecuniary profit to be made by shipping them. Labor was one of the few European importations which even the earliest colonists would sacrifice much to procure, and the system of indentured servitude was the most convenient system next to slavery by which labor became a commodity to be bought and sold. It was profitable for English merchants trading to the colonies to load their outgoing ships with a cargo of servants, for the labor of these servants could be transferred to colonial planters at a price well above the cost of transporting them. It was profitable to the colonial planter to buy them, for he could rise from mere subsistence to prosperity only by commanding the labor of others beside himself. Hence there was a constantly active stimulant to the emigration of servants, a powerful and resourceful group of merchants and shippers always ready to accept the services of volunteers for the new world, and, what was more important, to bring pressure to bear on doubtful candidates, to advertise the attractions of life in America, and even as a last resort to collect a shipload of labor by forceful means.

It is, of course, not intended to imply that the profitable nature of the trade in servants was the only cause for their going to the colonies. The peopling of the new settlements was a complex phenomenon and the activating forces behind it must be sought also in the expansive spirit of the age, in the economic and social maladjustments in Europe, and in the various obscure motivations of individual personalities. Everyone knows that America was a haven for the godly, a refuge for the oppressed, a challenge to the adventurous. Nor should the fact be forgotten, particularly when dealing with indentured servants, that it was also the last resort of scoundrels. A great many servants went to the colonies simply because, for one reason or another, they wanted to get out of their own country. Even so, they would not have had the opportunity to leave if the peculiar institution of indentured labor had not made it worth the while of shippers to take them.

The English government was well content that the handling of emigration should be in the hands of private business men. It liked to see the establishment and peopling of colonies go slowly forward without requiring from the state either financial commitments or moral responsibility. The government might indeed have taken charge of the migration of poor persons, and have worked out a system of getting them to the colonies which would have been less painful than that which the merchants contrived. Many schemes were drawn up and submitted with this end in view, but nearly all of them were ignored or turned down, and the state transported very few settlers. Even the convicts were handed over to private individuals. They shipped them to Maryland and Virginia and sold them at an excellent profit to the same planters who denounced the English government for allowing them to come at all. In one case, that of Georgia, the proprietors of the venture were liberally assisted with governmental subsidies; in two other instances, those of the Palatine Germans in 1709 and of Halifax in 1749, the government itself directly carried out both transportation and settlement. All three of these state enterprises were justified on the grounds of military and political strategy.

The fact was that although the best political and economic opinion viewed the expansion of empire in general with satisfaction, it was not so certain that emigration was a good thing for the mother country. Mercantilists after about 1660 came to look upon the swarming masses of the poor as forming an indispensable reservoir of labor at home, which ought to be used at home and not dispersed overseas. Emigration was therefore discouraged, though never within the colonial period was it stopped. If this attitude had obtained during the earliest and most critical years of colonization there might have been great difficulty in starting any colonies at all, but when the Virginia Company was commencing its operations people were chiefly impressed with the magnitude and difficulty of the unemployment problem. Various forces had caused a dislocation of the economic life of England, and everyone was made conscious of this dislocation by the large numbers of wandering, idle, and necessitous people who infested the highways and flocked to the cities. Being unable to offer a better explanation for the situation, contemporary opinion attributed the cause to over-population and held that new colonies would provide an outlet for the surplus inhabitants of the mother country. This belief endured long enough to get the new settlements firmly established, but disappeared almost completely after the Restoration. From our present point of view the chief result of this change in opinion was that the servant trade thenceforth got a bad name for depopulating the mother country, found its operations hindered by official obstacles, and transferred much of its activity to Germany, Scotland, and Ireland. Likewise the malodorous reputation which the servant trade has attained in most historical accounts is in part undeserved, for it springs from the testimony of persons who wished to see the business suppressed, and were not averse to arousing public opinion by accusations of kidnapping and other nefarious practices.

Concerning the servants themselves, as individuals in the new world, we do not read very much. Colonial society was not democratic and certainly not equalitarian; it was dominated by men who had money enough to make others work for them. Few of these men were descended from indentured servants, and practically none had themselves been of that class. In studying the servants we drop below the level of distinguished individuals to the undifferentiated body of the people: obscure shopkeepers, field laborers, mechanics, schoolteachers, pioneer farmers in the western valleys. These were the best, but there were many more: men and women who were dirty and lazy, rough, ignorant, lewd, and often criminal. They thieved and wandered, had bastard children, and corrupted society with loathsome diseases. There were still more whose role was most humble of all; they came to America, remained a few days or weeks, and then died of the familiar colonial fever. It would be presumptuous to say that even these contributed nothing, for the process of selection was capricious, and many had to emigrate in order that a portion might survive. This was the cruel system by which the colonies were peopled.

It was under the auspices of the Virginia Company that the customs and habits of indentured servitude were established essentially in the forms which became so familiar to later colonial history. That a man should become a bondservant by legal contract was not strange, for the ancient institution of apprenticeship was well known to all. Its application to colonial requirements had been suggested at least as early as 1582 by Sir George Peckham, who wrote that many people would be glad to go to the settlements and serve for a year for food and clothing only, in the hope that they might "thereby amend their estates."[2] The Virginia Company experimented with various forms of contract embodying different terms of agreement, and found to its discomfiture that none of them worked to the profit of the company in London nor to the satisfaction of those who emigrated under them. It was necessary to set most of the colonists free from their servitude and to try a different scheme. The new plan worked no more to the profit of the company than the old one, but it happened that servants were sent to Virginia and transferred to the use of the planters resident there, who reimbursed the company for the expense of transportation. This innovation, which was not deeply meditated nor seriously considered at the time, nevertheless accustomed people to the later practice of "selling" servants. Such a transaction smacked enough of the eastern slave markets to give occasional scandal to delicate-minded observers, but it was the one characteristic of the servant trade which was both indispensable and novel. Hence its development, as well as the other trials and errors of the Virginia Company with their emigrants under bond, must be traced in some detail.

The earliest information which exists of the terms on which people could go to Virginia is contained in a broadside issued by the company in 1609, which held out many false hopes. It announced that since many noble and generous persons were going to the colony, "Therefore, for the same purpose this paper has been made public, so that it may be generally known to all workmen of whatever craft they may be, blacksmiths, carpenters, coopers, shipwrights, turners, and such as know how to plant vineyards . . . and all others, men as well as women, who have any occupation, who wish to go out in this voyage for colonizing the country with people." All such were invited to come to Sir Thomas Smith's house in Philpot Lane, where they would be enrolled, "and there will be pointed out to such persons what they will receive for this voyage, viz. five hundred 'reales' for each one, and they will be entered as Adventurers in this aforesaid voyage to Virginia, where they will have houses to live in, vegetable-gardens and orchards, and also food and clothing at the expense of the Company of that Island, and besides this, they will have a share of all the products and the profits that may result from their labor, each in proportion, and they will also secure a share in the division of the land for themselves and their heirs forever more."[3] A pamphlet published in the same year makes it plain that the division of lands and profits was to be made after seven years, and that each person going to the colony was to be allowed a share equal to that of the investors at home who had put in £12.10.0 apiece.[4]

This first scheme for the transportation of English workers

to America is obviously not one of indentured servitude, yet it contains some of the elements of the later system. No wages are to be paid; all rewards are deferred until the end of the seven-year period of labor, and meanwhile the company engages to supply food, clothing, shelter, and a passage to America. The idea of profit-sharing may have seemed generous to those ignorant of conditions in Virginia, but it is scarcely necessary to say that the scheme did not work and the rosy prospects of the broadside proved wholly illusory. Instead of orchards and vegetable gardens the colonists found wretched hardship and want. They were marched out to labor in the fields in gangs, supervised by overseers, and browbeaten by the governor. As all the products of their work went into the common store there seemed to be no reward for individual diligence, and they complained that their condition was actually one of servitude rather than of partnership, as indeed it was. Great numbers died of fever; a few returned to England despite the prohibition of such return by the company, and the tales of these things told at home made it increasingly difficult to get new recruits. When the time eventually came for a division of profits there was nothing worth dividing, and the investors were required to make a new contribution of capital, while the colonists went unrewarded.[5] The company was forced to modify its system, to relax the strictness of the communal arrangements in the settlement, and to introduce limited rights of private property.

These changes were made between 1613 and 1619, and though the precise nature of the earlier ones is difficult to discover, it is plain that tracts of three acres were allotted to some if not to all of the old settlers, for which they paid a rent to the common store of two and a half barrels of corn. By working these tracts they maintained themselves in food, and the service they owed to the company was restricted to one month in the year, while any tobacco they raised individually was traded nevertheless through the company's "magazine." Meanwhile new colonists were sent over, and the most significant development from our present point of view was that some of the partially free tenants were allowed to rent these laborers from the company and employ them as servants, becoming responsible for their maintenance and paying for them at the rate of two and a half barrels of corn apiece per year.[6] The semi-independent farmers had become as desirous of obtaining labor for their own profit as the company had been, and thus was taken a most important step towards the later customs of white servitude.

In the year 1618 new officers took control of the company, new policies were adopted, and Governor Yeardley was sent out to the colony with elaborate instructions for undertaking many reforms.[7] Old settlers were now given substantial amounts of land for their own use, some of them receiving as much as one hundred acres. Later arrivals got less, and paid an annual rent for it to the company, but the principle of individual ownership was accepted and all traces of "servitude" were abolished. New tracts of "public land" were ordered to be laid out: three thousand acres for the governor, twelve thousand for the company, and other amounts for the maintenance of a college, of ministers, and of a fund for converting the Indians to Christianity. These public lands were to be worked by tenants, most of them newly sent over, and the company now offered fresh proposals to such prospective tenants in these words:

Every man transported into Virginia, with intent there to inhabit, as Tenants to the Common land of the Company, or to the publike land, shall be freely landed there at the charge of the Company: And shal be furnished with provisions of victuall for one whole yeare next after his arrivall, as also of Cattle: And with apparell, weapons, tooles and implements, both of house and labour, for his necessary use. He shall enjoy the ratable moytie of all the profits that shall be raised of the land on which he shall be Planted, as well Corne and Cattle, as other commodities whatsoever: the other halfe being due to the Owners of the Land.

He shall be tyed by Covenant, to continue upon that Land for the Terme of seaven yeares: which being expired, it shal be in his choyse, whither to continue there or to remove to any other place, at his own will and pleasure.[8]

Thus the company, though it could not bring itself to abandon completely the idea of public lands and collective farming, nevertheless recognized that the old profit-sharing scheme of 1609 would not work again, and endeavored to tempt new emigrants with the promise that they should enjoy half of whatever they could as individuals make their own labors produce. The terms were really very generous.

Beside these tenants the company sent two other classes of emigrants. First were about two hundred poor children taken off the streets of London, for whose transportation the City raised about £500 in 1618 and 1619.[9] These young people, nearly all boys, were distributed among the free colonists as apprentices. Also, beginning in 1619, groups of young women were dispatched to make wives for the planters. The company instructed its officials in Virginia to guard these women carefully, to see that they were not married against their wishes, and to make sure that every colonist who took one remitted the company 120 pounds of tobacco as the price of her passage. To this end the administrators were asked to prevent the girls from falling in love with servants or apprentices.[10]

A year later, in the summer of 1620, the company announced its intention of sending to Virginia "one hundred servants to be disposed amongst the old *Planters,* which they greatly desire, and have offered to defray their charges with very great thankes."[11] Except for the arrangements concerning the young women, this is the first clear example we have of the characteristic transaction of the servant trade: a colonist paying a lump sum to the importer, and thereby acquiring full right and title to the services of the immigrant. Though this is the first evidence of such transactions, there is no reason to doubt that they had been common for at least a year or two before 1620.

The colonists heartily approved of the company's scheme. "Our principall wealth," wrote John Pory from Virginia in 1619, ". . . consisteth in servants," and he told how one planter with six of them had cleared a thousand pounds by one crop of tobacco.[12] The system of tenancy at halves did not work at all well, if indeed it was ever seriously tried, for when the *Bona Nova* arrived with tenants in 1619, the council in Virginia, instead of assigning them to the company and the college land, rented them out to private planters, with the justification that they would thus become acclimated and their overseers learn to know the country.[13] Perhaps the real truth was that the planters could not bear the sight of so much good labor being spent on public and charitable works, and so contrived to secure it for their own profit. Those who did find their way to the public lands were, according to George Sandys, "neither able to sustain themselves nor to discharge their moiety, and so dejected with their scarce provisions . . . that most give themselves over and die of melancholy."[14] Meanwhile the planters made fair profits while the stockholders in London derived little or nothing from their investments. In 1619 the company sent out 650 emigrants, and in 1620 five hundred, but in the autumn of 1621 the deputy of the company reported that capital was nearly exhausted and but few could be shipped that year.[15] Company-promoted emigration rapidly declined, and the dissensions of the directors of the enterprise hastened a collapse which the failure to make a profit seemed to render inevitable. In 1622 an Indian massacre nearly finished the settlement, and it is plain that if the fortunes of the colony and of the company had been identical, Virginia would have been another Roanoke.

The colony was saved because private individuals took over the activities formerly reserved for the company, and made the profits of the free planters themselves the basis of the settlement's life. We have already noted some aspects of this process as reflected in the system of land distribution, and we have seen how from a kind of collective farming project a society of independent farmers had evolved. It remains to show how private enterprise began to participate in the management of emigration from England.

As early as 1617 the company granted to certain groups of men the privilege of transporting settlers to Virginia and establishing them in semi-independent plantations generally called "hundreds." Little is known exactly about these hundreds before 1620, but the rules and regulations obtaining in them seem to have been different from those outside, and their proprietors had the privilege of trading independently of the company's magazine.[16] Their existence marks the first relaxation by the company of its monopolistic control of emigration. What conditions may generally have been offered to prospective settlers in these hundreds we do not know, but from the papers of one of them comes the first genuine servant's indenture which has survived. Four gentlemen who had been granted the right to establish what became known as Berkeley Hundred made on September 7, 1619, the following agreement with one Robert Coopy, of North Nibley in Gloucestershire:

That the said Robert doth hereby covenant faythfully to serve the said Sr Willm, Richard George and John for three years

from daye of his landinge in the land of Virginia, there to
be imployed in the lawfull and reasonable workes and labors
of them . . . and to be obedient to such governors his and their
assistants and counsell as they . . . shall from tyme to tyme
appoynt and set over him. In consideracon whereof, the said
Sr Willm Richard George and John do covenant with the said
Robert to transport him (with gods assistance) with all convenient speed into the said land of Virginia at their costs and
charges in all things, and there to maintayne him with convenient diet and apparell meet for such a servant, And in thend
of the said terme to make him a free man of the said Cuntry
theirby to enjoy all the liberties freedomes and priviledges of a
freeman there, And to grant to the said Robert thirty acres of
land within their Territory or hundred of Barkley. . . .[17]

It happened that Robert decided not to make the voyage, and
perhaps that was the reason that his document of indenture
was preserved, for it cannot have been unique. The proprietors
of Berkeley Hundred as well as other similar groups probably
made many such agreements, and in fact the Virginia Company itself may have commonly used the same form.

Presumably these sub-corporations were the first to transport settlers independently of the company itself, but from
about 1618 private individuals were also granted land by the
company on condition that they transport persons to the colony.
This turned out to be one of the most satisfactory methods of
encouraging settlement; it became known as the headright
system, and was used in nearly every one of the colonies. There
is no certain knowledge of when or how it began; a document
of December, 1617, may indicate that it had not been worked
out at that time.[18] Soon afterwards, however, it became customary to make a grant of fifty acres for each person transported to the colony, and in April, 1623, it was reported to the
company that during the past four years, forty-four patents for
land had been issued to persons each of whom had agreed to

take at least one hundred men to Virginia. During the spring
and summer of 1621, according to the company's deputy, nearly
one thousand emigrants had gone out, but of these some nine
hundred were upon the charge of private men.[19] Doubtless
many of these emigrants were servants who did not pay their
own passage, and it may be assumed that some of them were
"sold" to planters already resident in the colony, but of this
there is no direct evidence.

Thus the handling of emigration passed from the hands
of the company into those of private individuals, and the unfortunate organization which alone had made the colony possible
saw its honors and profits turned over to others. After the
massacre of 1622 the courage of the undertaking was gone; the
land for the "colledge," situated up the James River nearly as
far as present-day Richmond, had to be abandoned, while the
pious hope of educating the Indians to true religion and civility
seemed ironic indeed. The colony itself barely survived that
terrible year, but it recovered quickly after the winter had
passed, while the company in London went through painful
days to its dissolution in 1624. By that time the customs of
indentured servitude had been fixed. In 1619 the first legislative
assembly in America provided for the recording and enforcing
of contracts made with servants before their departure from
England, and they became a distinct class in the community.
The census of 1624-1625 showed 487 of them in a population
of 1,227;[20] the idea of indenturing them in England, bringing
them to America, and transferring their services to resident
planters for a sum of money or tobacco had become familiar,
and the servant trade was ready to bring them in great numbers.

The usual form of indenture was simple. It was a legal contract, by which the servant bound himself well and faithfully

to serve the master in such employments as the master might assign, for a given length of time, and usually in a specified plantation. In return the master undertook to transport the servant to the colony, furnish him with adequate food, drink, clothing, and shelter during his service, and perhaps give him a specified reward when his term was ended. In the majority of cases this was all the agreement that was made, but it could be varied at will according to the bargain struck by the two persons concerned.[21] Skilled workmen sometimes secured a clause entitling them to annual wages or providing that they should do no common labor in the fields. A child's indenture might specify that he be given the rudiments of an education or taught a trade. German servants often entered into indentures providing that they be taught to read the Bible in English. The length of service varied considerably; it might be any number of years, but was generally four, and when longer terms were called for it was usually because the servant was a child. Diversity is also found in the "freedom dues"; some indentures named a sum of money, certain tools, clothes, or food, or a plot of land. In all colonies, however, these matters were regulated from early times by custom, and most servants depended upon this custom to direct their lives, contenting themselves with leaving their indentures in common form.[22]

By the year 1636 one could procure printed indentures, with blank spaces left for the names of the servant and master and for any special provisions desired. These forms were entered in the Stationers' Register by Nicholas Bourne, printer, and must have sold well, for in 1661 Bourne's executors petitioned against persons who "during the late disorders" had been illegally producing them.[23] Similar forms were used throughout the colonial period, and one may be quoted here as representative of all servants' indentures:

This Indenture made the *21st February 1682/3* Between *Rich. Browne aged 33 years* of the one party, and *Francis Richardson* of the other party, witnesseth, that the said *Rich. Browne* doth thereby covenant, promise, and grant to & with the said *Francis Richardson* his Executors & Assigns, from the day of the date hereof, until h*is* first & next arrival *att New York or New Jersey* and after, for and during the term of *foure* years, to serve in such service & imployment, as he the said *Francis Richardson* or his Assigns shall there imploy h*im* according to the custom of the Country in the like kind—In consideration whereof, the said *Francis Richardson* doth hereby covenant and grant to and with the said *Richard Browne* to pay for h*is* passing, and to find and allow h*im* meat, drink, apparrel, and lodging, with other necessaries, during the said term, & at the end of the said term to pay unto *him according to the Custom of the Country*

In Witness thereof the parties above mentioned to these Indentures have interchangeably set their Hands and Seals the day and year above written.

The servant took his indenture with him, and a copy might also be furnished to his master or even to the authorities of the plantation where he took up residence.[24] He could be sold for service only according to the terms of the contract, which thus became his protection against an unjust master. In most cases, and especially if the servant was less than eighteen years old, the indenture was chiefly useful to him as a certificate of the length of service required, but if generous freedom dues or any other particularly liberal provisions were included, it became of more obvious value. Colonial courts were always ready to enforce the terms of any servant's indenture which could be produced, and on occasion they even accepted the testimony of a servant's friends who had seen the document and would swear to its terms though it had since been lost. For one living the life of a laborer in the plantations it was not always an easy matter to keep possession of these small scraps of paper.

The pamphleteer John Hammond strongly advised all servants to make their contracts in this manner before leaving England, and to have them properly signed and sealed, so that questions and disappointments after arrival might be reduced to a minimum.[25] After 1682 the English regulations were so strict that this became almost necessary to protect the ship captain from a charge of kidnapping. Yet a great many servants, especially before the turn of the century, went to the colonies without written indentures. Some made verbal agreements with the merchants who shipped them, not realizing that such agreements were of no legal validity and would not be enforced in the colony. On their arrival they were sold as servants because they had not paid their own passages, and to regulate their treatment each colony evolved a certain standard known as the "custom of the country." Sooner or later this custom was set down in statutory law by nearly all colonies, and the earliest of these statutes were to specify the time which servants arriving without indenture should serve. Thus the new arrival, whether with or without previous indenture, found himself fairly well protected against capricious and excessive exploitation, while his importer knew with some exactness what could be expected in years of labor and expense of upkeep.

Few planters could journey to England and select their own servants. Hence they were practically always indentured to a merchant, an emigrant agent, a ship captain, or even to one of the seamen, and then exported like any other cargo of commodities. Upon arrival in the colonies they were displayed on deck, the planters came on board to inspect them, and they were "set over"[26] to the highest bidder. If the servant had a document of indenture, a note of the sale and of the date of arrival was often made on its back, and the transaction was then complete. The invention and acceptance of this system made it possible to handle emigration as a business proposition, and to treat white labor as a commodity. The trade in servants became quite an important part of colonial trade, and the peopling of English America proceeded according to the crudest manifestations of the law of supply and demand. Throughout the colonial period vast numbers of ordinary indentured servants were thus transported to the colonies, while convicts, rogues and vagabonds, political prisoners, all were sold in the plantations as servants and taken there by merchants as merchandise.

During all of the seventeenth century indentured servitude was practically the only method by which a poor person could get to the colonies or by which white labor could be supplied to planters. About the beginning of the eighteenth century, however, a new scheme made its appearance, and the "redemptioner" took his place alongside the "servant." At first this class of emigrant came generally from the Continent. The movement of Germans and Swiss to the colonies, which had been occasional and scattering since the 1680's, began to assume large proportions in 1708 and 1709. Large numbers of people descended the Rhine to Rotterdam, seeking a passage to the new world, and many of them found when they arrived at the seaport that their financial resources were insufficient to get them the rest of the way. Accordingly, merchants used to take whatever money the emigrant might have left, put him and his goods and his family aboard ship, and contract to deliver them in America. After arrival a certain period of time, commonly fourteen days, was allowed during which the passenger might try to find the balance which was due the shipper, the hope being that he might locate friends who would advance the money. But if the necessary amount could not be found within the time limit then he was to be sold into indentured servitude by the captain of the ship, for an amount sufficient to satisfy his indebtedness. Thus the length of his servitude would depend roughly upon the size of his debt.

The first contemporary references to this method of migration are of no earlier date than 1728, but they indicate that it had been familiar for some time.[27] Though confined at first to Germans, it soon spread across the Channel and was considerably used, particularly by those who transported Irish to Pennsylvania. Many English travelled under redemptionist agreements to the colonies, but the system never wholly replaced the older scheme of indentured servitude among them. Germans, on the other hand, seem rarely to have adopted the seventeenth-century method, and as far as we know nearly all who did not pay their own passage went out as redemptioners. In consequence the total migrations of the eighteenth century consist much more of this class than of ordinary indentured servants.

Between these two methods of transporting persons to the plantations there were certain significant differences which have commonly been overlooked. It is true that once a redemptioner had been sold for his passage money, he became in every respect an indentured servant, and there was no distinction between the two classes. But to the prospective emigrant in Europe, contemplating the possibilities for getting to America, there were virtues in each scheme, and his choice might depend upon his personal circumstances. In the first place, it was customary to supply an indentured servant with food, clothing, and shelter from the time he signed his contract until the end of his term of servitude; destitute persons in Britain, when all other hopes had faded, therefore, could and did sign up as indentured servants and get free of their worst immediate troubles from that moment.[28] Furthermore, since a servant made his agreement before departure he could perhaps secure for himself particularly favorable terms, while the redemptioner, who executed his indenture of servitude after reaching America, was apt to find it necessary to accept whatever was offered.

The most remarkable difference between the two was, however, that the redemptionist system applied generally to people who emigrated in whole families, bringing their goods and chattels with them and seeking a new home. Indentured servants nearly always came singly, in fact English regulations after 1682 required a declaration from each emigrating servant that he was unmarried and without dependents, as well as under no apprenticeship to a master at home. Redemptioners were apt to be people who had raised some money by the sale of their lands or other non-moveable goods; they came in families, and very often one or two members of a family would take the burden of service for the rest. Sometimes parents would come with the expectation of selling the services of their children in order to pay their own passage, while the children would thus become apprentices and learn a trade. At some expense of overstatement the point may be made this way: indentured servants came essentially as cargoes of merchandize representing a supply of labor; redemptioners came essentially as emigrants hopefully transplanting themselves to a new home in America. This statement does not do justice to the aspirations of many servants, but it helps to indicate why the redemptionist system flourished in the eighteenth century, after the colonies had achieved a stable existence such as would be inviting to newcomers, while indentured servants played a greater proportional part during the years of perilous beginnings.

There were, of course, a few times in colonial history when persons were sent to one plantation or another without being under the obligation of labor or servitude, except in so far as labor was obviously necessary to insure their own existence after the supplies furnished by their transporters had run out. When settlers were urgently desired for some locality previously uninhabited they were sometimes established as free men, and given food, shelter and tools for a year with the promise of subsequent land grants. This was the case at Halifax, Nova Scotia, where a settlement was founded by the British government in 1749 for strategic reasons, and over three thousand persons taken out at public expense in the first year, under the supervision of the Board of Trade.[29] The Georgia Trustees, with the considerable financial help of the government, sent 2,127 persons to their colony "on the Charity,"[30] and while the motives of the trustees were charitable, those of the government again were strategic. In this case as in that of Halifax, provisions and tools were supplied the colonists for one year. Charitable contributions sent six hundred French Protestants to America in 1687, and about seven hundred more in 1700.[31] On several occasions entrepreneurs secured large grants of American land from the Crown on condition of settling it with certain numbers of Protestant inhabitants; thus for instance de Graffenried settled New Bern in North Carolina with 650 Palatines in 1710, and Jean Peter Pury established some Swiss in Purysburgh, South Carolina, two decades later. Henry McCulloch, a London merchant, petitioned for no less than 1,200,000 acres in North Carolina, and was actually granted such a tract in 1737 on the understanding that he would take 6,000 foreign Protestants there to live.[32] Apparently he did not fulfill his part of the agreement, though he kept the land until the time of the American Revolution. The enormous schemes of Alexander McNutt for the settlement of Nova Scotia in the 1760's gave promise of depopulating Northern Ireland, and were sharply checked by the Privy Council.[33]

None of the above mentioned plans involved the servitude of settlers, and hence they do not come within the province of this study. A few cases involving modification or adaptation of the usual conditions of servitude require some mention, however, and of these the first group is composed of schemes similar to that of the Virginia Company and its "company servants." Essentially this meant, as we have pointed out, that servants worked for a corporation in England instead of for a planter in the colony, and usually they were rewarded with a share of the proceeds of their labors. Thus the Massachusetts Bay Company in its earliest years,[34] the Bermuda Company,[35] and the Providence Company[36] all tried this plan, and in each case it failed just as it had when attempted in Virginia. The Georgia Trustees, besides supplying servants for some of their planters, also tried to use "trust servants" on the common land with no better success.[37] The most grandiose attempt of this kind was that made by the British government itself, when it sent some 3,200 Germans to New York in 1710 for the purpose of making naval stores on the banks of the Hudson.[38] In this case also the project failed, though political conditions at home were in part responsible.

One curious modification of the redemptionist system, which was tried at Halifax, is worth noting. The Board of Trade engaged John Dick of Rotterdam to procure a number of Germans and Swiss for the colony, promising them food and tools for one year, but requiring them to pay their own passage. Dick was unable to find candidates with enough money for this purpose, and the Board, though anxious to have them emigrate, did not wish to pay it for them. Hence it agreed to advance the price of their transportation and since there was no one in the colony able to "redeem" them, it instructed the governor to set them at labor on the public works for such time as it should take them to earn the amount due, calculating their wages at one shilling a day. This was thought a particularly shrewd move because the prevailing wage rate in Nova Scotia was twice the amount allowed the Germans; it had unfortunate results nevertheless, for the foreigners were disgruntled at the bargain, while the price of labor in the colony was so driven down that free workers nearly starved.[39]

While schemes such as these were carrying their hundreds to the plantations, the regular trade in indentured servants and redemptioners was carrying its tens of thousands. This trade was the backbone of the whole migratory movement. Neither imperialist visions and necessities, nor charitable impulses, nor religious enthusiasms, nor desire for landed possessions kept it going, but simply the fact that colonists wanted white laborers and were willing to pay merchants and ship owners for bringing them. We must turn then first to the nature of this demand for servants, and the profits that were to be made by meeting it.

CHAPTER 2

THE TRADE IN SERVANTS:
TWO CONTROLLING FACTORS

THE DEMAND FOR WHITE SERVANTS

I T IS an old truism that in the development of new countries labor is the most scarce of the elements of production. Capital also is generally scanty, mainly because such large amounts of it are necessary and returns are apt to be precarious and long-delayed. Though many American colonies were founded like Virginia as capitalistic enterprises, none of them succeeded in paying adequate dividends to the investors, and the only people who made financial profits in the new world were those who actually emigrated, or those wise proprietors who contented themselves with exacting a modest quit rent. But any man who emigrated to the colonies and wished to make a comfortable living found himself faced with the problem of procuring labor. His free and enterprising neighbors, instead of offering their services as workers, were themselves seeking men to work for them. There was no surplus population, and the only possible recourse during the colonial period as well as for more than a century afterward was to Europe. But in the colonial period practically no one had sufficient capital to transport large numbers of workers for his own use. The device of indentured servitude made it possible for the colonial tradesman or farmer to purchase small amounts of white labor as he would purchase small amounts of any other European commodity, such as textiles or tools.

In so far as the migration of indentured servants satisfied the normal economic demand for workers its function does not require much explanation, and the colonists themselves fully recognized the importance of this labor supply. We have already found John Pory writing from Virginia in 1619 that "our principall wealth . . . consisteth in servants." Governor Sharpe of Maryland wrote in 1755: "The Planters Fortunes here consist in the number of their Servants (who are purchased at high Rates) much as the Estates of an English Farmer do in the Multitude of Cattle." A member of the council of Maryland said that experience had shown that in all plantations where servants worked in the tobacco fields their labors would produce a yearly profit of fifty pounds sterling apiece, and commonly more. The assembly of Barbados lamented in 1667 that in their island the planter "lyes under great charge and duty without much produce for want of such servants," and the president of the council of Pennsylvania told Governor Shirley of Massachusetts in 1756 that "every kind of Business here, as well among the Tradesmen and Mechanicks as the Planters & Farmers, is chiefly carried on and supported by the Labour of indented Servants."[1]

Free labor was procurable to an increasing degree as the colonies grew older, but in comparison with indentured it was exceedingly expensive and somewhat undependable. Throughout the period there is universal complaint of the intolerable rates of wages which were demanded, and to persons accustomed in England to paying around a shilling a day the figures of two or three shillings which obtained in America even for unskilled workers seemed extremely burdensome. Artisans and craftsmen demanded and received as much as eight shillings and sixpence. Hence the colonist who could board a ship and buy the services of a competent carpenter or mason for three or four years would be happy to pay twenty or thirty pounds, while even the most unlikely immigrant would probably be worth an investment of eight or ten. Thus Christopher Jeaffreson, a planter in St. Christopher, wrote home to his agent in 1681: "For a taylor, a cooper, a carpenter, a joyner, a mason, a smith,—which are the trades most necessary here,—I would allow to such an one, when a good workman, a thousand pounds of sugar wages, for each yeare that he should serve me, with what must be paid for theire passages, tools or instruments."[2] Had such candidates appeared on a servant ship, Jeaffreson would certainly have hastened to buy them.

Even more troublesome than the price of free labor was its uncertainty. The scarcity of workmen made it uncertain that an employer could find help when he needed it, and the excellent opportunities which the country offered for attaining a modest independence made workers indisposed to spend their lives as hired men. On the other hand, an indentured servant was purchased for a relatively small capital sum, fed and clothed as cheaply as possible, and could be kept to his work and his place by force if need be. All the facilities of colonial law and police were at the service of masters whose servants ran away. Hence such establishments as the iron works in Maryland generally used indentured labor, and we find them advertising their runaways in the newspapers, offering a reward for recaptures. It was not until the population increased enough to provide a surplus of men, making it possible to hire and fire at will, that free labor could be used to the satisfaction of employers.

Greatly preferable as indentured labor was generally felt to be, there seems to have been some opposition to its use in New England. "For its observed," wrote an unknown person in the middle of the seventeenth century, "that Virginia thrives by keeping many servants, and these in strict obedience. New England conceit they and their Children can doe enough, and soe have rarely above one Servant: and by their gross and foolish indulgence, slave themselves to their Children and Servants, giving them 2s. a day for their worke."[3] An illnatured letter in the year 1723 describes the Bostonians as possessing too many Negro slaves, "and yet their masters will rather be burnt in their beds by them than suffer English servants to come hither to work, obligeing all M[aste]rs of ships to carry them back again upon their owne charge, or else they must not trade in this country."[4] We know that the Irish who arrived in New England in 1718 and 1719 were given a cold welcome, and that Massachusetts was inhospitable to newcomers, especially such as were held to be ungodly. Certainly there were indentured servants in the original migrations of the 1630's, and in 1645 John Winthrop lamented that they had stopped coming because of the Civil War, making the price of labor in Boston impossibly high.[5] Other cargoes of them were landed throughout the colonial period, though not in great numbers, and it is evident that the demand for them cannot have been very lively. Perhaps the explanation is to be found in the lack of any large-scale commercial agriculture.

Negro slaves, of course, answered many colonial requirements even better than did white servants. Slaves were held to perpetual instead of temporary servitude, they were usually cheaper to feed and clothe, they replaced themselves to some extent by natural breeding, and they endured the hot climate of the plantation colonies much better than white men.[6] Hence the use of Negroes did in actual fact do away with the economic demand for white servants in those colonies which found them suitable, and especially in the West Indies. As early as 1676 Governor Atkins of Barbados said that three blacks would not only do more work, but also do it more cheaply, than one white man. By 1690 Dalby Thomas computed that a sugar plantation of one hundred acres needed only seven white men among fifty Negroes to run it; a hundred years later it was stated that such an enterprise could best be conducted with slaves only.[7] It was true that indentured labor called for less original outlay of capital, and we read in the seventeenth century that aspiring planters were advised to start in a small way with a few servants from England bought for ten or fifteen pounds each. After the first profits had been made slaves could be purchased to work with the white servants.[8] Small-scale planting in the West Indies had almost disappeared by the beginning of the eighteenth century, however, and with it went this motive for the acquisition of servants, while the increasing skill and docility of Negroes made white men continually less necessary as supervisors. It is evident that the natural economic demand for white servants dwindled almost to nothing. Planters would no longer go down to the shore and buy from a servant ship, though they eagerly took up the shipments of Negro slaves which arrived. It was reported from Barbados in 1682 that many servants had been brought to the island, exposed to sale, and then carried away for want of buyers.[9] The result was that the white population declined rapidly in proportion to the black, and even in some cases actually diminished in numbers.

Not long after the middle of the seventeenth century the island governments became aware that the proportion of white men in the population was getting dangerously low, and the French wars of the 1670's and 1680's brought this more pointedly to their attention. The militia was weak; the dangers from French and Negroes were great. They complained that not enough servants were being sent to them, and they made suggestions for increasing the traffic. Barbados in 1667 petitioned "that wee may have a free trade and a supply from [the] Kingdom of Scotland of Scotch servants with whom being supplyed in good numbers (as experience heretofore hath been had) will render both Comodity and Security to the planters."[10] Jamaica in 1676 was interested that trade with Ireland and England be increased at the expense of that of New England because no servants ever came from the latter place. During the reign of William and Mary the Jamaicans instructed their agent in London to try to encourage a trade with Scotland in order that more servants might be brought.[11] It is remarkable that there are in fact more vociferous demands for servants from the island colonies which did not actually have much economic use for them than there are from the continental colonies where they were more necessary to the productive system.

It was not long before the islanders realized that something more than exhortation was required before merchants would bring them cargoes of white labor. They proceeded to create an artificial demand, and to attempt to increase the supply by legislation. Barbados began in 1670 by giving special facilities to merchants for recovering in court any money owed them for servants; Jamaica in 1672 and Nevis in 1675 followed with similar enactments. In 1672, amid threats and rumors of war, Jamaica passed a law requiring each planter to keep one Christian servant for every ten Negroes on his plantation: Antigua and St. Christopher imitated this in 1677 and 1679 respectively. Barbados followed a slightly different plan, assessing the militia upon each planter according to the number of acres he held, and requiring him to furnish his quota of white men at musters.[12]

These laws did not prove adequate, however, and in 1679 Antigua led the way with a new scheme. By statute it was provided that anyone bringing to the island a good English, Scottish, or Welsh servant with four years to serve should receive for him from the island treasurer two thousand pounds of good muscovado sugar. The governor and two of the council were empowered to distribute these servants among planters who did not have their proper proportion under the law of 1677, and the recipients were to be forced to pay for them.[13] In 1682 Barbados passed the first of a series of acts encouraging the importation of white servants. If any captain brought good servants and could not sell them within ten days, he might turn them over to the island treasurer, who would pay £12.10.0 apiece for them. They were then to be apportioned among the planters according to the information received from colonels of militia, and the planters were to pay £13 each for them. This law, when renewed in 1688, changed the prices to £10 and £10.10.0 respectively, which may indicate either that the supply was increasing or that fear of war was lessening.[14] Meanwhile, Jamaica, where there were better opportunities for the employment of freed servants and consequently more stimulus for voluntary immigration, contented herself with the enactment in 1681, that any ship bringing fifty servants should be free from port dues.[15]

The wars of William III brought about a most acute and dangerous situation in the West Indies, to which Barbados responded in 1696 with a remarkable law. Not only was the treasurer directed to pay £18 for each common servant, but the servant himself was guaranteed wages of twenty-five shillings per year during his term of service.[16] Barbadians claimed in 1701 that they had spent more than forty thousand pounds in carrying out this act, and despite their reputation for hyperbole the statement is not wholly beyond belief.[17] In this law, as in her other for encouraging the importation of servants, Barbados carefully defined the food and clothing to which each servant was entitled during his term, and each successive act offered more liberal inducements.[18] Most exact and stringent provisions were made for distributing these servants among delinquent planters, and the existence of such regulations is an eloquent witness to the disappearance of a normal economic demand for white labor. In 1693 Montserrat offered 2,500 pounds of sugar per servant, and freed from port charges any ship bringing twenty or more. Nevis in 1701 offered £12, and fixed the proportion for each planter at one white to twenty Negroes. Jamaica passed an act in 1698 promising to pay £7 for the passage of any white man to the island, with forty shillings extra for the captain of the ship, and entire freedom nevertheless to the immigrant to hire himself out as he saw fit.[19] In 1703 Jamaica imitated the other colonies by a law offering £18 in war time and £14 in peace for each servant, but for Irish only £15 and £12 respectively, and for convicts, Jews, or Quakers, nothing at all.[20] An elaborate schedule of proportions between whites and Negroes was drawn up, provisions were made for distributing the servants, and any ship bringing thirty or more was freed from port charges. Even South Carolina, the only continental colony in which Negro labor was wholly preferred to white, found herself obliged to adopt similar devices; in 1698 she passed an act offering £13 to captains bringing a white servant, and required each planter with six Negroes to buy one. This law was repealed in 1700, its purpose having been accomplished, but a new one was necessary in 1712. The price offered this time was £14, and in 1716 it was raised to £25 on account of the Indian war, but in the following year the act was repealed.[21]

Schemes like these were desperate expedients for building up the white population in order to defend the colonies against the French. They could not form any permanent basis for the servant trade, and they were abandoned as soon as the wars ceased. Nevertheless the problem remained of insuring the social system against Negro revolts. Jamaica passed throughout the eighteenth century a series of what were called "deficiency" acts, which set up a certain proportion of whites to blacks and assessed a fine on each planter who did not maintain this proportion.[22] Instead of buying white servants, however, the Jamaicans often found it more convenient to pay the fines, and the deficiency acts became in truth revenue bills. Defense against the Negro menace was tolerably well provided for when small garrisons of British troops began to be stationed in the islands, and the planters could dispense with a militia. Hence the white population in the small islands steadily declined through the eighteenth century, while in Jamaica it rose only from about ten thousand in 1739 to eighteen thousand in 1768. There was no demand for servants whatever in Barbados and the Leeward Islands, and we read that by 1774 they were not even wanted in Jamaica.[23]

No such forces operated to destroy the demand for servants in the continental colonies north of South Carolina. Tobacco required greater skill in its production than sugar; Dalby Thomas stated that twenty-one white men were required with fifty Negroes on a plantation of 100 acres.[24] New lands were constantly being opened up by small farmers of the kind who were particularly anxious for the assistance of a few servants. As one travelled northward there was less inclination to use Negro slaves, and opposition was strong enough among the

Quakers of Pennsylvania to influence markedly the demand for white labor. Agriculture and industry were more diversified; much of the food eaten on the sugar plantations was grown in the Middle Colonies with the labor of indentured servants.[25] Philadelphia and Newcastle became their principal ports of entry, and though many shiploads were sent to Virginia and especially to Maryland during the eighteenth century, nevertheless persons came from those colonies to buy servants arriving in the Delaware River ports. Rarely does it appear that a merchant waited more than a few days to dispose of his entire cargo at Philadelphia, and the numbers sold in Maryland were at their greatest in the years just before the Revolution. Fewer came to New York, but those who did were speedily purchased, and the inhabitants of that colony expressed several times a desire for more. Only in New England, as we have already observed, did the demand for imported servants apparently lag behind the demand for labor.

THE PROFITS OF THE TRADE

Never during the colonial period did it cost more than five or six pounds sterling to transport a servant to the plantations. The Virginia Company paid six pounds in 1619, and in 1750 the Board of Trade contracted with merchants to take settlers to Nova Scotia at five pounds five shillings each. The Georgia Trustees usually paid five pounds for the passage of their free colonists, but shipped at least one lot of indentured servants for only four pounds apiece.[26] In 1708 a merchant tried to get £7.10.0 each from the government for taking Palatines to New York, and was told that his bid was too high.[27] Seventeenth century writers always figured five or six pounds as the cost of a passage.[28] It must be remembered, however, that in practically all the instances cited, the amount given represents not the actual cost of carrying the servant, but rather the price charged by merchants, who expected to make a profit on the transaction. Consequently if the merchant, instead of carrying passengers for the government or for one of the companies or for an individual, carried a cargo of servants on his own account, which he proposed to sell in the colony, his investment must have been well under five pounds each.[29] Since the price of transportation included food and drink for the voyage, it would vary somewhat with the quality of these necessaries which the shipper supplied, and also with the general price level.

To the price of transportation was generally added a charge for equipment and clothing for each servant, and also an indefinite sum for expenses while he awaited departure or travelled from his home to the seaport. The amount spent on equipment varied greatly. William Bullock drew up a scheme for the outfitting of two servants bound for Virginia, recommending that they be furnished with two cloth suits, two canvas suits, two waistcoats and two pairs of woolen drawers, six shirts, four pairs of stockings, four pairs of shoes, two monmouth caps, six neck handkerchiefs, eight ells of strong canvas to make a bed and bolster, one rug and two blankets. This all could be bought for £6.15.8, making the price of fitting out each servant £3.7.10.[30] Other estimates run a little higher, and indicate that Bullock may have been skimpy in his allowance of shirts and shoes. Littleton in 1689 wrote that the clothing of each servant sent from England cost just under five pounds; Sir Thomas Lynch, writing from Jamaica to Lord Cornbury in 1672 estimated it at just over five, while de Graffenried's Palatines were clothed before their departure in 1710 at a cost of only twenty shillings each.[31] All these estimates were made for persons who wished to emigrate, taking servants with them, and once again it is certain that the merchant who took out a cargo of laborers could equip them at less expense. We have evidence concerning one such trader, who bought rolls of cloth, took them to a tailor, and had suits, shirts, stockings and blankets made up very cheaply.[32] As the colonies grew older it became less necessary to supply each servant with full sets of clothing before departure, and in any case the merchant regulated his purchases of equipment in accordance with his judgment of the demands which would be made by colonial masters.

The expense of feeding and sheltering indentured servants after they had signed their contracts but before the ship departed would vary greatly according to the length of time they were kept waiting. The Virginia Company and the Providence Company found themselves embarrassed by the necessity of feeding their prospective emigrants, and had to send some of them home,[33] while the merchant trader already referred to refused to sign indentures until the ship was ready, lest his candidates after eating and lodging at his expense run away before the sailing. A man who raised a cargo of servants in Aberdeen in 1743 began to pay for the food and lodging of them on February 4; there were nineteen of them collected at this date, and the number gradually increased until the ship sailed on May 12. During all this time he fed them, some on the ship, but most at various boarding houses in the town.[34]

Thus it would seem that the cost of procuring a servant, equipping him, and getting him to the colonies, was about ten or twelve pounds for the individual going to his own plantation; for the merchant collecting a cargo to go on his own ship it need never have been more than ten pounds, and must have been generally much less, a minimum figure being about four pounds. In the case of redemptioners, nothing mattered but the "freight" of five or six pounds sterling; if they needed any advances of money for equipment the merchant merely charged such against their accounts and added it to the amount due him in America.

The price which an indentured servant brought in the plantations depended on his own worth and on the current demand for labor in the particular colony where he landed. Scottish servants were esteemed the best and Irish Catholics the worst;[35] artisans and skilled laborers were always in particular favor. In 1636 a shipload of servants sent to Virginia was sold off at various amounts ranging from 250 to 600 pounds of tobacco per servant;[36] it is difficult to be sure how much this represented in money, but at a rate of sixpence a pound this means that they brought from about six to nearly fifteen pounds apiece. The same year servants were sold in Barbados for five hundred pounds of tobacco each, which may be about twelve pounds sterling.[37] The average price in Maryland during the earlier seventeenth century has been estimated as from £15 to £20, and in Virginia as high as £40 to £60.[38] Sir Thomas Modyford said in 1670 that male servants sold in Jamaica for from £12 to £15, and females from £10 to £12.[39] We have already seen that the islands fixed prices by law ranging as high as £18 apiece for good servants, and this figure was intended to attract trade. In Jamaica a good "tradesman" was said to bring about £40 in 1739, and other less skillful servants went for £20 each.[40] On the other hand, a captain who took Irishmen to North Carolina in 1735 testified before a committee of the Irish House of Commons that he used to get about thirty-five barrels of pitch or turpentine apiece for them, worth "of our money" three-and-six or four shillings a barrel. This figure of six or seven pounds each, if accurate, is certainly very low, for we know that even convicts sold regularly in Maryland for from eight to twenty pounds apiece throughout the eighteenth century.[41]

Thus a merchant who spent from four to ten pounds on getting a servant to America could count on selling him for from six to perhaps thirty pounds. This was a comfortable profit, despite the large risks that sickness or death might scale down the value of the cargo, but it was not exorbitant, for the time involved in these transactions was long and the total value of any shipload not great. The real point was that servants provided a convenient cargo for ships going to the plantations to fetch tobacco, sugar, and the other raw products available.[42] It is obvious that merchants did not bring back money; they applied whatever money they might receive from the sale of servants to the purchase of colonial products, and brought these home where they could normally be sold at a good profit. Generally the servants were in fact directly exchanged for these products, for colonists had but little hard money, and but little use for it except as it would purchase European goods for them.

It is plain that the servant himself was grievously exploited, for he was generally sold not simply for the cost of his passage, as is often stated, but for a considerably higher figure. If he could have begged or borrowed five pounds, he might have paid his own passage to the plantations and then, if he desired, have sold himself into servitude, keeping the profit for himself. Few servants could raise the money, and few who could do so cared to spend it in emigrating, for the real stimulus to emigration was not the desire of servants to go to America but the desire of merchants to secure them as cargo.

The case of the redemptioners was rather different. Theoretically, as has been explained, they were sold in America for an amount only sufficient to make up the cost of their passage. It was customary to add about 15 per cent to this cost "as an Indemnity for the Charges & laying out of the money," or in other words as interest and insurance on the deferred payment.[43] A charge for the transportation of baggage was also commonly added, and through most of the eighteenth century a head tax of one pound charged in Pennsylvania was paid by the immigrant himself. Thus the actual charges might add up to seven or eight pounds sterling, payable in Philadelphia, for the passage of one redemptioner. Now a great mass of evidence shows that redemptioners in Philadelphia sold for amounts ranging from as low as £10 in 1722 to around £20 in 1772, with the figure in the 1750's being about £15.[44] It has always been claimed, in view of these facts, that the redemptioners were outrageously exploited, and that captains of ships contrived to doctor their accounts so that the helpless immigrant should be sold at a good profit. But this accusation takes no account of the fact that Pennsylvania currency, in which all these quotations are given, did not have the value of sterling after about 1720. It is not always possible in any given instance to say what the rate of exchange was, but in 1748 one hundred pounds sterling would purchase £180 of Pennsylvania currency. Two years previously we know that Irish redemptioners were sold for £13 each, which does not indicate that there was any exploitation whatever. Again, we have from the year 1775 a redemptioner's agreement made in England, by which the emigrant is bound by indenture, but if he pay £14.14.0 sterling within fourteen days of his arrival in the colony the indenture is to be void. It appears that this emigrant could not find the money, and on the back of his indenture is recorded a transfer of him to one Thomas Cloudsdale for £20.[45] It is probable that the difference is due not to exploitation but to the rate of exchange, and in fact it is likely that in this instance the captain had the worst of the bargain.

It would be foolish to assert that overcharging was never practiced, or that captains were always just and honest; indeed there is plenty of evidence to the contrary.[46] Making allowances for the rates of exchange, however, the trade in redemptioners was normally not so profitable as the trade in servants. Robert Morris thought it "so troublesome and precarious" by 1774 that he ceased to employ his ships in it.[47] Essentially it was not the transportation of a cargo of labor, but rather the carrying of passengers under slightly peculiar arrangements, and while a shipload of passengers was more profitable than a shipload of ballast, it brought no such returns as a cargo of slaves or servants, and under the circumstances it entailed large risks. Serious illnesses or a large number of deaths aboard ship might be impossible to balance by increased prices put on the rest of the cargo. Yet despite these things many merchants avidly sought for full complements of redemptioners to pay the way of their ships going to the colonies, and took means both fair and foul to stimulate the emigration of such people from Europe.

One minor method of making a profit from a cargo of servants needs to be noticed; this was by claiming land for their importation and then selling the claim. Practically all colonies offered a grant of land, usually fifty acres, to any person who should bring in an immigrant. This encouraged private individuals to assist in building up the population of the colony and generally proof was required that the immigrant had actually been settled upon the land before a grant was given to his importer. But in Maryland, before the year 1683, grants were given not to the planters who purchased servants but to any person who brought them to the country. Thus for example when Captain Benjamin Cooper arrived from London with seventy-one servants on board his ship in February, 1674/5, he was duly credited with 3,350 acres of land. Captain Cooper, of course, had no intention of settling; he sold off his claim on the day he received it to Robert Ridgely, an official of the colony, who in turn disposed of the land at leisure, to his own best advantage.[48] Thus Cooper made an extra profit on his cargo of servants, Ridgely speculated in land, and the true purpose of the head-right system was defeated. Such abuses led to the abolishing of the whole scheme in 1683. In other colonies a more careful administration of the system prevented its acting directly to increase the profits of the servant trade, though it certainly tended to increase the demand for servants, and especially to stimulate propertied persons to bring servants with them when they came to the colonies.[49]

Year after year throughout the colonial period the migration of servants and redemptioners thus rested primarily on the demand for their labor in the plantations. The convenient procedures of the trade, by which they could be "sold" individually to colonists of modest fortune, were necessary to make this demand effective, and the anxiety of merchants to provide their ships with a cargo of commodities which would be attractive in the new world acted as a stimulant to emigration. The merchants competed among themselves for recruits to make up such cargoes, and the methods which they used, as well as the nature of the people on whom they were used, require some description. We have seen why it was worth while to take emigrants to the colonies, even though they could not pay their own passage; it remains to consider why such emigrants came actually to start the voyage.

[CHAPTER 3]

RAISING A CARGO

I N DISCUSSING the motives for emigration, as in fact for nearly any historical occurrence, it is customary to examine the economic background. If it can be shown, for instance, that people were poor, discouraged, and exploited in their homes, and that there was a chance for improvement in another place, and that they were aware of this chance, then there appears to be a satisfactory explanation of emigration, and we are apt to be content. Yet the fact is that most people have always been poor and exploited, and nevertheless have rarely emigrated. On the contrary it has usually been only with the greatest difficulty that people, no matter how miserable their condition, have been persuaded to cut loose from their ancient moorings and try a new country. Poverty and discontent are not necessarily causes of emigration; they are favorable and perhaps indispensable attendant circumstances.

There is, of course, no difficulty in demonstrating that the majority of English people were poor. Gregory King, making his well-known calculations for the year 1688, estimated that more than half of the total population were to be regarded as diminishing the wealth of the kingdom, because their annual expenses exceeded their annual incomes, and the deficiency had to be made up by the poor rates. This poverty-stricken half consisted of 849,000 families, containing an average of three

and a quarter persons each, and the income of each family was
£10.10.0 per year. The total amount of poor rates collected in
1685 was £665,362, a figure equal to a third of the total revenue. These rates steadily increased, yet Davenant remarked that
despite them many of the poor died yearly from famine. Besides those who were aged, impotent, or infants, there was a
large class of able-bodied persons some of whom were willing
to work if they could find anything to do. The number of these
unemployed cannot be stated with any certainty; contemporary
estimates vary from 100,000 to 1,200,000, and thus prove nothing. Years of depression in trade and of high prices for food
were frequent, some of the worst periods being those of 1622-
23, 1660-63, 1693-1700. The problem of poverty and unemployment faced society as constantly and menacingly then as now,
and while many books and treatises advocated various methods
of meeting it, the steady mounting of the poor rates seemed
to indicate that the situation was hopeless.[1]

Yet the existence of poverty is not remarkable, nor had
deaths from famine been unknown in any age. More important is the fact that poverty, as it existed at the beginning
of the seventeenth and the end of the eighteenth century in England, was a symptom of the instability of society. It was a kind
of poverty which was not rooted in the ancient and permanent
order of things, but which appeared because those were years
of transition, first from a feudal to a commercial and then
from a commercial to an industrial economy. The circumstances of these transitions have been very often described: the
dissolution of the monasteries and cessation of their charities,
the disbanding of the private armies of feudal lords, the en-
closing of arable land for sheep pastures or for large-scale
cultivation, the rise of commerce and the decline of the gilds,
the adoption of labor-saving machinery. Amid these changes

a few of the aristocracy lost their heads and their fortunes, some of the middling sort of people attained wealth and titles, but many thousands of the poor were dislodged from their ancestral habitations and occupations, and turned out to wander in the world. A vagabond or a casual laborer might possibly have as much to eat and as good an expectation of life as a medieval villein, but he had no security of place and status, no certainty of decent work, and no assurance that his person and his labors would be of any value to society.

Thus there came into existence a large body of poor, characterized by their mobility and by their lack of anchorage either to place or to occupation. They drained into the towns and cities. These were centuries in which London grew with enormous rapidity. Not even the most stringent settlement laws could wholly prevent their wandering. Contemporary respectable opinion was alarmed and during the last years of the sixteenth and the first of the seventeenth centuries became convinced that the country was overpopulated.[2]

The consciousness of the problem of poverty, and the ascription of its cause to overpopulation, produced some cordial support for the first colonizing ventures and a general favoring of emigration. To "relieve the land of its surplus inhabitants" as well as to discover gold and convert the heathen to Christianity was the avowed purpose of early expansionists. Thus the climate of opinion was set towards emigration; it was in the air; it was encouraged and even financed by high authority. But it is well to note that this enthusiasm was confined to the respectable and the well-to-do; there is no evidence whatever that as a class the "surplus inhabitants" had any yearnings for a new and perilous existence in the colonies. When a fever of mass migration appeared, as it did among Puritans in the 1630's, it attacked the moderately prosperous and not the hopelessly indigent, though it might in time spread down in the scale for a short distance.

As mercantilist ideas of population became current after the middle of the seventeenth century, and a large amount of cheap labor was looked upon as a necessary though troublesome asset, upper-class enthusiasm for emigration ceased and opposition set in.[3] The maladjustment of population continued, varying in painfulness with the varying rate of change in economic life. London swarmed with destitute people, living from hand to mouth and consoling themselves with cheap gin. Workhouses were full, Bridewell and other prisons overflowed, idle and diseased wanderers infested the land. "There are few, if any, nations or countries where the poor . . . are in a more scandalous nasty condition, than in England," reported Henry Fielding in the middle of the eighteenth century.[4] "Compared to these people," wrote Franklin of rural workers in 1771, "every Indian is a gentleman; and the effect of this kind of civil society seems only to be the depressing multitudes below the savage state that a few may be raised above it."[5] Artisans and small farmers hovered always on the margin between subsistence and want, uncertain of their jobs, uncertain of their scanty holdings of land, not knowing when they might be depressed into the ranks of the wholly destitute. During those centuries the class which we know as the proletariat was in process of formation.

Contemporaries used to describe the impulse to emigrate as spreading through communities like an epidemic fever, and they were often puzzled by its virulence. The analogy is a good one, and may perhaps be pushed a step further. Diseases do not flourish in healthful or sanitary regions, nor does the fever of emigration occur where people are contented and prosperous. Yet it is not always easy to explain why a dirty and malodorous city may go for years without serious epidemic disorders, and then suddenly be attacked by a plague. Some point is reached where resistance breaks down, or some influence of extraordinary power may be brought to bear, and the population packs up its goods, sells its property, and decamps. This sort of mass migration is a different phenomenon from the ordinary, more or less regular, flow of individuals from one country to another. Such individuals are driven by their own personal inclinations, or perhaps they are merely too weak to resist the blandishments of an emigrant agent. As the Lord Justice Clerk of Scotland put it, "While individuals think and act for themselves, there is no great danger that many will go; but when they enter into associations, and go off in bodies from the same place, with their wives, children, and kindred, this removes the natural tie to their country." The causes of the particular movement he was describing were, he remarked, bad crops, unemployment, and a rise in rents, "but the great danger is that when these causes cease, the spirit of emigration may still continue."[6]

There were in our colonial period a number of important mass migrations of this epidemic variety. First was the Puritan movement of the 1630's. We consider that the "causes" of this movement lay in the religious discontents of the time and in the peculiar and temporary maladjustment of economic life in the eastern counties. What cannot be well understood, perhaps because of the lack of sufficient evidence on the point, is the mysterious way in which the spirit of emigration spread from one parish to another, so that not merely individuals but whole communities arose with their ministers and departed for New England.[7] Some twenty thousand persons migrated in ten years; then the fever subsided and the movement was over.

Nearly a century later Ireland showed the same symptoms, and a mass migration occurred for which the way had been prepared by a long-continued piling up of grievances. Placed outside the English mercantile system by the act of 1663, the Irish were forbidden in 1670 to share even in the victualling of ships engaged in the plantation trade. The exportation of beef to England was next forbidden, and when a promising woolen trade had been built up which began to compete with the English industry, it was ruthlessly throttled by a series of acts beginning in 1698. Then the unfortunate Irish artisans found insufficient employment in their linen production though it was left without cramping restrictions. Meanwhile farmers felt the perennial grievance of rack-renting absentee landlords, and the economic condition of the people became progressively more wretched. To these troubles were added religious disabilities when a High-Church faction came to power with Queen Anne in 1704. The Roman Catholics, who constituted the vast majority of the population, had long been deprived of political rights and forced to support the Anglican establishment, but Presbyterians and dissenters had enjoyed some favor under William III. New acts now forced all public officers to take the sacrament according to the rites of the Church of England, persons were prosecuted for being married by dissenting ministers, and schoolmasters who were not of the Anglican faith became liable to imprisonment if they performed their pedagogical functions. The Ulsterites of the north thus joined the Catholics of the south in political and economic misfortune.[8]

Though there was a preliminary movement to New England in 1718 by some Presbyterian congregations from the region of the Bann River, the full tide of migration was set going by three years of famine in 1725, 1726, and 1727. Rapidly the idea went around of abandoning the country. During the summer of 1728 more than three thousand persons departed, and the Lords Justices of Ireland reported that twenty thousand had declared their intention of going in the next spring, to the great prejudice of the linen trade and of the Protestant interest. The "humour," wrote Archbishop Boulter, "spread like a contagious distemper." James Logan of Pennsylvania wrote in 1729 that it looked as if Ireland was to send all its inhabitants to that colony; according to a newspaper account two thousand of them arrived in the Delaware River during one week.[9] After a few years the volume of migration diminished, but it often swelled again during the century when lean years made life unusually hard. Ireland was of all countries the one most subject to repeated attacks of the "contagious distemper" of emigration.

The same phenomenon may be observed in Scotland during the 1770's. Slowly but steadily since the middle of the century the condition of tenant farmers in the Highlands had deteriorated. The causes of this were several, and were related to the peculiar structure of society in that country,[10] but actual reports from many of the emigrants in this movement show that practically all of them left because their rents had been raised and there had been a bad year or two for cattle and crops.[11] A few of their number went to America and sent letters back telling of the good settlements there, of having purchased large tracts of land for trifling sums, and of living comfortably. These reports, said the customs collector of Wigtown, "raised a spirit of Emigration amongst others of the like station in this Country next to Madness. We hear that . . . some Tradesmen of different kinds and some farmers have entered into an association to emigrate themselves with their Familys to North America against the ensuing Spring or Summer."[12] It is notable that few of these Scots were penniless; they were able to sell what property they had and pay their own way to America, and a few even took indentured servants with them.

German migration to the colonies during the eighteenth century was nearly always of this collective kind. The peasants of the Rhineland and Palatinate, though not a little oppressed by their landlords, were much better off than those further east. Their land was more fertile and their trade more brisk. From about 1685, however, their country was periodically ravaged by the armies of Louis XIV, and when the time of open warfare ceased in 1715, they were exposed, for the rest of the century, to the capricious tyrannies and outrageous exploitation of their petty princes, who sought to emulate the French monarch in the extravagance of their palaces and the numbers of their officials. Some of the Catholic potentates persecuted their Protestant subjects for religious reasons. There was reason enough for discontent, but except for the extraordinary hardships of Louis XIV's wars there was no more reason for these Germans to leave their country than for the inhabitants of any other district in Europe to move; perhaps in fact there was rather less. Yet move they did, by the tens of thousands.[13]

We have already observed that the beginning of the great migrations of Germans took place in 1708 and 1709, when vast numbers of them set forth at the invitation of the British government to settle, as they thought, in New York. Some thirteen thousand were actually transported across the Channel to England, of whom about 3,200 were eventually sent to New York and the rest distributed to other colonies, or to Ireland, or sent back home. It seems to have been the enticements contained in the government pamphlets, as well as the other propaganda which had been circulating in Germany since the days of William Penn, that turned the minds of these people to America, but the distresses of an exceptionally severe winter fixed their determination to emigrate. From that time on the movement was continuous, fluctuating in volume according to the exigencies of particular situations. Far more generally than was the case in Britain these people left their homes in groups, by families, kindred, or even by whole communities. There would be a hard winter, or a persuasive emigrant agent would appear in town, or a series of enthusiastic letters would be received from someone in America, and this would be enough to stimulate a small mass migration. Arrangements would be made for selling whatever real property the family possessed, and a date would be set in the spring when all persons from the vicinity who wished to go would meet, load their movable goods, and commence the long journey down the Rhine to Rotterdam. The group impulse in these migrations, the influence of mutual emulation and encouragement, the contagious enthusiasm which spread like a fever, these were the things which converted people from passive endurance of economic misery to active seeking for a chance of betterment.

As might be expected, most of the people who were first involved in these movements were not the hopelessly indigent or the vagabond poor. They emigrated generally as free men, who had property enough so that by selling it they could pay their own way, or at least as redemptioners whose resources were insufficient but by no means non-existent. They carried with them, however, on the fringes of their movement, a considerable number of destitute persons as servants, and they showed the way to others with less initiative and enterprise. Thus we read that Germans before about 1728 were commonly people of substance when they went to America; one writer declared that the poorest master of a family had taken with him after paying his passage fifty pounds sterling, and many more than six hundred pounds.[14] The Puritan leaders were men of property; the Ulster Irish of 1718 were not servants. No sooner did such a movement get well started, however, than many of the desperately poor joined it. Archbishop Boulter stated that not one in ten of the Irish who emigrated in 1728 could pay his own way,[15] and the Germans coming to Pennsylvania seem to have become progressively less substantial people as the century went on.

Such mass movements to the New World as those described were of course godsends to merchants who sought a cargo for their ships, but they could not be relied upon to furnish a steady supply of emigrants. Generally the demand for servants and settlers, and the prospects of profit from their transportation, were much greater than the natural impulse of the poor to move to America. It was the problem of the colonial proprietor, the merchant, seaman, or emigrant agent to draw recruits from the great reservoir of population which existed in poverty at home, to persuade or encourage men to sign up as servants, to induce perhaps a local attack of the emigration fever in some German town, and to raise a cargo of laborers and settlers for the colonies. The methods of accomplishing this ranged from those which were wholly legal and aboveboard to others which were surreptitious and disreputable, and they extended even to forcible kidnapping. It is actually very difficult to fix the point at which legitimate means of recruiting blend into illegitimate, as will be seen in what follows, but the present chapter will concern itself mainly with the former.

A planter who was in England, or a man of substance who emigrated to the colonies, might find it possible to pick out his own servants; in fact he commonly took them from his own countryside. The early colonizing companies depended to some extent upon the local influence of their members, who brought forward people suitable for the venture. Thus in 1609 the Virginia Company requested the Earl of Pembroke to address letters to his officers in the stanneries for the recruiting of a hundred "mineral and laboring men."[16] The Providence Company in one of its first meetings resolved:

That eich Adventurer should entertaine into the Companies service so many men, and boyes, as are willing to undertake the same; and as they shall conceive fitt to be imployed therein; and to use the best Expedicon, that may be, in the same. And also should give notice to the Deputy, before Christmas next, how many they have provided, and of what age, and Condicon they be; that so the Deputy may take order to have so many, as the Company shall now thinke good to send, ready to be shipped by the 10th of January next.

A year later the Adventurers were again given notice to "harken out for honest men" who would be willing to go the voyage.[17] Most of the servants sent to Massachusetts in the early years were gathered in much the same way; in the next century the Georgia Trustees closely supervised the selection of candidates for their settlement, interviewing each one before allowing him to go.[18] Yet this method was by its nature infrequently possible, and it was outside the regular course of the emigrant trade. Far more common was the practice of colonists who wrote to their friends, family, or agents in England, and entrusted the selection of servants to their special care. Such a procedure was most apt to result in the acquiring of good and satisfactory servants, for it avoided the necessity of buying whoever became available on the decks of ordinary servant ships; it was not possible, however, for the greater number of colonists to enjoy this advantage.

For the encouragement of emigration in general, the usual practice was to rely in the first place upon printed inducements in the form of handbills or pamphlets. Beginning with the Virginia Company's broadsides, of which one example has already been quoted, practically all colonizing ventures issued a prospectus, setting forth the opportunities offered to emigrants in their particular colony, and sometimes enlarging upon the natural advantages of the locality chosen. Each person who would pay his own passage to the colony was generally offered fifty acres of land immediately, for himself, and additional amounts for each servant or member of the family who came in the party. As inducement to servants a promise was always given to assign them certain amounts of land, ranging from ten acres in the smaller West Indian islands to fifty or more on the continent, when their terms of servitude expired. Emigrant agents also printed handbills; according to William Eddis one could not help seeing on the streets of London numerous advertisements "offering the most seducing encouragement to adventurers under every possible description; to those who are disgusted with the frowns of fortune in their native land; and to those of an enterprising disposition, who are tempted to court her smiles in a distant region."[19] It was reported from Scotland that "enticing accounts of America published everywhere by the shipmasters and agents, have a great effect" in persuading men to emigrate. Georgia and Nova Scotia used the newspapers to gain publicity for their colonizing schemes.[20]

Of the large numbers of miscellaneous pamphlets concerning the colonies some were mainly for the purpose of encouraging emigration, though there are fewer of these after the general opinion had come to favor keeping the population in England. William Bullock, in the introduction to his *Virginia Impartially Examined,* says that he has written it because "many Gentlemen have unsetled themselves, with a desire to better their fortunes in remote places, and in this condition, inquisi-

tive after the severall Plantations abroad ... are much troubled
with the various relations both by books and men, whose onely
aime is to draw all men to themselves." John Hammond's *Leah
and Rachel,* describing Virginia and Maryland, seems to have
been written especially for the benefit of servants, for it devotes
much of its space to a favorable account of their condition.
George Alsop, author of the *Character of the Province of Maryland,* had himself once been a servant in the colony.

In Switzerland and Germany printed material was more
successful in procuring settlers than it was in Great Britain.
The writings of William Penn first turned attention towards
the English colonies, and a glowing pamphlet about Carolina
written by Joshua Kocherthal had remarkable influence at the
end of the seventeenth century. John Rudolph Ochs printed a
book for emigrants in 1711, and Jean Peter Pury was prodigal
with pamphlets, newspaper advertisements, and broadsides
promoting his schemes. "We have been informed," wrote some
Swiss about 1735, "by a little Boock printed in Bern that the
King of England wants Maun that are brought up to country
Buissiness and know how to improove Land and make Butter
and Cheese, in the Royal Province of Carolina wich as wee
heard is a land flowing with milck and Honey." [21] John Dick,
agent for the Board of Trade in procuring German settlers
for Nova Scotia, published his terms in the press of many towns,
and found himself engaged in a controversy with Joseph Crellius, similarly employed by the colony of Massachusetts. When
Dick's prospectus came out, Crellius countered it with another
denouncing Nova Scotia as a remote and uninhabitable region.
Dick thereupon sent copies of the *Frankfort Gazette* containing
Crellius's remarks to the Board of Trade, telling them that if a
similar story appearing in the Groningen newspaper was not
confuted, some ninety families whom he had enlisted would
change their minds and refuse to go. [22]

Most influential of all written persuasions were letters from actual settlers. These were sometimes printed by emigrant agents for distribution; the city of Berne on the other hand used them for the purpose of keeping its citizens at home, suppressing favorable accounts and printing unfavorable ones.[23] We have already quoted the account of the customs collector at Wigtown, in Scotland, relating how letters from settlers in America had actually raised the emigration fever to a pitch of madness. John Dick advised the Board of Trade that particular care should be taken to receive the first contingent of Germans kindly in Nova Scotia, "for all the future Embarkations of these people will depend upon the Letters they send home at their Arrivall," and he even recommended that their letters be sent first to the Board or to himself, so that a judicious censorship might be exercised.[24]

The consideration of this literature leads to one of the most interesting and at the same time most puzzling questions in the whole subject of colonial migration. Did the servants and redemptioners have a reasonably intelligent idea of what they were doing? Did they actually learn something about the colonies, about the conditions of servitude and the chances for success, and emigrate after realistically weighing these chances? A good deal of modern writing on the subject has indicated that most of them did, and has argued that they were exercising sound judgment in escaping from the economic, political, and religious maladjustments of the bad old world to the golden opportunities of the new. Most contemporary writers, on the other hand, charged that emigrants were all sadly deceived and imposed upon by false propaganda and lying agents, and that if they had known what they were doing they would have stayed at home. There were certain reasons, as we shall see, why contemporary writers may not have been strictly impartial in making these remarks, and their words cannot be taken quite at face value; nevertheless, it does not appear to the present writer that many servants knew enough about America to make an intelligent appraisal of their chances, or that many of them went after taking deep thought. We shall cite so much evidence showing how ignorant they were, and how irregularly they were prevailed upon to go to the colonies, that it is unnecessary to recapitulate the points here, but there are a few impressive facts on the other side of the argument which cannot be excluded from consideration.

Some servants certainly had informed themselves sufficiently well as to the terms which were being offered so that they refused to take inferior propositions. Thus for instance the Providence Company in 1637 tried to enroll candidates without promising the "freedom due" of £10 which was then being given in the West Indies, and was unable to get any.[25] In 1698 the island of Jamaica, in order to get white men, offered to pay the passages of servants and set them free upon arrival; the governor complained that the agents of the island in England had not published the act, and therefore not many servants had come.[26] He apparently expected that such offers, if made known, would receive intelligent consideration. But most striking of all evidences is that which shows servants preferring one colony over another. We are told that the number coming to Barbados fell off after the available land in that island had been granted out, and in 1683 Jeaffreson wrote that "Carolina and Pennsylvania . . . are in such repute, that men are more easily induced to be transported thither than to the Islands."[27] An agent of the Georgia Trustees wrote from Scotland in 1735 that it was difficult to procure servants, because many had been bound for Georgia and then shipped to Jamaica, which "frightens the Vulgar."[28] Many testimonies concur in showing that the Germans insisted on going to Pennsylvania rather than to other colonies.

These things show that in one way or another, whether by published literature or by word of mouth, a certain amount of sound knowledge and honest opinion got about among prospective emigrants concerning the relative excellencies of various colonies. Yet the effect of this must have been almost entirely on the more intelligent classes; the lower fringes of society can hardly have been touched at all by the influence of books and pamphlets. Some other encouragement was needed, some pressure far more direct and immediate than printed exhortations, before such people would make the final and irrevocable decision to move. This pressure was supplied by the emigrant agent, generally called during the seventeenth century in England a "spirit" because of his tendency to use improper methods of persuasion, and known in Germany as a "Newlander," or more venomously "Soul-seller." Such agents were paid by ship captains, merchants, or proprietors, generally at a fixed rate per head for all recruits whom they produced ready for transportation. Their activities were at the root of all emigration during colonial times except in those periods when a true "fever" was running its course.

There is reason to believe that the proprietors of Berkeley Hundred in Virginia had an agent recruiting servants for them as early as 1620; certainly the Providence Company was using one in 1633. In 1638 the same organization agreed with "diverse men" to "take up" servants for twenty shillings each, and an agent was sent as far afield as Wales.[29] In 1634 Lady Verney, who was engaged in fitting out her graceless son Tom for a plantation in Virginia, wrote to a man in Bucklersbury who told her he could have forty servants ready for shipment at a day's notice.[30] The Carolina proprietors sent a man to Ireland in 1669, and in 1735 the Georgia Trustees commissioned Hugh Mackay to raise a shipload of emigrants in the Highlands; they also had agents recruiting foreign servants in Holland and the Lower Rhineland.[31] As early as 1730 the Board of Trade employed a man named Hintz to recruit Palatine families for Nova Scotia;[32] this venture was not successful, but the activities of John Dick in 1750 and 1751 have already been mentioned. Dick, like Crellius for Massachusetts, had sub-agents living in the principal cities of the Rhineland, and the competition for emigrants was so great that when the Halifax colonists had been brought even to the borders of Holland they were set upon by representatives of the Rotterdam "monopolists," Hope and Stedman, who spread rumors of the insalubrious climate of Nova Scotia, won away some of Dick's men, and encouraged such dissension that there was finally a pitched battle between the two factions of emigrants.[33]

The foregoing examples are mainly from the accounts of large and relatively respectable enterprises. Moving a step lower in the scale there is the typical small-scale venture of some Aberdeen merchants and tradesmen, who decided in 1743 to freight a ship with servants and send it to the plantations. They employed one James Smith to recruit the cargo and manage all this part of the business for them; Smith operated from the beginning of January to the middle of May, when the ship sailed. He hired a drummer to go twice through the town of Aberdeen, announcing the voyage, and sent pipers about at the fair for the same purpose. As the servants came in he superintended their board and lodging, and sent emissaries to the country districts to bring in more candidates; his total expenses came to £160.18.9.[34] Similarly in Ireland Captain Cumming of the ship *George* sent his brother and his brother-in-law in 1735 to the counties of Monaghan, Cavan, and Meath, where they "dispersed publick notice through the country," and told great stories of the charms and comforts of life in North Carolina.[35]

Though a great many servants were thus recruited by the agents of particular enterprises, or by ship captains, still a larger number were collected by agents who were not connected with any particular voyage but were permanently in the trade. If we run over the names of the masters to whom servants are indentured in the records at the guildhalls of London or Middlesex, we find that there are very few of them: John Taylor, yeoman; John Dykes, victualler; Ambrose Cox, tobacconist; James Gerald, vintner; Christopher Veal, woolcomber; these five accounted for nearly all servants registered at the London Guildhall during the early 1720's. They were agents, or crimps, if a less pleasant name be preferred, who brought their candidates before the magistrate for a legal registration of the contract, and then turned them over, complete with indenture, to a merchant or ship captain sailing for the colonies. According to William Bullock in 1649 a person wishing servants for the plantations could get them at "Cookes houses about Saint Katharines" by paying about £3 to the agent, who would generally have plenty on hand.[36] At the turn of the century Ned Ward described the business thus:

We peep'd in at a Gateway, where we saw Three or Four Blades well Drest, with Hawks Countenances, attended with half a Dozen Ragamuffinly Fellows, showing Poverty in their Rags, and Despair in their Faces, mixt with a parcel of Young Wild Striplings like Run-away Prentices . . . that House, says my Friend, which they are entring is an Office where Servants for the Plantations bind themselves . . . [37]

William Eddis, near the end of the colonial period, gives a similar description.[38]

The German Newlanders are traditionally described as prosperous looking individuals with massive gold watch chains, who had returned from Pennsylvania and who told their victims tall stories of riches and ease in the new world. Having made an agreement with the shipping companies of Rotterdam by which they were to receive half a doubloon or a florin for each emigrant they should produce, they went about through the German towns collecting groups of people, and if possible getting them to sign contracts then and there for transportation to America.[39] Most observers agreed that these men were the principal influences stimulating the large annual movements from Germany and Switzerland to the colonies.

Public opinion, especially in the British Isles, was generally hostile to these agents. Despite the drummers which they sent through towns, their pipers at the fairs, their public advertisements, gold watch chains and flaunting stories, despite the fact that in the eighteenth century they generally saw to it that servants were legally bound before a magistrate, their success was held to be owing to secrecy, misrepresentation, and fraud. This was in part because some of them were actually kidnappers, and people who were not susceptible to their blandishments had a deep-rooted fear of them and of the vague terrors of the colonies. Here, for example, is the report of Robert Southwell, representative of the Carolina proprietors to Ireland in 1669:

I did fully inlarge and explain [the conditions of servitude] to all the persons that I thought fitt to take notice thereof, & consulted with all such as I thought intelligent in those affaires to advise mee how to raise such servants but hetherto I could not obteyne any, for the thing at present seemes new & forraigne to them, & withall they have beene so terrified with the ill practice of them to the Carib[da] Ileands, where they were sould as slaves, that as yet they will hardly give credence to any other usage; & withall they are loath to leave the smoke of their owne Cabbin if they can but beg neer it.[40]

Another reason for the unpopularity of emigrant agents was the state of opinion respecting emigration in general. It has been seen that after about 1660 official and respectable thought came to favor the keeping of people in England, and one consequence of this was an attempt to discredit all who had a hand in emigration. Naturally, most of what we read comes from the pens of the official and respectable class, a fact which probably causes the true popular distrust of agents to be magnified in the evidence. Nevertheless, these classes had a dominating influence upon opinion in their own day, and hence the emigrant agent, though he was the key man of the whole system of emigration and indentured servitude, remains generally an obscure and often a furtive figure.

In this account of how people came to emigrate as servants and redemptioners we have reached the point at which proper, legal, and open methods of persuasion blend into those which were improper, dishonest, and secret. Before giving a further description of the latter this chapter may conclude with the story of the ship *Abraham,* which collected a cargo of servants and took them to Barbados in 1636. It is worth telling not because of any strange or unusual features, but because it must have been just such an enterprise as numberless other ships carried out. The supercargo of this ship, Thomas Anthony, was sent on ahead to the south coast of Ireland to sign on servants; his letters to the owner, Mathew Cradock, and his expense accounts, have survived, and furnish the only complete history of one of these enterprises which is known.[41]

Anthony's instructions were to procure as many servants as possible up to the number of a hundred, indenture them for four years' service in Virginia, and hold them ready to be picked up by the *Abraham* when she arrived. On April 28, 1636, he was at Kinsale, where he found "a flymishe shippe of 140 tonns or thearaboutt of Amsterdam which hath gonn from heare at othear times which doth hope to clear 120 or 140 passingers for St. Christours & licke wise a shippe of thes towne which will carry about 100 and will be Ready within three wycks or a month. . . ." Undismayed by this competition, Anthony informed his friends and acquaintances of his purpose, "that they maye make it knowen in the Cuntry for the procuringe of servants," but he prudently decided that "untill the shippe be heer thear will be no providinge of servants the Resson so that as soon as wee have greed with sutch as will goe, They will be forthwith one our Chardge, and douttfull that after sume time of sutche Expence they will Runne away so thear is lettle to be don untill the shippe be heer to take them Abourd." While waiting he procured the services of Hugh Neal, tailor, of Kinsale, to whom he delivered woolen and linen cloth, and six dozen tin buttons, to make clothes for the servants. Neal also made stockings and blankets, and continued through the summer to work for Anthony, receiving the modest remuneration of eighteen pence per suit, eightpence per blanket, and eighteen pence per dozen pairs of stockings. The total cost of the suits was seven or eight shillings each, blankets nine shillings a pair, and stockings eight shillings and threepence per dozen pairs.

Curiously enough, Anthony found that "every mans mind in thes place" was inclined towards going to St. Christopher. An impression had got about that servants in that colony were given liberal wages by the year, and in view of this no one wanted to go to Virginia. It was probably untrue that such wages were paid, as no other evidence for it has been found, but it was the custom in the West Indian islands to promise a freedom due of £10, and it may have been of this that the Irish were thinking.

The *Abraham* arrived at Kinsale on August 27. Cradock had approved of the arrangements Anthony had made, and on September 13 the supercargo wrote as follows:

for peese & chees I persume you have made sufficient provizon . . .

And now it may plese you to be informed that uppon the fearst dayes of markett aftar the shipps Arivall, bothe heer at Bandon Corke and Yoghall we caused the drume to be Betten, and gave warninge to all those that disposed to goe servants for Virginea shuld repare to Kinsale whear I leay and uppon Condisons accordinge to the Cuntry I would intartayne sutche. . . .

The master of the ship, Anthony himself, and several hired agents went into the country to collect servants whenever they could find time. Money was spent on these trips, and from the accounts we learn that a glass of beer was generally given to the servant when the bond was signed. One Thomas Belchard of Bandon, who had assisted in procuring servants, was rewarded with a "pinte of wine & shugar." Probably there was something like kidnapping involved, for though Anthony is careful not to give himself away in his letters, it is evident that he spent a few days in jail, having been put there by the mayor of Kinsale until he released two of the servants he had signed. There are charges laid out at the "Blewe Anker" for the servants' food, and a total of more than twenty-five pounds was thus expended.

By the middle of October the business has progressed:

. . . And we dowe entartayne all comers both men & women. . . . And hethear untow we have entertained, and furth cominge the number of 61 persons whearof ther is 41 men servants the

rest women kind from 17 to 35 Eares and very lustye and strong
Boddied which will I hopp be meyns to sett them of to the best
Advantidg . . . ther cometh one or othear of men servants dayly
and for women they are now Reddear to goe then men, whereof we ar furnished with as many as we have Rome And for
procuringe of men servants hath bene veary Chardgable, as by
the acompt when it cometh to your hands will apeer. . . .

Upon the eve of departure Anthony purchased three pounds
and a half of tobacco for the servants, at a cost of nine shillings
and fourpence, and a shilling was invested in "peppar and
Gingar for the servants at seaye." Another shilling was given
"to a mydwiffe to vizat the women servants doutinge ther
behaviour." This last precaution proved insufficient.

On November 22 the *Abraham,* after some buffeting, had
been driven into the harbor at Cowes, where Anthony found
a letter from his owners giving him permission to go to Barbados if he wished. He considered this an excellent move, and
reported as follows:

Our passingers as in my formar I advized arr all well only have
bine seahe sicke and the worse by Reson of our weake and
Leacky shippe which nowe I hoppe will be Redrest . . . by
Reson that wee Could not furnishe ourselves with as many
men servants as we desired we were constraned to take Twenty
Women for whom the time beinge shortt aftar Entartayning,
And want of mony weare not able to provid them with lyninge
& smocks as we shuld have dun, whearfore if you maye Covenant to send as many as you see fetting which is a great
want . . .

A month later the ship was still at Cowes, with fifty-eight
servants on board. As was a common practice on such voyages,
the women were landed to wash their own and the men's
clothes; a guinea was expended for needful house room while
they were doing it, and a shilling for soap. Some of them ran
away, and ten shillings had to be spent in tracking them down.

Meanwhile Anthony discovered that three of the women were pregnant, and he set them on shore with passes to return to Ireland and five shillings sixpence "in the purses." Another woman, who had been taken aboard at Cowes, was found "not fette to be entartained havinge the frentche dizeas," and so was "left to herselfe."

The last letter to be quoted is from Barbados, dated February 13, 1636/7:

. . . my formar to you was of the 24th decemb and that daye at night wee set sayle from the Cowes with a hapaye and prospers winde. And feare weather which harbored us in the Iland of the barb bados the 25th of January, whear we hopp of good sales for that of our goods which you shipped from London and the licke of what came from Ireland . . . And from the Cowes we brought 56 servants for your accompts which weare desposed of to sale 10 of them to the governor of thes place in four hondreth and fiftye wayght apece and all the Rest in five hundreth to paye the 20th and last of Aprill for good to Bacca, which we hopp well be peayed at the tyme . . .

The account book for the sale of the cargo at Barbados may also be seen. Names of the servants are not noted; only the purchasers with the number and price of each purchase are given. Fifty-three servants were sold in two days, none save those to the governor for less than five hundred pounds of tobacco, and the total amount received for the servants was 27,650 pounds. The speed of selling indicates a brisk demand, and since there is no further entry of a sale of servants after January 29, it may be assumed that three died on the voyage, which was indeed a very low mortality rate for a servant ship.

CHAPTER 4

KIDNAPPING, SPIRITING, AND REGISTRY OFFICES

———

I N T H E stockholders meeting of October 23, 1622, the Deputy of the Virginia Company called attention to three matters having to do with the transportation of persons and goods which were faulty and would breed trouble. In the first place, said he, divers ships were going daily to the colony without any further reference to the company than the obtaining of a commission, and there was no register kept of the names of persons transported on these ships. Therefore he and the other officers of the company had been unable to give any satisfaction to persons that "did daylie and howerly enquire after their friends gon to Virginia." Secondly, the goods of passengers on board ship were open to appropriation by the sailors if the owner died, and his relatives on shore had no means of recovering such property. Lastly, it was necessary to provide by some means that covenants between masters and servants should be observed, and that no fraud should be practiced by either party. The wrongs suffered by servants were particularly serious, "it beinge observed here that divers old Planters and others did allure and beguile divers young persons and others (ignorant and unskillful in such matters) to serve them upon intollerable and unchristianlike condicons upon promises of such rewards and recompence, as they were no wayes able to performe nor ever meant." In November a plan was drawn up and a special office appointed to register the names of all persons going to Virginia, whether in the company's ships or not. Contracts were to be executed in writing, and to be drawn by a man who understood the situation in the colony.[1]

Although the abuses mentioned by the deputy are mild enough when compared with the later iniquities of kidnapping, his statement puts the problem very much in the way it persisted throughout the colonial period, and the solution devised was also the only satisfactory one which was ever worked out. In those early days the evil might be limited to an exaggerated promise made by a planter, or to the mild deceit of ignorant boys, but as the plantations developed and the demand for servants increased a situation was created which offered too great a temptation to the greed of many persons in England. Vessels were constantly leaving for the colonies, and their owners or captains, anxious to get a load of servants, would pay a pound or two for each candidate produced and ask no questions. There were plenty of unsavory characters around London and the seaport towns who would not scruple to collect a few wandering children, or simple-minded adults, or drunkards asleep in the gutter, and convey them on board the ship. Once aboard, the unfortunate victim never saw the light of day until the ship was at sea.

From this it was only a step to bolder means, but though force might occasionally be used the records indicate that "persuasion" was more common. The spirits, wrote Bullock, "take up all the idle, lazie, simple people they can intice, such as have professed idlenesse, and will rather beg than work; who are perswaded by these *Spirits,* they shall goe into a place where food shall drop into their mouthes: and being thus deluded, they take courage, and are transported."[2] If this method did not work, drink might be tried, and if the victim did not become sodden and manageable, he might even be forcibly kidnapped. Children were interested by presents of sweets, and were then concealed in obscure haunts until they could be shipped. All the various examples which might be quoted to show the methods of the spirits are as readily and accurately imagined, and to such methods the ignorant, credulous, and drink-loving multitudes of the poor were easy prey.[3]

This business rapidly grew in proportions and organization, and by the fifth decade of the century had ceased to be a casual occupation. Depots were established in less reputable sections of London, especially in St. Katherine's near the Tower, and the ordinary kidnapper could bring his victim to one of these houses, where he might be kept prisoner for a month or more until the master of a vessel should fetch him off. According to William Bullock in 1649 it was usual for anyone desiring a servant to procure him from one of these resorts, and the spirit's charges together with the expense of feeding in the "cook's-house," were commonly £3.[4] We have an animated description of one of these dives from the anonymous pen of the English Rogue, who fell in with a kidnapper, was taken to Wapping, and housed there:

To the intent he [the kidnapper] might oblige me to be his, he behaved himself extraordinary friendly; and that he might let me see that he made no distinction between me and his other friends, he brought me into a Room where half a score were all taking Tobacco: the place was so narrow wherein they were, that they had no more space left, than what was for the standing of a small table. Methought their mouths together resembled a stack of Chimneys, being in a manner totally obscured by the smoak that came from them; for there was little discernable but smoak, and the glowing coals of their pipes. Certainly the smell of this room would have outdone *Assa Foetida*. ... After I had been there awhile, the Cloud of their smoak was somewhat dissipated, so that I could discern two more in my own condemnation: but alas poor Sheep, they ne're considered where they were going, it was enough for them to be freed from a seven years Apprenticeship, under the Tyranny of a rigid Master . . . and not weighing . . . the slavery they must undergo for five years, amongst Brutes in foreign parts, little inferior to that which they suffer who are *Gally-slaves*. There was little discourse amongst them, but of the pleasantness of the soyl of that Continent we were designed for, (out of a design to make us swallow their gilded Pills of Ruine), & the temperature of the Air, the plenty of Fowl and Fish of all sorts; the little labour that is performed or expected having so little trouble in it, that it rather may be accounted a pastime than anything of punishment; and then to sweeten us the farther, they insisted on the pliant loving natures of the Women there; all which they used as baits to catch us silly Gudgeons. . . .[5]

The sinister and secretive practices of the spirits soon began to frighten the lower classes of London and excite their imaginations. We read that William Graunt and Thomas Faulkner were brought before the justices of Middlesex in 1645 "to answer for assaulting and pumping of Margarett Emmerson upon the false report of a spiritt or an inticer or inveagler of children . . . there beinge noe charge or accusation laid against her." Likewise Margaret Robinson was haled up to answer "for a ryott upon Mary Hodges, and sayinge shee was a sperritt," while a few years later Susan Jones was ordered to appear "to answer the complainte of Rebekah Allen for raisinge a tumult against her and callinge of her 'spirit.'"[6] These cases indicate that there was a growing popular apprehension and fear of the spirits, and this state of mind later made possible the persecution of harmless persons by unjust accusations of kidnapping, and so hindered the normal trade in servants.

Meanwhile the government made its first move to check the practice. An ordinance of Parliament, in 1645, charged all officers and ministers of justice "to be very diligent in apprehending all such persons as are faulty in this kind, either in stealing, selling, buying, inveigling, purloyning, conveying, or receiving Children so stolne, and to keep them in safe imprisonment, till they may be brought to severe and exemplary punishment." The marshals of the Admiralty and of the Cinque Ports were ordered to search all vessels in the river and at the Downs for such children.[7] A further precaution was taken by the Admiralty Commissioners, who ordered that Customs Houses should keep a register of all outgoing passengers to plantations or to foreign parts; this order was repeated by Parliament in January, 1646/7, and the governor of each colony was instructed to return a certificate of the arrival of such persons in his province.[8] Apparently all of these injunctions were ignored; certainly no such lists remain, and the spiriting of servants went on with increasing vigor.

Where Parliamentary orders failed, local regulation succeeded better. In 1654 the city of Bristol passed a corporate ordinance requiring the registry in the Tolzey Book of the names of all departing servants, together with their destinations and the terms of their indentures. A penalty of £20 was imposed on any captain who disregarded this order, and for twenty years it was observed. The registrations of more than 10,000 servants may still be seen at Bristol, and the two volumes containing the entries are almost the only systematic records of servant transportation during the seventeenth century which are known to exist.[9]

The only recourse of persons whose children or apprentices had been kidnapped was a special petition to the highest authorities. Thus a warrant was granted in 1653 for the master

of a ship to deliver to Robert Broome his son, aged eleven, who
had been spirited on board. In 1657 Sir John Barkstead, Colonel
Francis White, and Major Miller were directed to inform themselves what passengers were on board the ship *Conquer*, bound
for the West Indies. They found nineteen servants, of whom
eleven had been "taken by the spirits," and most of these stated
that they were unwilling to go. The ship was allowed to proceed
after setting these on shore.[10] In the summer of the Restoration
the Privy Council received information on the subject, and in
writing to the customs officers of London they described the
practices of the spirits, calling them "so barbarous and in-
humane, that Nature itself, much more Christians, cannot but
abhorre." Continuing, they said that they had been informed
"That, at this tyme, there is a Shipp, called the Seven Brothers,
lately fallen downe towards Graves-End, and two other Shipps
in the River of Thames in good forwardnesse to follow after
in which there are sundry such Children and Servants of severall Parents and Masters, so deceived and inticed away Cryinge
and Mourninge for Redemption from their Slavery." The
officers were accordingly ordered to search all ships, and especially to stop the *Seven Brothers*.[11] In 1663 the clerk of the
town of Plymouth took it upon himself to stop the ship *Reserve*,
bound for Maryland and legally cleared from Gravesend. A
number of servants on board informed the clerk that they had
been kidnapped, upon which he set them free. For this he
was soundly rebuked by the Privy Council, yet very likely he
was justified with respect to a part at least of the cargo.[12]

The need for a regular system of recording the names and
indentures of all emigrating servants had by this time become
obvious. In November, 1660, two men petitioned the king for
letters patent to keep a registry office, to which all servants
were to be brought to declare their willingness to go, as well
as the parents of all children who were to be transported. A

series of other petitions and suggestions poured in on the king and Council. The mayor of Bristol in 1662 recited the situation in his city. In 1664 the Lord Mayor and Court of Aldermen of London presented a memorial on spiriting, saying that it often caused great tumults and uproars in the city, to the breach of the peace and the hazard of men's lives. On July 12, 1664, a group of merchants, planters, and masters of ships trading to the plantations petitioned for the appointment of persons under the Great Seal to enter the name, age, quality, place of birth, and last residence of all those desiring to go to the colonies as servants. This time the matter was referred to the attorney-general, who reported that the mischiefs of spiriting were indeed very great and frequent, and that there was scarcely a voyage to the plantations without some persons being illegally carried away. He recommended a registry office, but remarked that such an office would never be effectually executed without an act of Parliament granting a sufficient salary.[13] The Council of Foreign Plantations favored the scheme, the usual formalities were seen through, and on September 14, 1664, the registry office was officially created. Roger Whitley, "at 40s." was given charge, and was expected to derive his principal reward from fees rather than from a salary.[14] Registration of servants was not, of course, compulsory; the point was supposed to be that if thus registered a servant could have no complaint against the merchant, nor could parents distress ship owners about their children if the children had been properly signed on.

No systematic records of the activities of Whitley's office exist, but specimens of the forms it used have been preserved, showing that a system was worked out, even if not much used. There is an affidavit made out by a servant in 1670, stating the terms on which he had agreed to go to Virginia, and that he was willing to go. With this is a long certificate signed by "Jo: Salladine, Deputy Registrar," which recites the substance of the affidavit, specifies the freedom dues which the master is to give the servant at the end of his term, and announces that he has been properly registered. A place is provided for the special seal of the office.[15]

Kidnapping nevertheless continued. Cases in the Middlesex court were as frequent as ever, and the series of petitions for individual redress kept on growing. Merchants petitioned again in February, 1670/1, and Parliament was appealed to, but refused in 1670 and 1673, as they had already done once in 1662, to pass any comprehensive act against the kidnappers.[16] Meanwhile, in January, 1670/1, a certain William Haverland was convicted before Justice Morton of being a spirit, and to save himself turned king's evidence, giving a great deal of interesting testimony. He told, for instance, of John Steward, of St. Katherine's parish, who had been spiriting persons for twelve years at the rate of 500 a year. Steward used to give twenty-five shillings to anyone who would bring him a victim, and could then sell immediately to a merchant for forty shillings. A shoemaker of East Smithfield had also been in the business for twelve years, and in one year had transported 840 persons. Robert Bayley had his headquarters sometimes in St. Giles and sometimes in St. Katherine's, and made his entire living by the trade. Haverland named sixteen persons who were spirits; a haberdasher, a hostler, a waterman, two victuallers, a seaman, a brewer's servant, and so on, all of whom had been conducting their activities for at least two years.[17] Some further evidence was taken of their methods, and the whole brought to the attention of the Privy Council. And still nothing was done.

A remarkable story has now to be related, in the course of which the business of kidnapping emerges for the moment into the realms of high policy, and others besides the unfortunate servants are seen to be victimized by the system. In March, 1679/80, a certain John Wilmore, or Wilmer, merchant of London, sent several workmen as carpenters and the like to Jamaica on wages, and with them two boys whose guardians had bound them to him for service in the plantation. On the day of departure Wilmore went with his party to take the water at Billingsgate, and while waiting for the tide the men and himself went into a house and bought "Pipes, Tobacco, and Brandy." The boys meantime went out to play on the wharf, and met there another boy named Richard Civiter, who told them that he also wanted to go to sea. The others brought him to Wilmore, who supposed he was someone's son or servant, and would have nothing to do with him. But Civiter said that he had no father, mother, or master, and he "cried and roared" at further refusals. Wilmore thereupon took him to Gravesend and consulted the mayor. With that officer's advice and consent he bound Civiter with an indenture in due form and sent him to Jamaica, thinking no more of the matter.

In Michaelmas Term of that same year, 1680, Wilmore served on the Middlesex grand jury, which defied Charles II and brought in a bill of indictment against the Duke of York as a Popish recusant. A year later Wilmore was foreman of the grand jury for London, and returned the indictment of Stephen College with an *ignoramus,* despite the great interest which the Court had in getting the man convicted. College's trial was removed to Oxford, and Wilmore, having got himself thoroughly disliked by the highest powers, spent fifteen weeks in the Tower for high treason, until he was released on £9000 bail.

Later in the year 1681 a man came to see Wilmore and told him that there was in Wapping a barber named Civiter, whose son had been sent to Jamaica by the merchant. Old Civiter admitted that his son had been disobedient, but he demanded money. Actually he was aided and instigated by agents of the Court party, and there now began a long litigation. A bill against Wilmore for kidnapping, which came back with an *ignoramus* from the grand jury, was later used as one of the pretexts for the *quo warranto* suit against the City of London.[18] A writ of *de homine replegiando* was then issued against Wilmore, requiring him to produce the body of Richard Civiter, and he made the return that the boy had been sent beyond seas by his own consent. When this was called an insufficient return, a writ of *capias in withernam* was issued, meaning that the merchant himself was to be taken as security for the return of the boy. The result of these tortuous processes was the ruin of Wilmore, who secreted himself for about a year in England and then fled to Holland; he returned in 1688 with William of Orange and published an account of his troubles.[19]

Wilmore was not alone in his misfortune. For one reason or another, Chief Justice Pemberton started a savage campaign against kidnappers, real or pretended. One Richard Owsley, who had shipped Richard Turner to the plantations with the consent of the searchers at Gravesend, was nevertheless brought into the Court of King's Bench in a manner similar to that by which Wilmore was prosecuted. Merchants ceased to ship servants, and Sir Thomas Lynch from Jamaica asked the Lords of Trade and Plantations to calm Pemberton down.[20] The following letter of Christopher Jeaffreson, a West Indian planter then visiting London, best explains the situation:

I designed to have sent more servants. But I have not yet had the leasure to make the enquiries that are now necessary on these occasions. I have had several in my eye; but, when we come to treat, they will not go on ordinary termes. And the Lord Chief Justice hath so severely handled the kidnabbers, and so encouraged all informers against them, that it is very difficult to procure any. One of the kidnabbers, a slopseller, hath been fined five hundred pounds sterling; and Mr. Bauden and Mr. Baxter, with several eminent men, have been in some trouble on this score; and poor Captain Winter is prosecuted and put into print. To avoide which scandal, and the inconveniences attending, I am told that several eminent merchants, who have dealt to Virginia, Barbados, and Jamaica, are glad to compound with their old friends, the kidnabbers, who, finding the sweet advantages of turning informers, Judas-like betray their masters. This is a general disincouragement to the merchant, the procurer, and the masters of ships, who are very scrupulous of how they carry over servants.[21]

Thirty years before the date of this letter, William Bullock had written that "the usuall way of getting servants, hath been by a sort of men nick-named *Spirits*."[22] From his remark, and from Jeaffreson's very revealing phrases, we begin to see that the kidnappers and spirits instead of being deplorable outlaws in the servant trade were the faithful and indispensable adjuncts of its most respected merchants. They were, in fact, the English equivalent of the later German "Newlander." Wilmore's story shows how personal or political grudges against a respectable merchant could be indulged by attacking him as a kidnapper. Now if Dalby Thomas may be believed, the true motive of Chief Justice Pemberton in prosecuting kidnappers was not to shield the innocent servant, but to check the emigration of poor laborers from Great Britain to the colonies. According to Thomas, the whole outcry proceeded "from the wrong Notion which has infected our Judges, as well as the less intelligent Gentry, that the People which go thither are a Loss to the Nation."[23] There was doubtless some truth in this; certainly we know that mercantilist opinion had turned against emigration, and many eminent persons doubted whether the colonies were of any real profit to the country.

These considerations help to explain why Parliament refused to take any steps which would regularize the servant trade. The members did not wish the trade to flourish, yet they could not bring themselves to prohibit it altogether. The merchants, on the other hand, found themselves in a serious predicament, and greatly desired some legislation by which they could continue to transport servants and yet not be exposed to charges of kidnapping. They were not able to procure it until 1717, and then in a form only partly satisfactory, but meanwhile the Crown, which had a sympathetic interest in colonial expansion, helped them as much as possible.

Shortly after the date of Jeaffreson's letter a group of important Jamaica merchants petitioned the King and Council and obtained a new order, dated December 13, 1682, that indentured servants should be taken before a magistrate, who should sign the indenture and file it on a special file. Furthermore, read this order, "The clerk of the Peace is to keep a fair book, wherin the name of the Person so bound, and the magistrats name before whom the same was don, and the time and place of doing therof, and the number of the file shalbe entred, and for the more easy finding the same, the Entries are to be made alphabetically according to the first letter of the surname." Servants over twenty-one might be bound in the presence of one magistrate on satisfying him that the service was voluntary. Those under twenty-one required the assent of higher officers, and the consent of parents or masters. No one under fourteen could be bound unless the parents were present, nor could such be embarked for a fortnight after the binding. There was no requirement that all servants be so registered, but only the provision that "such Merchants, Factors, masters of shipps, or other Persons that shall use the method hereafter following . . . shall not be disquieted by any sute on his Majestys behalf, but, upon certificate thereof, . . . he will cause all such sutes to be stopped, to the end they may receive no further Molestation thereby."[24] This was as much as the king could do; he could not prevent suits on behalf of private persons.

On the same day, December 13, 1682, a *scire facias* was ordered to be brought against Roger Whitley's patent for a registry office, which was found to be "of no use, but rather a prejudice to his Majestys service."[25]

The magistrates immediately began to perform these duties, and special forms of indenture were printed for the purpose, which they used until Charles II died.[26] But they looked upon the order as having "dyed with the King," and it was not until the customs searchers at Gravesend had remonstrated that James II renewed the order on March 26, 1686.[27] In June of the same year he granted to John Legg, Christopher Guise, and John Robins letters patent for a new registry office, several merchants having declared that the old one had served a useful purpose.[28] Petitions were later received against this establishment, and in favor of a new one to be granted to one Edward Thompson. The matter was debated at some length in the first years of the reign of William and Mary, and Guise claimed that he had spent £1500 on his office, and never misbehaved in its conduct; nevertheless a *scire facias* was ordered, and a new patent granted to Edward Thompson. This last grant was renewed to the descendants of Thompson, and the office functioned through the eighteenth century.[29] The fee paid by the merchants was five shillings for drawing each indenture, and sixpence for the registration. None of its records survive, but various evidences prove that its services were in frequent demand.[30]

But still the evils of spiriting and kidnapping were not

much abated. In 1685 occurred a famous incident at Bristol, when Judge Jeffreys berated the mayor and haled him to the criminal's bar where he pleaded his own case. Jeffreys had discovered that the mayor was wont to sell small rogues and pilferers to the colonies, they having been deceived into praying for transportation as the only means of saving themselves from hanging.[31] The petitions of merchants on the subject, which seem to have been agitated at regular ten-year intervals, continued, but they were now directed to the Houses of Parliament rather than to the Council. What these ship owners wanted was a statute which should relieve them of all responsibility once a servant transported by them had been registered. In 1691 a committee of the House of Commons reported favorably on a bill to aid them; it passed two readings and was defeated on the third by a vote of 90 to 29. Again in 1701-1702 such a bill was under discussion. Micajah Perry and other prominent merchants gave testimony before the Commons committee, which reported that the case in favor of the bill was fully proved. Again it failed. In 1717 the question came up yet again; this time Joshua Gee was the principal witness for the merchants, and this time finally some success was achieved. In the new act concerning the transportation of convicts a clause was inserted making it lawful for merchants to transport persons between the ages of fifteen and twenty for terms of service not exceeding eight years providing that such persons were brought before the mayor of London, or one magistrate of London, or two magistrates elsewhere, for the purpose of acknowledging that they went of their own accord. The contract was to be signed before the magistrate and a record of it kept, and after this had been done the merchant was to be safe from any prosecution "any law or statute to the contrary in any wise notwithstanding." Leonard Thompson, who had inherited the registry office from Edward Thompson, petitioned the House of Lords to be heard against this act before it should be passed; he was referred to a committee and there is no further record of his case.[32] We have already observed that the registry office continued to do business throughout the century.

Stimulated by this act, the magistrates, at least of London, once more began the registration of servants. In the Guildhall is preserved an entry-book of the names of servants and of the masters to whom they were bound; this runs from 1718 to 1732 and contains records of 3,257 indentures. Blank forms were also kept in addition to the entry-book, and one was made out for each servant, stating exactly the terms of his contract and the plantation to which he was going.[33] There are a few hundred of these remaining from years subsequent to those covered by the entry-book, but unless the documents have been lost it would seem that the magistrates' activities languished after 1736. Probably they continued to sign the indentures but stopped keeping a record of them, for William Eddis wrote that during the 1770's it was customary for servants to be brought before a magistrate before embarkation in order to give their assent to the terms of service.[34] The town clerk of Aberdeen, testifying before a court in 1765, said that he never knew of any indentured servants going abroad without having their contracts attested by a magistrate, but "as to keeping a Register of indented Servants who were attested by the Magistrates of *Aberdeen,* he never kept any; neither does he know of his Depute or Servants keeping any such Record or List; neither could he possibly keep the same, as the Indentures, when attested, were signed by the Magistrate or inferior Judge, and immediately carried off by the Owner thereof." It was the opinion of this clerk that without official indorsement indentures would be useless in America.[35]

We may assume, therefore, that during the eighteenth century all servants normally had their indentures either signed by a magistrate or executed at the registry office. Certainly no more complaints are heard from the merchants, though in 1724 Thomas Ludwell of Bruton could still refuse to procure servants for Philip Ludwell of Virginia because he was afraid of being accounted a kidnapper. There are still cases of real kidnapping, and in fact the most famous instance of the whole colonial period, when the son and heir of the Earl of Anglesey was carried off, occurred about 1728. The notorious Peter Williamson endeavored to prove that he had been spirited to America in 1743, and had a good deal of success.[36] But the public clamor of the 1670's and 1680's was not revived, and the servant trade pursued a tranquil, if somewhat disreputable course to the end of the colonial period.

Though the whole subject of kidnapping and spiriting has usually been passed off with a description of its cruelties and a fulmination against its wickedness there was actually much to be said for the merchant and ship captain, as the case of John Wilmore and the letter of Jeaffreson have indicated. It was extremely difficult for an emigrant agent, however honest his intentions, to know the true status of persons who presented themselves for transportation as servants. We must remember that the "spirits" were not only man-stealers but were also the hope and refuge of all persons who wished to fly the country for any reason whatever. In 1662 the mayor of Bristol wrote:

Among those who repair to Bristol from all parts to be transported for servants to his Majesty's plantations beyond seas, some are husbands that have forsaken their wives, others wives who have abandoned their husbands; some are children and

apprentices run away from their parents and masters; oftentimes unwary and credulous persons have been tempted on
board by men-stealers, and many that have been pursued by
hue-and-cry for robberies, burglaries, or breaking prison, do
thereby escape the prosecution of law and justice.[37]

It is plain that the majority of persons named by the mayor
went of their own free will, though all left behind them a storm
of protest. The animosity of abandoned wives or husbands, of
deserted masters and disappointed constables, would be vented
not upon the absconder but upon the helpful "spirit," or the
owner of the vessel in which the runaway emigrated. The
servant sailed contentedly away from his obligations while the
"spirit" received the blame.

A further means of victimizing the merchant was soon
invented. The petition of July 12, 1664, reveals that the wicked
custom of spiriting "gives the opportunity to many evil-minded
persons to enlist themselves voluntarily to go the voyage, and
having received money, clothes, diet, etc. to pretend they were
betrayed or carried away without their consents."[38] The obvious
remedy for this was a registry office, and the fact that registration in these offices was not compulsory shows that they were
founded not for the benefit of the servant, but for the protection
of the merchants, who therefore had to pay a fee. Yet such
protection was only partial, at least before 1717, because the
merchant was still open to the attacks of persons on shore
who might truly or falsely claim that the exported servant
was fleeing from some responsibility or obligation. Evidence
of the actual occurrence of such cases is plentiful. A memorial
of the merchants in 1670 declares that "several Merchants and
masters of ships are now prosecuted for servants that went over
voluntarily and were duly bound and examined in an office
erected by his Majesty which has so terrified all merchants

and masters that of late none will carry them over."[39] Micajah Perry testified in 1702 that there were many ill persons about town who made it their business to be troublesome to merchants by procuring servants for them. The servant would be properly bound in the registry office, would go aboard ship and be provided with clothes. Afterwards, "some of their own gang" would go and search for them and then sue the master of the vessel for a kidnapper, alleging that the servant had left his family or his master. Perry reinforced his statements by several specific instances, including one of a person who was in Newgate because he had accepted the bond of a servant who had registered under an assumed name.[40]

This sort of racketeering was only possible because of the fact that genuine child-stealing was frequent enough to give color to the procedure. We have also seen that persons like Chief Justice Pemberton were glad to denounce merchants as kidnappers because they disapproved of emigration. It was for this reason that the pamphleteer Morgan Godwyn wrote in 1680 that ten thousand people annually were carried out of the country by the trade of spiriting;[41] his figure is absurdly large, and can only have been given for purposes of propaganda. It is easy to imagine also that when common people who stayed at home and resisted the persuasions of emigrant agents, learned of the emigration of their fellows to the unknown terrors of America they should assume that such departures were brought about by criminal means, and raise an outcry accordingly. The inhabitants of Bruton, according to Thomas Ludwell in 1724, "will live meanly & send their Families to the Parish to be relieved, rather than hear of such a long journey to mend their condition."[42] Emigration, except when a "fever" was aroused, was against the instinctive feelings of most people then as now, and so they called the agents of emigration by the opprobrious name of "spirit."

Yet despite these things which may be said for the merchant, the truth which emerges from the evidence is that the methods of emigrant agents were generally unsavory to a high degree. It is not that a small minority of them, practicing these methods, were "spirits," but rather that all of them used the same devices, and only a few were denounced and brought to book. An official commission appointed in 1661 to look into the whole subject of servant transportation reported that the usual way of procuring servants was by "persuading" or "deceiving" ignorant persons to make the venture.[43] More than a century later Jonathan Boucher wrote that white servants "are decoyed from hence by romantic Promises," and William Eddis said that the agents used to "represent the advantages to be obtained in America, in colours so alluring, that it is almost impossible to resist their artifices." Eddis also said that servants went only as a result of their ignorance and the misrepresentations of the agents.[44] But these descriptions are no different from the descriptions of "spirits" in the Middlesex Sessions Records, where the words "entice," "inveigle," and "decoy" are constantly used. William Bullock makes it quite clear that these were the usual methods of raising servants, and that the emigrant agents were known as "spirits." Once having signed the indenture, the servant was apt to be imprisoned until the ship sailed, sometimes on board the vessel itself, often in houses on shore, and in a few instances, even in the town jail.[45] For this the merchant justified himself by saying that he could not afford to have servants run away after receiving food and clothing, perhaps for several weeks, but even so the method encouraged grievous abuses.

If now we dispense for a moment with evidence, and inquire by the light of common sense how the average unskilled, ignorant servant would be recruited for a voyage to America, we shall certainly conclude that it must usually have been an irregular and unpleasant business. The candidate's respect for contracts would scarcely be much developed, and it is improbable that his sense of moral obligation could be relied on very far. The emigrant agent could make only a very limited inquiry into the status and responsibilities of his victim even if he felt moved to make any inquiry at all, and his depiction of conditions in America would be precariously governed by the extent of his knowledge and the delicacy of his conscience. In the course of the negotiations, who is to say when "decoying" began, or "inveigling" was brought to bear? And when the servant was duly enrolled, how was the merchant to protect himself against a breaking of the contract except by more or less strictly incarcerating his recruit until the ship sailed? The line between what was legal and what illegal is very hard to draw, and the persons of that time, who have left us what evidence there is on the subject, drew it with as much attention to their own prejudices as to the actual facts. The methods of the emigrant agent were not often criminal, but they were almost always disreputable; the "spirit" was seldom a lawbreaker but generally a shady character. A much larger proportion of our colonial population than is generally supposed found itself on American soil because of the wheedlings, deceptions, misrepresentations and other devices of the "spirits"; a very small proportion indeed were carried away forcibly and entirely against their wills.

PART TWO

———

Penal Transportation

CHAPTER 5

CONVICT TRANSPORTATION
TO 1718

T HE INCREASE in England of thieves, robbers and other
criminals was one of the consequences of those changes
which substituted a mercantile for an agricultural economy
and widened the gap between rich and poor. Crimes had been
committed during the Middle Ages, of course, and since the
twelfth century the king had sent out his justices to detect
criminals and punish them with all the authority of royal
power. But crime, as a social problem, did not exist until great
numbers of poor people had been turned away from their
manorial occupations and set adrift in a society which was
learning to disclaim responsibility for their support. They
swarmed to the cities, idle, masterless, unwanted persons, and
they lived by whatever wretched devices they could invent.
Inevitably many of them stole and robbed. Respectable contemporaries viewed them with alarm, and endeavored to sup-
press them by a brutal code of punishments which were intended to act as deterrents.

The penalty of death was prescribed by law for all felonies,
and a judge was allowed no discretion in imposing this penalty
upon persons duly convicted.[1] Hence the definition of what
constituted a felony was of peculiar interest to the criminal

classes, and it was by enlarging this group of offenses that Parliament undertook to deal with the problem of maintaining law and order. During the seventeenth century some three hundred crimes were designated as felonies, and from the fact that house-breaking, or stealing anything of value greater than a shilling, was thus made punishable by death the severity of the code may be estimated. Thousands of persons, most of whom were guilty of what we should consider almost negligible crimes, were condemned to the gallows.

This system, which appears so cruel on the statute books, was nevertheless profoundly mitigated by two practices, the pleading of clergy and the granting of royal pardons. During the whole of the seventeenth century a person convicted of felony might "call for the book," and if when given a book he could read it, he would thereby become free from the penalty of death and subject only to a branding in the thumb, under the ancient theory that all who could read were in holy orders and therefore exempt from the heavier punishments of the secular arm. Absurd as it manifestly was, this practice was a boon to literate offenders. In 1705 Parliament made it more absurd but also more generous by providing that those wishing to plead benefit of clergy need no longer prove their ability to read, but at the same time it set forth a list of felonies which were "non-clergyable." This list included about twenty-five crimes, among which were petty treason, piracy, murder, arson, burglary, stealing from the person above the value of a shilling, and highway robbery. Other offenses were frequently added, until in 1769 Blackstone found 169, and in 1819 Mackintosh 200 crimes for which a convict could not plead benefit of clergy. The code thus gradually became even more drastic than it had been in earlier days, and a practice grew up of convicting prisoners of smaller offenses than those of which they were probably guilty, in order to allow them to come under clergy.[2]

The practice of granting royal pardons to ordinary offenders has not received as much attention from historians as it deserves. Beginning early in the seventeenth century, and continuing in increasing measure through the eighteenth, it was customary for judges after each sessions to send up a list of convicts whom they considered worthy of mercy, and a pardon was forthwith issued under the Great Seal for the entire list. Later in this chapter various statistics will be presented from which the extent of this practice may be illustrated, but it may be stated now that long before 1700 it was usual to pardon at least half and generally a greater proportion of felons sentenced to death. Convict transportation to the colonies before 1718 was closely related to the system of pardons, and that relationship was maintained in lesser degree after 1718. According to the common law and the Habeas Corpus Act it was illegal to inflict a penalty of exile or transportation. But it was not illegal to pardon a felon upon the condition that he transport himself out of the country, and the term of his exile might thus be fixed as the authorities desired.[3] From 1655 to 1718 this was the legal device by which convicts were transported. In the latter year Parliament passed an act modifying the common law so that certain offenders in clergy could be sentenced to transportation, and from that time the majority of transportees were of this class. The system of pardons continued nevertheless to apply to non-clergyable offenders, and a large number of them came to the colonies, their term of exile being generally longer than that of less flagrant criminals.

The transportation of convicts was thus a mode of introducing reasonable leniency into a criminal code of which the ruling principle was that of fearful punishment. From very early years the idea had been familiar. Criminals had occasionally been used in war, and for filling out the numbers of men bound on dangerous exploring enterprises. Cartier took some to Canada in 1534, and Francis I authorized a selection of malefactors to be made from the Breton prisons for the expedition of 1540. Frobisher had men from the jails with him, and the Spaniards used them in colonization. Towards the end of the sixteenth century a French penal settlement was founded on Sable Island, but without success.[4] Governor Dale of Virginia recommended to Lord Salisbury in August, 1611, that all offenders in the common jails who were condemned to die should be sent for three years to Virginia, "as do the Spaniards people the Indies," and he seems to have believed that they would prove better than the three hundred profane, diseased and mutinous colonists who had gone on his first voyage.[5] The planting of the colonies with convicts was an element in nearly all plans and proposals for empire. Yet it was a long time before the system was effectively established, and we must review the various experiments in legal procedure made before 1661, and the many shortcomings in actual transportation evident before 1718.

The first step was taken by James I, who addressed to his Privy Council a commission, dated January 24, 1614/5, which is worth quoting at length because it summarizes the motives and principles behind convict transportation:

. . . Nowe of late wee find by experience that with our people offences and offenders alsoe are encreased to that number, as besides the severitie of our lawes punishing offenders in felonies to death, It is moste requisite some other speedy remedy be added for ease unto our people. Wherein as in all things els tending to punishment it is our desire that Justice be tempered with mercie, Soe likewise it is our care soe to have our Clemency applied as that greate and notorious malefactors may not be encouraged, and yet the lesser offenders adjudged by lawe to dye may in that manner be corrected, as that in theire punishment some of them may live and yeild a profitable service to the Comon wealth in parts abroad where it shall be found fitt to imploie them. Wee therefore reposing greate trust and confidence in you . . . doe for us our heires and successors give full power warrant and authoritie by theis presents to you or any six or more of you whereof some of you the said Lord Chauncellor Lord Treasourer lord Cheife Justice of England, Sir Ralfe Winwood to be twoe, to reprive and stay from execucon such and soe many persons as nowe stand attaynted or convicted of or for any robberie or felonie, (wilful murder rape witchcraft or Burglarie onlie excepted) whoe for strength of bodie or other abilities shall be thought fitt to be ymploied in forraine discoveries or other services beyond the Seas. This to be done after Certificate in writing made unto you by any one or more or our Judges or Serjeants at Lawe before whom such felons have bene tried. . . .[6]

The remainder of the commission gives power to the same persons to bestow reprieved felons upon any specific foreign undertaking they may see fit, and for any fixed length of time. If such felons return within the time limit, or refuse to go in the first place, their reprieve is to become void and they are to be executed. Finally, it is directed that all proceedings in accordance with the commission are to be certified by the principal secretary of state at the time, and "to be entred and enrolled on Record by the Clarke of our Crown in the Office called the Crowne Office" of the Court of King's Bench.

Shortly after the date of this commission the first batch of convicts was reprieved, and seventeen unfortunates were ordered to be delivered to Sir Thomas Smith, governor of the East India Company, to be conveyed into the East Indies or other parts beyond the seas. On July 7 of the same year, three felons were similarly reprieved on certificate from a judge of Admiralty, and three more were added to the previous seventeen who had been certified by the recorder of London.[7]

This method of procedure in sending convicts overseas was followed until 1634. Six renewals of the commission were made by the king,[8] usually because of the death or resignation of officials previously named in the quorum, and in that of September, 1622, a change was introduced which indicates some dissatisfaction with the process of transportation. Reprieved felons might thereafter be sent to the plantations, or they might be "otherwise constrayned to toyle in some such heavie and painefull manuall workes and labors here at home and be kept in chaynes in the houses of correction or other places . . . which servitude, as it is conceived, wilbe a greater terror than death itself. . . ."[9] From this time few felons were sent to the colonies, and indeed such evidence as has come to light shows only about sixty in the whole period before 1634.[10] Apparently the method was too cumbersome or the Council too unenthusiastic; certainly the scheme was abandoned, and from 1634 until 1640, when political troubles began in the kingdom, criminals were transported by authority of the king's own warrant under the sign manual. This seemed to work more effectively; within these six years we have record of more than sixty persons reprieved for the colonies by this speedier process.[11] After the beginning of the Long Parliament there are a few scattered notices of convicts transported by the authority of that body, but no systematic pursuit of the business was attempted.[12]

During the whole period prior to the time of Cromwell evidence is too scanty and inconclusive to encourage much confidence in statements about the total number of convicts transported or the particular colonies to which they went. According to the terms of the king's commission there ought to be complete records in the Court of King's Bench, but if any such records exist, they have not been found. There should also be, for each reprieved felon, a certificate from some judge of his fitness, and a warrant from the Council granting a reprieve; of these one sometimes finds the certificate without the warrant, and more often the warrant without the certificate, while in other instances there is evidence that felons were actually transported, though no warrant or certificate can be found. At least 150 convicts were destined for the colonies in these years, and many others reprieved for wars foreign or civil, some of whom may eventually have drifted to the plantations. It is extremely likely that there were still more of whom no record has remained.

Up to the year 1619 all reprieved convicts save one of whom we have evidence were handed over to Sir Thomas Smith, and while he may have sent them to the East Indies it appears more likely that he would use them in Virginia. Thereafter, until 1640, all are listed as reprieved for Virginia. In the latter year, twenty-five were given to Philip Bell; we may presume that he took them to Barbados where he was governor.[13] Evidence concerning the others is uncertain, and indeed it would be foolish to state that even those mentioned as going to Virginia actually arrived there, for the clerks of that period were apt to use the name of Virginia to denote any part of America which was subject to the king.

This period of trial and error in legal procedure and of scarcity in surviving evidence ends with the year 1655, when the first use of conditional pardons marked the discovery of a method which was to prove satisfactory until the next century. On the Patent Roll for that year, dated August 2, appears a pardon granted to certain prisoners who had been convicted of small crimes at the Surrey Assizes. At the end this clause is inserted:

Provided nevertheles and upon this condition that they the said Richard Biggs . . . and every of them shallbee by the Care of our Sheriffe of the said County of Surrey transported beyond the seas to some English Plantacon with all Convenient speed and if they or any of them shall refuse to bee transported being thereunto required or make any Escape or retorne into England within tenn yeares after theire said Transportacon without Lawful Licence first had then this our present Pardon to them soe refuseing escapeing or retorning to bee null and voyd.[14]

Two other collective pardons were issued in the same year, and the condition of transportation was imposed upon twenty-five convicts, while more were added to the list during subsequent years of the Protectorate.[15] The restored government of Charles II did not immediately adopt this procedure. It required a petition from a group of Jamaica merchants before the first conditional pardon was granted, in the summer of 1661, to no less than seventy-three felons, who were required to be transported to Jamaica.[16] Thereafter the series is uninterrupted, and by consulting the Patent Rolls one may find that about 4,500 convicts were thus destined for the colonies between 1661 and 1700.[17]

The great advantages of this machinery of the conditional pardon were that it was relatively simple and that it did not require the intervention of important personages before it would work, as James I's procedure had. After a jail delivery or other major assize, the justices sent up to the secretary of state a pardon fully drafted for such of the convicts as they thought worth saving from the gallows. If sentence had already been passed on any of them execution was stayed. The document was always signed by two justices, or, in the case of the Newgate delivery, by the mayor and recorder of London. Its Latin text was followed by a docket, giving again in English the name of each prisoner, his crime, and sometimes the special reasons which had induced the judge to recommend mercy. This complete document was then signed by the king and countersigned by the secretary of state, and a note added that it was to pass by immediate warrant, or without the usual writs of signet and privy seal. It was then handed to the chancery and issued in the usual way.[18] The whole process became purely formal, and no case has been found where a pardon so recommended was refused, though the king frequently commanded that additional persons be included. The last step in the proceedings was for the prisoners to appear in open court and "plead their pardons," after which those who had been slated for transportation were available for shipment.[19]

The pardon which was issued for these felons was couched in the ancient formulas for granting royal mercy, but there was added to it, for such persons as were to be transported, the following section, which assumed a common form by 1664:

Proviso tamen quod si ipsi [here appeared the names of the convicts] aut eorum aliquis vel earum aliqua non exibunt vel exibit extra Angliam transituri super mare versus Insulam vel Insulas vocatam les Barbadoes vel Jamaica aut aliquam aliam partem Americe modo Inhabitatam per subditos nostros quamprimum opportunitas fuerit infra spatium sex mensium proximorum post datam presentem aut si ipsi vel ipse aut eorum aliquis vel earum aliqua infra septem annos immediate proximos sequentes eosdem sex menses proximos post datam presentem remanebunt vel remanebit aut redibunt vel redibit in Angliam Quod tunc hec nostra pardonacio sit et erit omnis vacua et nullius vigoris . . .

The term of seven years' exile became fixed, while the time allowed before starting varied according to the distance from a seaport, or to any other peculiar necessity.

Actual shipment of the convicts was performed by merchants trading to the plantations, and it was enjoined in the pardon itself that they should give good security for the safe

conveyance of their charges out of England. Arrangements
with these merchants were entrusted to the sheriffs, or to the
recorder of London, and the merchants made their profit by
selling the convicts as indentured servants in the colonies. It was
thus essentially a private business, with which the colonial authorities had little or no concern. During the 1660's, however,
there are various warrants from the king, directing sheriffs to
hand over certain groups of convicts to certain captains for
transportation,[20] and on November 29, 1664, a circular letter
informed all sheriffs that Sir James Modyford had been granted
for five years the privilege of taking all pardoned felons from
the jails of all circuits and sending them to his brother Sir
Thomas for the better improving of the island of Jamaica.[21]
Despite this instruction, the king granted twenty-one Newgate
felons to John Pate for Virginia in 1667, and it is possible to
trace their shipment and arrival in that colony. Others were
given to Robert Ingram in the same year,[22] but no further
special warrants of this type have survived. It is evident that
the sheriffs from that time must have made their own arrangements.

Only a very few transported felons can be certainly traced
to their destinations. In Maryland, shiploads of convicts had
their names entered in the books of the Land Office so that
the importer might claim headrights for them. By comparing
lists of names from the Newgate pardons with the lists in the
Land Books it may be ascertained that at least 152 convicts
entered that colony between 1672 and 1676, and the failure of
any felons to appear after that date indicates that the exclusion
law, passed to keep them out, was well observed.[23] Jeaffreson's
shipments may be followed to the Leeward Islands, as will
presently appear, but with these exceptions it is impossible to
say exactly which of the 4,500 convicts pardoned for trans-

portation reached the colonies. This part of the business has left no systematic records.

Various testimonies indicate that in fact the procedure did not work very well; that great numbers of convicts were never transported at all; that the sheriffs and especially the jailers were careless in their duties, and more interested in receiving fees than in attending to the safe departure of their charges. The justices at the Old Bailey in 1681 spread upon the sessions record their discovery that many persons pardoned for transportation had never left the kingdom, and that "by reason of the insufficiency of their manucaptors noe advantage can be taken of them." They ordered the "Town Clerke of the City of London" to use greater diligence in taking security from the merchants, and to report to the court all breaches of these obligations.[24] There is no evidence, however, that this dictum produced any improvement.

A good deal of light is thrown upon the processes of convict transportation of about the year 1680 by the story of a scheme hatched in the Leeward Islands, where the authorities, alarmed by the small numbers of the white population, decided to import three hundred convicts. In 1675 Sir Charles Wheler, governor of the islands, made this suggestion to the Lords of Trade and Plantations, who approved the idea and called in some merchants to consult about shipment. The merchants expressed their willingness to undertake the transportation, provided that they should not have to pay the jail fees, which they said were very high.[25] Thereupon the committee asked Sir John Shorter, sheriff of London, to prepare an estimate of the amount of these fees for each convict. Shorter reported that the average fee per convict was thirty-one shillings, about half of which went to the clerk of the peace for searching the records and drawing up the pardon, and the other half to the jailer and turnkey. Besides this amount five pounds was generally given to the recorder's clerk whenever a considerable number of convicts were transported.[26] Nothing further was done until June 1, 1677, when the king and council authorized the sheriffs to pay £465 in jail fees, promising them reimbursement from the Exchequer. The new governor of the Leeward Islands, Sir William Stapleton, was delighted, and said that the malefactors would be benefactors, but a year later he inquired of the Lords where the promised shipment was, for it had not arrived.[27]

In fact the zeal of the home government for spending money in peopling the colonies varied as the danger of French invasion rose or fell. In July, 1680, the council of St. Christopher addressed a long memorial to the Lords of Trade and Plantations, recalling the old proposition of the three hundred malefactors. Again the government was set ponderously in motion, and a year later they informed Mr. Hill, who asked leave to transport the convicts, that he must enter into two good securities of £5000 to carry them safely. Neither Mr. Hill nor anyone else was prepared to produce such enormous securities, but in September, 1682, the Lords announced their opinion that no convict should be transported unless security of £100 were given that he should remain in the colony for at least four years. They also composed a new and quite unnecessary *Proviso* clause for insertion in the transportation pardons. It is plain that the details of this business had never before engaged the attention of the colonial administrators.[28]

At this stage the letters of Christopher Jeaffreson, the Leeward Islands planter who has already been mentioned, begin to provide further information. On November 15, 1682, he wrote from London to Captain Phipps at St. Christopher:

It will not be impossible to procure some [servants]; but as to the 300 malefactors, I see small hopes of them . . . the prison keepers must be well feed; and at the best they are enemies to the order . . . Besides they are to be had only by tens or twenties at most at a tyme; and that so seldome, that the island will not be so advantaged by it, as was expected.[29]

Ten days later he had persuaded the Lords of Trade and Plantations to reduce the required security to £20 per convict, and they wrote to Stapleton recommending that he have a law passed enforcing eight years' servitude from transported felons. Jeaffreson believed that under these terms they could be sold for from 2,200 to 2,400 pounds of sugar apiece, and he determined to take the venture, though it would be quite impossible to assemble three hundred at once.[30]

Accordingly, armed with an order from the colonial authorities, Jeaffreson betook himself to the Old Bailey on the day when a group of felons knelt in court to plead their conditional pardons. Before the Lord Mayor and sheriffs left the hall, he applied to the jailer of Newgate for the prisoners, but he was told that they had already been allotted to other merchants. His special order had no effect; the other ship was ready, and provision had been made upon it for the accommodation of the convicts. The matter rested again.[31]

Jeaffreson's next letters reveal a further reason for his failure to secure any convicts. He had expected to pick and choose from the available groups, taking able-bodied men, and leaving women and children behind. The Jamaica merchants, he wrote, were not so particular; they took men and women, strong and weak, all together, and in consequence the jailers preferred to do business with them. When these circumstances were explained to the Lords of the Council, they informed Jeaffreson that the word "men," used in reference to malefactors for transportation, included women. This was discouraging. He did no more until September, 1683, when, conceiving the idea that the

Rye House Plot would put more men than women in prison, he accepted the Council's terms. After further delays and disappointments he eventually secured twenty-eight felons, and shipped them to the islands in September, 1684. Despite his economical efforts, he decided at the last moment to pay fifty-five shillings apiece for them, "Mr. Recorder having twice declared that this business of transportation of the convicts in this manner is £30 or £40 out of his way; which if so, will be a considerable loss in the 300." Obviously it was not well to antagonize the recorder more than was necessary. Meanwhile he gave bond of £500, to be redeemed when he should produce a certificate of arrival from the governor of the island.[32]

In March, 1685, the recorder informed Jeaffreson that about thirty more convicts would plead their pardons on the 20th, and that he might have them upon paying the fees. The jailer of Newgate was still very unfriendly, but nevertheless, early in April, a second lot was equipped for shipment. Having heard "that the last parcel threw off their cloathes overboard, and came as bare to the island as if they had had no cloathes, we thought good to save some of that charge." At six o'clock on Easter Eve Jeaffreson went to Newgate, collected thirty-eight felons, and marched them in procession to the river. The unruly gang, "notwithstanding a guard of about thirty men, . . . committed several thefts, snatching away hats, perewigs, etc. from several persons, whose curiosity led them into the crowd." Thus departed the long awaited contingent which was to assure white supremacy in the Leeward Islands. They sailed on the *Friend's Goodwill,* were "thrown on shore at Antegoa," then salvaged and shipped on to St. Christopher, where the inhabitants, who had had sore trials with the former lot, were not anxious to buy them. Jeaffreson had trouble with his partners over dividing profits and abandoned any further venture in disgust.[33]

From this narrative it is plain that the shipment of convicts had become a matter privately arranged between merchants and jailers, each for his own best profit, and Jeaffreson's letters indicate that ships trading to Jamaica did most of the business at this time.[34] Into this regular routine a political element was introduced when the Leeward Islands men tried to get convict servants without paying the usual fees. The Lords of Trade and Plantations took up the subject for the first time, and displayed their ignorance of it. In the end vested interests and long practice proved too much for the new project, and after Jeaffreson's last shipment convict transportation returned to its usual course. But since it was in 1681, at the very time when the Leeward Islands were vainly trying to get convicts, that the justices of London declared that many were not being shipped at all and that the bonds given for their transportation were inadequate, one is led strongly to suspect that there was a connivance between jailers and merchants, whereby the merchants took away all felons condemned to transportation, but actually shipped only those who would make good servants. The rest were turned loose.

In the last analysis, the success of this system of convict transportation depended on the demand for convicts as servants in the colonies. Even if the jailers' fees were as high as forty shillings apiece, this is still less than the three pounds which Bullock estimated as the average price paid at a "cook's-house" for a servant ready to ship. But the demand for convicts was not very lively. Though they were exiled for seven years, and though Jamaica in 1681 passed a law expressly stating that they were to remain in servitude for this period,[35] they were notoriously bad characters. In July, 1672, the governor of Jamaica issued the following order:

Whereas divers thefts, felonies, and other enormities have been committed lately on Port Royal, which cannot be imputed to anything but to the great numbers of malefactors and other convicts yearly brought from his Majesty's prisons in England, ordered that every master of a ship bringing out white servants from England shall before he enters his ship make oath of the number of such convicts brought, and that either himself or those to whom they are consigned give good security in the Secretary's office not to sell them to any person that shall keep them on Port Royal, nor to suffer them to remain there on his own account more than three weeks.[36]

An uprising among the servants in Gloucester County, Virginia, during 1663 was attributed to the factiousness of transported felons, and in 1670 that colony passed a law prohibiting their further importation. Likewise Maryland, after receiving less than two hundred convicts, excluded them by law in 1676.[37] Enactments such as these greatly narrowed the market, cramped the trade, and decreased the enthusiasm of merchants for carrying away felons. It was especially hard to dispose of women.

Eventually the machinery of convict transportation broke down completely at this point of shipment, and its collapse was publicly and shamefully displayed at the end of the century. On December 28, 1696, the merchants of Jamaica attending the Board of Trade refused the offer of eighty malefactors "because most of them were women, and because persons of bad character were not wanted in Jamaica." Thereupon the Board made investigation, and found that the only colony disposed to accept "persons of bad character" was Barbados, and even there women, children, and infirm persons were not wanted.[38] It will be remembered that this was the time at which Barbados was desperately trying to build up the numbers of its white male population.

During the summer of 1697 Newgate prison filled up with women convicts awaiting transportation, but no one could be persuaded to take them. The recorder despaired, and instead of inserting the usual phrase in their pardon, that they should remain in prison until transported, put *quamdiu justiciariis placuerit,* and earned himself an annoyed reproof from the justices.[39] Newgate in summer, with fifty malodorous women in it, was not a salubrious place. Neighboring residents having petitioned the recorder on the subject, the City of London addressed an official remonstrance to the government. Finally the Admiralty was called on to provide shipping, and demanded £8 per head for the business.[40] The Board of Trade being asked to recommend a destination, their secretary William Popple was instructed to write to the various colonial agents inquiring if their colonies would accept the women. The replies to this inquiry are instructive. The Leeward Islands were willing to take them. Virginia and Maryland refused, citing the laws they had made against receiving convicts. The Jamaicans would not have the women unless 150 men were also sent. Thornburgh, agent for Carolina, thought the women would be welcome, but said it would be necessary for him to consult the Lords Proprietors. New York would take them only if young and fitted for labor, and if consigned to special persons who would bear the expense. Barbados did not want them, as no English women were put to work in the fields, and the people of that colony would be unwilling to take them into their houses. The agent added that in such places as Virginia and Carolina, where white women did work outdoors, such convicts ought to be welcome. Massachusetts explained that from their first settlement the government and inhabitants of New England had earnestly desired to be excused from receiving criminals, and they sanctimoniously opined that Virginia, Maryland, Barbados, Jamaica, or the Leeward Islands would be glad to get them.[41] And so on July 26 the Council wrote to the Lords Justices, recapitulating the various answers received, and recommending that the women be sent to the Leeward Islands. The Commissioners of Transport were ordered to make the necessary arrangements, but on August 20 the women were still in Newgate, though all the men had been shipped. The Lords Justices, for their part, were scandalized at the perverseness of the colonies in thus defeating one of the principal ends of colonization.[42]

At about this time a further disgrace occurred, when twenty-five convicts were released from Newgate by properly signed warrants "upon a mere pretence of transportation." The men responsible were summoned to give an explanation, but no record of it survives. Finally the Privy Council, disgusted with this state of affairs, ordered the Board of Trade to consider how and to what place convicts pardoned for transportation might best be disposed of, or what punishment might be more proper for such convicts in lieu of transportation.[43] No report on this subject has been found, but the problem was temporarily solved when war broke out in 1701, providing good employment for able-bodied felons in the armies of William III and Marlborough. Meanwhile convict women in the City of London were confined at hard labor in workhouses, a procedure which was rather expensive and not very satisfactory to the authorities.[44] Not until the end of the war was a thorough reorganization of the system attempted; how effectively this was done will be considered in the next chapter.

The convicts thus bestowed upon the struggling plantation settlements were a sorry lot of human beings. It is hardly necessary to say that they were far different from the political prisoners with whom they are sometimes classed by writers anxious to cleanse the reputation of our early immigrants. Let us take a few examples from the first group which Jeaffreson shipped

to the Leeward Islands.[45] On December 6, 1683, a certain
Eleanor Adams was taken by a waterman and his boy from
Brandford to Queenhithe. An hour after she left them a male
infant was found dead "in the passage that goes to the common
vaults." Eleanor confessed that it was hers; said that she lived
with her father-in-law at Brandford and when found with child
was put out doors; and claimed that she bore it dead in the
boat. The testimony of her "father-in-law" seemed to prove that
he was actually the father of the child, and that Eleanor had no
husband. She was tried at the Old Bailey in December, and sentenced to death. Her pardon was dated May 24, 1684; on July 3
she pleaded it in court, and was shipped by Jeaffreson about
September 8. This kind of sordid and unhappy case is frequent
in the annals of transported convicts. More often, however, the
transportees were thieves. Stephen Bumpstead stole a grey geld-
ing, valued at forty-six shillings, from a person unknown. He
made little defense, but said that the animal had been lent him.
He was also sentenced to death. John Codd stole three petti-
coats, Richard Enos stole a silver tankard, Charles Atley, "a little
boy," stole twenty-eight shillings and elevenpence out of a shop,
Jacob Watkins took a "point Crevat" off the neck of George
Spence in Thames Street at ten o'clock at night, Silvanus Morris
killed a fellow soldier in a brawl. Of the twenty-eight persons
shipped by Jeaffreson in his first lot, twenty-six had been convicted of stealing, one of murder, and one of robbery with violence. Commonly murderers were hanged, unless as in the case
of Eleanor Adams there was some reason to doubt their guilt.
Petty thieves, on the other hand, were generally pardoned outright, without any condition of transportation, and the number
of these free pardons was at least as great as the number of conditional ones. Those who were shipped to the colonies, though
their crimes may sometimes sound mild enough when de-

scribed, were such as the judges thought useless and dangerous in England.

Yet there was some hope for their reform, and there is reason to believe that James I was sincere in wishing that lesser offenders might thus be corrected "as that in theire punishment some of them may live and yeild a profitable service to the Comon Wealth." Justice Kelyng in 1664 enjoined the Old Bailey Sessions:

> That such Prisoners as are Reprieved, with intent to be transported, be not sent away as perpetual Slaves, but upon Indentures betwixt them and particular Masters, to serve in our *English* Plantations for seven Years, and the three last Years thereof, to have Wages, that they may have a Stock when their time is expired . . . [46]

There is no good reason to believe that these instructions were literally followed, but they indicate at least that the Justice had good intentions. Even the genially cynical author of the "English Rogue" remarks of female convicts landed at Barbados, that "those that despaired of ever having Husbands in *England,* had them here ready made to their hands, and they with others found in this remote place a conveniency for raising a new credit and reputation, which they had irrecoverably lost elsewhere." [47]

What testimony there is from the colonies, and it is very scanty, does not indicate that the convicts generally reformed. We have already mentioned that Virginia and Maryland passed laws prohibiting their entry, and that Jamaica found it necessary to exclude them from Port Royal. In 1684 a certain Jenney Voss was hanged at Tyburn, and the usual pamphlet concerning her career was prepared for the edification of the young. These pamphlets are not remarkable for the literal truth they contain, but they may be worth something as presenting the sort of story which people were willing to believe was true. Jenney, it seemed, had once been transported for various crimes:

and accordingly served her time beyond Sea; during which time she could not forget her old Pranks, but used not only to steal herself, but incited all others that were her fellow Servants to Pilfer and Cheat what they could from their Master, so that he was glad to be rid of her; and the rather for that she had wheadled in a Son of the Planters, who used to Lye with her and supply her with Moneys, which she was always averse to the want of.

She returned to England before her time was out, and continued in her evil ways until retribution overtook her.[48] Whether the story be correct or not it is doubtless a typical instance of transported convicts' conduct. It illuminates the reasons for the refusal of so many colonies to accept female felons.

CHAPTER 6

CONVICT TRANSPORTATION
AFTER 1718

WITH THE ENDING of the French wars and the disbanding of armies after 1713 the problem of what to do with
convicted felons became so serious that a solution could not long
be postponed. It was no longer practicable to send surplus males
into the army, nor had any plan for disposing of females been
found which was even moderately successful. Still more difficult
was the situation caused by the changes of law made in 1705,
which allowed any convict to plead benefit of clergy, whether
or not he could read, unless his crime was one of a list expressly
designated as non-clergyable. Numbers of malefactors thus appeared likely to escape any punishment adequate to their misdoings, while at the same time public sentiment had become
too humane to permit their execution, and the penalty of imprisonment was practically unknown. The colonial market for
felons as servants had collapsed, mainly because the principal
plantation colonies which still used white labor, Virginia and
Maryland, refused to admit them. Their transportation to other
colonies would not reward the merchant for his expense and
trouble.

The major reorganization thus appearing necessary was accomplished by Parliament in "An act for the further preventing

robbery, burglary, and other felonies, and for the more effectual transportation of felons . . .,"[1] passed in 1717, which became the cornerstone of policy for the disposal of convicts throughout the century. The preamble of this statute called to mind that punishments then in use had proved ineffectual and that many who had been pardoned for transportation had neglected to perform the same; it also stated that in many of the colonies there was a great want of white servants. Therefore it enacted that "where any person or persons have been convicted of any offence within the benefit of clergy" and were still awaiting their mild chastisements, and also when "any person or persons shall be hereafter convicted of grand or petit larceny, or any felonious stealing . . . who by the law shall be entitled to the benefit of clergy, and liable only to the penalties of burning in the hand or whipping," it should then be lawful for the court instead of ordering these punishments to order the convicts sent "as soon as conveniently may be" to the colonies for seven years.[2] The court also "shall have power to convey, transfer and make over such offenders, by order of court, to the use of any person or persons, who shall contract for the performance of such transportation to him or them . . . for such term of seven years." Furthermore, any persons convicted of non-clergyable felonies for which death was the penalty, and whom the king should pardon for transportation, "and such intention of mercy be signified by one of his Majesty's principal secretaries of state," should likewise be handed over to the contractor for a period of fourteen years, unless another term should be specified. The person so contracting was to have property and interest in the service of such offenders for their terms of years, and the service of the term was to have the effect of a pardon.

It was also provided in this act that the penalty for returning prematurely from transportation should be death, and that contractors should give security for the proper transportation of their convicts and procure a certificate of their arrival from the governor or customs officer of the plantation to which they were taken. Two years later, a supplementary act provided that in the provinces the court might nominate two or more justices of the peace to make contracts with the transporter and attend to other formalities.[3]

This remarkable statute thus created a new legal punishment, that of transportation, for all offenders in clergy on whom the court should think fit to inflict it. It confirmed the old practice of pardoning convicts sentenced to death on condition of transportation, but lengthened the standard term of their exile to fourteen years,[4] and provided for a rather simpler machinery so that they should not have to wait until their pardons had been made out and sealed. It therefore tightened the whole criminal code very considerably; the old days were over when a criminal could by reading "the book" escape practically all consequences of his crimes, and a greatly increased number of candidates for the plantations would soon be available.

Meanwhile the Treasury had taken a step to make transportation more effectual, before the statute was passed, which was to form an important precedent for the rest of the century. On December 7, 1716, it made an agreement with one Francis March, that he should "on or before the 25th of the said Month of December at his owne proper Expence cause the Commanders of some of the Merchant ships bound to his Majesty's Plantations, to receive on board all such Malefactors (being in health) as his Majesty should direct to be transported, and would agree or consent to serve the said Francis March or his Assigns in some of his Majesty's Plantations for 8 years." For this March was to be paid forty shillings per malefactor upon producing a certificate signed by the captain of the ship giving the number and names of those embarked, witnessed by the jailers or by such persons as were trusted to convey them on board. March took fifty-four felons to Jamaica, and was duly paid £108, but soon afterwards William Pitt, Esq., keeper of Newgate prison, sent in to the Treasury a bill for £170.1.3, being the amount of his fees, the cost of "passing a Pardon," and of irons and conveyance to the ship. The Treasury allowed Pitt the full sum of his account.[5]

After this contract was executed the act of Parliament was passed, and had as one of its most important and far-reaching effects the opening of the market for convicts in Virginia and Maryland, for no one on either side of the Atlantic seems to have doubted that a colonial law flatly prohibiting their importation could not stand against the new parliamentary statute. Accordingly Jonathan Forward, a merchant of London with connections in Maryland, applied for the first lot of convicts early in the summer of 1718, loaded about forty of them on his ship, and sent them off. Soon afterwards, learning perhaps of the advantageous contract which had been made with Francis March, Forward approached the Treasury and proposed a similar arrangement for himself. He wanted to be paid £3 apiece for Newgate felons, and £5 for those from the provinces, and he explained that because of death, sickness and other accidents he could not continue to transport them without subsidy. The solicitor general reported on July 9 that no one else would do it as cheaply, and that although the last contract had been for only forty shillings a head, the charges for irons and prison fees had doubled the expense to the government.[6] On August 8, 1718, the agreement was signed, and Jonathan Forward began his long career in the business of transporting convicts. His contract was at first renewed annually, and the amount of his stipend was gradually increased; for prisoners out of Newgate

it went to £4 in 1721 after he had complained of losses due
to the low price of tobacco, and to £5 in 1727, where it remained for the rest of the period for him and his successors.[7]
Besides Newgate felons the Treasury paid only for the transportation of convicts from the "Home Counties" of Hertford,
Essex, Kent, Sussex and Surrey, and the amount was £4 each
in 1719, rising to £5 in 1722.[8]

The terms of these agreements remained practically the same
throughout the century. The contractor undertakes to receive
"all and every such malefactors" as are to be transported; later
it was specifically stated that he must not except or refuse any
by reason of age, lameness, or infirmity. He agrees to pay all
charges such as those for conveying them on board ship, supplying irons, and rewarding jailers. He promises that they shall not
return before their time is up by any fault of his, and that before
their delivery he will enter into bonds of £40 per malefactor
that they shall not return thus. And he "doth also further Covenant that he will as soon as conveniently may be procure an
Authentick Certificate from the Governour or the Cheif Cus-
tomehouse Officer of the Place whereto they shall be so transported of the Landing of such Offenders as aforesaid (the Dangers and Casualties of the Seas excepted)." He does not have
to await this certificate before receiving payment, however, for
the money is handed over upon presentation to the Treasury of
a certificate signed by the captain of the ship on which the
felons embark, giving their number and names, and witnessed
by the jailer or by the guards who saw them on board. Under
these conditions Forward continued as contractor for the transportation of Newgate and Home Counties felons until April,
1739, when the Treasury made a new agreement on the same
terms with Andrew Reid.[9] Reid was succeeded in March, 1757,
by John Stewart, whose ships had in fact been conveying the

convicts for some time.[10] Stewart died in February, 1772, and though his partner, Duncan Campbell, asked the Treasury to renew the contract with him they would not consent because the market for servants was by that time so good that several merchants were willing to do it for nothing; Campbell in fact continued to transport convicts without subsidy until the system broke down in 1775 as a result of the Revolution.[11]

Prisoners were also transported regularly from all the provincial circuits, and while an allowance from the Treasury was made for their maintenance in jail a county levy was raised to pay the expenses of conveying them to a seaport and transporting them. In early days the justices seem to have made contracts with whatever merchant presented himself at the right moment with the necessary qualifications; thus convicts were assigned to six different contractors by the justices in the Western Circuit during the period July, 1718–March, 1720.[12] Those from the Midlands were sometimes taken to London and turned over to Forward or Reid, who gave a receipt for them to the officer bringing them. Later on regular contractors appeared, some of whose names can be discovered; thus Jonathan Forward Sydenham, of London, wrote to the Earl of Shelburne in 1768 that he was "the Contractor with the greatest Part of the Counties in England for the Transportation of their Felons," and he sent many of his shipments from the port of London to Maryland.[13] Samuel Sedgley & Co. of Bristol were transporting nearly all convicts from the western part of England to Maryland by 1750; ten years later the firm was called Sedgley and Hillhouse. One William Randolph entered the business at Bristol about 1766, and later combined with William Stevenson to take over the convict trade formerly held by Sedgley.[14] These are the only ones of whose activity extensive evidence remains, but several others appear once or twice in the records; for example, William

Cookson of Hull is named as a contractor in 1747, James Baird of Glasgow in 1770, and Patrick Colquhoun, also of Glasgow, in 1772.[15] Some of the later contracts made with Stevenson and Randolph at Bristol may also be seen, and the terms are practically the same as those which the Treasury made with Reid and Stewart, providing also for a subsidy of five pounds for each prisoner transported.[16]

The number of convicts transported to America has been the subject of various calculations and speculations,[17] most of which could have been set at rest by a few days' work in the Public Record Office. Warrants for the payments of subsidies to Forward, Reid and Stewart are all entered in the Treasury Money Books, and the names of all the convicts, with the ships on which they sailed and the date of shipment, are transcribed in the same records. Hence it may easily be ascertained that from 1719 to 1772 the three contractors took 17,740 felons from the Home Counties and from Newgate, put them aboard ship, and started them for the colonies. Statistics for the provincial circuits are not quite so easy to procure, for most of the evidence is not available and has probably disappeared for good. Western circuit records happen to be nearly complete, and by taking three periods of five years each in the century we get an average annual transportation of fifty-one felons from this circuit.[18] The reformer Howard printed figures from the Norfolk and Midland circuits covering the years 1750 to 1772; these yield averages of fifty-four and fifty per year respectively.[19] Duncan Campbell, who had had twenty years' experience in transporting convicts to America, wrote in 1787 that he had always looked upon the number from the other parts of the kingdom as equal to that coming from London and the Home Counties.[20] Perhaps this was a generous estimate, in view of the figures we have from three provincial circuits, but accepting it as roughly accurate we should certainly be justified in saying that Great Britain bestowed upon America a total of 30,000 felons during the eighteenth century.

To get an idea of what this meant to the English penal system some figures collected by A. L. Cross from a set of Old Bailey Sessions Papers may be used.[21] Taking eight years from the period 1729-1770 as specimens, it appears that an average of 560 persons annually stood trial at the Old Bailey; of these sixty-three per cent, or about 352, were convicted of felony or misdemeanor. Of these, sixty were sentenced to death, and 235 to transportation. Cross appears to ignore the fact that about half of those condemned to death were subsequently pardoned on condition of transportation, while a few who were sentenced to transportation had that penalty remitted by the king's mercy.[22] It is plain that at least 70 per cent of those convicted at the Old Bailey were sent to America. Another calculation, taking into account only those convicted of felony, finds that about 7.5 per cent of them were executed "and the remainder, with very few exceptions transported."[23]

Very nearly all of these convicts were taken to Maryland or Virginia. Out of 190 ships leaving London with Newgate and Home Counties felons, fifty-three may be traced definitely to Maryland, and forty-seven to Virginia, despite the fact that the records which make this possible are incomplete and for part of the period non-existent.[24] Only two may be followed to other colonies; one to South Carolina and one to Nevis, while another probably sold some convicts in Barbados before proceeding to Maryland. As for the eighty-eight shiploads which cannot be traced, there are good reasons for believing that they must have gone to the same destination. They generally belonged to the contractors whose business connections were principally in those two colonies and who had perfected arrangements for disposing of convicts in them. Occasionally a group may have been turned over to another shipowner by the contractor himself, but such was not the rule. Duncan Campbell told a committee of the House of Commons that in his twenty years of business he had sold only in Virginia and Maryland. Maryland, wrote William Eddis, "is the only province into which convicts may be freely imported," and a French traveller in 1765 reported that they came only there and to Virginia.[25] Failure to find evidence of their arrival in the shipping returns cannot be considered as proving that they did not arrive, for the returns themselves are incomplete and can be demonstrated to have omitted mention of several convict ships which are known from newspaper sources to have reached the colony. It must be remembered, however, that ten or fifteen per cent of these passengers commonly died during the voyage, so that of the 17,740 carried on Treasury contracts not more than 14,000 or 15,000 lived to reach their destinations.

Convicts from the provinces can be traced with nearly as much accuracy as those from London and the Home Counties. It is plain from the Maryland shipping returns that the Bristol contractors traded there, and the number which they are credited with bringing is so large that it is difficult to believe that they had many left to take elsewhere. Sydenham also shipped to Maryland, and several of the other contractors. Yet it is certain that some convicts were taken to other colonies. The evidence for this is chiefly in the fact that laws were passed to regulate their admission in Jamaica, New Jersey, and Pennsylvania, and perhaps also in other places. One shipment has already been mentioned as sent to Jamaica by Francis March; one from Bristol arrived at South Carolina in 1729, and a group of seven found their way to Boston from Hull in 1747.[26] Irish felons were sent to Philadelphia in considerable numbers,[27] and also probably to Jamaica. Yet such evidence is only scattering, and there is no reason to believe that any colony received more than a small fraction of the number going to Maryland and Virginia.

The Maryland shipping returns show with absolute certainty that 9,332 convicts arrived there between 1748 and 1775; I would estimate that the total number actually reaching Virginia and Maryland during the whole century was slightly more than 20,000.[28]

After so many years of freedom from such undesirable immigrants the sudden influx of them after 1718 did not fail to arouse alarm and apprehension in all the colonies concerned. As early as the summer of 1719 the Maryland assembly discussed an act to deal with the situation, but the upper house secured its postponement, apparently on the ground that such hasty action would be unfair to Jonathan Forward.[29] The governor refused finally to sign it. Virginia was the first actually to pass a law on the matter, and in the session of 1722 the assembly inserted a long section concerning convicts into the act for regulating white servants.[30] Apparently they took it for granted that nothing like the rule of 1670, which forbade importation, would be allowed, and so they drew up elaborate provisions which may be outlined as typical of what various other colonies tried. After reciting that many frauds had been committed by the importers of convicts and crimes by the convicts themselves the law provided that, 1. Any shipmaster bringing in felons and selling them for less than their terms of transportation, or concealing from the buyer the true cause of their transportation, should forfeit £10 to the informer, and not be allowed to plead any statute of limitation. 2. Shipmasters allowing felons ashore before they had been actually and *bona fide* sold should pay twenty shillings to the person who should take them up and return them to the ship. 3. Shipmasters must declare under oath the number and names of all imported convicts, and give bond of £50 not to let them ashore until sold, while everyone having charge of the disposal of such convicts must give bond of £100 for their good behavior for two months after the sale. 4. Each purchaser of a convict must bring him before the first or second court after the purchase and declare his name with the cause of his transportation, and enter into recognizance of £10 for the good behavior of the convict, under penalty of twenty shillings for each court after the second during which this duty should be neglected.

This act was obviously designed to make the importation and sale of convicts so troublesome as to be unprofitable. No sooner had its terms been reported to England than Jonathan Forward sent a letter to the Board of Trade desiring them to have it repealed. On June 27, 1723, the Board heard Forward personally on the subject, and the same day sent their attorney, Mr. West, a copy of the act for his opinion. The whole business moved with extraordinary speed: West reported on July 3 that the act amounted to "a prohibition of any convicts being imported," and remarked that if this example should be followed in other colonies the execution of the act of Parliament concerning transportation would be rendered wholly impracticable. Two days later the Board recommended that the law be repealed, and on August 27 the Privy Council formally disallowed it.[31] An act couched in similar terms which the Maryland legislature passed in 1723 was disallowed by the proprietor in the following year because of its incompatibility with the act of Parliament, and the assembly of the colony appointed committees to consider a special address of remonstrance to the king himself on the subject.[32]

Later attempts by these two colonies to exclude convicts fared no better. In the revenue act of 1754 Maryland imposed a duty of twenty shillings on each servant imported "to serve for the Term of Seven Years or upwards," and of five shillings on those with shorter terms. The contractor Stewart again filed objection to this as being directed against convicts, though other shippers who transported from the inland prisons paid it without protest. Lord Baltimore wrote from London to Governor Sharpe that he had been roundly criticised by the attorney-general for this act, but had managed to pacify that officer by showing him that the word "convict" did not appear in it. "I will do what I can to keep quiet Mr. Stewart But fear it," wrote Calvert. "This Manifests the danger there is in touching upon Acts of Parliament, and upon which I have observed in my former Letters." Mr. Stewart was not kept quiet; his factors refused to pay the duty, and it was abandoned in 1756.[33]

In 1767 Stewart again protested to the Privy Council and to Lord Baltimore against laws passed both in Virginia and Maryland providing for the quarantine of convict ships. According to Governor Sharpe many of these vessels were grossly overcrowded, and the jail fever which raged on board was commonly transmitted to inhabitants of the colonies when the convicts landed. Stewart managed to get the Virginia law disallowed, but the Maryland one was permitted to stand, perhaps because it was more carefully drafted to escape the criticisms which the Privy Council managed to find against Virginia's rules of procedure. A similar act passed by the latter colony in 1772 was also thrown out.[34]

On the other hand, those colonies to which the large contractors did not send convicts were sometimes able to pass laws restricting their importation and keep them in force, at least for a time. In 1722 Pennsylvania levied a duty on imported

felons, and repeated the act in 1729 and 1743, the amount being
five pounds per head. None of these laws came to the attention
of the Privy Council until 1746, when they were all disallowed.[35]
Jamaica in 1722 levied £10 on each convict by its annual revenue act, and in 1731 raised this to £100. The Board of Trade
took notice of this latter huge figure, and instructed the governor that the law must not be reenacted, but since the act was
limited to one year's duration it did not trouble to recommend
a repeal. New Jersey imposed a duty on felons in 1730, and it
was two years before the Privy Council threw it out.[36] One may
be quite sure that if Jonathan Forward or Andrew Reid had
been shipping convicts to these colonies, no time would have
been lost in securing the disallowance of such laws; the whole
business is in truth an edifying example of the intimate relations
between vested interests and statutory law.

The profits made by the contractors were normally good,
and Governor Sharpe said that they were exorbitant. According
to his statement, convicts were sold for from eight to twenty
pounds apiece.[37] Duncan Campbell himself testified that the
price averaged ten pounds, females bringing eight or nine, and
men of useful trades going for from fifteen to twenty-five. The
old and infirm had to be given away to such people as would
take them, and with some he was obliged to give premiums.[38]
Campbell turned in an account of his operations from April to
July, 1772, after the Treasury subsidy had been discontinued,
which is the only piece of detailed evidence we have on the
profits of the trade.[39] From this it appears that he shipped 348
felons, at a cost of £1740.9.7, and sold them in Virginia for
£2957.9.0. Deducting ten per cent for bad debts, and allowing
also for a commission of £233.6.8 to his agent, this was still a
very comfortable margin of profit, and since during most of the
century his £1740 of expenses would have been fully covered

by the Treasury grant of five pounds per convict it may be seen that there was good reason for Sharpe's description of the trade. Nevertheless, on this particular series of ventures Campbell lost money. After the convict transactions he loaded his ships with 872 hogsheads of tobacco, which cost him no less than £7669.4.5. When brought to England this tobacco sold for only £4683.16.9, and after balancing all accounts, a loss of £2410.1.10 was shown. This is a good example of the way in which the trade in servants and convicts frequently depended for its profits on other factors than the selling price of the cargo in the plantations. In this case the tobacco market was bad, but obviously during most of the period merchants made a profit from the return as well as from the outward voyage.

Duncan Campbell submitted these accounts in the hope that his losses would move the government to restore the £5 subsidy. Observing that the losses were in tobacco and not in convict trading, the Treasury quite properly refused to do so, yet Campbell nevertheless continued transporting convicts to Maryland until the Revolution stopped the business.[40] He would not have done this if it had been unprofitable. Indeed it may be questioned whether at any time in the century after the Virginia and Maryland markets had been opened there was a real need of paying the subsidy. When Forward first demanded it he was having some trouble in getting the trade started, but in his subsequent communications to the Treasury he complains of the state of the tobacco market. It seems most likely that the real effect of the government's payments was to cover the contractor's losses in years when trade was poor, and enormously raise his profits in those when it was good.

When peace was signed in 1783 the English appear to have thought that the old system of convict transportation could be resumed, and they immediately set about arrangements for shipping more to America. One cargo of eighty felons was actually landed in Maryland, but there is no certain evidence of further successful shipments.[41] Occasional attempts were made, until finally in 1788 one Leonard White Outerbridge transmitted to John Jay information of the expected arrival of a considerable number. The matter was then brought up in the Continental Congress, which, on motion of Abraham Baldwin, "Resolved That it be and it is hereby recommended to the several states to pass proper laws for preventing the transportation of convicted malefactors from foreign countries into the United States."[42] This advice was speedily followed, and a permanent end put to the business. England was obliged to seek other outlets for her criminal population, and almost immediately established true penal colonies in Australia.

The populace of London and the provincial towns accounted it no small diversion to see the convicts leave for America. Three and sometimes four times a year a procession of these unfortunates would emerge from Newgate and wend its way with clanking irons through the narrow streets to Blackfriars, where a lighter waited to furnish conveyance to the ship. During this march it was the privilege of bystanders to hoot at the convicts, and even on occasion to throw mud and stones at them, while the departing reprobates replied with whatever abuse their wits could invent. We read of a scene at Bristol in 1752, when eleven felons were taken out of the jail, chained two by two on horseback, and taken off to Bideford for shipment. A large number of people turned out to see this sight, and were especially entertained by one Bishop, who had murdered his sweetheart, and who returned their obscene shouts with such interest that he was showered with dirt and stones.[43] No accounts remain of the long journeys which convicts had to make from inland towns to the seaport; they must have presented a strange and igno-minious sight, whether on foot or chained on horseback.

Some fortunate transportees did not have to mingle with the common herd. If a man had money and some influence, he might free himself from becoming the "property" of the con-tractor, and travel to America in whatever state his resources would permit. Thus four convicts in 1736 rode down to the shore in two hackney coaches, while a fifth, who was "a Gentle-man of Fortune, and a Barrister at Law" guilty of stealing books from the library of Trinity College, Cambridge, rode in a third coach with no less a person than Jonathan Forward himself. These five paid their own passage and had a cabin to themselves on board ship, while the inferior sort were put immediately un-der hatches.[44]

It was customary to keep all ordinary felons below decks and chained during the entire voyage. Like other cargoes of servants they were divided into groups of six, and fed with stated amounts for each group of bread, cheese, meat, oatmeal, and molasses. On Saturdays two gills of gin were allotted to each group.[45] The diet was probably better balanced than most of them had been used to; certainly the allowance of gin was uncommonly scanty. Conditions below decks were neverthe-less very bad, especially in the earlier years of the century. "I went on board," wrote a visitor to one of contractor Stewart's ships, "and, to be sure, all the states of horror I ever had an idea of are much short of what I saw this poor man in; chained to a board in a hole not above sixteen feet long, more than fifty with him; a collar and padlock about his neck, and chained to five of the most dreadful creatures I ever looked on."[46] Under such circumstances jail fever and smallpox carried off generally at least fifteen per cent of the convicts before they reached America. Sometimes the death rate was appallingly high; when the

Honour arrived at Annapolis in 1720, twenty of her sixty-one convicts had died; thirty out of eighty-seven perished on the *Gilbert* in 1722, and thirty-eight out of ninety-five on the *Rapahannock Merchant* in 1725. It was no wonder that Jonathan Forward protested to the Treasury that his profits were rendered uncertain by "death, sickness and other accidents," and asked for a regular subsidy to cover his losses.[47]

These conditions were somewhat improved in the late 1760's, when the Sedgleys of Bristol put a ventilator on their ships, while Stewart and Campbell "made theirs quite airy by opening a Range of Ports on each Side between Decks." Nevertheless Duncan Campbell testified twenty years after this date that he had been accustomed to losing more than a seventh of all felons. He remarked that smallpox carried off most of them, and that the number of women who died was only half in proportion to the men, which he attributed to their greater sobriety and stronger constitutions.[48] Apparently it was never worth the contractor's while to adopt strict measures for insuring the health of his cargo.

Many captains and ships continued in the convict trade year after year. One of the seamen longest in the business was Captain Darby Lux, who made his first voyage with convicts as master of the *Gilbert* in 1720. Subsequently he commanded eleven more trips, seven of them on the *Patapsco Merchant*. His last voyage was in 1738, and he appears then to have settled in Maryland as Forward's general agent, where he was still flourishing in 1749. The ship *Thornton* made eight trips to Virginia and Maryland with convicts between 1767 and 1775; she had been built in Maryland in 1765, was of 175 tons, carrying a crew of thirteen, and brought more than 1,100 convicts to the two colonies. Captain James Dobbins first arrived in Maryland with convicts in 1744; he made eight more voyages, and was esteemed in the colony as "a Gentleman of honour, in whom strict Discipline and Humanity are equally temper'd, in his Behaviour towards those unfortunate Wretches."[49] For five years he commanded one of the largest convict ships, the *Thames,* an English-built frigate of 210 tons, carrying eight guns and a crew of twenty. Captain Dobbins was involved in one of the most remarkable incidents of convict transportation, when on February 21, 1746, his ship the *Plain-Dealer* was overhauled by the *Zephyre,* "a French Man of War of 30 Carriage Guns and 350 Men." Turning the convicts loose, Dobbins fought an engagement "of two Hours and a Half, in which forty of the Convicts on Board behav'd well, and fought with great Courage." Nevertheless they were overpowered, and the Frenchman took Dobbins and a few of his passengers on board the man-of-war, leaving a prize crew on the *Plain-Dealer* with most of the convicts. Dobbins soon got safely back to England, but the *Plain-Dealer* was lost on the coast near Brest with everyone on board save seven Frenchmen.[50] One other ship is worth mentioning; the *Justitia,* which made at least seven voyages to Virginia after 1764, under the command of Colin Somerville. After the business of transportation broke down she was turned into a hulk, and used for keeping felons employed in dredging the channel of the Thames River.

The only other convict ship of whose wreck we have certain knowledge was one belonging to James Baird, the Glasgow contractor, and filled with felons from Northumberland and Durham. This came to grief on the coast of Kent in 1770, and was a total loss, though the convicts were saved and kept by the sheriffs of London and Middlesex until another disposal could be made of them.[51] It does not seem possible that more ships should not have been lost, but there is no record of further catastrophes. Vicissitudes of other kinds were not lacking, but they were neither very frequent nor disastrous. The first lot of convicts for which Jonathan Forward received payment from the Treasury was started for Maryland on the *Eagle* in 1718; while on the way the ship was captured by a pirate, then rescued by South Carolina vessels and taken into Charleston. The ship *Honour* set out for Virginia in 1720 with eighty convicts, of whom twenty came from the provinces. Fifteen of these mutinied, overcame the crew, and forced Captain Langley to put them ashore at Vigo in Spain; after this event the ship proceeded to Virginia with what was left of her cargo.[52] Another mutiny occurred on the *Sally* in 1741, and the convicts took her into Holland. In 1761 the French captured a shipload of felons and set them ashore in Spain. They found their way to Oporto and "committed some irregularities," whereupon at the request of the consul they were put aboard a British warship and returned to Spithead.[53] None of these incidents was of much moment, and it is remarkable that a trade extending over so many years should have left so few evidences of mutinies, wrecks, and misfortunes.

English opinion held that the transportation of criminals to the colonies was an excellent and humane thing. Sir John Fielding, writing in 1773, summed up the whole matter: ". . .the wisest, because most humane and effectual, punishment we have, viz., transportation,—which immediately removes the evil, separates the individual from his abandoned connexions, and gives him a fresh opportunity of being an useful member of society, thereby answering the great ends of punishment, viz., example, humanity, and reformation. . . ."[54] And indeed there was much truth in this. We have already remarked that the convicts, immediately upon embarkation, were put on a diet which was at least regular, and their gin consumption cut down to a minimum. Granted that they survived the voyage and the first weeks of colonial climate, they were then put to a life of physical labor in the open air, with adequate food and careful supervision. Such conditions were of no benefit to the physically and morally ruined, but they certainly gave some modicum of decent opportunity to those who could grasp it; they were better conditions than the convict could have found for himself in Newgate prison or in the slums of London.

But apparently the convicts themselves did not agree with this view. Fielding wrote that he had heard several give accounts of their sufferings, and declare that they would rather be hanged than transported a second time. They ran away when they could, and returned to England if possible before their times were out.[55] Nor was transportation regarded as a light punishment by those who inflicted it. Often the judges and the king's secretary were importuned to grant free pardons to those under sentence of transportation, and they did so often enough to arouse Fielding's protest that some very daring robbers were thus let loose, "to the terror of society."[56] It was assuredly as difficult a path of reformation as could well be invented, but at least the way was not altogether closed.

Colonial opinion could scarcely find the same satisfaction in contemplating the humanitarian aspects of the system, for the spectacle of thousands of thieves, robbers and murderers descending upon the settlements was calculated to make men fear for their lives and goods. There can be no doubt that the convicts vastly increased the amount of lawlessness and crime in those colonies where they lived. We read in the newspapers of brutal murders committed by them, of robbery and arson attributed to them.[57] His Majesty's Attorney-General in Virginia successfully petitioned for a raise in salary because of the extraordinary business he was put to in prosecuting so many criminals.[58] An article in the *Virginia Gazette* of May 24, 1751, had this sinister passage:

When we see our Papers fill'd continually with accounts of the most audacious Robberies, the most Cruel Murders, and infinite other Villanies perpetrated by Convicts transported from Europe, what melancholy, what terrible Reflections must it occasion! What will become of our Posterity? These are some of thy Favours Britain. Thou art called our Mother Country; but what good Mother ever sent Thieves and Villains to accompany her children; to corrupt some with their infectious Vices and murder the rest? What Father ever endeavour'd to spread the Plague in his Family? We do not ask Fish, but thou gavest us Serpents, and more than Serpents! In what can Britain show a more Sovereign contempt for us than by emptying their jails into our settlements; unless they would likewise empty their Jakes on our tables!

Benjamin Franklin's ironical letter suggesting that rattlesnakes be transported to England in return is well known.

Although direct statutory limitation of the importation of convicts was rendered impossible by the disallowances of the Privy Council, various measures more or less ineffectual were taken to deal with the special conditions which arose. The Provincial Court of Maryland in 1721 took notice of the increase of crime due to the influx of convicts and ordered that all such persons thereafter arriving were to be deemed persons "of Evill fame," from whom security might be taken by justices of the peace for their good behavior.[59] This order was repeated a year later, and reinforced by the act of 1723; it led to an acrimonious dispute between the magistrates of Annapolis and Forward's agents, who refused to give the required bonds.[60] The disallowance of the convict statute in 1724 seems to have settled the question in favor of the contractor. Nevertheless, in 1751, after a year of particularly heavy importations, the magistrates of Baltimore and Anne Arundel counties took it upon themselves to order a security of fifty pounds taken for the good behavior of every imported felon; this time the Provincial Court overruled the justices, saying that they had "exceeded their jurisdiction."[61] In 1736 Virginia passed a law requiring the masters of convict servants to give them the usual freedom dues, and this was supposed to be some small discouragement to those purchasing newly arrived felons. Four years later the same colony legislated concerning the raising of recruits for the campaign against Carthagena, and allowed the enlistment only of "able-bodied persons fit to serve his majesty who follow no lawful calling or employment." It has been suggested that this was an ingenious attempt to get rid of convicts, but this is at least doubtful.[62]

Curious problems arose because convicted felons were, in law, dead, and during the period of their transportation could not validly give evidence or act as witnesses to legal documents. Maryland in 1728 required by statute a statement from ship captains as to the offences of imported convicts, because some had been brought in as good servants and their testimony received at law; this act was strengthened in 1769.[63] In 1748 Virginia, and in 1751 Maryland, provided by statute that the testimony of convicts should be held good in cases involving other convicts, but not otherwise.[64] A problem of remarkable difficulty is exhibited in the Order Book of Lancaster County, Virginia, for 1740, where it is recorded that a proposition was sent to the General Assembly asking whether, if convict women-servants had bastard children, their oath as to the father of the child should be held valid in case the reputed father should be a free man.[65] What the answer may have been does not appear, but the question illustrates well some of the less obvious ramifications of the situation caused by the presence of these felons in colonial society.

It is sometimes said that Virginia and Maryland became practically penal colonies. In one sense this is true, for the convicts of England were sent there in great numbers certainly, but in another and more correct definition it is not. A penal colony is properly a place maintained and managed by the home government, to which convicts are brought in government ships and in which they live under constant supervision of official guards. This was the sort of establishment which England later set up in Australia, and France at Devil's Island, and of course it bears no resemblance to the colonies of Virginia and Maryland, where felons were brought by private merchants and blended into the civil population. Certainly the general character of society was lowered by the practice, and in particular the reputation of the servant population suffered, for William Eddis remarks that planters ceased to make distinctions between good indentured servants and the riff-raff which appeared on the convict ships.[66]

Resentment against the English government for this transportation has nevertheless been considerably overdone. Despite the loud outcries in the press and the ineffectual attempts of colonial legislatures to stop the influx of felons, the truth of the matter is that they were received with open arms by the greater proportion of planters, who wanted cheap labor. The British government never forced convicts on these communities, because it did not need to do so. All it did was to prevent the more responsible colonists from enacting laws which would keep the less responsible from buying them, and when no law forbade it, the ordinary planters of those two colonies made haste to the seaports, and eagerly purchased the commodity which was offered them. Had there been any united sentiment of opposition to convict transportation a boycott would have been perfectly effective for a time, and then the British government might have had actually to force them in. But the demand for cheap labor outweighed the sense of social responsibility. It was perhaps to the discredit of the English that they shipped their felons to America, though they had at least the virtue of a certain humanitarianism; but it was certainly to the discredit of Virginia and Maryland that those felons were shipped at a handsome profit.

NOTE ON THE TRANSPORTATION OF SCOTTISH AND IRISH FELONS

The penalty of banishment was not foreign to Scottish law as it was to English, and it was frequently imposed. Sometimes the sentence would require the convict to go to the plantations, but more often it was merely one of banishment from the country. In the machinery of transportation, however, felons were classed with rogues and vagabonds, and it will be more convenient to give what scanty information there is on the subject in the next chapter.

An examination of the Justiciary Records recently acquired by the General Register House at Edinburgh discloses that it was often the custom of an accused man to petition the judges as follows: "That whatever might be the result of the Petitioners undergoing a Trial he cannot after being Accused of such Crimes think of passing the remainder of his life in this Country with any degree of Comfort or Satisfaction and therefore and in order to save the trouble of a trial he makes this Application to Your Lordships to be banished to one or other of his Majesty's Plantations in America." Such requests, which I presume were instigated by the judges in the first place, appear never to have been refused. They are frequent in the eighteenth-century records.

The Parliamentary Act of 1717 respecting the transportation of felons did not apply to Scotland, but in 1766 its provisions were extended to cover that country as well as England.[67] No

changes as a result of this extension can be discovered in the
Justiciary Records. Two isolated documents prove that as early
as 1728 felons were being transported under the condition that
the transporter should give bond for their safe conveyance. The
fact that there was a contractor for the transportation of felons
in Glasgow in 1772 shows that many must have been shipped,
but I have not come upon any collections of statistics.

From the Ormonde Papers it is evident that felons were
reprieved and transported from Ireland to the plantations after
1661 in much the same manner as from England.[68] The Lord
Lieutenant issued the necessary reprieves and pardons. By an
act of the Irish Parliament passed in 1704, judges acting with
the grand juries were permitted to respite the execution of
certain classes of felons and allow merchants giving security of
£20 to transport them to the plantations, giving a certificate
within eighteen months that they had been properly landed.
Other acts modelled on the English statute of 1717 were passed
by the Irish Parliament in 1719 and 1722, and in 1726 the payment of a subsidy to the transporting merchants was authorized
by statute.[69]

The destruction of the Irish Public Record Office in 1922
together with all the records, both general and local, which
were deposited there, renders it impossible to collect statistics
for the whole century. It so happened, however, that a committee
of the Irish House of Commons investigated the whole subject
of convict transportation in 1743, and printed its report, together with complete statistics for the preceding seven years.[70]
According to these figures, 1,890 persons were transported from
Ireland during that period, and one would scarcely be far wrong
in estimating that nearly 10,000 must have been sent during the
century. Over half of the 1,890, however, were not felons but
vagabonds, condemned to transportation at Quarter Sessions.

Some other points of interest were brought out in this report. When any group of convicts and vagabonds were transported, a levy on the county was made of five or six pounds for each person sent away. The sheriffs collected this levy, but several of them testified that they paid merchants only £2.10 or £3 of it, and kept the rest for themselves. The committee also discovered that magistrates had been very lax in demanding certificates of arrival from the transporting merchants. One shipload of seventy-three was certified as having arrived at Annapolis. Another merchant produced an account of his sales of twenty convicts in Maryland, for whom he received two hundred pounds. Others gave lists of those shipped to Pennsylvania, but could not produce certificates in proper form. The committee did not suggest that many had not been transported, but they criticized the magistrates. Since it was also true in England that the certificates required by law were not filed, despite the fact that convicts were certainly shipped, we have no reason to believe that there was any great shortcoming in the shipping of Irish convicts.

It is also interesting that "Mr. Henry Gonne, Town-Clerk of Dublin, being examined, produced two Books to the Committee, where in [are entered] the Names not only of all convict Felons and Vagabonds ordered for Transportation, but also the Names of other Persons who enter into Indentures with Merchants Transporters to be transported to his Majesty's Plantations, and the Term of Years for which they bind themselves respectively, and that have been bound by Indentures before the Lord Mayors of the City of Dublin."[71]

[CHAPTER 7]

THE TRANSPORTATION OF
ROGUES AND VAGABONDS

IN A famous passage of the statute 39 Eliz., c. 4, Parliament defined what classes of people were to be esteemed rogues and vagabonds, and presented posterity with a curious list of reprobates which did duty for two centuries as a standard text for all English laws dealing with the subject. In subsequent enactments the spelling was improved and minor changes made in the list itself, but no fundamental alterations were found necessary. These, then, were the rogues and vagabonds of our colonial period:

All persons calling themselves Schollers going about begging, all Seafaring men pretending losses of their Shippes or goods on the sea going about the Country begging, all idle persons going about in any Cuntry eyther begging or using any subtile Crafte or unlawful Games or Playes, or fayning themselves to have knowledge in Phisiognomye Palmestry or other like crafty Scyence, or pretending that they can tell Destenyes Fortunes or such other like fantasticall Imagynacons; all persons that be or utter themselves to be Proctors Procurers Patent Gatherers or Collectors for Gaoles Prisons or Hospitalls; all Fencers Bearewards comon Players of Enterludes and Minstrells wandring abroade (other then Players of Enterludes belonging to any Baron of this Realme . . .); all Juglers Tynkers Pedlers and Petty Chapmen wandring abroad; all wandring

136

persons and comon Labourers being persons able in bodye using loytering and refusing to worcke for such reasonable wages as is taxed or comonly given in such Parts where such persons do or shall happen to dwell or abide, not having lyving otherwyse to maynteyne themselves; all persons delivered out of Gaoles that begg for their Fees, or otherwise do travayle begging; all such persons as shall wander abroade begging pretending losses by Fyre or otherwise; and all such persons not being Fellons wandering and pretending themselves to be Egipcyans, or wandering in the Habite Forme or Attyre of counterfayte Egipcians.[1]

Every such person found begging was to be stripped to the waist and whipped until his body became bloody, and then sent to his birthplace or place of last residence. In case neither place was known he was to be sent to the house of correction for a year, unless someone would give him employment.

This same statute also provided, however, that "Yf any of the said Rogues shall appeare to be dangerous to the inferior sorte of People where they shalbe taken, or otherwyse be such as will not be reformed of their rogish kinde of lyfe by the former Provisions of this Acte," then the justices of the peace at the next quarter sessions might banish them out of the realm, and have them sent at the charge of the county to such places beyond seas as the Privy Council should designate. Any rogue thus banished and returning without licence should be adjudged guilty of felony, and punished with death. Thus the legal penalty of transportation, which could not be inflicted on English felons until after 1717, could be pronounced on incorrigible rogues throughout the whole colonial period, and by no higher court than quarter sessions.

To be sure, when this act was passed, there were no English colonies to which rogues might be transported. Within six months of the accession of James I an order in council, according to the provisions of the law, designated "The New found Lande, the East and West Indies, Fraunce, Germanie, Spayne, and the Lowe Countries or any of them," as receptacles for English vagabonds.[2] But meanwhile one of the principal arguments for the starting of colonies was that they would provide an outlet for this surplus population, this "Surcharge of necessitous people, the matter or fewell of daungerous insurrections."[3] Sir Humphrey Gilbert had urged it in 1576, Hakluyt had given it his powerful support, Peckham, Carleill and Gorges had all insisted on the same point. We might expect to find a considerable business in the transportation of rogues to America, once Virginia had been established, and indeed there was no lack of talk and writing on the subject throughout the seventeenth century. Practically everyone who had anything to say on the subject of colonial development recommended that beggars, delinquents, "allsuch as lie on the parishes," all "lewed and lasy felowes," be forthwith collected and sent off.[4]

Yet the fact is that while there were many vagabonds sent to America, and certainly a vast number of lewd and lazy fellows, comparatively little of this was accomplished in proper form under the provisions of 39 Eliz., c. 4. An inspection of quarter sessions records scarcely reveals any evidence whatever of vagabonds sentenced to banishment or transportation, though hundreds of them are conveyed back to their original places of residence, and are whipped or sentenced to houses of correction. Needless to say, after the workhouse system came in at the end of the seventeenth century, and the attitude toward the emigration of poor persons changed to one of sharp disfavor, even less evidence can be found, and in 1713 the statute of Elizabeth was repealed. From that time vagrants without a legal place of settlement might be bound out as apprentices or servants for a term of seven years to serve either in Great Britain or in the colonies, and the master was bound under a penalty of

£40 to supply the vagrant with proper necessities and finally to set him at liberty. Such provisions made it difficult or impossible to inflict transportation as a penalty.[5]

Thus we cannot, as in the case of felons, discover lists of the names of transportees, and obtain satisfactory statistics of vagabonds sent to America. But there is a good deal of miscellaneous information to be had on the subject, and from it one may get a fair idea of the way in which the system actually functioned. The first evidence is from the year 1619, and is doubtless of later date than the first actual transportation of rogues, if statements concerning the moral character of the earliest Virginian colonists may be taken at face value. On January 13, 1618/9, King James I wrote to Sir Thomas Smith from Newmarket, saying that the court of late had been troubled with divers young people who refused to mend their ways despite several punishments. Having no other way to get rid of them, the king asked Smith to take them to Virginia and set them at work. Smith was not enthusiastic. He wrote to the lord mayor of London, saying that the company had no ship handy, and asking that the vagrants be kept for a while in Bridewell Hospital. This request was granted and the group eventually transported.[6] The king seems to have been pleased with this procedure, for he wrote once again in October about more "dissolute persons," and a month later insisted that at least fifty be sent at once to Virginia. The company was forced to assume the charge of maintaining them, and appointed a committee to make a hasty search for ships. A thousand pounds was appropriated as a fund "to be onely for the sattisfyinge of his Mats: desyres from tyme to time," and a hundred voted on December 15 for equipping the fifty persons. On December 23 a commission was given to John Damyron of the *Duty* to ship the lot as soon as possible.[7] They were all youths, sent for seven years' service to their masters, the time to be extended in case of wrongdoing. It was expected that the equivalent of £10 apiece would be paid for them by the planters, but in 1622 the company had received only £275.15.6, and two years later they were still trying to collect the balance. When the terms of the "Duty Boyes" had expired, they were instead of being set free ordered to serve the governor, since all his servants were freed and there were no others available to maintain the dignity of his position.[8]

During the next two decades, occasional notices may be found in the Court Books of Bridewell Hospital of vagrants and disreputable persons sent to Virginia or "kept for Virginia." In the course of the year 1631 fifty boys were bound apprentices to merchants and others for service in Barbados and Virginia. In April, 1635, it was ordered that if Mr. George Whitman and the treasurer thought fit to send any vagrants to Virginia, they should do so, and Woodall, "the contractor" was to have 26/8 per head for twenty-one sent overseas. Many are recorded as brought in by one constable or another and kept for Virginia; thus for example Ellen Boulter was in 1620 "brought in by the Marshall for a Vagrant, that will not be ruled by her father or her friends," and is kept at her father's charges to go to Virginia.[9]

Notes such as these are not available for later periods, but they make plain that Bridewell was in fact a source of supply for the servant trade. This is amply confirmed by further evidence, and by the remarks of travellers and residents in the colonies. In 1685 William Byrd wrote to his agent in London:

I am sorry you did not Send mee our apprentice Boy, they may (as I am confidently informed) bee had from the Hospital at any time, Such as are very capable of our businesse, Ime sure m^r. Paggens concerne is Supplyed that way. . . .[10]

The cantankerous John Urmstone, representative in North

Carolina of the Society for the Propagation of the Gospel, wrote in 1719 about his only maidservant, a "notorious whore and thief," who "was bred a Trader in Spitlefields but followed the Musick Houses most and other vile courses which brought her to Bridewell and from thence transported hither."[11] We are informed from the middle of the eighteenth century that it was customary for ship captains to visit the house of correction in Clerkenwell, ply the female inmates with drink, and invite them to go to the plantations. Richard Ligon, voyaging to Barbados in 1647, found on his ship many servant women, "the Major part of them, being taken from *Bridewell, Turnbull* Street, and such like places of education."[12]

There is nothing to indicate that the servants which as Byrd said might be had from the hospital at any time, were legally condemned to transportation. Some of them certainly were, as for instance John Sowell and John Rivers, tried and acquitted of felony in 1667 at the Old Bailey, then recommitted to Bridewell by the court to labor until transported or until pardoned by the mayor. These were taken to Virginia by John Pate.[13] But if the Elizabethan statute had been habitually put into operation, we should certainly find more frequent record of it in quarter sessions minutes. Sentence to transportation was in fact very sparingly inflicted, but of course a great many individuals were committed to Bridewell as vagrants or as incorrigible rogues. In the latter case they were apparently shipped to the plantations by order of the hospital authorities whenever a merchant appeared who desired to take them; in the former they were perhaps persuaded to express their willingness to depart, and this persuasion may not have been especially gentle. There was no one to protect the rights of obscure vagabonds, and Bridewell was generally so crowded that its officers would be happy to be rid of as many inmates as possible.[14] Thus the transportation of rogues and vagabonds to the colonies really depended not so much upon the imposition of sentences by justices of the peace as upon the frequency with which merchants and ship captains resorted to Bridewell in order to collect a cargo of servants.

During the Protectorate drastic measures were taken to rid the country of idle and loose-living persons, though it may be doubted whether actual accomplishment was very great. The instructions to the Major Generals in 1655 provided that persons of bad life who could not give an account of themselves should be "apprehended and transported into foreign parts," but it was not until August 14, 1656, that definite orders were issued to the same officers to send in lists of the persons they had taken up.[15] Meanwhile the zealous Major Generals had filled their jails with candidates for transportation who were not removed. Whalley wrote to Thurloe that "the not takeing rogues, such as our instructions ordered to bee sent beyond the seas, off our hands, makes us neglect the imprisoning of them; a better worke for the safety and satisfying the country cannot bee: I wonder it should bee soe much neglected."[16] A committee was eventually appointed to treat with merchants concerning their transportation, but unfortunately this is nearly all that is known about the matter. On July 24, 1656, Captain Christopher Keynell of Antigua was given "liberty to transport, at his, or their owne Charge, such and soe many persons, as he cann obtayne from the respective Major Generals of those who are to be transported beyond sea by virtue of their Instructions."[17] There is no evidence that Keynell ever took any. Martin Noell was granted 20,000 acres of land in Jamaica, and in view of the fact that he played a large part in superintending shipping to that island it is not improbable that he took some vagrants, but there is no record. Most remarkable is the evidence of the Venetian ambas-

sador, who wrote on March 3, 1655/6, that the soldiers of the
London garrison had visited various brothels and other places
of entertainment and forcibly laid hands on more than four
hundred women of loose life, whom they compelled to sail "for
the Barbados Islands," in order that by their breeding they should
replenish the white population. Another writer put the number
at 1,200, and a third reported that on March 4 some four hundred were already on shipboard.[18] One can hardly doubt in the
face of these testimonies that the islands were actually favored
with several shipments of prostitutes, but the total numbers of
rogues transported during these years cannot be estimated.

On May 9, 1661, the usual proclamation was issued by the
king for the enforcement of the laws against rogues and vagabonds. Mention is made in this of "those who will go to the
English Plantations," and such are excepted from the common
punishments of whipping and resettling.[19] In the following
year an act of Parliament provided that for the ensuing three
years justices of the peace might send to the Privy Council the
names of such vagabonds and sturdy beggars, not necessarily
"incorrigible," as they thought fit to be transported, to be disposed of in the usual way of servants for a term not exceeding
seven years.[20] At least eighteen persons were reported to the
Council under the terms of this act by the justices of Westminster and of Middlesex, and the Council ordered "That if
the said Prisoners will Petition to goe, and be transported, beyond the Seas...they will give Order, for the delivering of them,
to such Merchants as will transport them."[21] Such a cumbersome procedure was hardly necessary, and was not revived.
For the remainder of the colonial period Bridewell furnished
its large quota of indentured servants to those merchants who
could persuade its inmates to go with them, or who could pre-
vail upon the officials to make the inmates go.

SCOTTISH VAGRANTS AND FELONS

On November 21, 1617, the Star Chamber sent to the Scottish Privy Council a code devised for regulating the border counties. The thirteenth article of this code called for the appointment of a special commission to make a survey and census of the most notorious and lewd persons in those counties, and announced that his Majesty's purpose was, upon certificate from this commission, to send the worst characters to Virginia or some other remote place. Some objection was made to this scheme, but during the following year the Scottish Council acquiesced. The commission was appointed, and the survey made,[22] but what transportations there were seem to have been to Ireland rather than to Virginia. Later in the century, however, an act of Parliament provided that border ruffians might be sent to the colonies without the formality of a conditional pardon, and in 1666 Lord Carlisle stated that the transportation of thirty evil-doers had had a more beneficial effect than the bringing of a hundred to justice in the usual way.[23] Nevertheless, the total number of such folk who reached the plantations must have been small. Cromwell instructed the Council of Scotland in 1655 to collect rogues and vagabonds for the colonies, and a tax of sixpence Scotch was to be imposed on every £100 of rent in Scotland for paying persons watching and taking up such rogues. Lord Broghill wrote that the instructions would be followed, but we have no way of knowing whether many persons were actually shipped.[24]

Early in 1662 the magistrates of Edinburgh petitioned the Council to be allowed to send to Barbados many thieves and whores who were pestering the town.[25] The Lords of the Council at that time evaded the question, but it came up once again in 1665, when one George Hutcheson, merchant of Edinburgh,

"for himself and in name and behalf of his copartners, mer-
chands of the ship bounding for Gemaica and Barbados," wrote
once more. Out of a desire "to promote the Scottish and Inglish
plantations in Gemaica and Barbadoes for the honour of their
countrey," as well as "to frie the kingdom of the burden of
many strong and idle beggars, Egiptians, common and notorious whores and thieves and other disolute and louse persons
banished or stigmatized for grosse crymes," they had been
authorized by former acts of the Council to seize upon such
persons and transport them to the plantations. They had apprehended some of them by warrants from sheriffs, justices of the
peace, and magistrates of burghs, yet they feared that without
authority from the Council they might meet with some opposition. The Council, having considered the petition, granted the
warrant, "provyding always that ye bring the saide persons
before the Lord Justice Clerk, to whom it is hereby recom-
mendit to try and take notice of the persons that they be justly
convict for crymes or such vagabonds as by the lawes of the
countrey may be apprehendit to the effect the countrey may be
disburthened of them." [26] On the 7th of December in the same
year, "the Lords of his Majesties Privy Councill, taking to their
consideration that there are severall prisoners within the tol-
buith of Edinburgh who of their oune accord are desyrous to
be sent to Barbadoes, doe therfore give warrand and command
to the magistratts of Edinburgh to sett at liberty all prisoners
for crymes who of their oune frie will are content to goe to
Barbadoes; and ordaines them to be delyvered to George
Hutcheson, merchand in Edinburgh, in order to their transportation." [27]

From this date it became customary to grant warrants for
the transportation of vagabonds and small felons from Scotland
in this manner. James Hamilton, owner of the ship *Ewe and*

Lamb, remarked in his petition that it was "ordinary to take occasion of shipes bounding to Virginia and other remote islands to disburden the kingdom of strong and idle beggars."[28] The fact was that a cargo of Scottish servants, even those of less fragrant character, was probably the most profitable cargo a merchant could take to the colonies. As a result, during the twenty years from 1665 to 1685, there were at least twenty-six warrants for that purpose issued by the Privy Council to various merchants, fourteen of them being given before 1672.[29] The *Ewe and Lamb* received five, and was twice mentioned as going to Virginia. It is probable, though not certain, that other ships were similarly freighted without warrant from such high authority, and in view of the comparatively small number of ships going from Scotland directly to the colonies after the Acts of Trade, this dealing in vagabonds must have been a considerable item in the total of their commerce.

Despite the precautions which were taken, and the fact that these warrants were usually valid only for three months, they soon began to be abused. In 1668 it was necessary to search the *Ewe and Lamb* and the *Covertine* for kidnapped persons; in the following year Henry Hay was bound in 5,000 marks that he would give in a list of the persons he collected.[30] The sheriffs of Selkirk and Teviotdale complained in 1672 that Patrick and John Shaw, who had received a warrant for taking up vagabonds and thieves, had committed many outrages. They had plundered the sheriffs' own houses, and they continued "still oppressing and sorning upon the people under pretence of executing their commission." The warrant was withdrawn, the Shaws put in prison, and they were liberated only under cautions and penalties. Next year, when the *Hercules* was about to sail with a cargo of servants, fit persons were deputed to go aboard and call for an account of the causes and warrants by which each servant was put on the ship.[31]

Meanwhile the Privy Council availed itself of these ships for getting rid of any miscellaneous culprits whom they wished to dispose of. Two women, prisoners for a long time with no persons appearing to complain against them, and nearly starving, were handed over to a ship master in 1667, though it might seem that they deserved to be set free. One David Morton was sent to Virginia for unlawfully marrying a couple, and later Patrick Wilson was put on the same ship, for the same curious misdemeanor. Upon the petition of Mathew Brisbaine of Rosland his most unnatural son, who had turned against his parents with "many deids of violence which the petitioner cannot think or speak of without teares," was shipped to the plantations by order of Council. In 1674 George Mount and James Layng were likewise transported for misconduct and threatening while in the pillory, and of James Layng we hear from Barbados in 1676 that he "is dead, his wyfe liveth very weel." Such examples are all from the records of the Privy Council,[32] which in general would scarcely trouble itself with such petty cases. Yet they indicate the kind of riff-raff which was bestowed upon the colonies from Scotland during these years, and strange to say the colonies appeared glad to receive it.

THE TRANSPORTATION OF POOR CHILDREN

Among the State Papers may be found a letter of the year 1609 from Lisbon, in which it is stated that the Portuguese were sending 1,500 children and youths from the age of ten upwards to the East Indies, where they would become acclimatized and do good work. The writer suggested that a similar practice might well be followed in the colonization of Virginia.[33] Possibly this letter had some influence, for in that same year the Privy Council informed the mayor of London that the ills and plagues of the city were chiefly due to the numbers of poor in the streets, and they recommended that the Corporation together with the chartered companies should raise a fund to ship many of these persons to Virginia. The Virginia Company gave necessary information as to the expense, and as to the terms which could be offered each new emigrant in the colony. The mayor issued a precept to the companies, and a considerable sum was raised, but at this time no further action appears to have been taken.[34]

About 1617, however, the lord mayor, perhaps at the request of the Virginia Company, authorized a charitable collection for the purpose of sending a hundred poor children to Virginia. The City was to grant five pounds apiece for equipment and passage money, while the children were to be apprenticed until they reached the age of twenty-one, and afterwards to have fifty acres of land in the plantation, to be held in fee simple at a rent of one shilling a year. The necessary £500 was collected from various parishes and probably also from private donations, and the children were dispatched in the spring of 1619, to the great satisfaction of the colonists.[35]

So successful was this venture, that in November, 1619, the company wrote to the mayor, thanking him for the children furnished during the last year, and asking for a hundred more, for which the City should pay £500 as formerly. These children, however, at the expiration of their apprenticeships, were to be tenants on the public land, with houses and a stock of cattle to begin with, and later. one half of all profits.[36] The common council met on December 18, and authorized the sending of the children, providing this time for a levy on each taxpayer of one-eighth of his annual poor assessment to pay the expenses.[37] There was some haggling with the Virginia Company over the terms to be offered the children, and it was finally established that seven years after the expiration of their apprenticeships they should each have twenty-five acres of land in fee simple, at an annual rent of sixpence.[38] This was certainly a better arrangement for the children, and it indicates that the council had some genuine interest in their welfare. This second lot was duly sent off in the spring of 1620, although some of the victims did not wish to accept the boon, and it was unfortunately necessary to procure a warrant from the Privy Council to enforce their departure.[39]

It is difficult to say exactly how many more such shipments there were. More collections were certainly made for the purpose, and the Virginia Company in November, 1620, entertained a motion to obtain more boys from the City, reducing their charge to five marks as the price for which people could bind their children as apprentices at home. Meanwhile Sandys started a project for raising poor young people from the parishes generally, and the company mooted a bill to that effect to be introduced into Parliament, but these efforts were certainly unsuccessful.[40] In July, 1622, the common council of London again voted £500 for the transportation of a hundred children, just as they had in 1619, and announced that they did it with greater enthusiasm "being sensible of the great loss which [the plantation] lately susteyned by the barbarous cruelty of the savage people there."[41] A letter of the year 1627 quoted by Neill without further reference says that in that year fourteen or fifteen hundred children gathered up from divers places were being sent to Virginia.[42] Whatever may be the accuracy of these figures, there is evidence enough to show that during these decades several hundred poor young people were taken to the colony and their passage paid by the charitable contributions of more fortunate Englishmen.

From about 1622 the majority of proposals and projects for transporting poor children name New England as the destination. The Council of New England, no doubt drawing inspiration from the Virginia Company, often expressed a desire to have a hundred children from London, or to collect poor people from the shires by a warrant from the Privy Council. So far as anything was accomplished, however, it seems to have been done by private donations. Anthony Abdy, citizen and alderman of London, made his will in 1640 and left £120, "to be disposed and bestowed by my Executors upon twenty poore Boyes and Girles to be taken up out of the streets of London as vagrants for the Cloathing and transporting of them either to Virginia New England or any other of the Western Plantations there to be placed." Abdy's sons Roger and Nicholas, in 1641 and 1642 respectively, left identical bequests in their wills.[43]

On January 31, 1642/3, the House of Commons, upon a petition from the agents for New England, authorized a collection to be made in London and thereabouts on the two next Lord's Days, for transplanting various poor and fatherless children of the kingdom who were out of work. The collection was made, and money to the amount of £832.9.5 was entrusted to Mr. Weld and Mr. Peter, the agents, for the administration of the scheme. At least twenty children were sent, and perhaps more, but Weld and Peter were accused of misusing the funds, and the statement which they rendered about 1650 is not to be entirely trusted.[44] Winthrop's *Journal* gives a painful account of one of these children: "the boy had the scurvy, and was withal very noisome, and otherwise ill-disposed. His master used him with continual rigor and unmerciful correction." Eventually the boy died, and the master, it is agreeable to know, was hanged.[45]

There were no more wholesale transportations of poor children during the colonial period. Those which we have noted were motivated partly by the common desire to procure servants for the plantations, but also by a genuinely charitable instinct,

which sought to remove young people from their virtually hopeless situation in Britain to a place where they might have at least
a chance of improvement. Strictly speaking these were not instances of penal transportation; the attempt was in fact to prevent these children from growing up into the rogues and vagabonds and felons of our previous pages. They were, nevertheless,
a part of the "surcharge of necessitous people," of whom the
home country was glad to be rid. One group, as has been observed, had to be forced to go by a special order of the Privy
Council. It is to be feared that nearly all of them were persons
on whom charity descended as a heavy punishment rather than
a gentle mercy.

CHAPTER 8

THE TRANSPORTATION OF POLITICAL AND MILITARY PRISONERS UNDER THE COMMONWEALTH AND PROTECTORATE

SCOTS PRISONERS

DURING the last years of the Civil War, when the supremacy of the Parliamentary armies was unquestioned and battles were won on a large scale, a considerable problem was presented by the large groups of prisoners which were taken at the principal encounters. Although the Royalist armies which were defeated at Preston, Dunbar, and Worcester contained many Englishmen, the great majority were Scottish, and the prisoners were almost entirely of that nation. They could not long be detained in England, nor could they be sent home with full safety to the Parliamentary cause, and as their number rapidly increased it became necessary to send them into exile. Some of them were sold off to be mercenary soldiers on the Continent, but the disposition of the Parliament was rather to use them as far as possible in the colonies. Thus security at home and economic development in the plantations was to be accomplished, somewhat at the expense of political stability in Barbados and elsewhere.[1]

A beginning was made after Preston, when a Parliamentary committee in 1648 took charge of the disposal of prisoners, who were temporarily quartered on the various counties. Such men as had been pressed into service were allowed to return to their homes upon giving a promise not again to enter England as soldiers without the consent of Parliament. The remainder were ordered to be transported, and merchants were invited to contract with the committee for their shipment, undertaking to remove them from the charge of the shires at least fourteen days after receiving warrant, and to carry them away so that they should not return "at any time, to the prejudices of the Kingdom." Security was to be exacted for the true performance of this contract, and those merchants offering the best security were to have the first choice of prisoners. It was enjoined that the plantations be first furnished, and then the service of Venice, which city was in the market for mercenaries. Five hundred prisoners were accordingly granted to some "gentlemen" of Bristol, of whose actual shipment no record remains, and a certain Colonel Montgomery dispatched two shiploads to an unknown destination.[2] This is all that can be discovered about the Preston captives.

Immediately after the battle of Dunbar the Committee of Examinations was delegated to take into consideration the disposal of prisoners. Sir Arthur Haselrig was in command at Durham, and was entrusted with general charge of them as they came from the battle, with instructions to send as many as he saw fit to the coal mines, and to await the orders of the committee concerning the rest. For a week the matter was deliberated, and propositions of various kinds were received, including one for the use of a thousand Scotsmen in the armies of Turenne. The demands of the colonies and of Ireland eventually prevailed, and on September 19 Haselrig was given more detailed instructions. He was to deliver 900 prisoners to Samuel Clark for Virginia, and 150 to Joshua Foot and John Bex for New England, all of them to be well and strong, and free from wounds. Upon the same day, 200 more were ordered for one Isaac le Gay, to be sent to Virginia, and the Council of State gave a general authorization for more warrants to be prepared whenever anyone should desire to transport prisoners to friendly plantations. Careful precautions were taken through the Admiralty Commissioners to insure that the Scots should not be sent to any place, colonial or foreign, where they might be used against the Commonwealth, and for this reason, out of 2,300 ordered shipped to Ireland there were to be no Highlanders, "by reason of their affinity to the Irish," though in the next year at least three hundred were allowed to go to France.[3]

Meanwhile, in the north, the prisoners were undergoing adventures which greatly reduced their numbers. After the battle Cromwell had found himself with about 9,000 captives, and he set at liberty all those wounded and disabled for future service, sending the remaining 4,000 southward towards Newcastle. At Morpeth they ate some bad cabbage which made them very ill, a few stopped at Newcastle, and upon arrival at Durham there were only 3,000 left. Of these about 500 sick were put in the castle, and 600 healthy Highlanders were confined in the cathedral, where they fought among themselves. Haselrig meanwhile granted forty of them to the salt works at Shields, and locally disposed some fifty-two others. Having delivered according to the Council's order 350 to Major Clark, he explained the situation in a letter to London, and awaited further orders. The Council approved his disposals, and reduced the number ordered for Ireland from 2,300 to 500.[4]

On November 11 Haselrig was ordered to deliver 150 prisoners to Augustine Walker, master of the ship *Unity*, for conveyance into New England. By this time prisoners had arrived as far south as London to await shipment. Some of them fell sick, and were received into the pest houses around Blackwall at the expense of those who were shipping them. When complaints were heard that some who had been put on board ship had been cruelly treated, Major Clark was summoned before the Committee for Examinations to answer these charges. Of the remainder in the north, some were sent to France in the next year, and a few others stayed at Tynemouth Castle until 1655, when the governor was ordered to deliver those who were fit to Martin Noell, for transportation to Barbados. Those left at Durham were discharged and sent home by an order of March 1, 1652, upon their taking an engagement never more to bear arms against the Commonwealth of England.[5] It is apparent that no more than a small proportion of those at first allotted to the colonies ever reached their destination.

The news of the battle of Worcester, on September 3, 1651, led to the taking of similar action about prisoners. A special committee was constituted on September 8, and on the 9th Colonel Barkstead was ordered to view the artillery ground at Tothill fields to see what part of the captives might be kept there. The surveyor of works was detailed to make further preparations. On the 10th a grant of 1,610 prisoners was made to persons desiring them for Virginia, upon the assurance that Christian usage would be accorded them. Arrangements were made for the gathering up of stragglers in all parts of the kingdom. Finally a committee was given authority to dispose to the plantations all prisoners under the rank of field officer, taken at Worcester or since, and warrants for their departure were to be signed by the Lord President of the Council. It was decided to send those in the neighborhood of Worcester to Shrewsbury, or any other convenient place on the Severn, that they might proceed down that river by boat to Bristol, where 1,000 of them were to be collected for shipment. The governor of Bristol was warned of this influx, and told to provide at the rate of 2½d. per day for all the prisoners under his care until they should be transported. The group duly arrived, and remained at Bristol at least until December, when an infectious disease broke out among them, and the Council inquired why the merchants had not fulfilled their transportation contracts. That is the last heard of the prisoners at Bristol. It is most likely that the remnant were discharged and sent home.[6]

Meanwhile others were transported from London. A proposal was made to the merchants of Guinea, that they should take some for labor in the gold mines, but this cruel plan was not carried out.[7] On October 21 some were ordered for Bermuda, and numbers of others sent to drain the fens of the eastern counties. A considerable group may also have been sent to Ireland, while it is certain that at least 150 were dispatched on the fleet bound for Virginia, which joined Ayscue at Barbados on December 1. These 150 engaged, "for a gratuitie," in the military operations which Ayscue conducted for the reduction of that island. In December the committee began to consider discharging those that remained in England, and about twenty prisoners left at Shrewsbury were set free in March.[8] No further records of their transportation exist.

The seventeenth article of the instructions given to General Monck when he was sent to complete the conquest of Scotland in 1654 gave him full power to transport to any English plantation such of the enemy as he should take in arms, in as great numbers as he should see fit. Monck produced only about 500 candidates for the plantations, and recommended that the rest be sent to the service of foreign princes, as they were men not content unless exercised in war. Of those for the plantations, many were individuals of some position and wealth, whose habit it was to bribe the merchants to set them free instead of transporting them. A number of prisoners who were taken in small groups, or drifted in from the hills, were thus shipped to the colonies in 1654, and another shipload went in 1655, but the treaty with the Earls of Glencairne and Athol, signed in 1654, provided for the release of such of their followers as had been marked for this fate, and some of those already on shipboard were thus rescued.[9]

These Scottish military exiles were the finest kind of human material for the colonies, and they left their mark in many communities which received them. One hundred and fifty Dunbar prisoners arrived in Boston on the *Unity,* and were sold for six or seven years' service at prices ranging from £20 to £30 apiece. Sixty of them went to serve in the iron works in Lynn; others went on to Berwick, Maine, where they were set to work in sawmills, and received grants of land on their freedom in 1656. Of the Worcester prisoners an unknown number were selected for New England, and 272 were landed from the ship *John and Sarah,* being consigned to Thomas Kemble of Charlestown. They were marched from Boston to Lynn in two days, sixty-five pairs of shoes and two hundred pounds of tobacco were purchased for them, and they were disposed in adjoining towns.[10]

The arrival of prisoners in Virginia is known only by an increasing frequency of Scottish names in the Land Patent Books, though it may also be presumed that those embarked on the Virginia fleet duly arrived.[11] They settled and prospered, and in 1665 Alexander Moray wrote from that colony that many Scots lived better than their forefathers, and from so mean a beginning as their servitude after Worcester and Preston were now themselves the masters of many servants.[12] In Bermuda some of the Worcester prisoners complained, in 1656, that their servitude was being unjustly prolonged to seven years. A committee investigated the matter, and "upon search being made in the Admiralty Court," no duration fixed by the government could be discovered, so they were compelled to serve according to their indentures.[13] Here, as in Virginia and New England, there is ample proof that they were not sold into "perpetual slavery," in the phrase often used at the Restoration to describe their sufferings, but upon indentures in the usual manner of servants. Their exile may have been permanent, but not their servitude.

Their experiences in Barbados show that if they had means they need not serve at all. On August 1, 1654, Monck wrote to Cromwell reporting that prisoners being sent to Barbados boasted that they would return as soon as the ships that carried them. He recommended that the Protector should order Governor Searle to take measures for prohibiting the departure of any Scots from the island. In February, 1655, he complained again, and cited the case of "two arrant rogues" who had returned to Scotland after being bought in Barbados by a Scot, Lieutenant Colonel Browne, and immediately set free.[14] More of such instances continually occurred, and the Protector sent a strong remonstrance to Searle, which resulted in the issuance of a proclamation stringently regulating the departure of all individuals from the island. There is proof in Barbados also that the ordinary Scots prisoner was sold by the importing merchant for a term of from four to seven years, and never into actual slavery.[15]

No sooner had news of the Restoration reached the islands, than a stream of petitions from exiles began to come in to the new government, begging financial aid for their return or for their rehabilitation in England. In June, 1660, such a plea was submitted by Lieutenant-Colonel Thomas Hunt, concerning thirty of his soldiers who were sold in Barbados; upon this petition Treasurer Southampton reported in December that the governor of Barbados ought to be instructed to arrange for the immediate return of these men at the king's expense. A year later Michael Bland, with 340 other officers and soldiers, complained that they had been sent to Jamaica in 1654 as disaffected persons, and after suffering much misery there, were returned home without pay and in miserable condition.[16] These individuals were probably not transportees, but pressed and discontented soldiers, hoping to get money by an affectation of past loyalties. Yet considerable sums were expended by the government in returning persons who had been transported to Barbados and in giving relief to the dependents of unfortunates who did not return.[17] The whole matter was in 1662 placed in the hands of the Parliamentary committee which was then entrusted with the bill against kidnapping, but no report from them has been found. The West Indian Islands did not provide a hospitable and permanent abode, as did Virginia and New England. During the remainder of the century, ancient veterans in England would occasionally regale the casual listener with tales of their sufferings in Barbados, after "Worcester fight."[18]

ENGLISH

The large number of English who withdrew of their own volition to the colonies during the Puritan regime must not be confused with the very small number whose transportation was ordered by the government. Some of the Dunbar and Worcester prisoners were doubtless English, but apart from these none were transported against their wills but a few who were implicated in various plots to assassinate Cromwell, and a larger number from the uprising led by Colonel Penruddock in 1655.

In May, 1655, Cromwell ordered eight conspirators to be delivered to Martin Noell for shipment to Barbados. Three of
these were never embarked, but the other five, Somerset Fox,
Francis Fox, Rowland Thomas, Thomas Saunders, and Christopher Gardiner, were in Barbados by September 4. They were
consigned to one Edward Chamberlaine, but they bought themselves free from servitude and refused to stay on his plantation.
Governor Searle, who was having his troubles in keeping track
of prisoners thus foisted on his island, issued an order in the
following February requiring that each one should bring in a
security of £200 that he would not depart from the island.
Upon these terms they were to be allowed to reside where they
pleased. But they seem to have been very elusive. Rowland
Thomas rode about on a horse, attended by a footman, and
eventually escaped to France where he joined Charles Stuart,
leaving behind him in Barbados a debt of £200 which may be
supposed to be his security.[19] There is no account of the fate of
the others.

A considerable number of prisoners taken in Penruddock's
rising were, after long delays, marched to Plymouth and shipped
to Barbados on the *John of London*. They arrived at the island
on May 7, 1656, and were sold "to barbarous persons" by the
master of the vessel.[20] Some of them soon bought their freedom
and immediately "assumed a confidence and boldness to goe
from plantacon to plantacon to discourage servants from that
service and obedience they owe to their Masters . . . and endeavour to beget in them mutinous and seditious thoughts and
to drawe them if they might into rebellious practices." They
spoke "scandalous and reproachful language" against the authority of the Commonwealth, with misinformation and false
reports tending to sow sedition on the island. For this reason
the harassed Searle issued another special order that persons

conducting themselves in this fashion were to be apprehended and summarily dealt with according to the laws of the island, while anyone concealing knowledge of them was to be taken as an aider, abettor, and councillor of theirs.[21]

After the death of Oliver two of these worthies, with Rowland Thomas, of whom something has already been told, returned to England to fish in troubled waters. On March 25, 1659, the trio appeared in Parliament with a tale of woe, describing their hardships on the *John of London* in company with horses and convicts, and their torture while digging in the fields and grinding at the mills of Barbados. Parliament debated whether their petition should be received or not; Martin Noell gave some interesting testimony on the servant trade, Thomas Noell told of the career of Rowland Thomas in Barbados, and some legal questions arose. Annesley and Haselrig were scandalized at the violation of the common law by sentences of banishment, while Henry Vane looked upon the business as concerning "the liberty of the free-born people of England." Military officers reminded the assembly that if the petition were received, there would be the "two or three thousand" transported prisoners of war to deal with next. Haselrig tried to draw a distinction between a time of war and a time of peace, but in prudence the matter was finally dropped.[22] The more worthy petition of Lieutenant Colonel Hunt in 1660, already referred to, may have been for participants in this rebellion, for he mentioned that he had raised his men "at the action at Salisbury." Some years later a sum of four pounds was granted to one Honor Deyman, because her husband "at the tyme of the risinge of Colonel Penruddock" was sent beyond seas, where he died.[23]

During the domestic troubles of 1655, the Protector and Council issued an order in September that "all who adhered to the late king or Charles Stuart his son" were to be imprisoned or sent beyond seas.[24] Despite this comprehensive decree, issued in a particularly uneasy period of the Protectorate, there is no indication that transportation was inflicted upon any persons in England except those already mentioned, who had actually been in arms against the government. Cromwell was always anxious to keep as closely as possible to the common law, and the wholesale shipments of Irish and Scottish military prisoners have tended to create an exaggerated idea of the number of English who were thus treated. It may be remarked, however, that certain individuals designated as "pyrates," who were actually members of the royalist navy, were occasionally sent to Barbados. Such persons were of various nationalties, English, Scottish, Irish, Dutch, and their number is very doubtful.[25] It is improbable that there were a great many of them.

IRISH

In considering the transportation of English and Scots, it has been convenient and natural to separate the shipment of political and military prisoners from the regular dealings in rogues, vagabonds, and felons. A clear distinction was drawn at the time, and the two processes rested on different legal and social bases. But when we come to Ireland, though the same distinctions existed, we soon find that it would be practically impossible, and certainly unprofitable, to disentangle political from non-political transportation. By far the largest number of Irish who were transported to the plantations were taken up as rogues and vagabonds under the provisions of 39 Eliz., c.4., but the reason that there were so many candidates available was clearly a political reason, and the wretched condition of the island was due to the harassing of the English Puritans. Since the rebellion of 1641 affairs had grown steadily worse. Cromwell conquered a part of the island in 1651, and his government sought to remove the entire native population to the western counties of Connaught and Clare, and to replace them in the east with Protestant Irish, and with English soldiers to whom land grants would be given. Such a policy of course produced an appalling social disorganization, and the emigration or transportation of the Irish was but one phase of the total situation.

It will clarify the subject, nevertheless, if the several different aspects of Irish transportation be first outlined, before proceeding to a more detailed account. The vast majority of people who left their country during these years went not to the colonies but to Spain or to Flanders, it being customary to enroll large numbers of Irishmen in troops and take them abroad into the service of the King of Spain. A few of these "rebels" were diverted to the plantations, and in 1654 it was intended to send a troop of 400 thus to labor in the sugar fields. There were also a small and miscellaneous collection of felons, of persons who failed to transplant into Connaught, and of Catholic priests and teachers who were shipped to the colonies, while an unfulfilled project for peopling Jamaica with 1,000 Irish girls and 1,000 boys, which has enjoyed much celebrity, must also be examined. But as has just been said, most Irish who were transported to the colonies were taken up as vagrants by virtue of the Elizabethan statute, and it was the abuse of this authority, not by the English government at Westminster, but by the merchants and ship captains as well as the magistrates who administered it in Ireland, that led to the well-known horrors of the Irish "slave-trade."[26]

From the earliest years Ireland had been a fair field for the recruiting of indentured servants. The adventures of Thomas Anthony and the ship *Abraham* have illustrated the methods and extent of this trade, and shown that it was none too scrupu-

lous. A proclamation of the year 1625 urged the banishing overseas of dangerous rogues; kidnapping was common. In April,
1649, the Council of State ordered that some of 170 Irish taken
prisoners in a Dutch ship be transported, and Cromwell is
reputed to have sent prisoners captured at Drogheda to Barbados.[27] The wholesale removal of Irish began soon after this
campaign, and continued nearly to the time of the Restoration.

In the latter part of 1651 numbers of Irish soldiers and fight-
ers sought permission to submit upon condition of receiving
license to go to Spain, at the expense of the Spanish monarchy.
A certain Don Francisco Fayssot had been employed in the
country since 1644 as an agent of the Spanish government to
raise troops; his services now proved useful, and the English
authorities granted licenses for the emigration of many thousands of Irish in organized detachments.[28] By January, 1653,
nearly 13,000 men had thus gone into Spanish service, and when
the king was behindhand in paying for their transportation
Cromwell himself reimbursed the unfortunate shipowners, for
he was glad to be rid of his enemies. Sir William Petty estimated
in 1691 that 40,000 persons, of whom 34,000 were men, were
transported from Ireland between 1651 and 1654.[29] This figure
has been generally accepted, and as it was not until 1654 that
the numbers going to the colonies began to be considerable, it
may be seen that the emigration to Spain was of remarkable
dimensions.

Transportation to the colonies began on July 9, 1652, when
it was decided to write to the governor of Waterford to deliver
such prisoners as he had in charge to Robert Cann, Robert Yate,
and Thomas Speed, merchants of Bristol, whose ships were
trading to the West Indies and who would take the lot, as they
had accommodation. In the next month a license was given to
Henry Hazard and Robert Immans, also of Bristol, to carry 200

Irishmen from any port in Ireland to the Caribbee Islands, and on the same day Robert Lewellin, of London, was given 300 men. Thomas Speed is again mentioned in October, as the recipient of 200 Irish rebels, to be delivered to him by the commissioners.[30] These are, however, the only records of the transportation of military prisoners to the plantations, though a somewhat similar scheme was suggested in 1654. It may therefore be presumed that the number of such prisoners taken from Ireland to the colonies could not have exceeded 1,000, which is probably less than the numbers of Scots shipped.

In May, 1653, the commissioners appointed as overseers of the poor in various districts were ordered to deliver to Joseph Lawrence, or his agents, such vagrants and idle persons as were adjudged by any two of them to be incorrigible. In other words, the act of Elizabeth was put into operation, and a proclamation of May 23 expressly declared that all laws in force in England for the correction and punishment of rogues and idle people were to be enforced in Ireland. This order was amplified, and the seeds of trouble were sown, when on July 1 the overseers of the poor in every precinct were authorized to treat with merchants for transporting vagrants to America. The overseers were especially enjoined to ship only those persons, begging and wandering in the country, who came strictly under the act, but later events show that they did not observe this instruction.[31] It is impossible to say how many shiploads of unhappy Irish were dispatched to America by the sole negotiation of the commissioners of precincts. No mention of such shipments would be likely to appear in the State Papers, and no record of them is likely to be discovered elsewhere. They must have been very considerable in number. It is only in those cases of a merchant or captain who petitioned the government for special license to transport such vagrants that any information remains.

In September Mr. David Selleck, of Boston in New England, asked the Council of State for a license to transport 400 Irish children, and after a consultation with Edward Winslow the Council granted the request. Two ships, the *Good Fellow* of Boston, George Dalle, master, and the *Providence* of London, were designed for Mr. Selleck's project, and on October 28 they received permits to sail. Meanwhile on September 14 Captain John Vernon promised Selleck that upon application to the Irish commissioners he would be given 250 Irish women between twelve and forty-five years old, and 300 men from twelve to fifty. Lord Broghill was authorized to search them out and deliver them, and was particularly cautioned not to send anyone who had any means of his own or friends to support him, thus making his activities come within a broad construction of the Elizabethan statute.[32] The cargo was duly collected and shipped, and the reappearance of this matter in Boston several years later may here be noted as a description of the method in which such instructions were followed. In June, 1661, William Downing and Philip Welch came before the Essex County Court in Massachusetts and refused to serve their master, Samuel Symonds, any longer. A bill of sale was produced from George Dell, master of the *Good Fellow,* who "sould Mr. Samuell Symonds two of the Irish youthes I brought over by order of the State of England," for £26. A certain John King then gave testimony as follows: he

with divers others were stollen in Ireland, by some of the English soldiers, in the night out of theyr beds & brought to Mr. Dills ship. where the boate lay ready to receave them, & in the way as they went, some others they tooke with them against their Consents, & brought them aboard the said ship, where there were divers of their Country men, weeping and Crying, because they were stollen from theyr frends, they all declareing the same . . . and there they were kept, untill upon a Lords day morning, the Master sett saile, and left some of his water & vessells behind for hast, as I understood. . . .

The two men, despite their plea, were judged to serve two more years.[33] When such scenes as this were enacted where the highest authorities were concerned, the performances of local commissioners must have been far more discreditable. There was in fact a period of licensed kidnapping on a large scale, with the magistrates and officers of the law actively conniving at it under some pretense of statutory sanction.

Meanwhile many other warrants were granted: to Sir John Clotworthy on April 1, 1653, for the transportation of 500 "natural Irishmen" to America; to Richard Netheway of Bristol on September 24, for 100 Irish Tories to Virginia in the ships *Golden Horse* and *Amity;* to "some merchants of the city of Bristol" for 400 Irish Tories to the Caribbee Islands in January, 1654, and on January 20 a sweeping order for the governors of Carlow, Kilkenny, Clonmel, Wexford, Ross, and Waterford to deliver all vagrants to Captain Thomas Morgan, Dudley North, and John Johnson, for transportation to the West Indies. Again it was directed that no person should be apprehended under that order who was a member of any family, and for whose good behavior the master of the family would answer. The vagrants of Limerick and Cork were ordered for Captain John Norris in April, 1654; sixty women from Connaught were granted to Colonel Stubbers for the West Indies in June; and all persons in the jails of Clonmel, Waterford, Wexford, Kilkenny, and Carlow were entrusted to John Mylam, merchant.[34]

But now the abuses of this trade in vagabonds were beginning to attract public notice. On December 22, 1654, the Commissioners General were ordered to send some trusty men on board a ship bound for Barbados, to ascertain what persons were kept on the ship under color of the declaration for transporting vagrants, to see whether the ship's officers had any warrants under the hands of two justices of the peace, and in short to find out if the procedure had been by legal or illegal means. At the same time all other vessels were ordered detained until they could be similarly investigated.[35] During the next two years the trade continued; an occasional ship was searched and persons removed, but no more licences for transporting vagrants were granted by the Council, and the arrangements must have been almost entirely in the hands of local magistrates. Complaints continued to come in, and finally on March 4, 1656/7, the Council of State revoked all orders for the transportation of such individuals, and directed that henceforth they should be brought to justice in other ways.[36] The language of this decree shows perfectly that shipmasters had used all the familiar methods of the kidnapping trade under pretense of collecting rogues and vagabonds. They employed "persons to delude and deceive poor people by false pretenses either by getting them aboard the ships, or in other by-places into their power, and forcing them away, the person so employed having so much apiece for all they so delude." Likewise, "for the money's sake [they] have enticed and forced women from their children and husbands, and children from their parents, who maintained them at school," and they practiced such dealings not only upon the enemy Irish, but even upon English residing in the island. For these reasons the trade in vagrants was abolished, and no further licenses were granted, or arrangements made by the local officials. It is well to emphasize that the principal injustices connected with the transportation of Irish to the plantations arose not from the direct action of the government, but from the wholesale abuse of licenses granted under the provisions of 39 Eliz., c.4. Such abuses, if not effectively hindered by the Puritans, were at least no part of their expressed intentions, and indeed they made some effort to insure that no persons except genuine vagrants should be carried away.

We now return to the year 1654, when one Peter Bath, who had been sentenced to death for refusing to transplant into Connaught, had his sentence changed into banishment to Barbados. There are only two more notices of the transportation of persons under this particular condemnation, and it is extremely unlikely that more than 150 were thus sent away.[37]

Most famous of all projects of Irish transportation was that for collecting 1,000 young girls and shipping them to Jamaica, where they would breed up a population for that newly acquired possession. Diatribes have been written on this subject, and pictures painted, and it has become one of the stock incidents with which to illustrate the brutality of Puritanism. There is not, however, very much substance to the whole story, though the letter of Henry Cromwell to Thurloe on the subject makes painful reading:

Concerninge the younge women, although we must use force in takinge them up. yet it beinge so much for their owne goode, and likely to be of soe great advantage to the publique, it is not in the least doubted, that you may have such number of them as you shall thinke fitt to make use uppon this account.[38]

This was on September 11, 1655. On the 18th he recommended that 1,500 or 2,000 boys of twelve or fourteen years be sent also, on the ground that Ireland could well spare them, "and who knows but that it may be a meanes to make them English-men, I meane rather, Christianes."[39] On October 3 the Council of State duly voted in favor of shipping 1,000 girls and 1,000 boys of fourteen or under, the allowance for each limited to twenty shillings. Then the business dragged along through the month of October, Henry Cromwell assuring Thurloe that the girls could be ready at any time ships would call for them. Finally,

about the first of November, Thurloe told Henry that the next
ships would be equipped to take the girls, and that they should
be ready to depart about the end of December.[40] That is the last
record which exists concerning the matter. It is impossible to
believe that 1,000 girls were ever sent to Jamaica without leaving
a shred of evidence. The scheme, considering the state of Jamaica at that time, was fully as foolish as it was cruel.

We may well believe that when fuller information came in
concerning Jamaica, the shipping of boys and girls was abandoned in favor of the shipping of men. Henry Cromwell declared in September, 1655, that many of the soldiers of the Puritan army in Ireland could be used in colonization, now that
their fighting was practically finished. Accordingly he delayed
the dispersal of his disbanded army until he should have fuller
knowledge of the number required in Jamaica, and the terms
on which they could be sent. Not until the summer of 1656 did
the project really get under way, when Martin Noell undertook
the transportation of 1,200 men from Carrickfergus at £5.10.0
apiece, and then the ships went through so many misfortunes
that the number arriving at Jamaica was scanty.[41] Few things
were dearer to the hearts of the Cromwells than the development of the island which they had so recently conquered, and
there is scarcely any aspect of colonial history during these years
on which so much thought was expended and so many plans
drawn up as the "peopling of Jamaica." Ninety per cent of these
schemes came to nothing.

Last of all classes of Irish transported to the colonies were
those clearly sent away because of their religion. On July 22,
1654, it was ordered that all priests in Dublin should be transported into Spain, but this was altered, in the following January, so as to condemn all those in Dublin not found guilty of
murder to Barbados. In the month of October a murder in the

town land of Lackagh caused the entire population of some thirty-seven to be sentenced to transportation, and with them at least two priests were ordered shipped to the plantations. Three "Popish priests" were delivered to Mr. John Norris for shipment to Barbados in December, 1655, and the governor of that island was particularly instructed to see that they were so employed that their return to Ireland should be impossible.[42] Twenty-six priests and Catholic schoolmasters were gathered in Carrickfergus in the summer of 1656,[43] and it is highly probable that some of them went on the Jamaica ships that year, but no further evidence of their transportation to the colonies can be found. The ominous instruction to the governor of Barbados concerning the employment of priests so that they should not return has given rise to dire suspicions, and to charges that they were condemned to "perpetual slavery." This was not so; and while the English government would doubtless have been glad to hear of their death, there was never any such thing as perpetual slavery for any white man in any English colony.

The records of the islands, in fact, show that quite a different attitude was taken towards such priests as were landed. When three of them came ashore at Spike's Bay, in Barbados, the Council was much alarmed, and in May, 1656, finding that four priests were then in the island, the Council gave them fifteen days to get out of the domains of the Commonwealth of England.[44] Nowhere is there evidence that any priest was kept in servitude; their punishment must be understood as one of banishment rather than of transportation and sale.

In general the Irish were most unwelcome servants in the plantations, and the numbers of them who came out in these years have left evidences of tumult and disaffection. Large numbers of Irish patronymics appearing in the Virginia Land Books give proof of the arrival of many in Virginia;[45] the ship *Provi-*

dence, Thomas Swanley, master, which we have already mentioned as sent to Virginia by David Selleck, arrived in good
season and sold three servants to Colonel John Mottrom of
Northumberland County.[46] In Bermuda the arrival of seventeen servants, probably Irish, was recorded on July 17, 1657,
and in November of the same year an order was passed that
the Irish should "straggle not night or dai, as is too common
with them." Further purchases of Irish servants were absolutely
forbidden to any inhabitant of Bermuda; nevertheless in 1661
it became necessary to take measures for suppressing a threatened insurrection of Irish and Negroes.[47] Likewise, the Irish
became so turbulent in Barbados that a long order of Council
was necessary on September 22, 1657, disarming and restraining
the wanderings of all Irish and Catholics.[48]

About the year 1666, the Reverend John Grace set out upon
a mission to the Roman Catholics in the British West Indies.
His report[49] is detailed, and the figures he gives are perhaps
fairly accurate, though they apply of course to the whole Irish
population, and not merely to those transported during the
Puritan troubles. Father Grace computed that there were twelve
thousand Catholics in the eastern islands. Barbados, out of a
total of forty thousand souls, had eight thousand Irish Catholics,
who were destitute of all spiritual ministrations. About four
hundred were in St. Christopher, and Montserrat was entirely
settled by two thousand Irish, a figure which certainly seems
too large. Six hundred were to be found in Nevis, while many
others were scattered through the small islands, and some had
fled to the French. Many other testimonies concur in regard to
the Irish and Scots in Barbados; Governor Searle wrote in 1655
to point out the danger of receiving so many disaffected persons,
particularly those of importance, and other writers attribute the
royalist outbreaks which occurred there to the influence of these

exiles rather than of the older inhabitants.⁵⁰ A letter of one
of Thomas Povey's correspondents indicates that Barbados expected some favors because she had taken "above 12,000" such
persons, and rendered them useful instead of a menace to the
Commonwealth.⁵¹ This is almost certainly an exaggeration, yet
it must be remembered that many royalists in Barbados were
not transported persons but voluntary emigrants.

The most detailed and diverting evidence respecting the
Irish in the Leeward Islands is to be found in various accounts
of Catholic missions to those parts.⁵² There is for instance the
extraordinarily interesting story of Father John Stritch, who
founded a chapel in the French section of St. Christopher about
1650, and ministered to many Irish from the English part of
the island. After three months' labor the good father went to
Montserrat, where he disguised himself as a timber merchant
and conducted secret worship in the woods. Upon returning
to St. Christopher he found that the English had forbidden
their servants to go into the French quarter; nevertheless many
of the devout came secretly, even at the risk of great hardships.
The English eventually took 125 of the most zealous Catholics
and immured them upon the desert Island of Crabs, leaving
them there to perish. Some of them managed to put to sea, and
were driven far and wide by a storm, passing many days without food or water. They were sorely tempted to save themselves
by the sin of cannibalism, but piety asserted itself, and no sooner
had they resolved upon the alternative of death than a large
fish appeared, which obligingly allowed itself to be caught by
their unassisted hands, and provided them with food until they
reached land. According to another version of the same story,
three hundred Irish were carried in chains to the island, where
all but two perished. These two, in desperation, leaped into the
sea, where one drowned, but the other (who was truly "viribus

valentior") "ad continentem natando pervenit," and reported the sad fate of his companions. It is to be feared that these accounts were designed more to fortify faith than to increase knowledge.

Generally speaking, the transportation of the Irish has been interpreted in a political light and the process seen as the logical development of Puritan ferocity. This is not wholly just. The devastations of war and rebellion must have produced an exceptionally large number of vagrants and starving people of the same kind that were habitually shipped from England and Scotland. Emigration of servants from Ireland was always great in volume, in the eighteenth and nineteenth no less than in the seventeenth century, and it was due very largely to the unstable economy of that agricultural island. Without any government interference a large increase would have been expected during the 1650's. To be sure, the Irish refused to be conquered, and vast numbers of them went to Spain, under the command of their own officers, to live in a more congenial country than their own had become. Of those who stayed behind, however, relatively few were shipped to the colonies by the direct action of government exercising vengeance on its enemies. The Puritans should not be too harshly blamed. It is nevertheless true that the fundamental cause of the deplorable economic condition of Ireland in those years was political, and that the Saints very largely created the vagabonds whom they ordered to be transported. They did not supervise effectively the magistrates and merchants who collected vagrants; they took little trouble over the difficult distinction between an Irish rebel, an Irish neutral, and an Irish rogue. They were glad to be rid of as many as possible, whatever their classification. Hence we really do but little violence to historical truth in ourselves treating rogues, vagabonds, felons, military prisoners, priests, teachers, and maidens all under the head of political victims.

CHAPTER 9

THE TRANSPORTATION OF POLITICAL AND MILITARY PRISONERS AFTER 1660

QUAKERS

THE QUAKERS, like the Irish, were perpetually the objects of slander, ridicule, and persecution. Their devotion to religion was not to be doubted, but it was fanatical and vociferous, often respecting neither the decencies of civil society nor the exercises of orthodox worship. Their incurable propensity for wandering, in a hygienic condition not always to be distinguished from that of the common rogue, left them open to discipline as vagrants, and no estimate can be made of the number which may have been transported to the colonies on a pretext of incorrigible vagabondage. But during three years they could legally be condemned to transportation, for by the provisions of the Conventicle Act of 1664[1] persons convicted for the third time of attendance at an unlawful religious meeting could be shipped to the colonies (except Virginia and New England) for an exile of seven years. The sheriffs were entrusted with arrangements for embarkation, and if the exile could pay his own passage he need not become an indentured servant. This law was aimed primarily at the Quakers, and its enforcement was attended with divers remarkable circumstances, highly characteristic of the age and the persons concerned.

In the same year that the act was passed, a zealous mayor of Bristol collected twenty-three persons in jail under accusations of a third offense under the law. The mayor's term of office expired, however, before he had actually convicted more than three of these, and his successor allowed the rest to go free. On December 16, 1664, the three who had been sentenced to transportation were placed on board the *Mary Fortune,* of Bristol, and remained there for a week. They were then put back on shore, because of a temporary prohibition of the departure of ships, and returned on shipboard at the end of another week, when a pass had been received for the ship to depart. But during this fortnight, apparently, they worked on the minds of the captain and crew not only by tears and prayers but also by solid arguments and citations of colonial laws forbidding the entrance of people brought away against their wills. The result of their efforts is shown in the following extraordinary certificate from the master and crew of the vessel, dated January 7. After reciting the circumstances, this document continues:

But now going to depart, their Cry, and the Cry of their Family and Friends, are entred into the Ears of the Lord, and he hath smitten us even unto the very Heart, saying, *Cursed is he that parteth Man and Wife.*

And moreover, they that oppress his People, his Plagues shall follow them wheresoever they go, and assuredly we do in part partake of them already, for our Consciences will no wise let us rest, nor be in quiet, for the Lord hath smitten us with a terrible Fear, so that we can in no wise proceed to carry them. . . .[2]

Were it not for the facility with which all kinds of people wrote such language, one would be practically certain that the Quakers themselves had drafted this. The certificate goes on to quote the common law concerning transportation, and the act of Barbados regulating immigration. For these and other reasons the undersigned master and crew announced that they were setting the three Quakers at liberty.[3]

This was no isolated case. Seven Quakers were sentenced to transportation by Orlando Bridgman at the Hertford Assizes in August, 1664. The sheriff instructed the jailer to treat with a shipmaster for their conveyance, and the jailer contracted with Thomas May, of the *Anne* of London, but told him that the Quakers were free men and that six of them would carry their goods with them. This was very probably true, as they doubtless had money enough to pay their own passage. May, however, asked them if they were willing to go, and when they gave a negative answer he refused to take them. Five times they were put on board his ship by the authorities, and five times taken off again, because according to the captain his ship would not move with them on board, though other vessels sailed away with ease. Finally May left them ashore and went without them, sending a letter to the Privy Council which told of the strange reluctance of his ship to get under way, and mentioning also that his sailors would not make the voyage if the Quakers were taken. The Council ordered their further imprisonment until another ship could be found, but they remained in jail until 1672, when they were released by the Declaration of Indulgence.[4] When Captain May returned he was taken into custody, and considerable trouble resulted for him and his sailors.[5]

Apparently this transportation of Quakers was distasteful to the masters of ships, and the crews were influenced by some obscure superstition which the Quakers fostered. No vessels could be found to take the prisoners away, and it became necessary for the Privy Council, in March, 1665, to issue a warrant forbidding the departure of certain ships in the Thames until they should take aboard a number of Quakers and give bond to transport them safely. In accordance with this, the *Jamaica Merchant* took three and duly conveyed two of them to Jamaica, the other perishing on shipboard. The two who arrived lived prosperously, and one of them later returned to England. It is probable that six were carried to Barbados on the *John and Thomas,* and seven to Nevis on the *Amity,* but no certain account of their arrival exists.[6]

Meanwhile large numbers were being convicted and put into Newgate, where they remained without transportation. After some searching, the authorities found a mariner named Fudge, who said he would not stick to transport his nearest relations, and sixty of the prisoners were assigned to him. They were taken to his ship in a barge, but the sailors were less amenable than their captain, for they refused to hoist the Quakers on board, and as the Quakers would not hoist themselves they had to be returned to Newgate. A few days later, on August 4, a detachment of soldiers from the Tower was told off to act as stevedores, and this time the prisoners were safely embarked. At this point Fudge was arrested for debt, and it was not until February 23 that the party finally left for the plantations, by which time twenty-seven of the unhappy passengers had died of a pestilence. The second day out of Plymouth they were captured by a Dutch frigate and taken to Holland, whence they were sent back to England with a special passport, as not being likely to be exchanged for prisoners of war.[7]

In various highly-colored pamphlets written by the victims, scenes at the trials of these people are described, the judges are accused of partiality and injustice, the validity of the act of Parliament is denied, and the juries are said to have been persecuted for failing to convict. These things need not detain us, for such Quakers as were convicted were undoubtedly guilty under the act, unjust and cruel though that act certainly was.

One case only surely deserves to be held in memory; it is that of a certain John Otter, who was asked at his trial in the usual form to state his residence. He replied that his dwelling place was in God, whereupon the judge sentenced him to transportation as an incorrigible vagabond, and he was sent to Virginia with three felons, to the great scandal of his coreligionists.[8]

Besse, in his *Sufferings of the Quakers,* has collected all the evidence which he could find of their transportation, and has omitted no horrors which could embellish the tale. There are very few cases to be found which he has not included. A sessions book of Bristol lists twelve Quakers as sentenced to the alternative of transportation or a fine of £100 on September 13, 1665.[9] Their names are not in Besse's work, but Sewel tells us that some of the Quakers compounded with the authorities,[10] as the law permitted, and it may be that these paid the fine. Thirty-two were in Hertford jail in July, 1665, and were ordered by the Privy Council to be transported in the ship *Nicholas,* of London, and there are a few other Privy Council orders which indicate probable transportations.[11] All those listed in the Middlesex Sessions Records, however, are included in Besse, and it is evident that he gathered the facts concerning all those who lay in Newgate awaiting transportation, as well as nearly all who were convicted in the provinces. An analysis of his accounts, stripped of much verbiage, shows two hundred Quakers actually sentenced to transportation under the act of 1664. Of these, he follows the careers of nearly all. Ninety of them definitely did not arrive in the colonies, some of them having been in Fudge's ship or the others which have been noted, while others remained in jail until 1672, when they were freed. Twenty-two died of plague in Newgate, and fifteen were "placed on shipboard" with no notice of their fate. Only three of the two hundred can be followed definitely to the plantations. Besse would scarcely have missed an account of any considerable shipments, though it may be supposed that a few of whom he had no knowledge were transported. The highest estimate of the total number cannot well exceed one hundred, for the Conventicle Act expired in 1667, and the new law in 1670 held no penalty of transportation. Thus despite a considerable sound and fury about the business, the real importance of it was negligible, except, of course, for the unhappy individuals actually concerned.

SCOTTISH COVENANTERS

The years from 1660 to 1688 in Scotland were marked by continual unrest, provoked by the incessant effort which was made to enforce the discipline of the Anglican Church and the authority of the English government. One disturbance after another broke out, and all were suppressed with cruelty and the force of arms. The principal events which concern this subject were the battle of Bothwell Bridge in 1679, by which one major rebellion was destroyed, and the equally ill-fated rising of Argyll in 1685. After each of these conflicts great numbers of prisoners were transported to the colonies, and between them there was a fairly regular flow of banished Covenanters as well. In all, more than eight hundred Scots were sentenced to transportation between 1678 and 1685, and it is remarkable that they should have attracted so little notice in comparison with the same number of Monmouth rebels. To be sure, many of them were prevented from arriving by various calamities, but those who did reach the colonies made a most valuable addition to the population.

The first serious outbreaks in Scotland occurred about 1666, just after the new church ritual had been forced upon the unwilling Presbyterians. The prisons were filled with rebels. It was decided to hang all ministers, officers, and one in ten of the common herd, while of the remainder one in ten was to be forced to confess and the other nine sent to the plantations.[12] This was done as an act of royal prerogative. As early as September, 1666, two persons were thus sentenced for their guilt in being accessories and active instruments in the late tumult in Edinburgh; and, since twenty under a similar condemnation escaped from prison during the next February, it is safe to assume that there were large numbers involved.[13] In July, 1667, the prisoners in the tollbooths of Edinburgh and Cannongate were divided into four classes. Those who confessed to their participation in the rebellion and refused to take an oath of allegiance were ordered to be shipped to Barbados with the first ships to depart. An indefinite number of these rebels were assigned to various ships, and in September, 1668, six of them were given to Captain Lightfoot, of the ship *Convertin,* bound for Virginia, who gave bond of £300 to transport them safely.[14] These are the first of a long series of grants to various captains and merchants, but from the year 1670 the process becomes more systematic, and such grants were accompanied with exact lists of names.

On August 3, 1670, the Parliament of Scotland passed an act requiring those who should be called upon to do so, to "depone" concerning conventicles which they had attended or of which they had knowledge.[15] Anyone refusing thus to testify might be sentenced to transportation. On the 11th, one James Dundas, son to the laird of Dundas, was sentenced to transportation for refusing to tell what he knew about a conventicle at the Hill of Beath which he had attended. Nine more persons were similarly condemned on the 16th, while on the 18th Dundas was released because he reconsidered and gave the information which was required of him. The majority of those who had been sentenced on the 16th were set at liberty on bail in order to attend to their families, and their presence was not required until the following May.[16] There is no indication that they ever were actually shipped, though it is always possible that some covenanters were delivered to the masters of those ships who had petitioned for rogues, vagabonds, and felons.

Apparently the act of 1670 was not again brought into operation until the summer of 1678, when conditions began to grow much worse in Scotland generally. On May 31 four men were sentenced, and by August 2 some sixty or more were under confinement awaiting their transportation.[17] According to a private letter of this date, friends of these unfortunates interceded for them, and the Council remitted the case to the two archbishops, who ("good merciful men") ordered the immediate execution of the sentence.[18] One Ralph Williamson, of London, petitioned the Council, asking that he might transport the prisoners whom he understood to be available, and promising to give such security as might be required. He further requested that the king order the governors of plantations to admit the cargo and allow him to sell it off at the best advantage. The Council agreed, and the king instructed Governor Culpeper of Virginia to allow the entry of Williamson's prisoners, any law, order, or custom of Virginia to the contrary notwithstanding. Thus protected against any colonial disposition to exclude the Scots by virtue of the act against convicts, Williamson loaded sixty-eight captives on the *St. Michaell of Scarbrugh,* Edward Johnstone master, which was lying at Leith.[19]

He made a great mistake, however, in sending his cargo to the Thames, with intent to transship it there for Virginia. The Scots were landed at Gravesend, where Williamson made arrangements with Captain Eveling, of the *York Merchant,* to

take them on board for America; but at the last minute Eveling
balked at the job, and likewise the commander of a royal frigate
refused to take them. There are conflicting stories of what followed, but it is certain that the prisoners were eventually dispersed on shore. General sympathy was felt for their condition,
a public meeting collcted £80 for them on one Sunday,[20] and
after about nine months' absence they returned to Scotland.
Williamson was so unpopular in London that he could not walk
about the streets in peace, and the Presbyterians in Scotland
took such courage at the affair that they believed the threat of
transportation to be impossible of fulfillment.[21] As in the cases
of the Quakers, it is plain that popular opinion in England was
definitely on the side of the nonconformists, and against the
constituted authorities of Church and State.

After the battle of Bothwell Bridge the Scottish Privy Council wrote to Lauderdale relating the story and requesting the
authority of the king for transporting the "rabble" of captives
to the plantations. There were long delays, but on September 5,
1679, Charles wrote to the Council directing that William Paterson, of Edinburgh, was to have the transportation of some three
or four hundred prisoners. Still it was not until October 16
that a committee was sent to inspect them in the several tollbooths and to select those fit for transportation. On November
8 Paterson was called before the Council to explain why he had
not sailed, and on the 17th his ship was still at anchor. Since
the Lords of the Council feared that a design was on foot to
interfere with the transportation, they peremptorily ordered
that the ship should depart.[22] Accordingly, having stocked the
Crown with 258 prisoners and £1,500 worth of provisions and
other equipment, Paterson sent his venture forth. To escape the
"phanatick designes" which had ruined Williamson he sent
the *Crown* around by the Orkneys, though the weather was

"such as in no mans memory the like hath been heard of." On December 10 the vessel arrived in those islands, and anchored while the mate went ashore for water and fresh provisions. But the anchorage was not sufficiently far up the sound; a great storm came down from the north, the ship dragged her anchor, and was driven on the rocks, where all but thirty or forty of the passengers were drowned. The discomfited Paterson petitioned for some help in his misfortune, and his distress was relieved by the Scottish Privy Council, who gave no sign of displeasure at this effective and permanent disposal of the Bothwell Bridge rebels.[23]

During the next few years transportation lagged, though the act of 1670 was occasionally invoked and a few covenanters handed over to merchants.[24] By 1684, however, policy had again tightened up. The king approved the transportation of all rebels who appeared penitent but refused to take the Test Oath, and the Privy Council ordered that magistrates and commissioners in the various shires where there were rebel prisoners should send up lists of them, so that a few might be chosen for banishment.[25] In the summer of 1684 George Lockhart took at least ten rebels to New York, while sixty or more were brought to Carolina by Walter Gibson and Robert Malloch.[26] Many more were made available in the autumn when the king stimulated local commissioners to further activity.[27] Gibson asked for some of these, and was granted 180 on condition that he take convicts and vagabonds before covenanters; it does not appear that he proceeded with the business.[28]

On July 28, 1685, after the defeat of Argyll and his followers, the Privy Council ordered that those prisoners who were to be transported should be branded and have one ear cut off, so that they might never be able to return to Scotland without being recognized. Various merchants lost no time in petitioning for groups of these unfortunates, and each recipient of prisoners was dissatisfied with the number allotted him and the arrangements which he had to make. Great confusion resulted, and one cannot be certain that the record of shipments is complete, especially as no less than 103 rebels duly sentenced to transportation cannot be found in any of the shipping lists. But we know that John Ewing, acting as agent for Philip Howard of Jamaica, took 177 to that island; that George Scot of Pitlochrie received more than one hundred and conveyed them to New Jersey; and that Alexander Fearn shipped thirty or more, probably to Barbados. William Arbuckles was given fifteen prisoners, whom he said he would take to New England, but there is no indication that they arrived.[29]

The oppressed victims of seventeenth-century persecutions were not backward about relating the horrors of their experiences. Several narratives of the voyages and adventures of these Scots have been preserved, and they are full of remarkable occurrences. The members of Walter Gibson's shipment, on their way to Carolina in 1684, sang hymns and conducted worship below decks, though an unsympathetic crew closed the hatches on them.[30] George Scot of Pitlochrie's voyage was most ill-fated; he himself and seventy of the passengers, including twenty-two exiled covenanters, died. The surviving prisoners refused to sign four-year indentures, and the courts of East Jersey upheld their refusal to serve, and set them free on the ground that they had been brought against their wills. Other inhabitants of the colony treated them kindly, entertained them through the winter in a village, and saw many of them off to New England during the next summer.[31]

The wretched passengers in Ewing's ship, bound for Jamaica, were confined below hatches, and suffered so much from hunger and thirst that "several of them were put to drink their

own urine, and two and thirty of them died." Upon arriving at
Port Royal they were put into an open prison for ten days and
then sold as "slaves" for the benefit of Sir Philip Howard.
Gilbert Milroy, the relater of this history, suffered greatly because his master forced him to work on the Lord's Day, and
beat him when he refused. Nevertheless, Gilbert's excellence
and honesty finally made him an overseer of Negroes. He served
in this position until set free after the Glorious Revolution and
then returned to Scotland and his family, with whom he was
still enjoying existence in 1710. Milroy derived some comfort
from the horrid fates which befell his captors, for he tells with
relish how Sir Philip Howard fell into the Thames and was
drowned before getting any money from the sale of prisoners,
and how during the voyage to Jamaica forty of the soldiers
and sailors who were most cruel to the Scots went mad and
leaped overboard, while the captain gradually rotted and died.[32]
To the zealous Presbyterian, these things demonstrated that
"it appears to be but a hazardous Venture to make merchandize
of the suffering people of God."[33]

Perhaps the most remarkable of all testimonies from indentured servants is that of a Scot named John Menzies, who was
a servant in Barbados in 1676, and probably, though not certainly, banished as a Covenanter.[34] This worthy was a schoolmaster, very proud of his Latin. "As to my present happy con-
ditione," wrote he, "yow may *mihi gratulare abunde;* for, be
assur'd, God hath blissed me with the absolut best conditionat
master in this island; in nature meek, gentle, and kind and
noblie generous. . . ." Menzies' position was that of a schoolmaster, or tutor, to his master's children, and though indentured he received £25 per annum. He seems to have thought
that by producing evidence of his scholarly training in the form
of a "testificat" he would be set free from his indenture, and

might make a greater profit from his knowledge. The following sentences, describing the fortunes of others who had been transported as vagrants or felons, are interesting:

Samuel Steil, the Inglishman, that stoll Duncan Duncans cloak is heir ane usher of a school and married. James Lying, the wright that was in the coock stool with George [Mount], is dead, his wyfe liveth very weel . . . One Margarett Hamiltone, a pritty young girle, I have spok with, is a servant too. She cam out of the tolbooth. She lived in the Wast Bow there with a march[ant], lives very weell though, and is about to be married to a doctor of phisick.

The Scots were most valued servants, in whatever capacity they came, and this letter as well as the story of Gilbert Milroy shows how well they settled down. The excellent Menzies enclosed with his letter some very creditable heroic couplets which he had composed on his situation, and these may well have been the first poetic effusions to come out of Barbados. We may select a few lines:

> *To serve whats that? Lett me consider, stay,*
> *What comes it to give myself away?*
> *The right I have resigned pray lett me see,*
> *What is't to lett away my Liberty?*

> . . . .

> *But hold! proud thought! the wretch deserve his woe,*
> *They fatters fancy and quhen it is not so.*
> *Tell me the man can brage so free estat*
> *That not to some great power subordinate.*
> *Who he or that hath uncontrolled intents,*
> *Seas have their shores and Kings ther parliaments.*

> . . . .

> *Ile owe no blush then as a debt to shame,*
> *Because that I noe slavish servant am.*

MONMOUTH REBELS

Best known of all political transportees are the Monmouth rebels, those forlorn remnants of the rising against James II which was crushed at the battle of Sedgemoor in 1685. Made famous by Macaulay, they have always been mentioned but rarely studied, despite the fact that the records of their fate are almost complete. Their disposal became a model for the treatment of prisoners from the risings of 1715 and 1745, for it was the first instance of the transportation of political victims under a legitimate ruler of England.

In the summer of 1685 Judge Jeffreys left London for the Western Circuit, to carry out that series of trials which became notorious as the "Bloody Assizes." He was prepared to select an indefinite number of prisoners for service in the colonies, and awaited instructions from the king as to their disposal. It had become known in the city at least by August 1 that many hundreds would be shipped, and assiduous courtiers were busy trying to persuade his majesty to allot them a share of the booty.[35] The serious business of the assizes began at Dorchester on September 5, and there Jeffreys received a letter from Secretary of State Sunderland giving the first definite instructions concerning transportation:

His Majesty commands me also to acquaint you that of such persons as you shall think qualified for transportation, He intends Sir Philip Howard should have 200, Sir Richard White 200, Sir William Booth, Mr. James Kendall, Mr Niphoe, Sir William Stapleton, Sir Christopher Musgrave and a Merchant (whose name I do not yet know) 100 each, and his Majesty would have your Lordship accordingly give Order for delivering the said number to the said persons respectively, or to such as they shall appoint to receive them.[36]

The recipients were to enter into security to take the prisoners to "some of his Majesties Southerne Plantations, viz. Jamaica, Barbados, or any of the Leeward Islands in America,"and to have them kept there for ten years before they were set at liberty. Within ten days the prisoners were to be taken off the hands of the king, and maintained by those who were to ship them. A postscript to this letter particularly outraged Macaulay: "The Queen has asked a hundred more of the Rebels, who are to be transported. As soon as I know for whom, you shall heare from me again."

Even Jeffreys was disgusted with this method of handing out captives, and on the 19th he wrote to the king:

I received your Majestys commands by my Lord Sunderland about the rebels your Majesty designs for transportation, but I beseech your Majesty that I may inform you that each prisoner will be worth £10 if not £15 a piece, and that if your Majesty orders them as you have already designed, persons that have not suffered in your service will run away with the booty and I am sure that your Majesty will be continually perplexed with petitions for recompense for sufferers as well as rewards for servants.[37]

This remonstrance had no effect, and the business went on mainly as the king had at first instructed, with the courtiers enjoying this unaccustomed and profitable speculation in prisoners whom they had done nothing to help in capturing.

A careful system of checking, employed to insure the safe disposal of the rebels, makes it possible to trace nearly all the shipments. In the first place, each recipient of prisoners gave in a certificate of the number handed over to him by the king's officers. Most of these were in by the 26th of September and they show that the total number of rebels condemned to transportation and thus handed over was 890.[38] Then on October 17 Secretary Blathwayt wrote to each of the transporters asking the names and destinations of those whom he was shipping, and each one save Musgrave and White eventually replied with an invoice of shipment which has been preserved.[39] Leaving these two out of the reckoning, we find that of 720 rebels assigned, only 522 were actually placed on shipboard. From other sources it may be learned that at least thirty-five of Musgrave's men sailed, and probably about ninety, but of White's no record remains.

Meanwhile, on October 11, the king caused a letter to be drafted for each of the colonial governors, explaining the situation, requesting them to see that their assemblies passed a law for the ten-year servitude of the rebels, and requiring a certificate of the arrival and disposal of the prisoners in each colony.[40] With these circular letters were sent copies of the shipping invoices, so that the governors might check the lists very carefully. The only certificates of governors which have survived are those of Stede at Barbados, from which we learn that out of four hundred originally destined for that island and 329 actually shipped, 306 were disembarked and 304 lived to be sold into servitude. Reports of the naval officer at Jamaica throw some light on the number of arrivals in that colony; it is certain that 159 rebels landed, and it is practically certain that about seventy more came.[41]

A brief consideration of each shipment will show some of the misfortunes which occurred and difficulties which were encountered. Jerome Nepho, who received one hundred prisoners, was the queen's personal secretary, and must have been one of those against whose favor Jeffreys protested. The actual supervision of his shipment was in the hands of George Penne, a papist resident in the West country, and it is possible that Nepho sold off all his rights in the business to Penne. Of the hundred victims, one was left wounded in Exeter jail, and one, Azariah Pinney, was transported under curious circumstances which will appear later.[42] There is no record of what happened to the other eighteen who disappeared before reaching the ship.[43] The prisoners were consigned to Charles Thomas and John Penne at Barbados, and eight of them died on the voyage.

Sir William Booth and James Kendall were merchants trading to Barbados, and Kendall's hundred prisoners are listed in the returns under the name of Booth. Two of the victims, John Edwards and Edward Lloyd, were sent to York River, Virginia, instead of to Barbados,[44] probably by virtue of special arrangements made by themselves or their friends; these are the only Monmouth rebels who made their appearance in the continental colonies. Booth and Kendall consigned their men to a factor in Barbados named Browne, who died shortly afterwards in bankruptcy. Not only did the partners get no profit from their enterprise in rebels, but there was even a movement to levy upon their estates in Barbados for the payment of Browne's debts.[45]

Whether the queen actually received a group of rebels and profited by their shipment is still doubtful. The judges sent a list to the Treasury, dated November 12, 1685, giving the sentences of all rebels whom they had tried;[46] in this list a hundred rebels are described as having been assigned to the queen, but, except for this mention and that in the letter of Sunderland already quoted, her name does not appear in any transaction. By comparing names it is found that her prisoners were shipped by John Rose and Company, merchants, and were consigned also to Charles Thomas in Barbados. Presumably Rose either acted as agent for the queen, or else she sold him her interest outright, and like Jerome Nepho, sought profit in a quick transaction.

Sir Philip Howard, who has already been described as shipping 170 Scottish Covenanters to Jamaica in this year, received also two hundred Monmouth rebels. The prisoners were taken from Wells to Weymouth, spending their first night at Shepton Mallet and the second at Sherburne. Thirty-three escaped during the journey, and one was reprieved by order of the lord chancellor.[47] Many of the rest were sick or wounded, and of the entire lot only 121 arrived in Jamaica. Of the shipment of Musgrave's men we have only the knowledge that thirty-five went on the same vessel that carried the queen's contingent. Thirty-two of these were still alive when the ship got to Barbados, and they proceeded from there to Jamaica. The fact that fifty "convicts" arrived at Jamaica on January 5, 1686, strongly suggests that the remainder of Musgrave's allotment were duly transported, but there is no definite record of them.

A certain Thomas Heywood of Westminster, Gent., received twenty rebels, most of whom appear on the judges' lists of November 12 not as transported but as "remaining in custody." His certificates nevertheless prove that they were safely conveyed to Jamaica. Concerning Stapleton's hundred there is no information beyond the fact that they were shipped on the *Indeavour,* of Bristol, for St. Christopher and Nevis. Sir Richard White was badly served; he received only seventy rebels, together with twenty-one common felons, and the judges' lists assign most of his men to a Captain John Price. There is no record whatever of their fate.[48]

General conditions for the residence of these rebels in the islands, as laid down in the king's circular letter of October 11,[49] disclosed one refinement over earlier practices. It was ordered that these prisoners should not be allowed to free themselves from servitude, but should become indentured servants for ten years even though they might possess the means to buy themselves off. This had not been the case with Cromwell's exiles, as we have already seen, nor was it so for the Scottish Covenanters of the same year. On December 29, 1685, the king's

letter was read in the council at Barbados, and a committee
of four was appointed to draw up a statute conforming to the
royal requirements.[50] This act was passed on January 4, sent
to the Lords of Trade, approved by them on April 20, and it
even brought forth a special expression of satisfaction from
James II himself.[51] It provided that each rebel should serve for
ten years, any law or custom of the country to the contrary notwithstanding. Any shipmaster, or any purchaser of the rebels
who should free any of them, for any consideration, should be
subject to a fine of £200, should be imprisoned for a year without bail, and should be forever incapacitated from holding any
public office on the Island. Any rebel attempting to escape was
to receive thirty-nine lashes, spend an hour in the pillory, and
be branded on the forehead with the letters F.T., signifying
"Fugitive-Traytor." Other provisions no less drastic completed
a law which was a model of ingenuity and loyalty. Jamaica and
the Leeward Islands were not so speedy in their responses, and
the former did not pass a suitable statute on the subject until the
summer of 1686.[52]

By the time these rebels had been settled into the life of the
colonies, had taken their places as servants, and had lent their
strength to the white population, James II was dethroned, and
the new monarchs had no moral right to keep the prisoners in
servitude. On July 3, 1689, the Lords of Trade agreed to represent to the king that instructions were needed in Jamaica concerning the Monmouth rebels. Early in the following January
the laws of Barbados, Jamaica, and the Leeward Islands concerning the prisoners were disallowed and in the next month
a free pardon was issued for all of them.[53] Yet the unfortunate
men were perforce detained in the colonies, and a letter from
Governor Kendall of Barbados, dated June 26, 1680, expresses
the difficulty of the situation:

I have not announced the repeal of the Act concerning the Monmouth rebels to the Council and Assembly. It seems that, when they arrived, the Lieutenant-Governor received positive orders from King James that their servitude should be fixed by Act at ten years. The planters accordingly bought them, and thinking themselves secure of them during that time taught them to be their boilers, distillers, and refiners, and neglected to teach any others as they would otherwise have done. If these men are freed, the loss to the planters will be great. . . . [54]

This matter was carefully considered at Whitehall, and on November 20, 1690, new instructions were sent to the colonies concerned which provided that acts should be passed repealing the laws fixing prisoners' servitude at ten years but reimposing such conditions as should be necessary to keep them in the islands until the king should permit them to leave. If any assembly should refuse to pass such an act, the king's disallowance of the former law was to be announced. The obliging assembly of Barbados duly passed an act of repeal on March 17, 1690/1. It provided that none of the rebel servants should receive the usual reward of servitude according to the custom of the country, and that they should all be liable to military service until released by the king. The law went on to impose the same penalties on them for attempting to escape as were provided for regular servants, but their terms of service were to expire in January, 1691, when they should finish the customary five years.[55] This act could scarcely be called a great amelioration of the prisoners' lot; it was in fact a disreputable device of Barbados planters to cheat some excellent servants out of freedom dues.

Despite precautions somewhat similar to these, half of the rebels in Jamaica had returned home before the king's instructions arrived, while the rest had entered voluntary service. The governor reported that danger from the French was great because of the withdrawal of so many white men; a remark which need not be taken too seriously, but which nevertheless indicates that scarcely more than one hundred able-bodied men made a great difference in the strength of Jamaican defense forces.[56]

Stories written by two of these rebels have survived. Henry Pitman was a physician, and did not fight at all for Monmouth, but was nevertheless condemned to transportation and handed over to Nepho.[57] George Penne persuaded Pitman's relatives to pay a sum of £60 so that the brothers would be free on reaching Barbados, but they were none the less sold to one George Bishop, who treated them cruelly. Bishop was apparently unable to pay for them, and eventually returned them into the hands of the merchants. With five other rebel prisoners Pitman soon afterwards managed to escape from the island in a small open boat, and sustained adventures worthy of Robinson Crusoe. He got to New Providence, went thence to Carolina, New York, and finally back to England, where he found that he had been pardoned and could set up a small business dispensing medicines.

John Coad was of a very religious turn of mind. After substituting himself for another man who did not wish to be transported, he was shipped to Jamaica in the *Port Royall Merchant,* Edward Brooke, master.[58] Ninety-nine prisoners were shut below deck in a place not large enough for them all to lie down, and were not allowed on deck for "air or easement." Smallpox, fever, calenture, and the plague carried off twenty-two of them, while fearful cries, groanings, and torments troubled the remainder, "yet we did pray, and sing praises to our God, and he was a light round about us." Finally, through the good offices of some other passengers, they were allowed on deck, and were then troubled only by the scarcity of food and water. The tyrannous insolence of Captain Brooke was also hard to bear, but Coad notes with satisfaction that Brooke never prospered again. Upon arriving in Jamaica, where they were consigned to Mr.

Christopher Hicks, a certain nonconformist minister named Robert Speere managed to persuade Hicks to use them well, and in particular Coad was most fortunate in his treatment. His master fed and housed him well, and gave him some stock, with which he eventually made a considerable profit. At the news of the Revolution of 1688, Coad presented a petition to the governor, who informed him that there were orders to send the rebels home. A man-of-war was actually procured for this purpose, to the tremendous joy of the exiles, and though it was detained for a long time by the local gentry while they offered a petition for the continued servitude of their captives, yet they were finally set free, and many of them found their way to England. Coad's own master gave him £10, but the ungrateful servant thought he deserved £36.

One other peculiar story has been preserved. Azariah Pinney was the black sheep of a large flock belonging to the Reverend Mr. John Pinney, a Presbyterian minister of some distinction.[59] He became involved in the rebellion, and was sentenced to transportation in the contingent of Nepho, but his devoted sister Hester managed to raise £65, which was paid to George Penne as a ransom. Instead of accepting promises of freedom in Barbados as Henry Pitman did, Pinney was sent secretly to Bristol, and an affidavit of his departure was made and sent by Penne to Nepho. After ten days in Bristol, during which time Azariah was fitted out with clothes, a bed, beverages, tobacco, and other necessaries, he shipped himself to Nevis, paying his own passage money of £5. Upon arriving in the colony he joined the business of Mr. Merewether, a sugar merchant, and himself carried on also a trade in lace. He remained in the island for many years, and took great care to ascertain his exact legal status after the Revolution had freed him from the necessity of exile. An opinion obtained from Richard West, counsel of the Board of Trade, assured him that he could hold property despite the act of attainder, which had been sufficiently annulled by the pardons of William and Mary. The case of Azariah Pinney is the only one of a Monmouth rebel substituting mere exile for the servitude which was prescribed, unless perhaps the two men who went to Virginia were similarly fortunate. Pinney founded a wealthy family in Nevis, and his son held several important administrative posts in the Leeward Islands.

REBELS OF 1715 AND 1745

The most remarkable difference between the transportation of rebels after the 1715 Jacobite rising and that of the Monmouth prisoners is that the transporter this time asked payment from the government for doing the job. On February 28, 1715/6, Sir Thomas Johnson of Liverpool, a merchant and "parliament man," sent in a proposal to the Treasury for taking off rebels at forty shillings each, they to serve him or his assigns for seven years in the plantations. The Treasury completed an agreement with Johnson on these terms in April, and it was provided that he should get his money upon producing a certificate of shipment from the mayor of Liverpool and the collector of customs. It was also expected that certificates of arrival from the governors of plantations should be produced in the course of time.[60] On the 23rd of April instructions were sent to the governors of colonies concerning these rebels; when landed they were to be guarded, and if there should be some who had not already entered into seven-year indentures they were nevertheless not to be set at liberty, but forced to sign contracts of servitude. There were, however, a few individual exceptions made by the home government, and several persons were thus sent out with special letters to insure their freedom.[61]

What happened to the prisoners themselves may be told by one of them, writing April 28, 1716, from Chester Castle:

On Thursday we were all taken out of our apartments before the Sheriff, the officer of the Guard, and Sir Thomas Johnston's son-in-law (who, they say, have bought us from the King) and were all offered indentures to sign for 7 years' service in the plantations, as the said Sir Thomas should please to dispose of us. They have prevailed with a great many of the common sort to sign them, the last of whom were carried off to Liverpool this morning. But the gentlemen unanimously refused to do the same, alleging we were no ways bound thereto by the nature of our petition presented to his Majesty, but only to simple transportation, which we were willing to undergo at his Majesty's desire, whereupon we were severely threatened, and, without getting liberty to return to our rooms for our bed clothes and linen, we were all turned into a dungeon or little better, and fed only with bread and water.[62]

It is evident from the instructions already sent that these prisoners were doomed to servitude, whatever their intentions when petitioning for mercy may have been.

During the spring and summer of 1716, at least 639 rebels were transported to the colonies by Johnson and his agents. The dates of shipment, number of prisoners, names of ships, and destinations are given in the Treasury records made when Johnson received his final payment in March, 1717.[63] They are as follows:

30 March	95	rebels on the	Scipio	for	Antigua
21 April	81	" " "	Wakefield	"	So. Carolina
26 April	47	" " "	Two Brothers	"	Jamaica
7 May	104	" " "	Susannah	"	So. Carolina
24 May	80	" " "	Friendship	"	Md. or Va.
25 June	30	" " "	Hockenhill	"	St. Christophers
29 June	126	" " "	Elizabeth & Anne	"	Va. or Jamaica
14 July	54	" " "	Goodspeed	"	Virginia
15 July	1	" " "	Africa	"	Barbados
15 July	1	" " "	Elizabeth & Anne	"	Virginia
28 July	2	" " "	Goodspeed	"	Virginia
31 July	18	" " "	Anne	"	Virginia

Not all of these ships can be followed certainly to their destinations. The *Anne,* and the *Elizabeth and Anne* duly arrived
in Virginia;[64] the *Friendship* and the *Goodspeed* went to Maryland,[65] while the *Two Brothers* found its way to Montserrat.[66]
Concerning the *Scipio, Wakefield,* and *Susannah* there is no
further record, though it is certain that some of the rebels were
bought in South Carolina and thus that at least one of the ships
must have arrived.[67] The *Hockenhill* sailed on the 25th of June,
but on August 3 its passengers mutinied, put the master, mate,
and supercargo in irons and forced the unwilling crew to take
them into Bordeaux, where they arrived early in September and
went free, selling the ship's cargo to their own advantage.[68] The
Elizabeth and Anne, which set out for Virginia with 127 rebels,
arrived with only 112. When an investigation had been made,
it was found that the captain had been bribed to allow a number
of his passengers to escape in Liverpool and Cork. No action
against him seems to have been taken either for this enormity
or for cruelties of which he was accused during the voyage.[69]

These rebels were tenacious of their rights and liberties. No
sooner had they arrived in Virginia and Maryland than they
petitioned the governor, protesting against their servitude, and
quoting the Habeas Corpus Act to prove even their deportation
illegal. This was of no avail, nor did another appeal, five years
later, sent to both governors requesting that their servitude be
terminated at the end of the customary five years, fare any
better.[70] There are more evidences of happy endings to their
colonial careers than can be found for the Monmouth rebels.
One named Francis Hume became Governor Spotswood's factor at Germanna, while Dr. John Browne managed to secure
his freedom at an early date and settled down as a physician.[71]
From Maryland comes an extraordinary letter in Highland dia-
lect, written for "Tonal Makaferson" by a fellow Scot who had

himself once been a servant.[72] "I kanna komplin for kumin to dis Quintry," says Donald, whose master kept him only at work which he enjoyed, and never denied him a pot of bitter ale. Nor had he any intention of making haste back to Scotland, for freed servants "grou unco rich." He observed one who was "now wort mony a Tusan Punt," and another who "has sex Plakimors wurkin til him alrety, makin Tumba Ko ilk a Tay."

We learn from the same reporter that the exiles had been healthy during their voyage; another source reveals that only one prisoner on the *Elizabeth and Anne* died at sea, despite the complaints which the passengers made after landing.[73] As usual, the Scots improved their situation in the new world with the greatest diligence, and it is quite uncommon to find that one of them, who ran away from his master, was described in the newspapers as "full of Words and little Performance."[74]

Thirty years later another desperate rising was suppressed by the Hanoverian armies, and a new flock of prisoners, nearly 3,500 of them, occupied the attention of the English government. We need not enter here into the painful details of their trials, their conveyance into England, their imprisonments and hardships, all of which have been the subject of a recent careful study.[75] On September 25 and 26, 1746, however, the Treasury made agreements with Richard Gildart of Liverpool, merchant, and Samuel Smith of London, for the transportation of such rebel prisoners as should be delivered to them or to their agents. These contracts called for a payment to the merchants of five pounds for each person taken; while half of the amount was to be given on presentation of a certificate of shipment, the other half would not be paid until receipt of a notice that the prisoners had arrived in the plantations.[76] It was even proposed that they should be branded in the face, to prevent their return, but this cruel plan was not carried out. Nevertheless, those who remembered the 1716 transportation informed the government that greater precautions would have to be taken this time to insure that rebels did not come back to Scotland too quickly.

On February 24, 1747, a pardon was issued under the Great Seal to 744 persons implicated in the rebellion, containing the condition that each should "seal an Indenture" with Smith or Gildart "to serve them or their Assigns in our Colonies in America during the term of their natural lives." This drastic clause is somewhat modified by the next sentence, which seems to indicate that in each colony they are only to remain servants for the period fixed by the custom of that colony. Within a week of the issuance of this pardon authorization was given to hand over 739 prisoners to the transporters. What had happened to the remainder we do not know; presumably they had either died in prison or succeeded in getting themselves free pardons. Of the prisoners handed over, four hundred were to be shipped from the Thames, the rest from Liverpool.

These numbers were further reduced before actual shipment. On March 31, Smith sent out three ships from the Thames with 270 prisoners on board, and this seems to be all of the four hundred who were really transported. On the other hand, Smith and Gildart together dispatched three ships from Liverpool on May 5 with 340 rebels; this number may include some persons later scheduled for exile and not put into the original pardon. Whatever the reasons may have been, the total number of rebels transported by the contractors was only 610, out of a pardon list of 866.[77]

The three ships from the Thames went to the West Indies, and safely delivered 254 of their prisoners. One, the *Frere,* landed 128 at Barbados, the other two went on to Jamaica with the remainder. Of the Liverpool ships one, the *Veteran,* with 150 prisoners on board, set out for the Leeward Islands and was captured near Antigua by a Frenchman; the prisoners were carried to Martinique and set at liberty. The other two Liverpool ships went to Maryland, landing 153 of their passengers. Upon presenting proper certificates both Gildart and Smith received from the Treasury the balance of their money.[78]

While these 610 persons were all that were transported by the contractors, there were many more who went to the colonies at this time, some as a result of pardons bearing a condition of banishment, and others perhaps out of sheer despair over conditions at home. We read particularly of them in North Carolina, where Governor Johnston was accused of notoriously favoring them at the expense of older inhabitants.[79] Contemporary accounts indicate that more than a thousand left Liverpool for the plantations during the same period that Smith and Gildart were shipping their groups.[80] Since there were only 936 in all whom the English government condemned to transportation or banishment, a considerable number must have departed of their own free will. This fact has produced an exaggerated idea of the number who were "sold into slavery."

When one of Gildart's ships reached Maryland on July 19, 1747, the supercargo made a speech to the prisoners, explaining the goodness of the country, and requesting them to sign seven-year indentures.[81] This they refused to do, enlisting the sympathies of the captain, who actually ordered the carpenter to take all their irons off. He then performed his greatest service by writing letters to neighboring Roman Catholic gentlemen and others friendly to the Jacobite cause, "so that we might not fall in the common buckskins' hand, for so the people that are born their are called." On July 22 the sale was held, and the friendly gentlemen rallied round in amazing fashion. Mr. Edward Diggs, Mr. John and Mr. Joseph Lancaster, and Mr. Thomson from St. Mary's County attended, while Mr. William

Diggs was commissioned by the gentlemen of St. George's County to represent them. These purchased all but three or four of the eighty-eight on board that vessel, and apparently set them free at once, for the narrator of this story took passage in the following January for Scotland. Indeed the precautions of the English government for keeping their exiles in the plantations were ludicrously inadequate.

Concerning the other shipments no further account has appeared. Governor Ogle of Maryland issued a proclamation in September, setting forth the terms of the pardon which had brought them to the colony.[82] This may indicate that the second of Gildart's shipments was not so fortunate as the first. On the whole, however, the colonies were esteemed a fair place for Scotchmen. From the time of this rebellion the normal migration of servants and freemen was gradually increased until it reached the huge proportions of the 1770's and the government turned its attention to restraining rather than compelling the departure of its subjects.

PART THREE

The Servant in the Plantations

[CHAPTER 10]

VOYAGE AND ARRIVAL

G IVEN good quarters, agreeable company, and a bit of luck
with the weather, much pleasure and instruction were
to be gained during a voyage to America, as many entertaining
histories bear witness. Even the travel diary of such an amiable
and curious man as Richard Ligon, however, cannot blind us
to the fact that the Atlantic crossing of the seventeenth and
eighteenth centuries was perhaps the most arduous and dangerous adventure in which large numbers of ordinary people
have ever engaged. It meant eight or ten weeks, more or less,
in a vessel of fifty, a hundred, or two hundred tons, usually
cooped up with many other passengers, threatened by pirates
and hostile navies as well as by ordinary perils of wind and
sea, and frequently tortured by seasickness if by no worse ills.
The prospect would appall nearly anyone nowadays, and indeed it appalled most people in those times. Few undertook
the voyage without foreboding, and fortunate were those who
survived it without pain, discomfort, sickness, and fear. The
amenities possible for free and well-to-do passengers were rarely
available for servants or redemptioners, and the sufferings they
bore were often of terrible intensity.

Germans and Swiss had a long and tedious way to go before embarkation, and many were the tribulations which they
endured before facing the dangers of the sea. A journey down

the Rhine from Heilbronn to Holland took from four to six weeks, and in the middle of the eighteenth century involved a stop at each of thirty-six customs houses, where a toll had to be paid.[1] The expense of this part of the trip averaged about £3, but it varied so greatly by reason of unforeseen delays or the dishonesty of agents that many emigrants found themselves on the borders of Holland without money enough left either to continue their journey or to return home. This problem first appeared in 1709 and 1710, when great numbers of those who were bound for New York descended upon the city of Rotterdam and had to be fed by the public charities until the English took them off.[2] Eventually the redemptionist system, invented in the 1720's, enabled such persons to pay for their passages after arrival in America, but another result of the situation was that the Dutch government, tired of having to support colonists for the English, took restrictive measures which considerably affected the whole trade. "Till of late," wrote the British secretary of legation at The Hague in 1739, "there was but one Merchant at Rotterdam, with his Associates, who was allowed to answer for, & transport These Emigrants." This merchant was an Englishman named Zachary Hope, a man who more than anyone else was responsible for the beginnings and early development of the trade in redemptioners.[3] Apparently the Dutch government made its rules somewhat more flexible in the same year 1739, for the frontier guards were then ordered to stop only those emigrants who could not produce "a Certificate of some sufficient Subject of This State having given Bail for their orderly Passage thro' & contracted with Them for their immediate Transportation out of it."[4] John Dick in 1751 gave a bond of this nature to the States General for the settlers he took to Nova Scotia.[5]

The redemptioner trade thus begun by Zachary Hope tended

under the influence of such regulations to stay in the hands of a few great merchants resident in Rotterdam, who kept their own agents in the hinterland to collect recruits. Groups of German emigrants were usually conducted down the Rhine by one of these agents, armed with the certificate which would permit them to cross the frontier into Holland. The merchants resented any intrusion into their business, and the recruiting agents themselves resisted and hindered the efforts of outsiders to collect colonists for other purposes; an example of such interference with the Nova Scotia project has already been cited. John Dick himself wrote from Rotterdam in 1750 that he had "apprehended as soon as the Affair became Publick, Messrs Hope & Mr Steadman of this Place, who had hitherto Monopolised that Buissiness would Oppose me as much as Possible, this is now the Case."[6] He reported a rumor that Steadman had gone to England to protest. In the late 1760's, though Hope was still in the trade, the monopoly had certainly disappeared, and such Philadelphia merchants as Willing and Morris, and Samuel Howell, were carrying large numbers of Germans in their ships.[7]

No such evidences of monopoly appear in the English trade, and indeed there was no reason or opportunity to establish one. Anyone who chartered a vessel and sent forth a venture had full right and opportunity to collect as many passengers as he could. Servants sailed from every important port in the British Isles, but by far the greater number came from London, Bristol, Liverpool, Dublin, and Cork, and doubtless it was principally the merchants of Bristol, Whitehaven, and Liverpool who conducted the trade from Ireland. Colonials occasionally participated; Samuel Galloway of Maryland, for example, brought over one or two cargoes of servants each year during the early 1750's and sold them in the West River. There is no evidence that Yankee shippers had much part in the business.[8]

Governmental formalities upon the departure of servant ships from Britain were not usually onerous. On the way down the Thames each vessel stopped at Gravesend, and the customs searchers came on board, perhaps accompanied by a doctor, to see that all was in order. One of their duties, as we have seen, was to look for servants who had been kidnapped, but the effectiveness of this procedure was slight. An official of the Registry Office was also available at the same place to fill in indentures in proper form.[9] During periods of political stress there was apt to be a long detention of the ship at the Downs, or perhaps it would be necessary to wait in port for special permits to sail. It was often also a matter of weeks before the weather would allow a vessel to get out of the Thames and through the Channel into the open sea; many passengers remarked that one of the most tedious parts of the voyage was the long wait for a favorable wind. Ships generally called at one of the western English ports for additional supplies of water and fresh food before starting on the long pull across the Atlantic. As for the Rotterdam ships, it was necessary for them to stop at an English port, usually Cowes, in order to obtain proper clearance papers under the provisions of the Acts of Trade.

The size of vessels on which emigrants were transported during the seventeenth and eighteenth centuries changed very little, though there may have been some tendency to use smaller ones in the earlier years. They varied from thirty-five or forty tons to three or four hundred, and in very few instances more.[10] The greatest number of people came on ships of from one hundred to two hundred and fifty tons, which were of course much smaller than those commonly used in the East India trade. Fares were paid, and accommodations ordered, according to a system by which each adult was counted as one full "freight" or "head," and children were rated proportionately to their age. Thus the

Georgia Trustees voted to send out Salzburgers, calling each person over twelve one freight, each child from seven to twelve half, and from two to seven a third, of a freight, while infants under two travelled free.[11] The Board of Trade in arranging for colonists to go to Nova Scotia asked that one ton and a half of shipping be allotted for each passenger carried, but this was certainly a counsel of perfection, for we read that during several years vessels averaging less than 200 tons carried generally about 300 German passengers to Philadelphia.[12] The *Thornton,* of 175 tons, brought 152 convicts to Maryland in 1767, and 202 in 1774.[13]

It was customary in the German trade to measure the accommodations and allott them according to rule. Pennsylvania passed an act in 1750 which, as explained by John Dick, required that a "Bed Place" six feet square be provided for each four whole freights, thus allowing them to sleep in pairs, by turns, with fair comfort, or to sleep all at once by crowding.[14] A freight, however, was a passenger above fourteen years of age; children between four and fourteen counted as half a freight, and those under four were not counted at all. Thus, even according to this rule, there sometimes occurred such incredible overcrowding as that on one of Dick's own ships sent to Nova Scotia. The vessel measured for 223½ freights; Dick put 228½ on board, but the actual number of souls was 322. He claimed nevertheless that his ship was much less crowded than many which went to Philadelphia, and from the chorus of protests against this abuse we may infer that he probably spoke the truth.[15] There was little complaint of overcrowding on ships carrying English servants, however, and sometimes cabins were fitted out so that small groups of even the poorer passengers had comparative privacy.[16] As for the Irish trade, its customs were nearer the German.

Provision for feeding passengers and servants during the voyage was made by dividing them into "messes" of four, five, six, or sometimes as many as eight persons, and allotting food in fixed amounts to each mess. Josselyn gives one account of the common allowance during the seventeenth century: for three days each week, a group of four persons received each day "Two pieces of Beef, of 3 pound and ¼ *per* piece, Four pound of *Bread,* One pint ½ of *Pease,* Four Gallons of *Bear* with *Mustard* and *Vinegar.*" On the other four days of the week, each mess received "Two pieces of *Codd* or *Habberdine,* making three pieces of a fish, One quarter of a pound of *Butter,* Four pound of *Bread,* Three quarters of a pound of Cheese, *Bear* as before." Besides these things, a gallon of oatmeal was allowed per day for fifty men.[17] In 1735 the Georgia Trustees drew up a scheme for victualling passengers which may be quoted in full as a model of what was considered good and liberal provisioning:[18]

> On the four Beef days
> Four Pounds of Beef for every Mess of Five Heads
> And Two Pounds and a half of Flour
> And half a Pound of Suet, or Plums.
> On the two Pork Days
> Five Pounds of Pork
> And two Pints and a half of Pease, for every Five Heads.
> And on the Fish Day
> Two Pounds and a half of Fish,
> And half a pound of Butter, for every Five Heads.
> The whole at Sixteen Ounces to the Pound
> And allow each Head Seven Pounds of Bread, of Fourteen Ounces to the Pound, by the Week.
> And Three Pints of Beer, and Two Quarts of Water, (whereof one of the Quarts for Drinking, and the other for boiling Victuals) each Head by the Day, for the Space of a Month; and a Gallon of Water (whereof Two Quarts for Drinking, and the other Two for boiling Victuals) each Head by the Day after, during their being on their Passage.

It is remarkable that this menu contains no cheese, but perhaps it was understood that this would be supplied, as it was on another contract, if the weather was such that the kettle could not be boiled.[19]

This food allowance cannot be regarded as typical of what most servants could expect, for the Georgia Trustees set rather a high standard. Certainly the Germans got no such solid fare, but as a matter of fact they did not really want it, and viewed it perhaps very much as we should at the present day. When the Board of Trade reproved John Dick for his inadequate provisioning, and sent him a schedule very much like that quoted, he replied that "however Agreeably it might suit with the Constitutions of Britons, Experience has Evinced the Contrary with these sort of Palatines, Especially where there are Women & Children, as their Chief Diet at home is upon Vegitables, Flower, Oatmeal, Eggs, Fish, Butter, Cheese, &c." The Board relented, and Dick took some of his recruits out with him in the city of Rotterdam to choose their own provisions, which they did much more in accordance with his ideas than with those of the Englishmen.[20] When one contemplates the diet furnished in the seventeenth century, it becomes wonderful that any passengers ever survived a voyage through the tropics.

Ships setting out for the colonies with servants were victualled on some such scales as these generally for twelve weeks, or for fourteen if liberally inclined. But it is to be noted that this provisioning was for "freights" or "heads" and not really for persons. When Dick sent out the *Speedwell*, victualled for 162½ freights for fourteen weeks, there were actually 229 souls on board, many of whom must have been boys just under fourteen with lusty appetites. Thus the provisioning of ships in the redemptioner trade, where many children were carried was usually not so adequate as that of ships carrying servants, even though the same general principles might be followed. One reads occasionally of vessels which had the ill fortune to be kept at sea too long. Thus the *Good Intent*, sailing rather late in 1751, arrived off the American coast in the winter and was unable to make port on account of particularly bad weather conditions. After twenty-four weeks at sea she finally put in to harbor in the West Indies, nearly all of her passengers having long since perished.[21] The Reverend John Henry Helffrich sailed from Amsterdam on September 6, 1771, and did not reach New York until January 14. His ship must have been well furnished, for it was only on Christmas Day that "they began doling out the water" and then everyone got about two pints and a half each day.[22] The sloop *Sea-Flower*, on the contrary, sailing from Belfast with 106 passengers in 1741, was at sea only sixteen weeks, but lost forty-six passengers from starvation. Six of these were eaten by the survivors, before help appeared.[23]

Most voyages, however, fell comfortably within the twelve weeks limit, and hardship was generally caused not so much by scarcity of provisions as by their poor quality. Sometimes this was almost unavoidable, for after two months at sea barrels of beef spoiled, fresh water stank, and butter became unmentionably bad. Beer was never expected to last longer than the first month. Usually, however, it was the incompetence or corruption of those who supplied provisions which was at fault, and sometimes large amounts of food had to be thrown overboard because completely unusable. Another frequent cause of trouble was the dishonesty of captains, who sometimes refused to give out provisions as the contract required, and starved their passengers for their own profit. Upon arriving in America the grateful passengers of a ship on which they had been well treated would often join in a testimonial of appreciation to the captain, while others would register their complaints with the local authorities.

Provisions might be adequate, and captains merciful, but no one could control the wind and sun. Probably the greatest single misery of our immigrant forebears was simple seasickness; and in this respect their wretchedness cannot be measured, and hardly imagined. Bad as it is today, this affliction was unutterably worse then. Whenever there was a storm the hatches had to be battened down, and all passengers under them, no matter how overcrowded the ship might be, and the results are painful to contemplate. John Harrower, who had a relatively pleasant voyage, relates nevertheless that soon after a storm began "there was the odest shene betwixt decks that ever I heard or seed. There was some sleeping, some spewing. . .some daming, some Blasting their leggs and thighs, some their liver, lungs, lights and eyes, And for to make the shene the odder, some curs'd Father, Mother, Sister, and Brother."[24] Mittelberger's list of woes is the most impressive; according to him the immigrants suffered "terrible misery, stench, fumes, horror, vomiting, many kinds of sea-sickness, fever, dysentery, headache, heat, constipation, boils, scurvy, cancer, mouth-rot, and the like."[25] John Coad's story of his trip with the Monmouth rebels is equally unpleasant: "we had enough in the day to behold the miserable sight of botches, pox, others devoured with lice till they were almost at death's dore. In the night fearful cries and groning of sick and distracted persons, which could not rest, but lay tumbling over the rest, and distracting the whole company, which added much to our trouble."[26]

Seasickness was only the prelude to worse ills, and the truly serious diseases which afflicted many cargoes, especially of Germans and Irish, became a problem to the colonial authorities. In 1754 the official doctors of the port of Philadelphia wrote that the people on most passenger ships sooner or later contracted diseases from the foul air, but they opined that this was

not generally communicated to healthy persons on shore.[27]
Sometimes, on the other hand, smallpox, yellow fever, typhus,
or dysentery wrought havoc on a crowded vessel. In 1738 it was
written that out of fifteen ships arriving that year at Philadelphia
only two had come with those on board relatively well, and
1,600 passengers had died. Sauer estimated that two thousand
Germans died at sea in 1749, which was the heaviest year of immigration; on one ship in 1752 only nineteen out of two hundred survived, on another in 1745 fifty out of four hundred.[28]

Such things were primarily due to the total lack of ventilation between decks, to the overcrowded conditions of ships from
Rotterdam and Ireland, to bad food, and to the diseases which
many low-class emigrants brought on board with them. Ships
were periodically washed out with vinegar during the voyage,
which helped to sweeten accommodations, but there was for
many years no solution of the problem of ventilation. John
Coad's party of rebels was finally, upon the intercession of other
passengers, allowed to come on deck for short periods; this was
of course generally permitted all servants who were not rebels
or convicts, but the experiences which a few ships had with
mutinies of these passengers must have discouraged the charity
of other commanders.

Meanwhile work was being done on the problem of ventilation, and when the Board of Trade prepared to send its settlers
to Halifax in 1749 it summoned a certain Mr. Sutton, inventor of
"Sutton's Air Pipes," and asked him to give an estimate for fitting up the transports with his device. He offered to do so for
£30 per ship, or £35 "if with the furnace," and said that it
would take three weeks. The Board accordingly ordered them
put on eight of the twelve transports, and had ventilators cut on
the other four.[29] It would appear that Sutton had worked out a
system of forced draft ventilation, which could even be con-

nected with a furnace for heating the air. Thereafter the governor of Halifax and the Board itself were very much impressed to find that the English on the transports arrived in excellent health, while John Dick's Germans, who came on a ship without ventilation, were all sickly. For the next year's contingent Dick was ordered to have ventilation provided, and an Englishman was sent to Rotterdam to install the apparatus on the ships which would carry Germans.[30] This enlightening experiment seems to have made no immediate impression on other merchants in the trade, though we have already seen that late in the 1760's, after quarantine legislation passed by Virginia and Maryland, the transporters of convicts opened up portholes on their ships, and secured enough ventilation to reduce the amount of jail fever which they customarily imported with their cargoes.

Thus there was no real need for the diseases, epidemics, and misery suffered by so many of the Germans. An intelligent and humane supervision such as that given by the Board of Trade under Lord Halifax, or by the Georgia Trustees, or by occasional private merchants and captains, would have prevented most of their woes. For a healthy voyage, even before the era of ventilation, it was only necessary to use decent care in providing food, to clean the ship thoroughly before starting, and frequently during the voyage, to have a little luck with the weather, and above all to avoid overcrowding. Everyone knew that scurvy could be prevented by a little lemon juice or fresh food. The Georgia Trustees, according to a man who travelled out in one of their ships, "were so careful of the poor people's health, that they put on board turnips, carrots, potatoes, and onions, which were given out with the salt meat, and contributed greatly to prevent the scurvy."[31] In 1741 it was stated that out of some fifteen hundred people who had gone to Georgia at the public charge, not more than six had died on the passage.[32] A traveller to Jamaica in 1739 related that the servants on his ship "had lived so easily and well during the Voyage, that they looked healthful, clean and fresh, and for this Reason were soon sold," but he also observed that "another Vessel, from the same Port, brought in a little after a Multitude of poor starved Creatures, that seemed so many Skeletons: Misery appeared in their Looks, and one might read the Effects of Sea-tyranny by their wild and dejected Countenances."[33] This writer nevertheless thought that very few captains were guilty of treating their passengers badly.

Since at one time or another in their history nearly all the colonies had some kind of regulation respecting immigration, the formalities which a servant ship had to go through might be irksome. Most common was a requirement that all servants, and possibly all immigrants, be registered, usually in the secretary's office.[34] This was sometimes called for by statute, as in Nevis in 1672, and in this case the reason for it was to provide a method for determining the length of time which incoming servants should remain in bondage. But more often the registration was called for by administrative decree, adopted to provide for public order and safety. Thus the governor of Barbados in 1656, and the governor and Council of Pennsylvania in 1717 and 1727 ordered that the names of immigrants be taken. The municipal authorities of Boston required the registration of immigrants at the impost office during the eighteenth century, and enforced their order with rigor. A regulation adopted in New York in 1721 provided that masters of vessels should file passenger lists with the mayor within twenty-four hours of arrival. Pennsylvania and New Jersey by 1684 were taking similar measures. Whether all these regulations were duly carried out is doubtful, for except in the case of Pennsylvania

Germans after 1727 none of the registration lists survive except in a few scraps and pieces.

During the eighteenth century Pennsylvania, Maryland, and New Jersey required declarations from incoming captains that their passengers were not convicts, or descriptions of the crimes which any convicts on the list might have committed.[35] Maryland during most of the century required that all immigrants take an oath to determine whether or not they were papists; thus the collector of the port of Oxford in May, 1742, took £2.8.0 from Captain Nathaniel Stokes of the *Milford Factor* for "swaring 40 servants," and six shillings for filing the list and oath concerning convicts.[36]

Quarantine rules were at first applied intermittently, and only when ships came from plague-stricken ports or had themselves been visited with plague during the voyage. Boston was most efficient in this regard, and from early days maintained a pest house on an island in the harbor, exacting severe penalties from all captains who disregarded the regulations. During the eighteenth century, grievous conditions among incoming Germans and convicts led several other colonies to attempt more permanent measures. After much delay and talk, Pennsylvania secured Province Island for the purpose, and built a pesthouse where sick immigrants might be maintained.[37] In the 1760's Maryland and Virginia passed acts providing for the quarantine of convict ships, but as we have already seen, the Virginia law was disallowed through the influence of the London contractor. In 1750 Pennsylvania passed a law to prevent overcrowding on immigrant ships; this secured the special approbation of the Board of Trade, and was followed by another in 1765 which was supposed to be even more effective.[38]

In an earlier chapter some account has been given of the head taxes placed upon convicts, and the restrictive legislation adopted respecting them, and it was there shown that in most cases such acts were ineffectual because the contractors for importing convicts secured their disallowance. Many colonies were almost as much alarmed by the influx of Irish Catholics as by the convicts, and some of them adopted similar restrictions. Maryland in 1699 taxed Irish immigrants twenty shillings each, and in 1717 provided that an additional twenty shillings should be imposed on Catholics, who were to be distinguished by their refusal to take the oath. By 1732 the duty on Protestants was repealed, but put on again in 1754, this time at a rate of five shillings on all servants, and twenty on seven-year passengers. This act, obviously aimed against convicts, was protested and allowed to expire.[39] Jamaica in 1730 imposed a £50 fine on captains who should import servants from Ireland without knowing them to be Protestants.[40] Pennsylvania, becoming alarmed at the number of Germans arriving, put a tax of forty shillings on foreigners in 1729, and twenty shillings on Irish; in the next year, after a protest by Germans, the former was reduced to twenty shillings, where it remained for the rest of the period.[41] Rhode Island in 1729 required the captains of all ships to post a bond of £50 for each passenger from any place except England, Ireland, Jersey, and Guernsey.[42]

Only Virginia and Maryland levied a head tax for revenue rather than restrictive purposes. In 1695 and 1698 Maryland collected 2/6 from each incoming servant in order to raise money to pay for building a capitol.[43] Virginia in 1699 put a tax of fifteen shillings on each servant not born in England or Wales, and avowed that the money was to be used for the same purpose, but the motive must have been partly one of restriction. In 1705 and again in 1710 the same colony levied a flat rate of sixpence per head on all incoming servants.[44] There is some possibility that the Pennsylvania taxes may really have been for revenue purposes, but this seems unlikely. Most southern colonies were far more concerned with encouraging the importation of white servants than with collecting head taxes on them.

As a servant ship approached the shores of America its cargo received what furbishing up was possible; faces were washed, hair cuts administered, and perhaps clothes put in slightly better condition. A clean list was made of the names and accomplishments of surviving passengers, and perhaps also of the equipment with which they were furnished.[45] Sometimes a little fraud was practiced; convicts were adorned with wigs to increase their respectability, and fictitious handicrafts were credited to some of the cargo.[46] Usually the captains of ships made contact with their owners' representatives on shore, and entrusted to them the selling of servants, but this was by no means necessary.

In later days a merchant might insert into the local newspaper an advertisement of his wares, giving more or less information about the kinds and qualities of servants available, and announcing the date for the commencement of sales. This practice was common, but by no means universal, and most shiploads were disposed of without any such assistance. Upon the appointed day buyers came aboard ship. The servants were produced from their quarters, the prospective purchasers walked them up and down, felt of their muscles, judged their states of health and morality, conversed with them to discover their degrees of intelligence and docility, and finally, if satisfied, bought them and carried them off home. The whole scene bore resemblance to a cattle market; a number of servants afterwards compared themselves to horses displayed for sale. Towards the end of the colonial period "soul-drivers" took over part of the trade, coming on board ship and buying considerable groups of servants, then driving them through the country "like a parcell of

Sheep," and selling them here and there to the best advantage.[47]

It is difficult to find much evidence about how speedily cargoes were disposed of, and it is impossible to make generalizations on the subject which are wholly satisfactory. Obviously much depended on the current demand for labor in the colony, as well as on the quality of the servants, their health, nationality, religion, and skills. An example or two have been quoted earlier in this study; one of fifty-three servants sold in two days at Barbados in 1636, for instance, shows the system at its most effective. But we know also that occasionally they went slowly. On September 22, 1745, the *George* arrived at Philadelphia from Ireland with a cargo of servants; most of them were speedily disposed of, but the last one did not go until the following March 14.[48] Since his time of servitude began on the day of the ship's arrival, his master lost six months from his term of five years, a fact which must have reduced the price he brought. John Harrower arrived at Hampton on April 28, 1774; he was sold at Fredericksburg on May 23, after the ship had progressed up river with its wares. Sick, weak, old, and lame servants naturally were not in great demand; we read in a Virginia court record of one who agreed to stay with his master an extra year "in consideration of his sd masters having purchas'd him from ship board at his Request while in a sick and weak Condition."[49] The convict contractors had to give away sick felons, and sometimes even to pay a premium with those who were most useless.[50] During the eighteenth century laws in the continental colonies forbade the landing of "lame and impotent persons," and perhaps on occasion merchants would have to leave port with some of their wholly unsalable servants still on board ship, but such was apparently not often the case.

In the West Indies, those acts for encouraging the importation of white servants which have been already mentioned, generally provided that all who were not sold within ten days from the arrival of the ship might be turned over to the island treasurer and a stated sum received for them. Jamaica in 1681 required, on the other hand, that no servants be sold off a ship for ten days after its arrival; at the expiration of this period a gun was fired and the proceedings begun.[51] The reason for this delay was presumably to allow planters from the country, who were deficient in the numbers of their white servants, to get to the port before the merchandize had been exhausted.

However distressing to the dignity of men the purchase of servants may have been it was nevertheless the accustomed thing, and they had no particular reason to resent it. Redemptioners, on the contrary, were often outrageously victimized, especially the Germans who landed at Philadelphia. Their baggage was sometimes plundered by emigrant agents before they ever left Rotterdam; more often it was stolen by dishonest seamen, and this the more readily because it often came in a different ship from the one on which its owner travelled. Most of the Germans could not understand English, and so became easy victims to unscrupulous merchants and captains, signing agreements which they could not understand and which occasionally deprived them of their rights and property. If a passenger died during the voyage his children, or his wife, or even his friends, might find themselves charged with the cost of his passage and forced to work it out after arrival. Sometimes they were not allowed ashore to seek their friends who might "redeem" them, but were kept closely on the ship until they could be sold to the greater profit of the captain. And finally, despite the circumstances which have been cited to disprove this point, they were often overcharged, and sold for longer periods of servitude than their just debts would have required.[52]

In 1764 some charitable Germans of Philadelphia formed a

society which had for one of its objects the alleviating of conditions among the poorer immigrants. From the petition which this society addressed to the legislature in the same year a further idea of the principal troubles may be obtained.[53] It asked that a German interpreter accompany customs officers on board incoming ships to explain to the passengers the laws of the province respecting their landing; that masters of ships be required to give each passenger a receipt for his baggage at the time of embarkation, and that no passenger who had paid his full fare should be denied possession of his goods; that no one should be held responsible for the passage of others who had died on the voyage, or for any other person's fare, except a man for his wife and children; that any contract by which an immigrant bound himself to pay more than his own freight was to be held invalid; and that indentures were to apply only in Pennsylvania, no passenger being sold out of the province without his consent. The society also drew up a bill for submission to the legislature respecting overcrowding on ships and the handling of immigrants' baggage. The latter provision was vetoed by the governor, who was accused of being in league with those making unjust profits in the trade, but the law against overcrowding was duly enacted. Perhaps the greatest service of the German Society was in giving assistance to individual immigrants who were particularly unfortunate in their circumstances.[54]

No laws could assuage the pain of those families which after arrival were separated and sold into remote parts of the province. Children between five and ten years old were regularly bound out to serve until they reached the age of twenty-one while those under five had to be "given to somebody without compensation to be brought up, and they must serve for their bringing up until they are 21 years old.[55] Nevertheless the actual indenturing of redemptioners was perhaps the most carefully supervised of any part of the business, for they had to be taken before the mayor of Philadelphia for a registration of the terms of their contract and of the place to which they were going. An entry-book of servants and apprentices bound before Mayor Hamilton in 1745 and 1746 still exists, and a much larger record of those appearing before Mayor Gibson from 1771 to 1773 is one of the best sources for a study of indentures as they were at the end of the colonial period.

[CHAPTER II]

THE CUSTOM OF THE COUNTRY

I T IS a familiar story that mankind, when confronted in America with a vast and trackless wilderness awaiting exploitation, threw off its ancient shackles of caste and privilege and set forth upon the road to freedom. Among the social institutions found most useful in the course of this march were those of African slavery and white servitude. While the former boasted extensive precedents from the remotest antiquity, the latter was less familiar, and in fact was to a considerable degree the peculiar creation of Americans themselves. The "custom of the country," by which the lives of white servants were governed in practically all matters, grew up gradually. At first it was no more than the common average of relationships between a thousand masters and servants; later it was more carefully defined, sometimes in written indentures, more generally in the decisions of colonial judges. Before long its more important particulars were embodied in acts passed by the colonial legislatures. The mass of this legislation became very large, while the number of judicial decisions based upon it was truly imposing, and we have finally a legal, social, and economic institution which is a monument to the peculiar necessities and native ingenuity of the early Americans.

The proceedings of the "first legislative body in America" at Jamestown in 1619 excellently illustrate the beginnings of this development. Concerning servants this assembly first formulated into law certain instructions which the governors had received from England, and provided "that all contracts made in *England* betweene the owners of lande & their Tenants and Servantes wch they shall send hither, may bee caused to be duly performed, and that the offenders be punished as the Governr & Councell of Estate shall think just & convenient." Then they turned to another sort of laws "suche as might proceed out of every mans private conceit," or, we may put it, such as colonial conditions had demonstrated to be necessary. Under this head they provided for the registration of servants' contracts and conditions, they forbade servants to trade with the Indians, prohibited women servants from marrying without the consent of their masters, and provided that for crimes such as swearing and Sabbath-breaking, for which freemen were fined, servants should be whipped. Finally, sitting rather as a high court than as a legislative body, they heard a petition of Captain William Powell against one of his servants for various misdoings, and sentenced the culprit to stand four days with his ears nailed to the pillory.[1]

The series of legislative enactments respecting servants which has survived does not begin to be copious until about 1640, but from that time numerous laws exhibit the general structure of the system.[2] Whatever rules were deemed necessary at the moment were laid down; the most frequent were those fixing the length of time which servants arriving without written indentures should remain in bondage, and those prescribing penalties to be imposed for various crimes, and especially for running away. In the year 1661 Barbados drew together all the various orders of council and acts of assembly concerning servants which had previously been passed, added a great many details, altered others, and produced the first comprehensive statute, which might indeed be better called a code, "for the good governing of Servants, and ordaining the Rights between Masters and Servants." This dealt with practically every contingency in the careers of indentured servants; it remained in effect throughout the colonial period with only minor changes, and very little additional legislation proved necessary except for temporary purposes. Jamaica, by order of the governor and council, adopted specifically many of the Barbados enactments, and in 1664 her assembly passed a statute precisely copying the very words of the Barbados law of 1661, except in a few points of detail which had to be changed to fit Jamaican conditions. Not until 1677 did Jamaica even change the wording of the law, and then only to make it more concise. In 1681 she finally passed her own law in a different form, and this remained in force at least until 1769 with a few amendments. Antigua passed a comprehensive statute in 1669. St. Christopher drew up a series of similar acts which finally took permanent form in 1722 with "An Act for the Good Government of Servants, for ordering the Rights between Masters and Servants," etc., and it is plain that all the West Indian colonies derived many of the provisions and some of the phraseology of their servant codes from the great Barbados statute of 1661.

Among the continental colonies, though the volume of legislation concerning servants in Virginia and Maryland was great throughout the seventeenth century, the first comprehensive "code" was that of Maryland in 1676, "An Act relating to Servants and Slaves." This had to be reenacted in 1692, 1699, 1704, and 1715, and the last was allowed to become permanent. Virginia did not pass such a statute until 1705; there was a new one in 1748 which was disallowed by the Privy Council, and another in 1753 which was left in force during the rest of the colonial period, though with some important amendments.

Pennsylvania in 1700 passed "An Act for the better Regulation of Servants in this Province and Territories," but it was not nearly so broad in scope as those of the more southern colonies. Likewise New Jersey, though in 1714 it passed "An Act for regulating of White Servants," concerned itself only with the treatment of runaways, and the law of New York in 1684 was also narrow in scope. The fairly complete codes of North Carolina concerning servants are dated 1715 and 1740, and of South Carolina 1717 and 1744, but there seems to have been no general law of Georgia on the subject until 1796. The New England colonies never had such laws, though occasionally servants are mentioned in their codes; it is worthy of remark, however, that the courts of those colonies administered justice to masters and servants upon principles similar to those obtaining where there was legislation on the subject.

We may begin our account of the custom of the country at that point which was of most lively interest to the many servants who came without written indenture: the time of service required. Earliest of the many laws on this subject which have survived is one passed at the first Maryland assembly in 1638/9, which provided that menservants over eighteen were to serve for four years and under eighteen until they reached the age of twenty-four. Maid servants over twelve were to serve for four years, and under twelve for seven. To avoid abuses under this act another was passed in 1654 requiring that servants considered to be eighteen or under should be brought before a court and registered, and their ages judged by the magistrates. In 1662 penalties were attached to violations of this law, and it became fully effectual. This method of fixing the times of service for servants without written indenture became general in all the colonies, though only those on the continent required a judgement of age before a court, and these provided that any servant not thus judged, usually within six months of his arrival, should be kept in bondage only for the minimum term provided for adults.

Five years soon became the usual term for a "custom of the country" servant of mature years, though Antigua and Nevis from the 1670's and New Jersey and Jamaica from the 1680's required only four, while North Carolina fixed no specific time in her law of 1741, but provided that all disputes were to be settled by the county court. Having said this much, however, it becomes almost impossible to give any further account of these time-of-service acts without descending to wearisome detail. It is extraordinary that so much variation was possible between neighboring colonies in a matter of common custom. For example: the five-year term applied to all servants over sixteen in South Carolina from 1717, to all over nineteen in Virginia from 1666, and to all over twenty-two in Maryland from 1699. Servants younger than these ages served for longer terms which varied among these colonies. If a nineteen year old servant came to Virginia without indenture in 1700 he served for five years, but if he came to Maryland in the same year his term would have been seven, and after 1715 six, years. The four-year term applied to servants over nineteen in Antigua from 1669, but to those over sixteen in Nevis from 1672. In Barbados, throughout the colonial period, a servant of eighteen or over served five years, while one under eighteen, whatever his age, served seven. Perhaps the law of Virginia, as it took shape in 1666, was most sensible; it provided that those nineteen or over should serve five years, while all others should serve until reaching the age of twenty-four.

It is impossible to discover any rational explanation for these intercolonial differences. There is no reason to believe that they were due to mutual ignorance, for we know very well that the colonies knew each others' laws. One might imagine that the more generous enactments, such as those of Jamaica and Nevis, were intended to attract servants, but there is no evidence that these laws were published in England for that purpose. A committee of the Jamaican assembly once declared that no servant ought to be held under indenture for more than four years,[3] but one would scarcely be justified in believing that the shorter term in that island was a proof of the greater humanity of its inhabitants. Probably the true origin of these differences, at least in the continental colonies, lay in the fact that the laws were based on true "customs," which having once been locally established, more or less by accident, could be altered only with the greatest difficulty.

During the seventeenth century there were certainly a great many servants brought to the colonies without indenture who were under age. In the six years from 1668 to 1674 the court of Northumberland County, Virginia, passed judgment on the age of 134. Talbot County, Maryland, recorded 128 in the period 1662-1674. Lancaster County, Virginia, received about the same number as Northumberland in the 1670's; in its court there were eight judgments of age in 1697, sixteen in 1698, and forty in 1699.[4] Most of the servants thus appearing were from thirteen to eighteen years old; the youngest I have come across was aged nine. Towards the end of the century the number tended to diminish, and from about 1719 practically no judgments of age are found in the court records. Since the laws of these colonies continued to require that if any master expected more than five years' service from his indentured laborers he must bring them to court within six months of their arrival, and since any negligence of the master in this respect was punished by a heavy fine, we may conclude that the greater number of such servants were properly registered and provided in England with written indentures. This is altogether probable, for we have already seen that the system of registration was progressively improved after 1682, and especially by the Parliamentary act of 1717. Whether it is also true that fewer young servants came cannot be stated.

The time of servitude as fixed by law thus became of less significance, so much so, in fact, that Virginia in 1765 repealed the clause of her servant statute which dealt with the subject. Most servants had written indentures, and by inspecting the various collections and registries of these documents which still exist one finds that the usual term called for in them was one of four years, both in the seventeenth and eighteenth centuries. Generally speaking, a servant who made his contract in England thus saved himself one year of servitude in the colonies.

It would be expected that much more variation would be found in the terms served by redemptioners, for their periods of bondage were presumably determined by their indebtedness rather than by custom. The only good evidence concerning them is to be found in the registers kept by the mayor of Philadelphia, which have been analyzed for two years by C. A. Herrick.[5] He found that from October, 1745 to October, 1746 there were 769 indentures recorded, of which 423 were for four years, 84 for five, 72 for three, 50 for seven, and so on in diminishing numbers. In the year 1772 there was greater variety: of 1,135 registrations before the mayor, 284 were for four years, 266 for two years, 145 for three, 127 for five, 88 for six, and so on. Such a short term as one of two years is decidedly characteristic of redemptioners and not of indentured servants, and it may be assumed that the average length of servitude throughout the colonies was considerably diminished during the eighteenth century by the increasing proportion of redemptioners coming into the country. To offset this in part, convicts served for their full terms of seven or fourteen years, a fact which helped to make them desirable laborers to the planters of Maryland and Virginia.

The status of an indentured servant was that of a chattel of the master, protected by the terms of his indenture, the "custom of the country," and the right of appeal and complaint to a county court or to the magistrates of the locality. He, or rather his service as expressed in the indenture, could be bought and sold freely in every colony save Pennsylvania and New York, where the consent of a court of sessions was necessary in assigning over a servant for more than one year.[6] He could be alienated temporarily by his master so that his services might pay off a debt, or he could be taken by the sheriff for the satisfaction of his master's debts.[7] He could be disposed of by will; his own freedom might be left him also. He might be won or lost in a card game. A Dutch traveller was scandalized to see such play in Virginia;[8] on the other hand one Virginian servant won a year's freedom from his master on a bet about the date of Easter.[9] A servant was subject to corporal punishment for various offences, and throughout the seventeenth century it was expected and in many colonies expressly provided by law that masters be allowed to whip their servants. Jamaica in 1672, however, laid it down that no master or overseer for any offence whatever should whip a Christian servant naked, and this law is found in other colonies during the eighteenth century. This may be taken to refer to a ceremonial whipping, with the victim tied to a post, stripped to the waist, and flogged for a certain number of times; such punishment according to these laws was to be prescribed for servants only by justices of the peace or other duly constituted magistrates. Milder corporal correction was certainly allowed the master at all times, and in the earlier years apparently he might whip servants as he liked.

A servant could not marry without the consent of his master. He could not vote.[10] He could hold property, but he must not engage in trade, and there were severe penalties in all colonies for freemen who traded with servants, presumably because the latter would steal or embezzle their masters' goods and dispose of them to unscrupulous freemen. The servant's special abilities, if any, were exercised for the benefit of the master, and if he earned money in his spare time it might be taken by the master. If he ran away, he was brought back under the auspices of rigorous laws and he suffered heavy penalties. Although the point was not often discussed, the colonists felt that masters had property in the labor of their servants, and that the master's rights were thus property rights,—a theory which became important only when the king's officers took to enlisting colonial servants in the royal army.

Whether property or not, indentured servants were Christian and they were white, and hence they were protected against arbitrary and unnatural cruelties, as well as against insufficient maintenance and other injustices, by their right of complaining to the magistrates. A Virginia act passed in 1643 expressly provided that servants might repair to the nearest commissioner and make complaint; Barbados in 1652 prescribed that servants be given reasonable time to commence suits at common law in the court of the precinct, and all other colonies had similar statements of a right which servants doubtless exercised long before the statutes specifically granted it. The phrasing of the Barbados act reminds us that there were two aspects to the complaints of servants; on the one hand they might have to bring suit against their masters for freedom dues or other advantages to which they were entitled by the terms of their contracts, but on the other hand they might wish to complain against cruel and oppressive treatment, a thing which it was perhaps not very easy for them to establish before an unsympathetic magistrate. In the early days of the colonies, when the processes of law were somewhat doubtful and the justices not much skilled in procedure, it became a custom to receive the petitions of servants and pass on them in an informal manner. The obvious inability of penniless servants to prosecute suits at law led to the regularizing of this procedure, and in such statutes as that of Virginia in 1705 it is stated that servants may bring their complaints to court "without the formal process of an action." Thus nearly all servant cases in the courts started with a petition, and proceeded without undue formality. Further discussion of the subject of these complaints must be postponed; at present it may be observed that there are great numbers of such cases to be seen in county court records, especially of the seventeenth century, and there is good reason to believe that they received fair hearings.

The right of servants to sue in court, the fact that their evidence was accepted in other suits exactly as that of freemen, unless they were transported felons, their right to hold property, and their duty in some colonies to serve in the militia, indicate plainly the great differences in status between an indentured servant and a slave. The master's privilege of inflicting corporal punishment cannot be considered as any degradation of the legal status of servants, for in England masters could whip their servants and husbands their wives to a reasonable degree without criticism. The servant in the colonies was liable to the public as well as to his master for any crimes he might commit; yet a very remarkable case from Virginia indicates that a servant, when commanded by his master to commit a crime, was not liable to punishment for that crime.[11]

Some further legislation, mainly in the West Indian colonies, assured special rights and privileges to the servants. After the middle of the century the main purpose of importing servants to the islands was, as we have seen, to increase the number of white men available for defense. Each servant was required under certain circumstances to serve in the militia, and a Barbados law of 1652 provided that any one of them that should "manfully and like a true soldier fight" should have half of his service remitted to him, and his master was to be reimbursed out of the public treasury. In 1673 Jamaica enlarged the reward to complete freedom, and Barbados followed this example in 1685, providing furthermore for the cure of wounded militiamen at public expense and for a grant of 2000 pounds of sugar to them.[12] The statute of 1661 in Barbados provided for the release and satisfaction of kidnapped servants. Barbados and Virginia, as well as Jamaica and the islands which adapted the Barbados statute, required servants to go to church and learn the catechism, but it cannot be proved that this was enforced, or that the moral tone of these colonies was thereby much elevated. In Barbados and Jamaica masters were compelled to use all possible means to care for sick servants, under penalty of forfeiting 2200 pounds of sugar to the authorities, who would then take charge of the invalid's cure. Nearly all colonies forbade the deplorable practice of granting freedom to servants who had become sick or disabled,[13] in order to avoid the charge of maintaining and relieving them. In the northern colonies from New England to Pennsylvania it was provided that a servant maimed or disfigured by his master should be set free, but this was not intended to remove the responsibility of the master for support and cure. Virginia and the West Indian islands prohibited the private burial of dead servants, lest masters thus conceal evidences of murderous treatment. Finally, no colony recognized the validity of contracts between master and servant, or indeed of any contracts made by a servant, which were executed during the time of servitude, unless both parties appeared before a magistrate and gave assent. This was one of the most important protections for servants. It prevented masters from coercing them into additional servitude, and it even prevented them from getting into debt, for no promise to pay by them would be held binding.

Only the West Indian colonies passed acts prescribing the amount of food and clothing to be allowed servants. This was because of their extreme anxiety to attract immigrants, and the regulations of this nature are found mainly in their laws for encouraging the importation of servants. Jamaica in 1672 promised three and a half pounds of good meat or fish per week, together with sufficient plantation provisions, and in 1677 raised the allowance of meat to four pounds, while Barbados in 1682 fixed it at five, and in 1696 raised it to six pounds.[14] Ligon had remarked, in the late 1640's, that the servants rarely had meat "unless an Oxe dyed," and that the planters themselves ate it only twice a week. It may well be believed that the later diet according to law was less healthful than the earlier, and in 1700 it was said that one reason for the continuance of pestilential fevers in Barbados was the fact that servants were allowed a pound of flesh or fish each day, which was usually salted.[15] But the laborer could complain at court if he did not receive his pound of flesh, and doubtless he died more happily on a meat diet. As for clothes, Antigua led the way in 1669 by prescribing that each servant should have three pairs of shoes, three shirts, three pairs of drawers, and one cap per annum. Barbados raised this bid by one pair of shoes in 1682, and in 1696 promised four shirts, three pairs of drawers, two jackets, one hat, four pairs of shoes, and wages of twenty-five shillings per annum, which when taken with his six pounds of meat each week rendered the Barbadian servant an aristocrat among his kind. Jamaica kept pace with Barbados in allowances of clothes; Nevis in 1701 prescribed that each servant have three canvas suits with hats and shoes each year.[16] No continental colony passed laws like these; yet it was stated to be an established custom in York County, Virginia, by 1661 to give the servants meat at least three times a week, and in 1640 a man under indenture successfully complained to the General Court about the insufficiency of his clothing.[17] The existence of written law on the subject in the islands is no true indication of better treatment, nor of worse, for these acts were motivated not by humanity but only by a desire to increase the white population, and most of them did not last long. Nevertheless they are not uninteresting examples of colonial "social legislation."

Finally we must notice an exceedingly important "custom of the country": that fixing the amount of "freedom dues" given servants at the expiration of their terms. Most indentures executed in England, and most of the indentures made in America for redemptioners, specified that these dues were to be according to the custom of the plantation. So universal was this practice and so great the importance of freedom dues for the servants, that it is worth while to assemble information on the subject in tabular form, with the dates of laws establishing each.

BARBADOS
>   1647   Land in Nevis or Antigua. (Proclamation by the Earl of Carlisle; not of permanent effect.)[18]
>   1661   400 lbs. muscovado sugar.

NEVIS
>   1672   £10, "according to former custom."
>   1675   800 lbs. sugar
>   1681   400 lbs. sugar
>   1701   400 lbs. sugar, or fifty shillings.

ANTIGUA
>   1669   400 lbs. sugar or tobacco.

ST. CHRISTOPHER
>   1722   Four pounds of current money, or 600 lbs. sugar.

JAMAICA

    1661/2   30 acres of land. (Instructions to Governor Lord Windsor)[19]

    1661   400 lbs. sugar. (order of council)

    1664   Forty shillings, or thirty acres of land.

    1681   Forty shillings.

SOUTH CAROLINA

    (During the proprietary period, various amounts of land were promised and allotted.)

    1717   One new hat, a good coat and breeches either of kersey or broadcloth, one new shirt of white linen, one new pair of shoes and stockings. For women servants: a "Wast coat and Petticoat of new Half-thicks or Pennistone, a new Shift of white Linnen, a new Pair of shoes and stockings, a blue Apron and two Caps of white Linnen." (Continued in Act of 1744)

    1730   The crown offers fifty acres of land, free of quitrent for ten years.

NORTH CAROLINA

    (During the proprietary period, land was given, e.g. in 1686, 50 acres at one penny quitrent.)

    1715   Three barrels of Indian corn and two new suits of a value of at least £5.

    1741   Three pounds proclamation money and one sufficient suit.

VIRGINIA

    1705   Ten bushels of corn, thirty shillings or the equivalent, one musket worth at least twenty shillings. To women servants: fifteen bushels of corn and forty shillings in money or goods.

    1748   Three pounds ten shillings of current money.

    1753   The same.

MARYLAND

    1640   ". . . one good Cloth suite of Keirsy or broad cloth a Shift of white linen one new pair of stockins and Shoes two hoes one axe 3 barrells of Corne and

fifty acres of land . . . women Servants a Years
Provision of Corne and a like proportion of Cloths
& Land."

1699   The corn is omitted and instead is given a hat and a
gun. Continued in 1715. (Land was not given after
1683.)

PENNSYLVANIA

(Penn promised fifty acres of land during the first years.)

1682   One new suit, ten bushels of wheat or fourteen of
corn, one axe, two hoes.

1700   Two complete suits of clothes, one of which is to be
new; one new axe, one grubbing hoe and one
weeding hoe.

1771   The same, but minus two hoes.

NEW JERSEY

1682   Seven bushels of corn, two suits of clothes, two hoes
and an axe. (Also land.)

NEW YORK

There seems to have been no law fixing freedom dues, except for the provision in the Duke of York's Laws, identical with that given below for Massachusetts.

MASSACHUSETTS

1641   Servants after seven years' labor must "not be sent
away empty." (N.B. This is a provision piously
taken from the Old Testament—Deuteronomy 15:
12, 13—and should probably not be taken very
seriously as an act passed for the sake of servants.)

The laws as abstracted here do not quite tell the story of
freedom dues. It is, for example, established by a great deal of
evidence that early custom in the West Indies called for a payment of £10 to the servant out of his time, but only one short-
lived act of Nevis embodied this generous provision.[20] Land
grants are usually not mentioned in the statutes, because relatively few colonies had the power to grant land, reserved as it
was to the proprietor or to the crown. Particular attention

should be called to the absence of any provision for a grant of land to freed servants in Virginia. Many of the indentures registered at Bristol show that servants bound for that colony were promised "Land according to the custom of the country," or even "50 acres according to custom," but John Hammond pointed out that this was a delusion, and that they received none.[21] In 1679 Governor Culpeper was instructed by the king to set aside land in Virginia for freed servants; perhaps he did so, but it cannot be proved. The absence of any statute whatever in Virginia concerning freedom dues during the seventeenth century is remarkable, especially as it is almost certain that they received dues practically like those in Maryland, but without the land.[22] In general, the continental colonies intended to equip the freed servant for life as a hired man, and wages were high enough so that he should have had no difficulty in buying whatever plot of land he desired before long. The scanty rewards given in the West Indies were practically useless.

The general outlines of the servant's status in the colonies, of his expectations according to the custom of the country, have now been described, at least as far as they appear in the statutes. Except in those concerning time of service and freedom dues, very little change or development occurred in these laws during the whole period, nor were there any significant differences between the various colonies apart from those noted. Though Barbados was the first to collect them into a statute, other colonies were not behind her in applying the same rules, and even those far northern colonies which passed little legislation respecting servants allowed their magistrates to erect a similar system. Granted that there should have been white servitude at all, the regulations under which it was established seem to have been as intelligent and humane as could reasonably be expected, and judged by the standards of a century more accustomed than the present to corporal punishment and personal subjection they are beyond serious criticism.

The real problem, however, is to determine how far these regulations were effective; how truly the servant was protected from excessive cruelty and exploitation; how far his right of complaint to local magistrates meant that he was given justice. In attempting to answer these questions few generalizations can be made which are capable of full proof, but a good deal of evidence can be cited, and the opinions of the present author given for what they are worth, as based upon the reading of a considerable amount of material.

In the first place, it can be definitely stated that when a servant produced an indenture in proper form its provisions were upheld and enforced by the courts. Likewise, when he appeared in court demanding some right or remedy specifically established by law he was given it. Most cases of this nature arose over the payment of freedom dues, and I have found not a single instance in which the court did not award the servant what was due him and force the master to pay, sometimes even ordering the sheriff to confiscate some of the master's property for the purpose. But there were other types of cases which arose over the indenture, and a few examples will illustrate the sort of trouble that appeared and the attitude of magistrates towards the servant. One John Dyllam petitioned the court of Chester County, Pennsylvania, in 1746, saying that he had been brought into the country and sold to John Bell by Robert Allison for four years, and now it appeared that the word "four" in his indenture had been altered to "five." Allison appeared and swore that he had sold Dyllam for the shorter term. The court examined the document, and could not be sure whether it had originally read four or five, but they released Dyllam from servitude, instructing him nevertheless not to try and collect wages for the time beyond four years which he had already served.[23]

Another example comes from Lancaster County, Virginia, in 1700. Catherine Douglas, servant to Mottrom Wright, petitioned for her freedom. Wright produced an assignment from John Gilchrist, who had sold her to him for seven years, but Catherine through her attorney declared that when she arrived in the country she had had indentures for four years' service only, which had been subsequently destroyed without the consent of any justices. She brought three witnesses who swore that they had seen her indentures, and that they were as she declared. The court decided that her case was "within the reach of the Law," and ordered her set free.[24] From Spotsylvania County comes the case of Thomas Mills, who petitioned for freedom, having served out his time by indenture. The court discovered, however, that Mills was a transported convict, and was bound to serve for the period of his exile, and the case was dismissed.[25] It does not appear whether Mills actually produced a written indenture for the shorter period; if he had done so the proceedings would have been much more interesting.

From Stafford County, Virginia, come three cases well worth citing. In 1689 two servants stated that the indentures which they had made in England had been lately stolen from their rooms, and their master refused to free them or to give them the prescribed clothes and corn. "On due examination" the court set them free. On the same day another servant complained that his master had forged a document by which he would be compelled to serve two extra years; this time the court decided in favor of the master. Finally, there is the remarkable case of a Negro named Benjamin Lewis, who told the court in 1691 that he was an indentured servant, bound in

England for four years, but that his master would not let him go free though the time was up. The master claimed that the indenture was a forgery, and that Benjamin ought to be a slave, and he produced another indenture for fourteen years' service which he said he had made with the Negro merely in order to persuade him to work better. A jury was impanelled to pass on the first document; it was pronounced valid, the second was therefore declared invalid because made while the first was in effect, and the Negro set free.[26]

These examples represent quite fairly the manner in which local courts judged questions respecting written indentures, and they show a real intention to do justice without taking advantage of the servant's menial status. One case from Maryland exhibits a different attitude, and it is the only one of the kind I know. In this instance a master informed the court that he had purchased a servant without indenture "for the Costum of the Cuntrys," and the servant after four years demanded his freedom, producing not an indenture but a certificate under the seal of the Registry Office in London. The court ruled that this certificate was "of Noe effect agst th^e Law of this Province for th^e Limittacon of Sarvants times," and ordered the servant to do one more year.[27] This was certainly a disreputable subterfuge, unless there was more to the case than appears in the record. In general servants were fairly and even generously treated; nevertheless, if their indentures were lost or stolen, they were at a great disadvantage, and we should probably be correct in supposing that many such cases never came before the magistrates at all, for lack of hope of a favorable decision.

Even more serious questions remain, however. How far did the courts protect servants against cruel treatment and insufficient maintenance? Were the laws allowing them to complain to magistrates mere pious formulas, and was John Fiske correct in saying that their rights were protected only in theory? Ligon saw in Barbados "such cruelty done to Servants, as I did not think one Christian could have done to another," and thirty years later it was written from the same island that white servants were "used with more barbarous cruelty than if in Algiers . . . as if hell commenced here and only continued in the world to come."[28] From the 1670's it was necessary for the English government constantly to instruct its colonial governors to take measures for preventing cruelty to servants, yet Eddis wrote from Maryland in the 1770's that the servants "groaned beneath a worse than Egyptian bondage."[29] Such testimonies are not scarce, though not always as emphatic as those quoted, and it is plain that we can give no such favorable account of this matter as of the former.

Before examining various records of the appeals of servants for relief and justice a few facts should be called to mind. Throughout the colonies, after their first scanty years, there were established in each locality county courts or the equivalent. The magistrates who sat on the bench were designated according to the English fashion, from among the few men of property and responsibility in the neighborhood, and the dozens of these courts during the colonial period exhibited a wide variation in the character and capacity of their magistrates. All of these men belonged to the planter class, to the group of those who employed labor. All of them must have attained moderate prosperity and influence in times when prosperity and influence did not go to the meek and pure of heart. The servants, on the other hand, were for the most part men and women of low grade, lazy, unambitious, ignorant, prone to small crimes and petty evasions, an unsavory and sometimes a dangerous class especially in those regions where there were many transported convicts. When a servant brought a complaint to court, he was appearing against one of the magistrates' own class, probably against one of their friends, and perhaps even against one of themselves. Under such circumstances one would hardly expect equal justice in all cases; on the contrary one would expect to find a high degree of injustice, and an encouragement of legalized exploitation. And certainly one would find that conditions varied from time to time and from court to court. Cases could, of course, be appealed to a higher jurisdiction, but it was very rarely that a servant could make such an appeal.

The fact is that the court records reveal a high proportion of cases in which the servant received fair treatment, and a great many in which the humanity displayed by the magistrates did them credit. It must be understood that we are speaking now only of the legal aspects of the servant's existence, and of whether he received fair treatment before courts. Later some of the great hardships which colonial conditions inevitably entailed will be described, and it does not follow that because duly constituted human authorities generally rendered substantial justice the servants therefore had no troubles. But it has often been intimated that they were quite unprotected from the arbitrary and capricious tyrannies of their masters; this can, I think, be refuted.

Complaints by servants of scarcity of food and clothing are not so plentiful as other kinds of petitions, yet there are a fair number of them in the court records. Here is an example from the Spotsylvania, Virginia, proceedings in 1758:

On Complaint of William Hust a servant man belonging to William Miller for not Cloathing him according to law Ordered that the said Miller Give him one Cotton and Kersey Jacket and britches, 3 Ozanb^g shirts and sufficient Diet and 1 pair shoes and stocking, 1 hat, and that he do not correct him without first carrying him before a Justice of the peace &c.[30]

The remedies in this case are rather more detailed than is usual. The following example is from Plymouth colony, in 1633:

Robt Barker, serv^t of John Thorp, complayned of his m^r for want of clothes. The complaint being found to be just, it was ordered, that Thorp should either foorwth apparrell him, or else make over his time to some other that was able to provide for him.[31]

By far the larger number of servants' complaints specify cruel and abusive treatment, often in addition to insufficient food and clothing. The variety of these is great, and the judgments of the courts diverse. Sometimes the cruelty was mainly negligence:

It appeareing to this Court by the petition of Margaret Roberts, that her Master Samuell du Molyn doth take noe care for the cure of both her Leggs, which if neglected are in danger of rotting, It is ordered by this Court, that if the said Molyn doe not within six dayes provide for the cure of the said servants leggs shee is by this Court declared free and at her own disposall.[32]

The decision in this unhappy case was not brilliant, for it is doubtful whether Margaret's legs would have been any less likely to rot after she had been set free. The discharge from servitude of healthy servants who had been badly treated was by no means frequent, but neither was it unknown. One was thus turned loose in Baltimore County, Maryland, in 1758.[33] Henry Hawkings, servant to Jonas Davenport of Conestoga, Indian trader, was given his freedom by the justices of Chester County, Pennsylvania, because his master had abused and ill-treated him, and finally sold him to an Indian.[34] A maidservant in Boston complained of her master "for wanton and lascivious carriages towards her & cruell beating"; the court set her free and punished the master.[35]

Cruelty is most often noted in connection with abuses of the master's right of chastisement. One of the first pieces of information about Barbados is a note concerning the career of Sir William Tufton, in 1630, and it is there related that he gave great offense to the planters by removing servants from estates where they had been ill-treated and transferring them elsewhere.[36] In 1640, Francis Leaven and Samuel Hodgkins punished their servant John Thomas by hanging him up by the hands and placing lighted matches between his fingers, thus doing him permanent injury. For this the servant was awarded 5000 pounds of cotton from each of his masters and was set free, while the masters were put in jail at the governor's pleasure. Similarly Patrick Miller, who complained of being inhumanly beaten and abused, was ordered to be set free if two justices should find his complaint well founded.[37] One can never predict what the verdict will be in any case of cruelty, for the justices seem to have followed no particular rule. A master in Essex County, Massachusetts, who punished his servant by "hanging him up by the heels as butchers do beasts for the slaughter" was merely rebuked by the court.[38] A maid servant in Maryland complained that her mistress kicked her in the belly; she was examined by a woman who reported that the complaint was probably true. The court ordered the husband of this mistress to make his wife stop kicking the servant.[39] Another servant told of excessive beating and abuse; he was sent back to his master with a letter from the court, instructing the latter to be less violent.[40] Another master was fined 500 pounds of tobacco for maltreating his servant.[41] Two servants who complained that their indentures had been signed under duress were set free, though there was no question that they had been free and competent to make contracts when the signatures were given.[42] In Virginia the General Court of 1679-1680 gave an order forbidding a woman who had become known as a cruel mistress to keep any servants at all.[43]

The foregoing examples have been intentionally chosen to exhibit the more ordinary and normal procedures found in court records. There are cases of appalling and incredible cruelties to be found, for example, in the printed records of the Maryland local courts. Two or three masters beat their servants to death, and were themselves hanged for it; two or three more apparently did the same thing, and nevertheless got away without punishment.[44] Other accounts in the same volumes display a coarseness of language and conduct among both servants and masters which though not surprising in itself is rarely set forth in print. Such extreme brutalities show what was possible under colonial conditions, but not what was typical; even the court entries, it must be remembered, concern only the small proportion of servants who ever had occasion to come or be brought before the bench of justices.

It is probable that many servants' complaints do not appear in the court records at all, but were adjusted by one or two magistrates without coming to the attention of quarter sessions. Thus for example the Chester Court in February, 1736, ordered Abiah Taylor and his servant to come before "the Justices at Chester the Twenty fifth day of March next" and settle their differences, and presumably they did so, but no entry was made in the quarter sessions records of the following May.[45] Again, a servant in the same county complained to two justices that his master "Did beat him unlawfully, More than Common Correction for servants," and the master was summoned to appear at quarter court. But during the interim master and servant appeared together at petty sessions and forgave each other; the only reason this was recorded was to explain why the summons had not been answered.[46] In 1742 a master brought "an Appeal from an Order made by two Justices Relating to a Servant said to be disabled in his Eyes"; after "mature Deliberation" the quarter sessions judged the order "to be Affirmed," but did not even trouble to enter what it was.[47] These instances we know more or less by chance. It is plain that for any major readjustments the authority of a full bench of justices would be necessary, but one may well suppose that a great number of minor complaints were settled with the help of one or two men of prestige and substance, without leaving any record.

"Servants complaints," wrote Hammond of Virginia, "are freely harkened to, and (if not causlesly made) there Masters are compelled either speedily to amend, or they are removed upon second complaint to another service; and often times not onely set free, (if the abuse merit it) but ordered to give reparation and damage to their servant."[48] Governor Stede reported from Barbados in 1688 that servants could, and did, complain to justices of the peace, and that when such complaints were reported to him he went carefully into them.[49] In all colonies nevertheless, severe penalties were prescribed for servants who went to court without good cause, and occasionally one finds evidences in the court records of such penalties being inflicted. Naturally, not all complaints were justified; some of them were plainly trumped up by servants in the hope of gaining freedom; others may have had their origin in ways suggested by the following:

Whereas diverse lewd people have raysed false scandals of Col St Leger Codd, importing, not only his barbarous usage of his servants but also murder, as if he had killed severall of his servants; And whereas it appeareth to this Court That Corderoy Ironmonger hath been guilty of divulging the said scandalls; It is ordered that in open Court the said Ironmonger doe ask the said Col Codd forgiveness for the same.[50]

This was not the only time that Corderoy Ironmonger had been in trouble for his scurrilous habits and divulging of scandal; it turned out on this occasion that he owed Colonel Codd 952 pounds of tobacco.

No one can deny that the indentured servants suffered many great cruelties and hardships, many more than they should have suffered, many which were quite unredressed by the constituted authorities. The evidences of fair treatment which have been presented in this chapter are matched by many examples of fantastic miseries. Here we have proved only what we set out to prove and no more: that servants could complain to magistrates if they were ill-treated, that they often did so and received justice, and that any generalization concerning them which does not take this fact into consideration is false.

Finally, a word should be said about the obscure and not very important subject of "settlement." It was generally considered, and in some of the colonial laws specifically provided, that an indentured servant acquired legal settlement in the locality where he did his service; therefore after his freedom he became eligible for poor relief in that neighborhood if it became necessary for him to receive it. Two cases in this connection which I have come across are not without interest; the first is from the town of Dedham, Massachusetts, in 1685, and excellently illustrates the New England attitude toward the servants.[51] At the town meeting of March 10 John Hunting appeared and said that his maidservant Abigail Littlefield had worked out her time; Hunting wished to be rid of her and asked the town to support her, as she was incapable of supporting herself. The "town" answered that he had brought her into the vicinity against the order and advice of the selectmen, and had taken her into his family, and therefore he ought to support her; nevertheless they agreed that she should continue with him for the next year and they would allow him four pounds of current money towards the expense of keeping her. A year later Abigail made her own complaint: "that she was under a great afliction by extrordinary burning." The town gave Hunting twenty-four shillings towards her cure and five pounds for her next year's maintenance. Thereafter the case disappears from the records.

The other example is from Chester County, Pennsylvania, in 1724.[52] Inhabitants of Haverford township petitioned the quarter sessions, stating that one Elizabeth Roost had served her time in their township and gained a settlement thereby. Then she went away "in divers places," and by her own statement had gained a new settlement in a place called Cold Spring, county Sussex. She had been away from Haverford for more than eight years, but had now returned and was so lame and indisposed that she had not been in a condition to be sent back to her legal settlement. The town had given her some assistance out of pure charity. On this the court judged her to be supported as a county charge; Haverford was to send bills for her maintenance to the county treasurer and look after her until she should be in a condition to be returned to Sussex.

CHAPTER 12

THE SERVANT IN THE PLANTATIONS

ACCOUNTS rendered by contemporaries of the life and labor of white servants are extraordinarily inharmonious. Having read a letter from Barbados saying that they were used as if hell had already commenced for them, one may turn to Dalby Thomas, who declared at about the same time that they lived much easier than in England, or to John Wilmore, who reported that in Jamaica none of them worked as hard as they would at home.[1] "I thought no head had been able to hold so much water as hath and doth daily flow from mine eyes," wrote a servant from Virginia in 1623, but John Hammond announced some years later that none had gone to that colony without commending the place in letters to their friends, and urging others to come.[2] The Maryland court records show that a significant number of servants committed suicide under their burdens, but a Scot in New Jersey declared in 1684 that they worked not a third as hard as in Britain, and had much better food.[3] William Eddis wrote that servants in Maryland groaned beneath a worse than Egyptian bondage; a visitor to Jamaica in 1739 reported that some of them dined as well as their masters, and wore as good clothes, while all were better off than at home.[4] Gottlieb Mittelberger, after filling the air with denunciations of life in Pennsylvania, himself went on to write that "an English servant-woman, especially in Philadelphia, is as elegantly dressed as an aristocratic lady in Germany."[5]

Such conflicting testimonies, of which these are only a few examples, are to be expected from observers of various sentiments concerning any diversified society. It would not be difficult to subject them to criticism, based on the known predilections of the authors, and thus to whittle away the important differences until they came to a fairly common and colorless agreement. The same result, however, may be reached more instructively by other means.

Of all those things which caused misery to white servants, the first and most important was not the temper of their masters nor the unfairness of magistrates, but simply the climate of the country in which they landed. Men and women of menial status were accustomed to obey masters in England, and often to suffer grievous cruelties from them,[6] but they were not accustomed to the heat and glare of tropical countries, nor even to the milder temperatures of Virginia. The English, masters as well as servants, had to learn about such countries, and their knowledge was gained at the price of the lives and happiness of many thousands from both classes. In early days mortality from fevers and pestilences was very high indeed; Governor Berkeley reported in 1671 that in previous years four out of five servants had died of disease soon after their landing.[7] If the unfortunate immigrant did not perish of the "bloody flux," he was apt to be taken off by the "dry gripes," while malaria, until the use of "bark" began to be understood, wrought havoc among all. A period of one year was supposed to "season" the new arrivals, and servants thus partially immunized to the climate sometimes brought a higher price than newly imported ones.

It was learned eventually that people should be landed towards the beginning of the winter season, but though this became the rule for ships from Rotterdam it does not appear that British and Irish emigrants were particularly favored in this way. They fared better as conditions in the colonies themselves became more stable, and as intelligent masters provided against the worst effects of the climate. Colonel Walrond, of Barbados, about 1650, provided his servants with a change of clothes when they came in wet from the fields, and not content with this he sent to England for rugs to cover them while sleeping, supplying them also with hammocks so that they should not rest on the ground. He was rewarded both by their better health and by their greater regard for his service.[8] Hours of labor, furthermore, had to be suited somewhat to climatic conditions. The instructions given Gates when he went to Virginia in 1609 directed that the men have three hours' rest at noon in summer and two in winter.[9] Ligon says of Barbados:

They are rung out with a bell to work, at six o'clock in the morning, with a severe Overseer to command them, till the Bell ring again, which is at eleven o'clock, and then they return, and are set to dinner. . . . At one o'clock they are rung out again to the field, there to work till six, and then home again. . . .[10]

These hours were by no means excessive according to English standards, but they eventually proved too long for white men in Barbados. Hammond declared that the servants in Virginia had five hours of rest in the heat of the day; a statement which seems scarcely credible. Three hours was the rule in Maryland. Saturday afternoons and Sundays were free from labor in all colonies, and in Maryland at least masters were haled into court for working their servants on the Sabbath.[11] Though doubtless these regulations were for religious rather than humanitarian reasons they were none the less necessary if white men were to survive at all.

Servants commonly lived in huts or cabins which they built for themselves; apparently they never lived with the Negroes, though the two races worked side by side in the fields. Food in early years consisted largely of a mess called "lob-lolly," made from ground Indian corn; in Barbados servants drank a liquid brewed from potatoes called "mobbie," or a concoction of spring water, orange juice, and sugar. With one accord Englishmen complained if they did not eat meat three or four times a week, and by the time Ligon left Barbados they were getting it.[12] From New Jersey it was written in 1684 that servants had "beef, pork, bacon, pudding, milk, butter and good beer and cyder for drink," fare of which no one could complain.[13] In Maryland, during the 1660's, a group of servants went on strike because they were given no meat, and complained bitterly to the Provincial Court that their master made them live on bread and beans. The court was unsympathetic, particularly when their master explained that this was a temporary shortage and that he had been utterly unable to buy any meat. The servants were condemned to thirty lashes, but this punishment was remitted and they returned amiably to work.[14]

Of the various kinds of plantation labor which servants had to perform one was certainly more difficult and exhausting than commonly fell to the lot of English workers; this was the preparing of new land for planting. Trees had to be felled, trimmed, and dragged away, brush had to be cleared, and the soil turned for the first time without benefit of good plows and sometimes even without draft animals. However long this might be postponed by expedients learned from the Indians it had eventually to be done on every respectable property, and immigrants groaned under the unaccustomed burden. The skilled American axeman was a colonial product, not a European importation, and he learned his art painfully. Once this had been done, however, there is no reason to believe that the regular processes of colonial agriculture were more toilsome than those of Europe. The cultivation of tobacco and sugar called for a somewhat different technique, to be sure, and the harvesting, curing, and refining of these products was a matter for new and special skills, but the physical labor involved was not impossibly arduous.

It is plain that work in the fields was generally required of all servants. This was what they were primarily wanted for, at least until the Negroes came, and even artisans were employed in this fashion unless their indentures specifically released them from the obligation. There were a few schoolmasters, clerks, and accountants, but it was written of Virginia that men who could chop logs were more valuable than those who could chop logic, and Jeaffreson said that one who could handle a pen rarely got as much as an artisan, for such were in fact more plentiful.[15] The court records show that servants attempted to escape the burden of field work, often in a manner shown by the following typical entry from Lancaster County, Virginia, in 1667:

Robert Clark servaunt to Robert Beverley, appeareing at this Court is willing to serve his master one yere longer than hee came in for provided his said master will during all his tyme free him from workeing in the ground, carryeing, or fetching of railes or loggs or the like things and beateing at the morter, and keepe hym to his trade either at home or abroad, which the said Beverley doth promise. All which the Court doth order to bee entred upon record.[16]

Servants who made their indentures before leaving England were oftentimes careful to include a provision that they should work only at their proper trades or crafts. In 1741 the Chester County Court of Pennsylvania ordered a certain master to keep his servant to the trade of a weaver "according to the Tenour of his Indenture," and not to employ him at field labor under penalty of having the servant set free.[17] Such cases also are frequent in the records, but it appears that the servant had to have a clear statement in his indenture in order to liberate him from toil "in the ground."

These facts provide a basis for understanding the true difficulties of the servant population. Contemporaries, observing their shorter hours of labor and other advantages, compared them with agricultural workers at home and found them well off. Those who wrote thus generally were interested in giving a favorable account, and they ignored the important fact that a large proportion of servants were not bred to agricultural labor, and hence found it extremely burdensome. The honest English farmer or German countryman found no great hardship in his tasks in the new world, but it was far otherwise for the tailor, or shoemaker, or weaver who was forced into the tobacco fields. Perhaps it was worst of all for the idle rogues, the thieves, pickpockets, and miscellaneous vagrants who were thus transplanted to unwonted toil; they suffered grievously, and few wasted sympathy on them. Put broadly, the fundamental human problem in colonization was simply that of adaptation, and the white servants did not come from the most adaptable levels of society. Men who had been idle had to work; men whose occupations had been sedentary found themselves tilling the soil. They had to go without fresh meat; they had to eat Indian corn instead of wheat and rye; they had to wear cotton or linen instead of wool, and sleep in hammocks instead of beds; probably for the most part they had to drink water. It was these things that made life painful for so many servants. For these reasons we can understand that while hours of labor might be shorter in the colonies than in Britain, and rewards for diligence might be greater, the servant unable to adapt his habits to colonial conditions and his muscles to physical labor could be said, without gross exaggeration, to be in bondage worse than Egyptian.

Probably the women servants had slightly less extraordinary burdens to bear than the men. They were not worked in the fields in Barbados, and Hammond claimed that they were not in Virginia, at least unless they were "nasty, beastly, and not fit" for other services.[18] They cooked and cleaned and wove and mended, like women in Europe, and indeed any plantation with a considerable number of menservants required several women to look after their clothing and food. Some evidences indicate that they took a hand in tobacco cultivation; certainly there are several examples of women appearing before the Virginia courts and promising extra service in exchange for freedom from this heavy toil.

The labor of servants was supervised by overseers on the larger plantations who were not apt to be men notable for Christian charity. It was unfortunate and tragic that so much should depend not only upon the servant's own character and adaptability but also upon the temper of his immediate superiors. "I have seen an Overseer beat a Servant with a cane about the head, till the blood has followed," wrote Ligon, "for a fault that is not worth the speaking of; and yet he must have patience, or worse will follow."[19] The greatest cruelties occurred in the earlier years, for colonial enterprises had to be put under way by the hardest types of adventurers and pioneers, men who bore tremendous difficulties themselves, extended small mercy to shiftless or weak servants, and punished them excessively when they fainted at their labors. Ligon noted that as time went on "discreeter and better natur'd men" took control of affairs, and there was a marked improvement in the treatment of laborers. Hammond and Alsop, as might be expected, give a favorable report of the relations between servants and masters. A traveller to Jamaica in 1739, after describing how handsomely good servants were treated,[20] goes on to say that stupid and roguish ones were hardly used, set in the stocks, and beaten. "Their salt Provisions are weighed out, and they have nothing but what the Law obliges the Master to give." Ligon remarked that "as for the usage of the Servants it is much as the Master is; merciful or cruel."[21]

On three or four occasions there was an attempt at concerted rebellion among the servants in a small locality, but information about these is too scanty to permit much description. Father John White, accompanying the first voyage to Maryland, landed in Barbados on January 3, 1634, and found a full-fledged conspiracy of servants in process of being put down. Their idea was, according to White, to kill all their masters, take the first ship which arrived thereafter, and put to sea, presumably as pirates. One of the plotters gave the scheme away, and on the very day that White landed eight hundred men were in arms to oppose the design. This indicates that the danger must have been formidable, but since only one ringleader was punished, though the nature of men at Barbados in those days was not mild, it may well be that the conspiracy was exaggerated.[22] Ligon reports that in 1649 just before he left the island there was a rebellion worse than any before. Some leading spirits among the servants, unable to endure their sufferings longer, resolved to break through their slavery or die in the attempt. This project was communicated among the servants, and a day appointed to fall on their masters and cut their throats. On the eve of this attempt it was given away by one of the servants involved, and the affair was crushed. This time eighteen of the leaders were executed, and the assembly appointed an annual day of thanksgiving for the deliverance of the islanders from such a peril. It was probably in this rising that Colonel Guy Molesworth was suspected of being a ringleader; he was deported, and returned in 1661 to petition for reinstatement, charging that although the servants had been tortured with lighted matches between their fingers they had refused actually to implicate him. No doubt there were political as well as class interests involved.[23]

A disposition to general rebellion seems scarcely to have existed among servants on the continent, perhaps because the chance of success was negligible as compared with that on a relatively small island. A curious affair occurred in York County, Virginia, in 1661, when a certain William Clutton told the servants they were not getting the food that ought to be given them. One Isaac Friend proposed that they "get a matter of Forty of them together, & get Armes & he would be the first & have them cry as they went along, 'who would be for Liberty, and free from bondage,' & that there would enough come to them & they would goe through the Countrey and kill those that made any opposition."[24] This valorous scheme petered out, to be followed two years later by a more serious conspiracy in Gloucester County. A general rising was said to be contemplated, and the servants intended to demand of the governor that they be released from a year's servitude, or perhaps be given full freedom. One of their number gave the plan away; the legislature felt that it had escaped from a "horrid plot," and resolved that the servant who revealed it should have his freedom and 5000 pounds of tobacco.[25] Many of the planters believed this rebellion to have been schemed by transported convicts, and it formed one argument against allowing more of them in the colony.

Far more significant are the speculations which were sometimes indulged as to whether servants would join and assist a foreign invader. Sir Henry Colt, visiting St. Christopher in 1631 and commenting on the possibility of defending it, said that it would be easy if the servants would fight, but that generally they preferred the Spanish to win in order that they might be free.[26] This idea was often repeated and was given some support during the later wars, when Irish Catholics joined the French and attacked the English from the rear.[27] Some of these were doubtless servants, but in these instances nationality and religion were stronger forces than class. Nothing indicates that in the many vicissitudes of the island wars servants as a class ever assisted the invader. During the eighteenth century the colonies of Pennsylvania, Maryland, and even Virginia were much alarmed by the number of foreign and Catholic servants and other inhabitants who might lean in sympathy towards their French Catholic brethren. Again there is no evidence that they had any real desire to do so, but since French troops never got near enough to many servants to tempt them we cannot say that the idea was groundless. In 1765, after the war was over, a French traveller declared that if any foreign power invaded and promised freedom to those under indenture, they would certainly give every assistance. Later on representatives of the French government reported that servants were ripe for rebellion against England.[28]

The most ambitious plans for this sort of thing were drawn up by the Anglican clergyman Jonathan Boucher, who returned to England in high dudgeon just before the Revolution. He addressed a letter on the subject to an English official, and after explaining what servants were, continued:

It appears to me to be worth while to send Troops thither, if for no other Purpose than the enlisting of these men whom, I cannot but think peculiarly fit for the American Service. They will bring with Them an ill Humour & Prejudice against the Country which it will not be unuseful to have propagated amongst those with whom they may be incorporated; They have some Knowledge of the country . . . &, above all, They have been seasoned to the Climate.[29]

Boucher, reported that a gentleman of Baltimore, "not addicted to random Declarations," was positive that five hundred could be enrolled in that city and its environs; "it is certain," wrote Boucher, "the richest Harvest of Them may be gleaned there, at Elk-Ridge, the Iron Works & Annapolis." He recommended that plans be carefully drawn for dispatching at one and the same time parties in armed vessels to the heads of rivers in Pennsylvania, Maryland, and Virginia, so that notice could be spread "to the back Settlements, where most of these People have been carried." Many servants, he said, had already run away to join the king's army in Boston.

So far as we know the parson's detailed plans were not followed, nor did the servants manifest any united determination to turn the Revolution to their own ends. Boucher's opinion of their willingness to rise against their masters deserves credit, for he was in a position to know. Yet the situation was surely far more complicated than he represented it; it would scarcely have been a politic move, for example, to seduce away the servants of good Loyalists, nor would it have been easy to avoid doing so if a general campaign to enlist servants had been started. Furthermore, a great proportion of persons under indenture in those years were serious redemptioners, unlikely to be turned aside from their purposes by political adventures. The sentiments of servants during the war were determined by the same fortuitous circumstances that established other peoples' opinions.

We may conclude that the indentured servants and redemptioners, who certainly formed a distinct social and economic class in all the colonial communities, were practically never "class-conscious" to the point of seriously threatening the order of society, either by rebellions of their own or by joining the forces of an invader. It is nevertheless significant that the idea occurred to men like Sir Henry Colt and Jonathan Boucher. There was always a vague fear that servants might join with Negroes in a servile rising, but the West Indian islands, where this danger was most real, soon became convinced that white men would stick together, and looked upon the importation of more servants as adding to the general security rather than imperilling it.

Though the servants were not much disposed to engage in organized conspiracies, they were very prone to individual misdoing. Colonial laws concerning servants are mainly devoted to fixing penalties for their usual crimes and misdemeanors, and the proceedings of county courts are full of judgments respecting them. We have already seen that the masters were expected to discipline their servants by various means, including mild physical punishments, for smaller departures from grace or for laziness and carelessness in work. But just as certainly masters were forbidden to take into their own hands punishment for major crimes. Since the only penalties which could be inflicted on an indentured servant were physical ones, such as whipping or setting in the stocks and the prolongation of the period of servitude, it was necessary that these penalties be administered only by legal authority or gross injustices would have been the rule.[30]

The most common misdoing was that of running away, and the statute books are full of prescriptions against it, while the records show that this was the most frequent cause for the appearance of servants before the magistrates. The natural desire of the planters to retain their laborers was reinforced, especially in earlier years, by a lively fear that servants would join with Negroes or Indians to overcome the small number of masters. Hence the extraordinary harshness of early laws, the worst being that of Maryland in 1639, which enacted that a servant convicted of running away should be executed.[31] There is no evidence that this drastic punishment was ever actually inflicted. Legislation on runaways began in Virginia in 1642/3, when they were condemned to serve double the time they had been absent, after the time of the original indenture should expire. For a second offense they were to be branded on the cheek or shoulder with the letter R, and were to be deemed incorrigible rogues. In 1658/9 it was provided that the hair of returned runaways should be clipped, for easier identification in case they resumed their wanderings. The penalty in Barbados in 1652 was an extra month's service for every two hours' absence, and in 1661 an extra day for every two hours, but the total extension of time was not to be more than three years.

From the confusion of early laws and procedures on the subject of runaways several definite problems and solutions gradually appear. We may distinguish first preventive measures, designed to make running away difficult. Most important of these was the provision in all colonies from very early times that all persons travelling had to have a pass, and that no person should be hired as a servant or harbored as a guest without presenting a certificate from competent authority showing that he was free. Presumably such laws were administered with some discretion, for there seem to be few cases of the prosecution of innocent men for travelling without a pass.[32] Servants would occasionally forge such a certificate, and in one instance a very enterprising convict forged a pass for himself under an assumed name, to travel about Maryland searching for himself under his real name.[33] In addition to these provisions for certificates and passes there were stringent laws in all colonies against the "harboring" of runaways. Any persons receiving and keeping individuals who had no pass or certificate were subject to fines, the amount of which varied greatly from colony to colony, but which were levied at so many pounds of tobacco or sugar per hour, or per twenty-four hours, that the fugitive was sheltered. It is plain that one of the principal motives for these laws was that of preventing servants who stole their masters' goods from taking them to free confederates and dividing the spoils. Lastly, all the southern colonies, and especially the islands, had severe laws regulating the keeping of boats and wherries, and providing that before any persons left the colony their intention to depart should be public posted for a certain number of days. Often ship captains were put under bond not to take away any persons not thus posted. Such regulations were directed as much against free debtors as against servants.

The most difficult problem was to get a servant back after he had run away. Early laws provided for the pursuit of such servants by hue and cry, thus depending upon the ancient obligations of Anglo-Saxons to insure recovery. Since in every colony this proved inadequate, new acts directed the public officials to pursue at public expense, pressing into service men, boats, and whatever assistance might be necessary. But the most effective method was simply that of offering a reward to anyone who brought such a servant back, or lodged him in a jail whence he could be procured by his master. Sheriffs were granted so much a mile for bringing back absconding servants, and in the eighteenth century rewards to those taking up runaways eventually became fixed amounts: twenty shillings in South Carolina, 200 pounds of tobacco in Virginia and Maryland, fifteen shillings in Jersey, and so on. Some colonies provided that runaways, once caught, should be returned by passing them from constable to constable until they reached home, as was done in England with rogues. When a servant was picked up by the authorities for travelling without a pass and refused to tell who his master was, the sheriff might take him to jail and keep him there for a definite time until the master claimed him; if no master appeared the sheriff was authorized after a suitable time to sell the servant at auction to pay his jail fees. On several occasions a runaway servant was incarcerated and his master refused to take him back, whereupon the magistrates usually instructed the sheriff to sell him.[34]

Last come the penalties inflicted upon the servant. These were dual in purpose; first to reimburse the master for his expense and trouble incurred in recovering the runaway and for the days of labor which were lost, and second to punish the servant for his misdoing. The punishment was clearly set forth in the statutes, though it varied greatly from colony to colony: for each day absent the servant was to serve two days extra in New Jersey, Virginia, North Carolina, and St. Christopher; five days in Pennsylvania, ten in Maryland, and seven in South Carolina. In a few colonies the scales of extra service to be enforced for reimbursement of expense are also provided by law; thus Virginia specifies one and a half months' extra service for every 100 pounds of tobacco paid out, but in general this matter was left to the discretion of the justices.

By the eighteenth century the considerable numbers of runaway cases which came before the local courts were being adjusted in a perfectly cut and dried fashion. A sample entry from the Chester County, Pennsylvania, records will show what happened:

Ephraim Jackson having Petitioned this Court prays Relief for sundry Charges Occasioned by the Runing away of his servant Paul Whitton amounting in the whole to [£3.2.0] with Eight days run away time which the Court allows of and adjudges the said servant to serve his master or his assigns Forty days for Runaway Time after the Expiration of his former servitude and to pay his said master [£3.2.0] Expended in Costs and Charges in Retaking of him after the Expiration of his former servitude or serve his said master or assigns nine months in Liew thereof.[35]

The same procedure was followed in Maryland and Virginia, with the changes made necessary by different laws. It may be remarked that the Maryland act allowed the magistrates some discretion in adjudging ten days of service for each day absent, but they seem nevertheless to have generally prescribed the full penalty, unless the servant had been away so long that his time was thereby hopelessly extended.

The courts seem always to have accepted the word of the master as to the length of time the servant had been absent, though the servant was present in court, and the entries occasionally indicate that he "had nothing to say for himself." Usually the unhappy victim was silent, and I have never come across a successful protest by a servant against one of these judgments.[36] There must have been many abuses. A case from the Anne Arundel records illustrates a highly unpleasant mode of procedure. Here a maidservant was brought to court in March, 1719, with 133 days of absence claimed against her, beginning with four days in 1714. What had happened was that her master had kept an account, as the years went by, of various short absences, and as she approached the end of her five-year term he brought her to court, produced a tabulation of all these small delinquencies, and was actually awarded 1330 days of extra service. The unfortunate woman stood in the court, and "sayes she has nothing to say against the said account."[37] It may have been a true account, but obviously she would have had an almost impossible task to prove that it was not, and with her habits being what they apparently were she had small chance of ever becoming free, unless the courts became more merciful than Maryland courts generally were.

Procedure respecting runaways was more irregular in the seventeenth century, but it followed the same principles, and has been so often described that there is no need for further elaboration here. A few cases illustrating the situation in Barbados may nevertheless be of interest. In August, 1654, one Thomas Carter was given permission by his master to visit some friends for the day. Being "overtaken in drink" he stayed out an extra day, and was haled by his master before John Colleton, Esq., who ordered that he serve an extra year. Governor Searle and his council heard the evidence, however, and reversed Colleton's decision, freeing the servant from this outrageous penalty. Similarly, when some Scottish servants absented themselves from their master "upon a pretence of freedom," the whole party, masters and servants, appeared before the Council and the masters agreed to take no advantage of the statute, while the servants promised to return peaceably to their labors.[38]

Probably the majority of runaways got successfully away. Governor Stede wrote in 1688 that many escaped even from the island of Barbados, by joining together in groups and seizing fishing boats; John Urmstone of North Carolina went so far as to declare that most servants never completed their times, but ran away and could not be recovered. Scharf calculated that there was an average of 150 advertisements for different runaways, including Negroes, each year in the *Maryland Gazette*; certainly there were not more than four or five cases of recovered servants each year in any of the county court records, and usually the number was even less. Complaints were heard in early years that servants escaped into the Dutch colonies, and also that they went north into Connecticut, where there were no laws by which they might be recovered. In general, however, they were returned from one colony to another whenever found without undue formality, and the newspapers of Pennsylvania carried large numbers of advertisements for servants who had escaped from Maryland.[39]

The institutions of indentured servitude appear at their worst in this matter of runaways, and there is little to distinguish a servant from a slave. Obviously the penalties of extra service were imposed principally for the enrichment of masters; there can be no possible reason for the Maryland law with a punishment five times as severe as that of Virginia except that the planters of that colony more openly pursued their own advantage. Newspaper advertisements for absconding servants make painful reading; often the fugitives are described as having iron collars about their necks, and the whole spectacle was a degrading one. Nevertheless, it has received a disproportionate amount of treatment from writers on colonial labor; as compared with the total number of indentured servants the number who ran away was probably not great, and certainly the number brought back and condemned to extended servitude was almost insignificant. It is the plentiful evidence rather than the actual importance of runaways that makes their history so well known.

Scarcely less conspicuous in the court records than the offense of running away was that of fornication, and the begetting of bastard children. The moral delinquency involved was expiated in all colonies by a ceremonial whipping, usually of twenty-one lashes, and commonly applied to both man and woman. But colonists took rather more seriously the economic consequences, which consisted of the loss of time by maidservants having chil-

dren, and the expense involved in bringing up the child. This
latter by English practice fell upon the county, and the laws provided that the father of an illegitimate should be discovered by
the oath of the mother, and a sum exacted from him sufficient
to bear the cost of supporting the child until it could be bound
out to work. Such a sum could rarely be got from a manservant,
and hence would either be paid by his master, in which case the
court judged extra service, or would be temporarily borne by
the county and the servant taken by the sheriff after his time
was up and sold again for the amount necessary. As for the
maidservant, some colonies prescribed a year's extra service to
make up for her lost time, while others left the period to the
discretion of magistrates, who rarely gave less than a year. In
fact a good deal depended on her master's story; if he had expended any considerable amount of trouble and money when the
child was born the length of service judged to repay him would
be greater. In many cases a master paid a fine, usually of thirty
shillings, for his maidservant rather than having her subjected
to the prescribed whipping; he was of course reimbursed by
several months of extra service, properly adjudged by the court.
Once again it is plain that the maidservant generally served far
more extra time than she can possibly have lost through her
misdeeds; sentences of two and even three years are quite common, though childbirth can rarely have incapacitated a woman
for more than a month or six weeks.

Legal marriage between servants without the consent of
masters was always forbidden; Pennsylvania held such mar-
riages invalid in 1682 and provided that they were to be proceeded against as for adultery or fornication, and children were
to be accounted bastards. Penalties were always heavy, and as
usual were in the form of extra service. We may cite one case in
illustration: James Hall and Margaret Ryan ran away from

their master in Chester County, stayed thirteen days, got married, and were eventually brought back at a cost to the master of £9. The court judged each to serve thirty extra days for their runaway time, five months for the £9, and one year for marrying.[40] Penalties in other colonies were generally one year's extra service, though Barbados and the other West Indian islands in 1661 required an additional four years of any manservant who secretly married.

When a freeman got a maidservant with child he merely had to satisfy the county for the child's maintenance in most cases, though a few colonies made him pay a fine to the woman's master. In all cases he suffered the usual penalty for fornication, a whipping or sometimes a fine of thirty shillings. More serious were instances in which a master got his own maidservant with child; the court might be forced to decide between her word and his, and though it was the rule in such cases to accept the statement of the woman, made when the child was born, the court could not always discover that such a statement had been made, and so was forced to hear evidence which was apt to be rather colorful. If the case was proved, the maidservant was generally taken away from her master and sold elsewhere, but not set free. The heaviest penalties were reserved for those white women who bore mulatto bastards; long periods of extra service, extending to seven years, were inflicted, usually in addition to a sound whipping.[41]

The fact is that one of the most troublesome and least satisfactory aspects of the whole system was that of sex relations among the servants. The early trade brought to America many more men than women; practically all of them were unmarried, and a very large proportion were of bad character. The prohibition of marriage tended to encourage illicit relations between servants who might under other conditions have lived in conventional fashion. It is true that masters sometimes made generous arrangements for their servants who wished to marry, and that the eighteenth-century redemptioners often had families before beginning their service. Nevertheless the average servant found his chances of marriage reduced below those of persons of similar economic status in England, and the consequences were not healthy. To illustrate one of the less obvious possibilities we may quote the following pathetic plea of a certain Sarah West to the Baltimore County Court:

Humbly Sheweth That your Petitioner having now the Misfortune of an Illegitimate Child, Which I am very sorry for and by Gods Grace I hope I shall never be Guilty of the like again I Doe Declare to your Worships in this Petition the Father of my Child which I hope will be sufficient without publication to any Persons Else (I Do Desire that Favour of your Worships) the Father of my Child is John Michael my Fathers Servant Man. I must beg your Worships to take my Obligation for my fine for I Cannot Gett Security Noe neither have I any Ready Tobacco or Money this year to pay but I have sold three head of Cattle this Spring for Tobacco to pay you this Ensueing year. I hope your Worships will take this into your Grave and Wise Consideration to Use me kindly. I must stand to your Worships Clemency.[42]

The justices spared Sarah a whipping but required her to come to the next court and swear publicly as to the father of her child, and to give security for payment of the fine and for any expense to the county from the child. These were given by Robert West, presumably Sarah's father. As for John Michael, he escaped with ten lashes.

It may be that the newspaper writer who claimed that the convicts, besides their other crimes, "pox'd" the daughters of the colonists, was guilty of exaggeration. Yet the number of illegitimates begotten by servants was large, and since many of the lower grade of servants remained in the colonies only as long as their period of service or of transportation lasted, it may well be that they left behind memorials of their character which were more enduring than their own careers in the new world. One's estimate of the importance of this factor will be influenced by his views on the relative importance of heredity and environment, and in any case the proportion of such baseborn elements in the population was not large; yet this is an aspect of the servant trade which cannot altogether be neglected.

Women servants, besides doing a great deal of domestic and some field labor in the southern colonies, contributed much to make life a bit more tolerable by becoming the wives and mistresses of settlers, or even by merely existing as amiable parts of society. This last function may be thought harmless enough, but the island of Nevis found it becoming a problem, and faced the situation boldly in an act entitled "Women Servants Inveagled."[43] This recited that complaints had been made by masters of families that their women servants had been "inveagled" by idle persons under pretense of marriage or freedom, and had therefore been careless and neglectful in their work. It enacted that any man, free or servant, who should "keepe often company with such women servants, and thereby allure them soe that they neglect their dutyes, or entice them under the afforesaid pretences of marriage or freedome, without knowledg or consent of their said masters," should be subject to penalties. Life on the island of Nevis in the 1670's had few enough amenities, and it was a pity that free men should be deprived of the right of enticing, alluring, and inveigling women servants, to say nothing of the pleasure this must have given the women. We know nothing about the enforcement of this decree, but its text suggests a good deal concerning life and servitude on the islands.

Of the other misdoings of servants little need be said. Most colonies provided by law that those committing theft should forfeit double the amount stolen, which meant, of course, extra service. Those who spent time in jail had to serve extra time for their fees and for the days lost from their masters' work. All colonies prescribed extra service of six months or a year for servants who resisted their masters, or struck them. Other misdemeanors, which if committed by a freeman were punished with a fine, were in the case of servants punished by whipping,[44] South Carolina providing that nine lashes be given for every twenty shillings ordinarily levied. Otherwise they were treated by the courts just as other inhabitants of the colony were. In the records of the sessions held in Chester County, Pennsylvania, for example, one may read long lists of cases in which no mention is made of the status of persons involved, though many of them can be recognized as servants because they appear as such in some other entry.

One who attempts a comparative summary of colonial penal codes concerning servants may perhaps first be struck by the similarities and relationships among them. We have already described how the Barbados statute of 1661 spread to Jamaica and in its principles through all the islands. The continental colonies found it necessary to deal with most of the same special problems by special enactments. Thus in every colony from Barbados to New York there was erected substantially the same mechanism for pursuing and returning runaway servants; the same sorts of penalties were applied to the recovered wanderer by extending his service, the same complicated enactments punishing those who "harbored" runaways were found necessary. Likewise, every colony found it desirable to pass laws concerning servants having bastard children, servants striking their masters, servants stealing from their masters, servants trading with freemen or with natives. Everywhere it was necessary eventually to provide by statute that a servant should not be whipped "naked" save by order of a magistrate. Above all, everywhere the same familiar penalty appears again and again: an extension of the culprit's servitude, usually for a time apparently out of all proportion to the magnitude of his offense. These regulations, together with those concerning freedom dues and customary times of servitude, constitute a body of statute law peculiarly colonial in its nature, though in some respects derived from older English practice. In some cases, as for instance when the Barbados law of 1661 was adopted in Jamaica, we know that there was conscious and deliberate copying of these codes among the colonies, but in most instances we should probably be right in supposing that similarities originally arose merely because the same problems were being met in the same way, under the compulsion of colonial circumstances. No doubt there was much conscious imitation later, as for instance when South Carolina in 1717 enacted freedom dues for women in the same words used by Maryland in 1692.

But after observing these relationships one would probably next be impressed by the considerable differences in detail among the colonies. Many of these have already been mentioned and it has been pointed out that most of them seem impossible of rational explanation. Why, for example, should the laws of Maryland in general have been so much more harsh than those of her neighbors, and this before the wholesale introduction of convicts gave her some excuse for severity? Why should a runaway serve ten days for one in Maryland, and only two for one in Virginia? Why should a person who harbored a runaway forfeit five hundred pounds of tobacco for every night in Maryland, and only sixty pounds in Virginia? And most remarkable of all, why, when most colonies progressively made their penal codes milder, should Maryland after abandoning her original death penalty for runaways and substituting double service, progressively make her code more severe? I know of no answer to these questions, except to assume that the planters of Maryland were a harsher breed than those of Virginia and Pennsylvania. This assumption appears foolish, but one certainly gains the impression from reading court records that not only the laws but also the magistrates of that colony were less merciful.

Year after year the courts from Pennsylvania southward found a considerable proportion of their time taken up by the troubles and the misdoings of indentured servants. Most of our information about servants comes in fact from these court records, and indeed it is difficult not to draw all conclusions about them from the evidences of their clashes with the law or with their masters. Perhaps this section had best be ended, therefore, with a summary view of the relations between the servant and the authorities in one typical locality, by which they may appear more nearly in their true proportions. Lancaster County, in the "Northern Neck" of Virginia, was neither so old and rich as those counties on the lower James River, nor so new and raw as those in the Piedmont. In the year 1665 one hundred and eighty-one persons in the county made returns of 965 "tithables," from which we may guess that there were about 500 white servants.[45] During that year the county court judged the age of eleven young servants, heard the cases of four runaways, of three maidservants having bastards, of four servants applying for their freedom, and of four others appearing for miscellaneous reasons.

In 1698 Lancaster County having been split into two, returned 708 tithables, 257 persons making the returns, and there may have been three hundred white servants. That year there were seventeen judgments of age, one case of bastardy, and one registration of an indenture. The year was hardly typical in not producing any runaways. In 1725 there were 1,249 tithables, but since Negroes were coming in we had best not assume that there were more than about 500 white servants. Four runaways appeared before the court, one maidservant on a charge of having a bastard, and six servants for various reasons, two of them for misdemeanors. In 1740, with 1,579 tithables and perhaps still about 500 servants, there were seven runaways, five cases of bastardy, and four miscellaneous affairs involving servants. In 1757 there were no servant cases, nor in 1764, from which it may be inferred that slaves had practically replaced white servants, and that individual magistrates attended to whatever small disputes may have arisen over those who were left.

These figures are fairly typical, as far as I can discover, of any colonial county in those regions. Even if the numbers of white servants have been overestimated it is still plain that only a very small proportion of them appear in court records. The vast majority of them worked out their time without suffering excessive cruelty or want, received their freedom dues without suing for them, and left no evidences from which to tell the stories of their careers. These points need to be emphasized, for nearly all accounts of white servitude are principally based on the records of courts of justice.

For the most part, American colonists succeeded in treating their indentured servants as private property. They bought and sold them, sued each other for possession of them, and set up engines of law for the protection of their rights in them. Though on occasion the state took a servant away from a cruel master without providing due compensation, this was certainly avoided as often as possible, and many cruel masters, though losing their servants, received the sum procured by selling them elsewhere. To be sure, the servant had rights, but while he was in servitude these rarely conflicted with the conception of him as property.

It was not the rights of servants which conflicted with their masters' conceptions, but rather their duties, as citizens, not as servants. Most of these duties were of course not imposed upon them; they did not vote, hold office, or serve on juries. But the primary duty of a citizen was that of defence, and here trouble eventually arose. In early years servants were required to appear in the colonial militias, usually with arms furnished by their masters, and indeed this duty continued into the eighteenth century for those in the West Indies. But the continental colonies soon grew more secure, and relaxed the obligation of militia duty, providing in several cases that servants should be expected to appear only in times of exceptional emergency. This was really no more than a concession to the interests of the masters; servants would be useful when someone had actually to be killed, but for the normal routine of drilling, accompanied as it might be by agreeable conviviality, they were not deemed necessary. Their duties as citizens bowed to their status as property.

But while the planters could control the institutions of the militia to suit their own ideas, they could not control the British army, which on various occasions appeared in one or another of the colonies to collect recruits for service against the French or the Spanish. A nice question immediately arose: were indentured servants primarily British subjects, with the privilege and perhaps the duty of serving in his majesty's armed forces; or were they primarily the private property of their masters, which might not be taken even by his majesty, without due compensation?

The first clear case of trouble between the home government and the colonist on this issue came at the time of Cromwell's expedition for the taking of Jamaica, in 1654-1655. While the fleet paused at Barbados General Venables recruited no less than 3,500 men, many of whom were indentured servants. The recruiting was carried out by the English officers, not by the Barbadian authorities, and the islanders registered vociferous complaints. Apparently the officers then returned all servants who had still more than nine months to serve, and Admiral Penn was reported to have ordered a search of the fleet for runaways. Even so, a witness declared that the islanders felt the loss of this nine months' service as more considerable to many of them than an assessment of twenty pounds sterling would have been. The fundamental question at issue was evaded.[46]

Once more in the 1690's Barbados complained that the royal fleet was impressing and carrying off servants. According to their law of 1696, the island treasury itself paid for such servants as came to the island and could not be sold, and the planters said they had impoverished themselves without accomplishing any purpose except the replenishing of the royal navy with men. Apparently they could think of no good argument against this practice, except that they did not like it, but their own militia law of 1697 provided that if a servant were killed in action, his master should be recompensed out of the public treasury.[47] They did not urge this on England, nor did New England do so, though during the same wars many servants from there were enlisted in the various campaigns against the Indians and against Canada.[48]

It was the Pennsylvania Quakers who first took it into their heads to hold the sovereign liable for the loss of servants. In 1711 they complained of the "great inequality and hardship which appears to fall upon such masters as lose their servants and yet pay proportionately their rates." The assembly accordingly set aside some of the funds which they had granted to the queen, and provided that they should be used to reimburse masters for servants who enlisted. Probably no money was actually paid, and this episode served only as the introduction to a full-fledged controversy beginning in 1740, when recruiting for the Spanish war commenced.[49]

This time the question was openly argued whether servants were to be regarded as property, or as British subjects liable to military service. Governor Thomas took the latter view, and held that it was the privilege of a servant to enlist if he wished to do so, and the duty of army officers to receive him. Seeking an opinion from John Kinsey, attorney-general of Pennsylvania, the governor got a series of answers directly contrary to this proposition, holding in fact that it was illegal for officers to enlist servants.[50] Some of the townspeople of Philadelphia announced their intention of commencing a suit at law against the officers, and hired two lawyers from New York, but the prosecution was certainly without success. Controversy on the subject between the governor and the assembly dragged wearily on for two years, the assembly refusing to pass necessary legislation or to grant supplies until the governor should meet their demand that the recruiting of servants be stopped. About three hundred servants were nevertheless enlisted, and eventually the assembly voted £2,588 as compensation to the masters. The governor thought that the whole affair was merely a pretext under which the assembly could withhold support for the war, which as pious and thrifty Quakers they were very anxious to do. The fundamental legalistic question was again not settled.

In no other colony was there such argument over enlistment in 1740 as there was in Pennsylvania. Virginia passed an act providing that justices of the peace might raise a levy of all able-bodied men who followed no lawful calling or employment, were no one's indentured servants, and had no vote.[51] A considerable force was raised and sent to Carthagena, and may have ridded the colony of some undesirable inhabitants, for the sheriffs were permitted to search out recruits, and there was little likelihood of anyone's returning from such an expedition.

With the beginning of the French and Indian war in 1755 the question arose once again. At first British officers refrained from enrolling servants, and the colonial legislatures in their acts for raising recruits generally forbade the enlistment of any servant without his master's consent.[52] But about the beginning of 1756 when the officers began to take on servants, opposition to this procedure became violent. In Kent and Baltimore counties of Maryland there was armed resistance to the recruiting officers, and open rioting. Governor Shirley of Massachusetts, first commander of the royal forces, argued once again that the king had a right to the services of his subjects; the colonists answered with a barrage of lawyers' opinions to the contrary. Sir Charles Hardy wrote to Lord Halifax that the greatest trouble in the whole recruiting service was that over servants: "the Lawyers. . .hold indented & bought Servants to be Property, &, as such, have no Will of their own, & cannot be withheld from their Masters; I much doubt if His Majesty's Attorney General was to try a Cause of this Sort, but he would find both Court [and] Jury of this Opinion."[53]

It would have been interesting to have had a final answer given to the question of whether servants were property or not, but the problem was treated, no doubt properly, as one of expediency rather than of principle. In 1756 Parliament took a hand, enacting that it should be lawful for officers to enlist indentured servants, but that if the master or owner objected, the servant should be returned, or the master should be paid whatever two justices of the peace should decide to be proper compensation. In deciding what should be paid, the amount originally given for the servant was to be taken into consideration, and the proportion of his time which was still to be served out. Accordingly, the inhabitants of Pennsylvania turned in a list of about six hundred servants who had been recruited, minutely specifying original costs and time served, and working out the amount of money due to the last farthing.[54] Nevertheless Lord Loudoun objected to paying this money, as insufficient proof was furnished that the men had actually been servants, and apparently the money was eventually voted by the disgruntled assembly itself. In Virginia Governor Dinwiddie rebuked an officer for enlisting servants "by hav'g 'em valued," for he opined that some of them were being rated at a figure higher than their first cost.[55] The county court records of Maryland show that compensation was paid to masters in that colony, but they do not reveal the process of fixing the amounts.[56] On the whole, it must be said that the burden of opinion inclined towards the doctrine that servants were property; yet it was hardly necessary to go to such an extent in justifying the payment of compensation to masters, for they had indeed invested money in their servants, and those who lost them to the recruiting officer suffered inequitably as compared with those whose laborers stayed at home.

Needless to say, at the time of the Revolution, American opinion was either entirely opposed to the enlistment of servants in the provincial army, or at least it was insistent that compensation be paid. We have evidence of several soldiers being discharged upon testimony that they were servants, and the assembly of Pennsylvania in 1778 granted money to those whose servants had enlisted. This act was in answer to such sentiments as those expressed by a committee from Cumberland County, which sounded oddly in the midst of the battle for freedom, "Resolved that all Apprentices and servants are the Property of their masters and mistresses, and every mode of depriving such masters and mistresses of their Property is a Violation of the Rights of mankind. . . ." The Provincial Congress of New York instructed its officers not to enlist servants, but by 1784 sentiment had altered, for in that year a group of the citizens of New York, beholding a newly arrived cargo of servants, declared that the "traffick of White People" was contrary to the idea of liberty, and voted to pay their passages and set them free, reimbursing themselves by a small rateable deduction from the immigrants' wages.[57]

CHAPTER 13

FREED SERVANTS

A N OBSERVER from the home country who visited Barbados in 1655 and looked it over with some care announced that it was a dunghill, on which England cast forth its rubbish. "Rodgs and hors and such like people arc those which are gennerally Brought heare," he continued. "A rodge in England will hardly make a cheater heare: A Baud brought over puts one a demour comportment, a whore if hansume makes a wife for some rich planter."[1] Lest this sweeping declaration tend to reflect unduly on the islands in comparison with their continental sisters, we may quote also the remark of a customs officer of London, who, instructed to stop persons emigrating during the 1630's replied that there was no point in hindering passengers to Virginia "because most of those that go thither, ordinarily have no habitations, & can bring neither certificate of their conformity nor ability and are better out than within the Kingdom."[2] Indeed, all plantations according to a publication of the year 1632, were no better than common "sinkes," where the commonwealth dumped her most lawless inhabitants.[3]

There has certainly been no lack of ink spent in describing the characters and qualities of early emigrants to America. The white servants have received their due share of attention, and since at least half, and perhaps two-thirds, of all immigrants to the colonies south of New York were servants or redemptioners the subject is not without importance. The nature of society in the new world, the manners and customs of people, the rate of economic advance, perhaps also the inherited characteristics of Americans, depended to some degree upon the nature of these immigrants. Accordingly, modern writers have generally viewed them with generous tolerance, and magnified their virtues either out of patriotic pride or out of a wish to demonstrate how grievously worthy persons were exploited by economic overlords in the bad old days. But almost with one accord their own contemporaries, who knew them and saw them, denounced them as next to worthless. A few more quotations will show the spirit of their remarks.

Charles Davenant, a highly competent publicist, wrote in 1698 that a considerable number of persons emigrated each year to the colonies, "but then 'tis generally of such sort of People as their Crimes and Debaucheries would quickly destroy at home, or whom their Wants would confine in Prisons or force to beg, and so render 'em useless, and consequently, a Burthen to the Publick."[4] And although Davenant may have had an axe to grind, the General Assembly of Virginia, in 1699, entered in its Journal the observation that "Christian servants in this country for the most part consist of the worser sort of people of Europe, and since the Peace, such numbers of Irish and other nations have been brought in . . . that in our present circumstances we can hardly govern them."[5] Likewise Governor Stede of Barbados told the Lords of Trade: "most of the white servants sent here [are] taken from the gaols, and [are] men whose lives have taught them all kinds of villainies and reduced them to such misery that they come to the Colonies to escape from starving."[6] Even that enthusiastic champion of Virginia, John Hammond, admitted that at the first settling "then were Jayls emptied, youth seduced, infamous women drilled in."[7] And

Hugh Jones, no enemy to the same colony, characterized the Virginian servants in 1724 as "the poorest, idlest, and worst of Mankind, the *Refuse of Great Britain and Ireland,* and the *Outcast of the People.*"[8] It would not be difficult to multiply such opinions from men of that time, and one will hunt long for favorable verdicts on servants, though redemptioners came off better.

These estimates, however, cannot be taken too literally, for just as it is the fashion among some nowadays to exalt the virtues of the lower classes, both past and present, and blame their vices on the treatment they received from their betters, so it was certainly the fashion then to decry the poor with equal unrestraint, and ascribe all their shortcomings to inherent wickedness. In those days it was rarely necessary to curry favor with the mob, and there was no reason to use caution or care in talking about the poor. Idleness, vice, poverty, and wickedness went conveniently hand in hand for nearly all writers, and consequently one must expect to find persons described as vicious rogues who were in fact only poor, unfortunate, and dirty. Another and actually more important consideration is that many of the writers quoted were favorable to the colonies, and wrote their remarks partly for the purpose of demonstrating that valuable inhabitants of England were not being drained away. This is especially true of Davenant, for instance, who was doing his best to argue down the mercantilist opponents of emigration. The worse the servants could be painted, the less hindrances would be placed in the way of their departure from England.

Nevertheless, after making due allowances for middle-class arrogance and the necessities of argument, there cannot remain the slightest doubt that in the eyes of contemporaries indentured white servants were much more idle, irresponsible, unhealthy, and immoral than the generality of good English laborers. Common sense, without evidence, would in fact indicate much the same thing. It is foolish to suppose that many persons of stable position in England would come to the colonies as servants, especially in the earlier years. There would be a few capable fortune hunters, some well-bred young men escaping from their debts or their amours, perhaps a penurious schoolmaster or two, and perhaps a fair number of farmers whose qualities of character were excellent but whose lands had been taken away from them. But the majority of servants would naturally be more or less worthless individuals who drifted to the colonies as a last resort, who were kicked out of England by irate fathers or expelled by the machinery of Bridewell and Newgate. These were the servants who had to be whipped for idleness, who ran away, committed thefts, and disturbed the peace. These, and in the eighteenth century the many convicts, were the servants whom the writers and travellers of the age saw and recorded, and whose exploits got into the records of the county courts, while the industrious and honest minority by virtue of their very qualities passed unnoticed.

The qualities of a good colonist were physical health, practical intelligence, and diligence, and if the virtue of obedience be added to these they are also the qualities of a good indentured servant. There can be no doubt that towards the end of the colonial period better servants came, and the large migrations of 1773 did not bring nearly as much riff-raff, proportionately, as did the smaller movements of a century before. Redemptioners, coming as they did with wives and families, were far more apt to be good colonists than were the casual servants, and though Franklin said the Germans were stupid and some other observers grumbled at their diminishing excellence as the century went on, they were in general of good quality, and welcomed in their new environment. The point was, of course, that the colonies had settled down into a stable existence; men could go there not as on a wild gamble, but with fair certainty of making a decent and even a comfortable living. It had become a reasonable project for the sober and industrious farmer, or the ambitious laborer. Contemporaries scarcely ever praise the qualities of servants, even at the end of the colonial period, but there is rather less pungent criticism of them, and the talk of depopulating Britain becomes far more powerful, resulting in actual measures to stop the movement.

Various types of servants can be distinguished, though this has to be done carefully. Rarely was any criticism levelled against the Scots, and the West Indian colonies complained bitterly when after 1663 the direct trade with Scotland was cut off, preventing the arrival of servants. Even though they had been rebels or vagabonds at home, they were looked upon as unusually ambitious, industrious, and intelligent, working faithfully through their servitude with an eye always on the time when they should be free to set up for themselves. Irish were least favored, and some colonies taxed or even forbade their importation. This was partly because of their religion, which was held to be politically dangerous, but mainly because of their tendency to be idle and to run away. Jeaffreson wrote that many of them were "good for nothing but mischief"; we read that they "straggled" in Bermuda, that they rioted in Barbados, that they would never settle down to an obedient servitude, satisfactory to their masters. Welsh were highly esteemed. Germans came in for little criticism except from those who objected to their language and customs; in Georgia they did not make good servants, but when given their own plots of land became admirable colonists;[9] in the north they seem generally to have worked out their terms of servitude patiently. Convicts were, of course, anathema to all who had the general social good in mind; they committed many brutal crimes, and dragged down the whole laboring population in reputation, but they were favored as servants because they could be kept in bondage for a longer period than the others, and because no one was disposed to shelter them from the severest discipline.

When one departs from these general estimates and comes down to specific cases, examples can, of course, be produced to fit any theory. The crimes of servants which are exhibited largely in court records and in the newspapers range all the way from trivial misdoings to deeds of spectacular viciousness. It would be quite wrong to base an estimate of the whole servant population upon such records; it is just as wrong to depend on the shining examples of faithful and diligent workers who emerged into prosperity and respectability. Many and diverting are the descriptions of runaways which were inserted in the newspapers when advertising for their recovery; an Irishman is a "complaisant pallavering fellow," an Englishman "very talkative, but foolish," a convict "of a very amorous disposition," another convict "writes a very good Hand, and has been used to keeping School." There was "Anne Young, about 30 Years old, very much pitted with the Small Pox, middling tall, and slender . . . has run away several times, and knows a great many noted men." Edward Coalman, an Irishman, "is very talkative, and much addicted to swearing . . . very positive in his answers"; Daniel M'Inniry, also an Irishman, "is very apt to use the word *really,* talks very broken and backward, and is fond of strong drink."[10] At "Hampton," home of the Ridgelys in Baltimore, a small manuscript book was recently found entitled "Description of the White Servants taken January 1772," which gives the names, ages, heights, and other data concerning ninety-one servants. Seventeen of these were from Ireland, one from Wales, and sixty-seven from England; two were women and four were Negroes. The average age of all was 25.27, only nine could read and write, one could read, write, and play the fiddle, and the average height of the group was only 5'6¼".[11] Perhaps this was a typical group of servants, but we have no means of knowing.

For the ambitious and intelligent servant, his term of servitude was by no means time lost. He became seasoned to the colonial climate, if he did not perish first, and he became accustomed to the modes of living and working which colonial conditions made necessary. He learned the best methods of farming, and the system of marketing farm products. He made acquaintances which might be worth something to him among the planters of the vicinity; if he was an artisan he became known as one, and might have customers ready when he set up on his own. According to Hammond and Bullock, a decent master often gave his servant a plot of land, or even a few beasts, which he could have in possession during his servitude, and which would build him up a small substance before his term was over. Even the worst servants might perhaps profit from physical labor and strict discipline sufficiently to improve their habits slightly.[12]

The time of servitude was also a time of apprenticeship, and might be used for learning a trade. Many indentures drawn for children specify that they be taught thus, just as if they had been bound out to a craftsman in England, and sometimes it was provided that they should be given opportunity to learn reading and writing. There are a number of cases in the Virginia records of servants who agreed to stay an extra year or two with their masters in return for being taught a trade; thus one in Lancaster County in 1721 promises to serve six months longer than his proper term "in case that his said Master doth obleidge himself to learn the said John the sawyer's trade." Another promised three months extra if his master would let him work with one Matthew Nathan, "for his further insight in the taylor's trade."[13] These were recorded simply because they involved extensions of time, which could not be allowed without the consent of magistrates. Many servants must have learned much without finding it necessary to contract for extra service. With a little good fortune in his master a servant might gain his freedom far better qualified to use it advantageously than he had been when he arrived in America.

In 1782 Hector St. John de Crevecoeur published in Britain his *Letters from an American Farmer.* A famous passage of this work set forth the attractions of life in the colonies as well as they have ever been stated. The European, wrote Crevecoeur,

does not find, as in Europe, a crowded society, where every place is overstocked; he does not feel that perpetual collision of parties, that difficulty of beginning, that contention which oversets so many. There is room for every body, in America. Has he any particular talent, or industry? he exerts it in order to procure a livelihood, and it succeeds. . . . Is he a laborer, sober and industrious? he need not go many miles, nor receive many informations before he will be hired, well fed at the table of his employer, and paid four or five times more than he can get in Europe. . . . I do not mean that every one who comes will grow rich in a little time; no, but he may procure an easy, decent maintenance, by his industry. Instead of starving, he will be fed; instead of being idle, he will have employment; and these are riches enough for such men as come over here. The rich stay in Europe, it is only the middling and the poor that emigrate.[14]

No doubt this description was overoptimistic in some respects, but fundamentally it was accurate, insofar as it referred to the continental colonies. There was always a scarcity of labor; always land to be had; always a decent livelihood to be won by those who had the qualities necessary to win it. Thus the freed servant with his new clothes and his small stock of corn need never have lacked for employment. If he desired land and independence he could certainly acquire them in time, even if not immediately on his freedom.

The West Indian islands, however, presented no such satisfactory prospects. Excepting Jamaica they were all of small size, and it was not long before the land was taken up. Barbados was the first to become crowded. In the early days of the colony servants seem to have been allotted grants of ten acres, but this practice soon had to be abandoned, and they were later promised small plots in the Leeward Islands.[15] As late as 1672 Governor Sir Charles Wheler reported that St. Christopher differed much from the other Caribbean plantations, being populated mostly by persons who had formerly been servants, and whose small tracts of ten or twelve acres were managed generally with English servants rather than slaves.[16] Opportunities were good in those parts even into the 1680's. Christopher Jeaffreson wrote that ingenious and industrious men seldom failed to raise up their fortunes in any part of the Indies.[17] A true success story may be read among the papers of the High Court of Admiralty, where one Nicholas Leech deposed that he had gone to St. Christopher about 1640, served for seven years, married, had two children, visited home once, and come to own jointly a plantation with between forty and fifty servants and slaves.[18] Those were good times.

But the inevitable filling up with people progressed—the consolidation of landholdings, the growth of large-scale sugar planting with slave labor, and the freezing out of small men. By 1695 the situation in Barbados had reached a sad state:

I dare say [wrote the governor] that there are hundreds of white servants in the Island who have been out of their time for many years, and who have never a bit of fresh meat bestowed on them nor a dram of rum. They are domineered over and used like dogs, and this in time will undoubtedly drive away all the commonalty of the white people and leave the Island in a deplorable condition. . . . Nor can we depend upon these people to fight for defence of the Island when, let who will be master, they cannot be more miserable than their countrymen and fellow subjects make them here.[19]

The governor recommended that royal action be taken on their behalf, or that they be given the right of suffrage so that aspiring assemblymen might dole out a little rum and meat in exchange for votes. Yet nothing effective could be done, for there was no economic need for poor white persons on the island. Despite their miserable condition, it was necessary in the very next year to pass the most liberal of all laws encouraging the importation of white servants, and to promise that at least during servitude they should be well rewarded. Only the establishment of a military garrison remedied the situation.

Those freedmen who escaped such evil fortune did so only by leaving the island; and even in 1680 the exodus was great.[20] At first they went to the Leeward Islands, and also to Carolina and Jamaica. In 1720 a correspondent wrote from Barbados that many hundred families had gone to Carolina and Pennsylvania, "such for the most part who had run themselves more in debt than they were worth in Barbados, and could have been no longer useful in that Island, and yet are now some of the toppingest inhabitants where they are, and many of them have paid their old debts."[21] Insofar as this could happen the servants had small reason to complain, but freedom dues in Barbados were so scanty as to make emigration difficult, and sometimes it was necessary for them to commence a new period of servitude.

Jamaica had of course far more land to be distributed than the other islands, and it was colonized by the English at a later date; hence opportunities tended to be better there. John Wilmore wrote in 1690 that some servants whom he had personally known had gone to Jamaica in low condition, "yet now have arrived to Estates of above One Thousand pound Sterling, per annum, and these are Planters."[22] Wilmore was anxious to prove that white servants, far from being objects of exploitation, were actually unprofitable to everyone but themselves, and his story must be accepted with reservations. Dalby Thomas, a more reliable writer, remarked that many persons, by carrying to the sugar islands "the remains of their shipwrackt fortunes, have recovered their lost estate, and very much conduced to that Increase of Wealth to this Nation as well as to the increase of Shipping."[23] Even Thomas was arguing against the mercantilists who would discourage emigration. The fact was that Jamaica fell into the hands of capitalistic and absentee sugargrowers even as did the other islands; small farmers found, soon after the turn of the century, that they had no chance of surviving. In 1735 a Jamaican investigating committee, pursuing the perennial problem of why there were not more white inhabitants in the island, reported that the chief obstruction to an increase in their number had been that exorbitant grants of the best land were given to a few favored people and there was none left for newcomers. Four years later a visitor to the island reported that the freed servants were in wretched condition, "for, after the Expiration of their four Years, no Body is fond to employ them, and they generally remain in a low abject State, thro' the whole Remainder of their Lives."[24]

It is plain that no intelligent and informed man or woman would emigrate to the West Indies as a servant after the first years of settlement were over. Circumstances were all against them. The genuine economic demand for their labors even while in servitude was slight and the chances for their success after freedom were almost non-existent. Yet we know from the estimates of Long and from the census of 1730 that as many as a third or a half of the white inhabitants of Jamaica were servants. The governor remarked that these were mainly Irish, imported to make up "deficiencies" and serve in the militia, and nearly worthless. No doubt there were some good servants, and some successful careers even in the eighteenth century, but we must look upon the white servant in the West Indies generally as being an unfortunate individual, prized mainly for the color of his skin, unable to find work, apt even to conspire with slaves, a tragic outcast in the colonial world.

Turning to the continental colonies, and surveying them generally at first, a few parallels strike us. The granting of land in New York was not unlike that in Jamaica, based principally on favoritism and corruption, and resulting in the engrossing of huge amounts by a few astute manipulators of the governor's favor. Freed from his indenture, the servant might look forward to life as a tenant farmer or as a hired man, but it was expensive and difficult for him to become fully independent.[25] The tightly closed social system of New England, the strictly controlled expansion, carried on in groups and often under the auspices of speculators, were unfavorable also to the ambitions of freed servants, though here also they might usually find work at good wages. There was plenty of land, but it was not to be had for the asking. On the other hand, the authorities of Pennsylvania, Maryland, Virginia, and the Carolinas were anxious above all things to get their lands into the hands of settlers. They encouraged expansion, granted lands on easy terms for moderate quitrents, and though speculators were by no means unknown, they did not succeed in appropriating all the fertile territory.

In early years people went directly westward. "The inhabitants of our Frontiers," wrote Spotswood in 1717, "are composed generally of such as have been transported hither as Servants, and being out of their time, settle themselves where Land is to be taken up and that will produce the necessarys of Life with little Labour."[26] Later began the steady flow of people southward from Pennsylvania through the mountain valleys even to Carolina and Georgia; this was the route of many Scotch-Irish and German redemptioners who came into the port of Philadelphia. The point is plain; it was on the frontiers of Virginia and her northern and southern neighbors that the land of opportunity was to be found. That was one reason why most servants went to those colonies.

The land of opportunity indeed was there, but how many freed servants took advantage of it? What proportion of the indentured immigrants actually became independent and prosperous citizens? Do their careers after freedom bear out the unsavory reputation which contemporaries gave them during their servitude? Of course no colony ever took a census to determine how many of its inhabitants had once been servants. Figures even of immigration and population are so conflicting and doubtful that it is almost impossible to answer the questions which have been posed. Such facts as that seven servants from the muster of 1624 in Virginia were sitting in the assembly of 1629 as burgesses are interesting because they show that we cannot regard the servants as hopelessly and permanently downtrodden;[27] but such facts tell us little about the great mass of those who came in through the colonial period.

There is, however, one way of getting some light on the problem; this is by using the records of the distribution of land. Professor Wertenbaker concludes from a study of the Virginia Land Books that up to the year 1666 perhaps thirty to forty per cent of the landholders in the colony had come in under indenture; if we compare this with the fact that probably seventy-five per cent of all immigrants during the same period were servants, we perceive that a good many fell by the wayside. Three-quarters of all immigrants were servants, yet only one-third of the landowners were ex-servants. This is not a very good record; nevertheless if it is read beside the extremely unflattering estimates of the servant population which have been quoted, it does not appear to be a very bad record either. The figures are rather vague, however, and perhaps they cannot be accepted as accurate enough to be indicative.[28]

From the Land Books of Maryland much more precise knowledge is available, though only for a limited period during the seventeenth century when each freed servant, by law of the colony and grant of the proprietor, was entitled to fifty acres of land.[29] When an indentured servant in those years became free, he appeared at the secretary's office and "proved his right" to his tract by showing his certificate of freedom. The secretary entered this transaction in his books, and if the servant desired it, straightway granted a warrant for the survey of the land. In due course the surveyor returned his certificate, a patent would be drawn up in proper form, and the whole series of steps recorded. Thus plentiful evidences of these transactions remain, and since the clerk always specified that such a grant was "due for his time of service performed in this province" there is little trouble in attaining reasonable accuracy. Furthermore, immigration figures derived from the entries of head-rights give a fair guide to the numbers of servants arriving in the colony.

Choosing the ten years from 1670 to 1680 as a fair sample, the following facts may be learned, all from the Land Books. Not less than 5,000 servants entered the colony within the decade, but only 1,249 proved their rights to fifty acres of land as freedom dues, and of these no less than 869 sold their rights immediately to other persons, and took no land themselves. Only 241 clearly took warrants for land, while 139 proved their rights but took no warrant, and my search did not reveal what happened to them. Assuming that 241 freed servants actually settled each on fifty acres of land in the space of ten years, they represent a little more than 4 per cent of the total number of servants who came into the colony. Probably at least a quarter of the servants died during their terms, however, or were sold out of the colony; after making this deduction we conclude that no more than 7 per cent of freed servants availed themselves of the right to fifty acres of land on which to settle.

These figures are accurate, and they give the nearest to a statistical estimate of the fortunes of indentured servants which can be made for any part of the colonial period. Perhaps they are slightly unjust to the servants, nevertheless, for the Land Office did not, by that period, have the best tracts available, and some of the servants may have found it possible to purchase a few acres in more satisfactory locations from speculators. Yet even after relaxing the final conclusion a bit more on this ground, we still see that it is foolish to describe the seventeenth-century indentured emigrant as a land-hungry pioneer. If he would not take a tract when it was handed to him for nothing, in a colony so relatively favorable to freed servants as Maryland, he did not want land.

My own inferences from the general mass of evidence are that of indentured servants, about one in ten was a sound and solid individual, who would if fortunate survive his "seasoning," work out his time, take up land, and wax decently prosperous. Perhaps another one in ten would become an artisan, following his trade in some town, or perhaps a hired overseer on a plantation, and thus live a useful and comfortable life without owning any land. The other eight either died during their servitude, returned to England after it was over, or became "poor whites," and occupied no substantial position in the colonies either as workers or as proprietors. They were no sturdy pioneers. Doubtless they were not the vicious wretches observers claimed them to be, but certainly they were shiftless, hopeless, ruined individuals, raked up from the lower reaches of English society by emigrant agents, kidnappers, and officers of the law. There is no reason to believe that they improved measurably in the eighteen century, and we might adopt as a text the melancholy reflection of the Georgia Trustees, who, after doing their utmost for several years in a most competent fashion, sadly realized that "many of the Poor who had been useless in England, were inclined to be useless likewise in Georgia."[30]

Concerning the one servant in ten who made a success of his career and became a landholder, more information may be found in the Maryland Land Books. There is, for instance, the case of Richard Gurling, who on October 13, 1674, took out fifty acres of land as his own freedom due, and also received 150 more acres assigned over to him by other servants. William Home, in the same year, got a warrant for 100 acres as his own and his wife's freedom dues, and another warrant for the same amount because he had transported two servants to the colony. In 1672 two servants assigned their rights of land to Katherine Layton, while a third servant, Bonham Turner, proved his own right, received a warrant, married Katherine, and entered into possession of her newly acquired tracts. John Slater, who finished his service in 1663, proved his rights only in 1672, but was then able to purchase an additional fifty acres. Philip Lynes, who is dignified by the title of "gent.," took out warrants for his own and his wife's freedom dues in 1674. Robert Ridgely, an official of the colony and a great land speculator, got fifty acres for his wife's freedom dues in 1671, and Nicholas Painter, whose speculative transaction ran into thousands of acres, took out the accustomed amount in 1680 as the reward of his own servitude. One might be tempted to think that there was dishonesty involved, if it were not that none of these names appears more than once in applying for such rights.

Seven burgesses in the Virginia Assembly of 1629 were ex-servants, as we have already remarked. In the Maryland Assembly of 1637/8 fifteen former servants had seats.[31] Naturally the proportion was far higher in those early years than it could be after the country was more fully settled. A few individuals of some fame came to the country as servants or redemptioners. Charles Thomson, who was for many years secretary of the Continental Congress, Matthew Thornton, a signer of the Declaration of Independence, Matthew Lyon, the belligerent congressman, and Daniel Dulany, a distinguished lawyer of the early eighteen century in Maryland, all began their careers under indenture. Benjamin Franklin's maternal grandmother was an indentured servant named Mary Morrils, whom Peter Folger bought for twenty pounds and afterwards married.[32] William Buckland was a skilled craftsman from Oxfordshire, who came in under indenture in 1754; he built Gunston Hall, the home of George Mason, and the house of Mathias Hammond in Annapolis, and Hammond had a portrait of him painted by Peale, to hang in the reception room of the house.[33]

Of redemptioners, as distinguished from indentured servants, no evidence remains which permits a statistical statement of their fortunes after serving out their time. It has already been pointed out in the first chapter of this study that the circumstances of their emigration, coming as they did in families, with furniture and equipment, and seeking definitely a new home, made them generally a much sounder group than the mere servants. We may be sure that a greater proportion than two out of ten of them attained independence and esteem, but just how many more it is impossible to say.

Probably the opportunities for success offered to women servants were greater than those which presented themselves to men. At least during the early years they were in great demand as wives; the Maryland Land Books show many husbands, probably themselves originally freemen, coming to the office and claiming the fifty acres of land due to their wives. Bullock remarked that he could never keep a maidservant long at his plantation, "except a poore silly Wench, made for a Foile to set of[f] beautie, and yet a proper young Fellow must needs have her, and being but new come out of his time and not strong enough to pay the charges I was at in cloathing and transporting her, was content to serve me a twelve Moneth for a Wife." The same author advised "that man that's full of Children to keepe his Sonnes in England, and send his Daughters to Virginia, by which meanes he shall not give but receive portions for all his Children."[34] Certainly the most entertaining description of the arrival of a cargo of servants is that given by old Du Tertre, who tells how some women were brought to one of the French islands:

A peine estoient-elles décendües à terre, qu'on couroit tout ensemble au marché & à l'amour; on n'y examinoit bien souvent, ny leur naissance ny leur vertu, ny leur beauté, & deux iours apres qu'elles estoient arrivées, on les épousoit sans les connoistre.[35]

No doubt the Anglo-Saxon pioneers in Virginia exhibited less conspicuous ardor, but there must have been just such a scene presented when the London Company's shipment of prospective brides put in at Jamestown.

As for the convicts, their ultimate fate is shrouded in mystery, where it is perhaps as well that it should remain. William Eddis remarked that most of them either found their way back to England after their seven or fourteen years was finished, or else they moved to different parts of the colonies and took up a new career under assumed names.[36] It is unlikely that any of them who became successful and esteemed would allude to their former disgrace. Watson, the annalist of Philadelphia, claimed that he knew of several substantial citizens of that town who had originally appeared in the colonies on transport ships bringing criminals, and who had since amassed wealth and respectability. He tactfully omitted to give their names, and it is unlikely that they could be discovered now.[37] Further knowledge of what families are descended from convicts will have to await genealogical research in the lists kept by the Treasury, meanwhile it is probably safe to assume that a good many less than ten out of every hundred of them actually settled down comfortably in the colonies. It would be surprising if twenty thousand or more felons did not include some of ability and character, who contributed excellent qualities to the building of the country, but certainly most of them were worthless and dangerous.

The system of white servitude was cruel, to our modern way of thinking, because it subjected such large numbers of persons to an exceedingly hard, laborious, and dangerous way of life, in strange regions and difficult climates, when these persons were generally unfitted for such a life, undesirous of pursuing it, and incapable of making a success of it. Once started upon it, furthermore, they could not draw back, they were subjected to masters who often exploited them, and they were constrained by the whole machinery of colonial law to keep at their tasks, even if it killed them. And kill them it usually did, at least in the first years, when fifty or seventy-five out of every hundred white servants died without ever having had a decent chance of survival. Certainly these same persons would not, for the most part, have enjoyed either an easy or a prosperous career if they had stayed at home; they would in general have been rogues, vagabonds, and convicts, or they would have been chronically unemployed and existing miserably on the poor rates, or they would have been pressed into the army or navy. Life seems to have been harder for the poor then than now, but one cannot help feeling that transportation to the colonies increased the burden.

It cannot be denied, however, that despite the crushing hardships of pioneer life which both master and servant had to endure together, America presented to the average man a far better chance of attaining decent independence than did Europe. Even the man of less than average capacity, providing only that he had good physical health, would find in the colonies the best opportunities then existing of expending his abilities to his own best advantage. Hence, though it might have been kinder to choose only the ambitious and the strong for emigration, it would not necessarily have been more just. Servitude enabled all alike to come to America and remain a few years with support assured; afterwards each individual chose his own path in a society where many paths were open.

The real discouragement, of course, fell on those persons who did not want to attain a decent independence by such painful means, and who found themselves laboring in America when they would have preferred to take their miserable chances in the old country. It fell also on those who were unlucky in their masters, who were overworked, underfed, beaten and abused; no doubt many honest and gallant spirits were broken.

It fell on those who realized that four or five years' bondage was far more than they justly owed for the privilege of transportation and support. Finally it fell most heavily on those who found themselves in the West Indies after the land had all been taken up, and who saw that they were at an unfair disadvantage as compared with those on the continent. This was, in truth, the most serious inequality of the system of white servitude.

It is worth asking whether this system was necessary, and whether a less burdensome method might not have been devised. One can easily invent schemes of colonization much more pleasant than that actually used; plenty of people did so in those days and have done so since. But the practical difficulty with all these schemes was that they were much too expensive, considered in relation to the wealth of society generally. A plan which worked well in the nineteenth century could not have been financed in the seventeenth or eighteenth. Thus, theoretically, the original project of the Virginia Company was more generous and equitable than the individualistic system of white servitude, but it did not work because it was too expensive for the time. The most attractive schemes actually carried out were those of Georgia and Halifax, where men were transported, fed and sheltered for a year, and then turned loose with a grant of land to fend for themselves. But these again were both very costly; small as they were they strained the available resources which the British Treasury itself could devote to them. One is forced to the conclusion that if colonization was to be carried on at all, the only way to do it without rearranging society in some utopian fashion was to set up the system of indentured white labor. This does not, of course, mean that masters had to be cruel, that servants had to be kidnapped, or even that they had to serve for as long a time as four years. Many details could have been improved, but generally considered the system was sound and well adapted to the practical necessities of the situation, both for servants and for masters.

Essentially it was simply a workable means of supplying white settlers and cheap labor. Its social consequences were by no means altogether good, for it certainly tended to make the colonies "sinkes" into which the refuse of Europe could be thrown. Perhaps it was a fortunate thing that pioneer conditions were as difficult as they were, if there is any truth in theories of heredity, for the weak, diseased, and unenterprising were not preserved. The strong and competent survived, and if this manner of separating sheep from goats put too great a premium on sheer physical health, that at least was something well worth distinguishing and preserving. There was a speedy winnowing of the vast influx of riffraff which descended on the settlements; the residue, such as it was, became the American people.

THE NUMBER AND DISTRIBUTION
OF INDENTURED SERVANTS

Some of the most obvious and important questions about indentured servants are the most difficult to answer. How many of them came to the colonies, and how did the number compare with that of free emigrants? How were they distributed among the colonies, and what proportion of the population of each consisted of servants? Needless to say, there are no complete statistics of population and immigration for the colonial period; those which do exist are very inadequate, and many of them do not fit together acceptably. Yet a few figures can be collected, and since some of the most interesting of them have not previously been printed, it seems worth while to put them together in this appendix, and afterwards see what conclusions may be derived from them. For the most part only those which specifically mention servants will be included, but in the case of the Germans and Irish it is necessary to work from statistics of general migration because practically no others are obtainable. First will be given data on emigration from Europe, then the available information for each colony will be summarized separately.

a. 1654-1686. Emigration of Servants from Bristol.

The following figures (on facing page 309) were taken from the "Tolzey Book," in the Bristol City Archives. For an explanation of this record see above, page 71.

For the years 1655 to 1678 the average annual emigration of servants from Bristol was almost exactly 400.

No other evidence exists by which the accuracy of these statistics may be checked. One may be sure that the figures are no larger than they should be; it is not so certain whether or not they are smaller. I believe them to be substantially correct, but the destinations seem a bit open to suspicion. Those servants bound for the West Indies doubtless went there, but it seems unlikely that so many went to Nevis and so few to Jamaica, or that so many went to Virginia and so few to Maryland.

b. 1684. Emigration of servants from London.

From September 1, 1683, to August 31, 1684, the magistrates at the Middlesex Guildhall recorded the indentures of 641 servants: 249 for Maryland, 172 for Virginia, 104 for Barbados, 72 for Jamaica, and the rest for other colonies. During the same period, the mayor of the City of London approved 123 indentures: 51 for Maryland, 40 for Virginia, 11 for Pennsylvania, and the rest elsewhere.

Total emigration of servants from London in this year: 764.

These figures certainly represent something less than the actual number of servants departing. Those from Middlesex were obtained by tabulating data from the file of indenture forms kept by the clerk; each form is numbered, and it is plain that many are missing, so that the proper total should probably be about 800 for Middlesex alone. The mayor of the City appar-

Year	Vir- ginia	Bar- bados	Nevis	New Eng- land	Jamaica	Mary- land	other colonies	destination not given	Total
1654*	40	16	1	—	—	—	—	—	57
1655	115	150	2	—	—	—	1	1	269
1656	136	194	—	—	—	—	—	6	336
1657	79	357	2	1	—	—	2	176	617
1658	172	273	27	6	—	—	17	276	771
1659	254	415	11	—	—	1	—	105	786
1660	167	277	72	—	—	4	14	58	592
1661	334	117	233	—	—	—	13	18	715
1662	510	105	179	27	13	4	4	—	842
1663	157	61	130	28	—	4	18	1	399
1664	120	62	54	11	—	—	10	1	258
1665	241	24	29	1	1	2	10	—	308
1666	255	70	2	3	—	4	—	—	334
1667	221	106	22	1	—	—	—	—	350
1668	280	83	18	9	—	2	—	—	392
1669	199	43	72	11	7	—	1	—	333
1670	158	45	75	9	10	14	14	4	329
1671	147	41	63	8	14	4	5	3	285
1672	192	10	20	—	7	16	8	1	254
1673	63	12	9	—	2	5	—	1	92
1674	186	46	108	13	—	6	2	3	365
1675	283	22	48	12	10	9	9	—	393
1676	158	27	9	—	9	13	3	4	223
1677	120	22	10	2	32	9	6	—	201
1678	133	12	16	7	—	5	4	1	178
1679†	37	15	21	8	6	—	5	1	93
1680	45	6	5	—	7	16	—	—	79
1684‡	24	33	4	1	49	9	11	—	131
1685	47	17	5	1	299	10	9	—	388
1686§	1	17	—	3	2	—	1	—	24
TOTALS	4874	2678	1247	162	468	137	167	661	10,394

*Entries begin September 25.

†From this point the books are incomplete. Figures for 1679 are to August 27.

‡From April.

§To June 12. In the column headed "other colonies" are included 67 servants going to St. Christopher, 35 to Montserrat, 31 to Antigua, 14 to Newfoundland, 3 to New York, and 17 to Pennsylvania. The 299 going to Jamaica in 1685 may have been Monmouth rebels.

ently kept no special record of servants indentured, and the figures were compiled from entries in his "Waiting Book," which may or may not be complete. For explanations of these recordings see above, pp. 78-79.

c. 1697-1707. Emigration of servants from Liverpool.

See below, p. 355, n. 30 for a description of this record. About 1,500 servants were registered as departing for the colonies during this period.

This record is not clear enough to permit a tabulation of dates and destinations which would be accurate. It is plain, however, that the registration was not systematically made, and one cannot assume that it is nearly complete, especially after 1701, when names become scanty. Probably half the total number of servants were registered in 1698, 1699, and 1700. It may be inferred from this evidence that the annual emigration of servants from Liverpool about the turn of the century was at least 200.

d. 1720-1732. Emigration of Servants from London.

The following figures are tabulated from "A Register of the Names and Surnames of those persons who have Voluntarily Contracted & bound themselves to go beyond the Seas into his Majestys Colonys and Plantations in America and Certified to the sessions according to the directions of the Statute in that case made and provided." Found at the Guildhall, London. See above, p. 81.

Destination	Number	Destination	Number
Maryland	918	Barbados	31
Maryland or Virginia	44	Jamaica	1146
Virginia	223	Antigua	165
Pennsylvania . . .	423	St. Lucia (in 1723) .	24
Carolinas	27	Nevis	22
New England . . .	32	elsewhere and uncertain	202
		Total . 3,257	

This registry book commences with scattering entries from 1718, which are not included in the tabulation. Dates are not clear enough so that an annual tabulation would be accurate, but there is no very wide variation from year to year, and the annual number departing must have been very close to 300.

e. 1736. Emigration of servants from London.

After the conclusion of the registry book summarized in the last section, a few loose forms of indenture remain from subsequent years, but only from 1736 are there enough to make a tabulation worth while. 222 servants were registered that year, of whom 169 were for Jamaica. It is extremely unlikely that the figure is complete, but the proportion going to Jamaica is interesting.

f. 1718-1772. Annual transportation of convicts from London and the Home Circuit.

Taken from the Treasury Money Books, in the Public Record Office. These figures may be accepted as complete, but it must be carefully noted that they apply only to London and

Date	Number	Date	Number	Date	Number	Date	Number
1719	301	1732	220	1746	272	1760	178
1720	207	1733	162	1747	149	1761	216
1721	181	1734	349	1748	280	1762	216
1722	300	1735	149	1749	440	1763	364
1723	271	1736	463	1750	557	1764	513
1724	308	1737	202	1751	312	1765	424
1725	341	1738	378	1752	475	1766	480
1726	282	1739	348	1753	367	1767	516
1727	309	1740	421	1754	417	1768	569
1728	241	1741	327	1755	333	1769	521
1729	250	1742	306	1756	317	1770	475
1730	338	1743	277	1757	274	1771	295
1731	319	1744	265	1758	332	1772	228
		1745	138	1759	240		

Total 17,470.   Number of shiploads   190

the Home Counties, not to the rest of Great Britain and Ireland.

The contract expired in 1772; figures for that year are therefore incomplete. The dates are of sailings; hence a variation in numbers from one year to the next does not mean much, as a ship leaving in January or February would take felons from the previous year's condemnations. Attention may be called, however, to the lower numbers carried during war times; this was due to the fact that many were used in the army.

g. 1774. Emigration from England.

Beginning in December, 1773, and continuing to May, 1775, records of emigration from Great Britain were kept by customs officials and are among the Treasury Papers. Those for Scotland are of little use in a study of servants. Those from England are printed in the *New England Historical and Genealogical Register,* Volumes 62 to 65, *passim.* Here are presented tabulations only from those of the calendar year 1774; that of servants from London is taken from George, *London Life in the XVIIIth Century,* p. 145

SERVANTS				TO			
FROM	Mary-land	Vir-ginia	Phila-delphia	Georgia	Caro-lina	Ja-maica	TOTAL
London	1,124	548	456	35	23	8	2,194
Bristol	119		40				159
Liverpool			4				4
							2,357

Free emigrants: from London, 492; from other ports, 858.

The most striking thing about these figures is the relatively large number of indentured servants sailing from London, as compared with free emigrants. Many of those who were free were children, travelling with their parents, others were colonists returning after a visit home, a few were leaving for the continent of Europe. Hence the true proportion of servants is even greater than the figures show. As for those leaving from other ports, it is not necessarily true that so large a proportion were free; they are not described as under indenture however, and so are counted as being their own masters.

It does not seem to me that these statistics are accurate for ports other than London. Reference to statistics for Maryland shown below will indicate how far they may be checked; and will show also that this was a year of very heavy emigration, which cannot be taken as typical of the century.

II. EMIGRATION FROM IRELAND

a. 1725-1727.

W. H. G. Flood, in the *Journal of the Irish American Historical Society,* XXVI (1927), 204, after examining the files of the Dublin newspapers, writes: "Between the years 1725 and 1727 there are records of about 5000 persons emigrating including 3500 from Ulster, many of whom had contracted with masters of ships for four years' servitude."

b. 1725-1728.

Archbishop Boulter stated in 1728 that "above 3200" had been shipped off in three years, and that only one in ten could pay his own passage. Hanna, *Scotch-Irish,* II, 180.

c. 1725-1768.

"A writer in the *Dublin University Magazine* for 1832" calculates that from 3,000 to 6,000 annually emigrated in these years. *Ibid.,* I, 622.

d. 1750-1800.

200,000 emigrated during this half-century; and during the three years 1771-1773, by exact statistics, 28,600. Sir Thomas

Newenham, *A Statistical and Historical Inquiry into the Progress and Magnitude of the Population of Ireland* (London, 1805), pp. 59, 60.

e. *1773.*

Emigrations from Ireland, from August 3 to November 29, according to statistics "taken in Philadelphia, and the other Towns, upon the Emigrants being landed there, and transmitted by the Isabella, Capt. Fleming." *Gentleman's Magazine,* XLIV (1774), 332.

At New York	1,611
At Philadelphia	2,086
Charles-town	966
New-Jersey	326
Halifax	516
Newport, Rhode Isl.	717
	6,222

f. *1769-1774.*

July 25, 1769, to June 25, 1774. 152 ships sailed to America with passengers from Londonderry, Belfast, Newry, Larne, and Portrush. Total tonnage, 43,720, and "the number of emigrants is supposed fully to equal the number of tons of shipping." *Gentleman's Magazine,* XLIV (1774), 332.

Except for the quotations under *d* and *e,* the above figures are all estimates, rather than exact statistics. They are by no means the only estimates available, but are given here as perhaps the most reliable guides in forming some idea of the volume of migration. There is no definite clue whatever to the proportion of these people who were servants or redemptioners.

III. EMIGRATION FROM GERMANY

a. *1750.*

2480 emigrants went from Wuerttemberg to America. Daniel Haeberle, *Auswanderung . . . der Pfaelzer im 18 Jahrhundert* (1909), p. 304.

b. 1752.

The following ships cleared at Gosport with Germans for America. (Dick to the Board of Trade, December 22, 1752. C.O. 217/13, H. 106.)

	No. of Ships	No. of Freights
Nova Scotia	5	868½
Philadelphia	9	2344
Charleston	7	1713
Maryland	1	262
Boston	1	271½
New York	2	421
Georgia	1	137
Total	26	6016

c. 1765.

"The transporting of Germans to America, which was interrupted during the course of the last war, began again last summer, when above 4,000 Persons young and old, were Shiped here, mostly for Pensilvania and Maryland." (Report from the British Consul at Rotterdam. C.O. 388/95.)

Practically all estimates of the volume of German migration in the colonial period have depended on Philadelphia statistics, for which see below. The above figures, especially those in section *b,* are thus interesting. Since Dick wrote to the Board in order to prove that his own ships, departing for Nova Scotia, had not been late, he gives the dates of sailing of all ships cited. His figures are almost the only ones to show that Germans went in considerable numbers to other ports than Philadelphia; he tends to confirm the opinion of A. B. Faust, that the number arriving by sea in South Carolina has been underestimated (*Pennsylvania Magazine of History,* LIX [1935], 435). But Dick's letter does not by any means show all the ships with

Germans which went to America in that year; nineteen arrived in Philadelphia alone, as shown by the lists in R. B. Strassburger, *Pennsylvania German Pioneers,* ed. by William J. Hinks for Pennsylvania German Society, *Proceedings,* XLII (Norristown, Pa., 1934). Only one of the ships listed by Dick as going to Philadelphia fails to appear in the lists published by Strassburger; from the eight other ships, which Dick describes as carrying 2179 "freights" to Philadelphia, only 826 persons took the oath upon arrival. When it is remembered that 2,179 "freights" may have meant nearly 3,000 "souls," this proportion appears smaller than the editors of those lists decided was usual (*ibid.,* I, xxxi). Our examples here are too few, of course, to refute their calculations.

IV. SERVANTS IN NEW ENGLAND

a. 1620-1650.

Charles Henry Pope, listing the names of about 6,000 persons in Massachusetts during this period, found the social position of 471 specified in the records; of these 240 were described as servants or laborers. *The Pioneers of Massachusetts* (Boston, 1900), p. 524.

b. 1665.

4,000 servants in New England (an estimate). Greene and Harrington, *American Population before the Federal Census of 1790,* p. 9. See also the quotations above, pp. 28-29.

c. 1676.

". . . no servants but on hired wages, except a few who serve four years for the charge of being transported thither. . . ." Edward Randolph, in *C.S.P. Colonial, 1675-1676,* no. 1067.

d. 1708.

Rhode Island, census. 1,015 freemen; 1,362 militia; 56 white servants; 426 black servants; total inhabitants 7,181. Greene and Harrington, p. 62.

e. 1716.

New Hampshire, "very few white servants." *Ibid.,* p. 71.

f. 1717-1718.

Arrival of servants at Boston. Governor Shute, answering the Board of Trade's inquiries as to the number of servants arriving, gave the account from June 29, 1717, to June 29, 1718, as 113 males and 13 females. Of these, 61 came from England, 5 from France, 9 from Ireland, 5 from Glasgow, 21 from Jersey, and the rest from other colonies. The governor said that there had been no great difference for the seven years last past. C.O. 5/867, f.310.

V. NEW YORK AND NEW JERSEY

For these colonies there are no statistics whatever which throw any light on the numbers of servants, and no records of immigration of more than fragmentary nature. See McKee, *Labor in Colonial New York,* p. 93.

VI. PENNSYLVANIA AND DELAWARE

Statistics for immigration to Philadelphia abound, and estimates are even more plentiful, but when put all together they are extremely confusing, and few of them are very helpful on the question of how many passengers were indentured. The following examples illustrate the possibilities, and include the most reliable sources, but I have not tried to include every estimate that has been made. First come a few general statistics, then some concerning Irish immigration, and lastly those of German arrivals.

a. 1729, June 16, to 1735, August 25. Port of Newcastle.

"An account of the Numbers of Passengers landed at the Port of New Castle...."

In the year 1729 . . Passengers . .	1376
1730	539

1731	.	.	.	.	.	.	.	85
1732	.	.	.	.	.	.	.	244
1733	.	.	.	.	.	.	.	330
1734	.	.	.	.	.	.	.	505
1735 till the 25th August					.	.	588

3667

Penn Papers: Papers Relating to the Three Lower Counties, p. 175, Historical Society of Pennsylvania.

Though these figures are for "passengers" it is notable that the account is sworn to by one David French of Newcastle, who said that it had been taken from the books of Robert Gordon, Esq., late collector of the duties imposed on convicts and servants imported into this country. Compare this with the next quotation.

b. 1729.

"In New Castle government there arrived last year, says the Gazette, forty-five hundred persons, chiefly from Ireland; and at Philadelphia, in one year, 267 English and Welsh, 43 Scotch—all servants; also, 1155 Irish, and 243 Palatines, of whom none were servants." Watson, *Annals of Philadelphia,* II, 266.

"New-Castle, August 14, [1729.] There is come in this last week about 2000 Irish People, and abundance more are daily expected. In one Ship about 100 of them dyed in their passage hither. It is computed that there is about 6000 come into this River since April last." Quoted from *The New-England Weekly Journal,* August 25, 1729, in *New Jersey Archives,* 1st ser., XI, 185.

c. 1773, May 12 to October 4. Philadelphia.

During this period, 3511 persons came into Philadelphia, of whom 1127 were Germans and 1774 Irish. From "another Book of this Year" 1486 immigrants are added to the total number, but nationalities are not distinguished.

These figures are taken from the first page of a manuscript volume, "Record of Servants & Apprentices Bound & Assign'd before John Gibson Esq. Mayor, Dec. 5, 1772 to May 21, 1773." (Historical Society of Pennsylvania, Am. 3795.) This volume appears to be a rough draft of the transactions between those dates which were afterwards entered into the larger record now preserved by the American Philosophical Society and printed in the Pennsylvania German Society, *Proceedings,* XVI (1907). On its first page is entered a list of vessels arriving between May 12 and October 4, with no year given. By comparing the names of these ships with the lists published in *Pennsylvania German Pioneers,* the correct year may be established. The figures are probably accurate, but there is no reason to believe that they represent only redemptioners.

   d. 1729, June, to 1735, September.

   "Passengers & Servants imported from Ireland . . ."

In June 1729	1865
1730 noe Account	
In 1731	271
1732 noe Account	
In 1733	322
In 1734	755
In 1735	343

Penn and Baltimore MSS, p. 167, Historical Society of Pennsylvania. The statistics are written on a small piece of paper; no source is given, and no reason why they should have been written down. They are contemporary, however, and reasonable, and hence I give them for what they may be worth.

   e, 1745.

      In the record of "Servants and Apprentices Bound and Assigned before James Hamilton, Mayor of Philadelphia, 1745" are the names of 736 persons, most of whom were newly arrived redemptioners. 529 of these were Irish. M. J. O'Brien, in *Journal of the American Irish Historical Society,* XXVII (1928), 179.

Further statistics and estimates of Irish immigration to Philadelphia can be found in another article by Father O'Brien, *ibid.,* XXII (1923), 132-41. It must be said, nevertheless, that his conclusions are to be viewed with much scepticism. For example, the first article cited establishes that 72 per cent of all persons bound before Mayor Hamilton in 1745 were Irish, and infers that such a percentage might hold for the whole century. The fact is that 1745 was a year when no German ships whatever arrived; hence any figures for that year are very far from being typical of the century. In the second article much is made of the fact that vessels from Ireland came from the south rather than from Ulster, as evidenced by customs records showing their port of clearance. The port of clearance, however, is no very good indication of where the passengers came from; for example most German ships cleared from Cowes, and if we applied Father O'Brien's test to learn how many Germans came in we should scarcely realize that there were any at all. Of course the test works much better for Irish than for German immigrants, but that is not a good reason for working it too hard.

f. 1727-1776. Germans Arriving in Philadelphia.

Total, 65,040. (R. B. Strassburger, *Pennsylvania German Pioneers,* I, xxxi.)

From 1727 incoming Germans were required to be registered and to take an oath before the mayor of Philadelphia, or another constituted official. Various lists made in the course of these transactions have survived. It is plain that not all German passengers signed these lists; the number coming on 178 ships is known, however, and proves to be 2½ times as many as signed the lists for those ships. Hence by multiplying the total number shown on the lists for this period by 2½, the figure given above is reached.

These are the most reliable statistics available for any colonial immigration over a considerable period of time; the lists are scrupulously edited, and all the information sound. Nevertheless, I am convinced that the total number given by the editors is definitely too small. The statistics cited above from John

Dick's letter to the Board of Trade tend to prove this; the figures cited in the next section below, if accepted as accurate, tend the same way. But the principal argument for a higher total is that the editors of these lists, though stating that the number of passengers on 178 ships was known, were not quite accurate; in a considerable number of cases, what they knew was not the number of passengers, but the number of "whole freights," which was quite a different matter, counting as it did only those over fourteen separately.

g. 1740-1750. Germans arriving in Philadelphia.

"A List of the Number of Palatines arrived in the Port of Philadelphia from the Commencement of the Year 1740 to 19th November 1750."

1740 . . . 870					
1741 . . . 1500	To be added				
1742 . . . 890	1741 . . . 620				
1743 . . . 970	1742 . . . 550				
1744 . . . 1609	1743 . . . 1200				
1745 . . . 0000	1747 . . . 1000				
1746 . . . 676	1748 . . . 1500				
1747 . . . 300					
1748 . . . 1061	4870				
1749 . . . 8778	20523				
1750 . . . 3869					
20,523	25,393				

Penn MSS.: Land Grants, VII, 73, Historical Society of Pennsylvania.

There is no indication of the source from which these figures were taken, nor of the name of the writer, nor of the purpose for which they were written; which means, of course, that it is almost impossible to receive these figures with any confidence. Yet they are correct in showing that no Germans arrived in

1745, and also in putting the largest importations in 1749. Furthermore, if these figures be checked with the Strassburger lists for 1750 (up to November 19), it will be found that they agree as exactly as they possibly could, in view of the fact that "freights" and not passengers are given. I believe them to be accurate.

This leaves a considerable discrepancy between the two sets of figures for 1749. The editor of *Pennsylvania German Pioneers* states (I, xxxi.) that in 1749 twenty-two ships arrived, bringing 6,787 Germans, and that the largest number on any ship was 550. He deals harshly with the historian Proud for reporting that there were twenty-five ships, bringing about 12,000 souls, and some of them carrying six hundred each. The manuscript of the statistics we have quoted above appears to indicate that there were twenty-five ships in 1749; in fact *Pennsylvania German Pioneers* itself lists twenty-four, for there are two noted on page 409 which did not immediately land their passengers because of sickness, and which the editor ignored in his summary. Furthermore, in stating that there were only 6,787 passengers the editor was also wrong, for he used statistics for passengers on only twelve ships, while on nine he took "freights," and on one it was necessary to make an estimate. Finally, the largest number of "freights" on one ship was 550, which probably meant at least six hundred passengers; another ship came with 503 "freights," which must have been nearly six hundred. Perhaps Proud was not ill-informed after all, but we must still doubt his 12,000 total; I think that the 8,778 given above is nearer than the 6,787 given in *Pennsylvania German Pioneers*.

It is difficult to discover just what relation the number of freights generally had to the number of passengers because so few examples can be found when both figures are given. For nine ships, five of which were sent from Rotterdam to Halifax by John Dick with Germans, and four of which come from the lists in *Pennsylvania German Pioneers,* the ratio works out at 1.28 passengers for every 8 freight. This is far too small a sampling to prove a rule, but we may be justified in believing that the total number of Germans coming to Philadelphia was nearer 75,000 than 65,000.

How many of these Germans were redemptioners? Unhappily, this question cannot be answered definitely. The concensus of opinion as summarized by Herrick, *White Servitude in Pennsylvania,* p. 177, has been that half or more of them discharged their debt by servitude; Geiser believed that two-thirds did so. I have found little or nothing to support or detract from these conclusions. Two slight indications may be submitted nevertheless. On September 30, 1772, the ship *Minerva* arrived from Rotterdam with 97 freights; she was the first of the season. Before October 16, when the next ship came with Germans, 51 persons from Rotterdam registered their indentures before Mayor Gibson. (See *Pennsylvania German Pioneers,* I, 739-40, and Pennsylvania German Society, *Proceedings,* XVI, pp. 134-40.) It is fair to conclude that at least 51 persons out of 97 freights were redemptioners. The same plan followed with the first of the 1773 ships shows that 126 persons out of 193 freights were redemptioners. The obvious method of ascertaining how many Germans arrived during the whole period of Mayor Gibson's entry book, and comparing them with German names in the book, is impossible.

VII. MARYLAND

a. 1633-1680. Immigration of servants.

Total, about 21,000. This figure is taken from the records in the Land Office, Annapolis, where in twenty-six volumes are registered the names of more than 21,000 immigrants for whose importation a headright of fifty acres each was claimed. Practically all are described as servants. It is unlikely that all arrivals were registered, as headrights became a drug on the market (see McCormac, *White Servitude in Maryland,* pp. 17ff.) If we assume that the annual immigration of servants was about 500 by the year 1670, some checks will be provided by the quotations given below.

b. 1660.

1,078 servants in a population of 12,000. Estimate by McCormac, pp. 28-29.

c. 1698. Servants imported.

600 or 700 servants, "chiefly Irish" were imported during the year. Estimate of the governor, *C.S.P. Colonial,* 1697-1698, p. 390.

To November 1, 1698, there were 901 servants imported, according to the Naval Officers account, kept for the sake of levying the duty on servants. From a Journal of the committee appointed to inspect the public accounts of the revenue of the province, in C.O. 5/749, no. 6.

d. 1707. Census.

33,833 souls; 3,003 servants; 4,657 slaves. Greene and Harrington, p. 124. N.B. To maintain a population of 3,000 servants, with an average term of five years each, would require an annual importation of 600.

e. 1755. Census.

98,357 free whites; 6,871 servants; 1,981 convicts; 3,592 mulattoes; 42,764 Negroes.

f. 1752-1755. German Immigration.

1,060 arrived. Society for the History of Germans in Maryland, *Fifth Annual Report,* p. 19. This is an underestimate, based on the Port Books. Newspapers show more cargoes of Germans arriving; Scharf estimated that at least 3,000 came in 1752-1754 (*History of Maryland,* I, 373).

g. *1745-1775. Immigration of servants, mainly to the port of Annapolis.*

The following figures were tabulated from the Naval Officer's Returns, of which two volumes are at the Mary-

Year	from London	from Bristol	from Ireland	from Gt. Britain other ports	Total servants	Convicts	Total servants and convicts
1745	—	—	218	63	281	—	281
1746	—	—	124	—	124	7	131
1747	—	—	29	4	33	21	54
1748	—	—	—	3	3	153	156
1749	—	43	—	—	43	222	265
1750	2	40	—	29	71	225	296
1751	262	7	—	8	277	206	483
1752	120	30	—	31	181	297	478
1753	126	—	199	—	325	465	790
1754	233	118	39	—	390	352	742
1755	153	107	34	7	301	366	667
1756	43	53	1	1	98	298	396
1757	8	18	—	39	65	459	524
1758	3	2	—	—	5	133	138
1759	3	—	—	—	3	321	324
1760	1	7	—	—	8	197	205
1761	—	3	—	—	3	159	162
1762	11	—	—	—	11	215	226
1763	20	—	—	—	20	81	101
1764	157	—	55	—	212	164	376
1765	15	—	40	—	55	464	519
1766	—	—	176	61	237	564	801
1767	78	1	189	35	303	430	733
1768	185	—	139	92	416	581	997
1769	152	12	237	54	455	498	953
1770	156	35	553	—	744	362	1106
1771	9	22	667	21	719	288	1007
1772	43	13	636	2	694	320	1014
1773	304	17	616	75	1012	589	1601
1774	910	101	1175	83	2269	507	2776
1775*	415	78	708	1	1202	416	1618
	3,409	707	5,835	609	10,560	9,360	19,920

*To October 1.

land Historical Society, Baltimore, and one at the Hall of Records, Annapolis. Others are in the Public Record Office, but do not add any statistics on this matter.

The figures given in this table are by no means complete for the colony of Maryland. Except for a few years when returns from Port Oxford and Patuxent are available, the records cover only the port of Annapolis, and that not completely. The *Maryland Gazette* published notices during the early 1750's of ships arriving with servants or convicts, and from these notices several hundred servants were added to the list, though they did not appear in the Returns. The *Gazette* soon ceased to print more than a very occasional notice of a servant ship's arrival, and hence further checking is impossible. Sometimes a convict ship, whose name we know from the London records, is entered in the Naval Officer's Returns without any mention of its human cargo; the *Gazette,* however, confirms the arrival of the felons.

As for servants entering other ports than Annapolis, we know only from various examples that they did so, and that they were not recorded by the Naval Officer. For instance, the brig *Grove,* owned by Samuel Galloway, came in several times from London during the early 1750's with servants which were sold in the West River, and advertised in the *Gazette.* After finishing the sales the *Grove* proceeded to Annapolis, and registered as arriving from London in ballast. Likewise the *Charles,* from London with forty-five servants, took them to "Patapsco," but registered at Annapolis as arriving in ballast. Were there no other proof, a reference to the census of 1755, showing 6,871 servants in the colony, would demonstrate that the annual immigration must have been far greater than that shown in our table, even granting that many came in overland after disembarking at Philadelphia.

Nevertheless these figures are valuable. They illustrate the numbers of Irish coming; the remarkable falling off during the Seven Years' War, and the even more remarkable increases of the early 1770's. One check may be applied to them which works fairly well. According to the Treasury figures for 1774, cited above, 1,124 servants left London for Maryland during that calendar year. These began to arrive during March, and if we add together all servants from London registered in the returns from March 1, 1774 to March 31, 1775, the figure is 817. Apparently about 300 servants died during the voyage, went to a different colony than they were registered for, or entered Maryland at a port other than Annapolis.

The convict statistics seem rather more satisfactory, and doubtless more care was used in collecting them. They may be checked from the census of 1755, which showed 1,981 convicts doing their time in Maryland; during the seven years before 1755 the returns show the entry of 1,920 felons. Some of these died, some ran away, and on the other hand a number of fourteen-year exiles from previous shipments were still serving their time. The figures agree well enough to indicate that nearly all convicts must have entered at Annapolis and been properly registered at least in those years.

The preceding table gave total figures for convict importations to allow comparison with figures for servants. We now present a table showing the ports from which these convicts came, most useful as indicating the number from Bristol, for which no English statistics were available. It must also be remembered that those coming from London were shipped not only by the Treasury contractors, but also by such men as Sydenham who disposed of those from the Midlands and the south coast. Of the total of 5,428 coming from London, only 2,881 are in fact specifically noted as coming on ships owned by Reid and Stewart, the Treasury contractors, but it may be presumed that these contractors often shipped on vessels belonging to others. This can be proved in a few instances by comparing the names of ships in the Treasury Money Books with those in the Maryland Returns, and checking the owners.

h. 1746-1778. Convicts entering Maryland.

From the Naval Officer's Returns, supplemented in a few cases by the *Maryland Gazette.* (See facing page 329.)

Again it must be said that this list cannot be taken as complete. For example, the *Dolphin,* Captain Dougal McDougal, sailed from London with 141 convicts on June 2, 1764. She is registered in the Annapolis returns as arriving on August 14, but no mention of convicts is made in the record. Thus these 141 are not included in the above table, though it is morally certain that they came to Maryland. For 1763, on the other hand, though the same ship is recorded as arriving in the same way, the greater number of London felons went on two vessels which sailed to Virginia, and are recorded as entering by the Naval Officer's Returns from Rappahannock and South Potomac respectively.

VIII. VIRGINIA

a. 1624-1625. Census.

Total population, 1,227; servants, 487; Negroes, 23. Greene and Harrington, p. 144.

b. 1665.

10,000 servant men. *Ibid.,* p. 136.

c. 1671.

6,000 servants in a total population of 40,000, with 2,000 black slaves. Estimate of Governor Berkeley, *ibid.,* p. 136. Professor Wertenbaker, using the Land Books, computed that the annual immigration throughout this period remained be-

Year	from London	from Bristol	from other ports in Great Britain	from Ireland	Totals
1746	—	—	7	—	7
1747	—	—	18	3	21
1748	114	—	39	—	153
1749	176	35	11	—	222
1750	113	33	79	—	225
1751	170	34	2	—	206
1752	179	46	51	21	297
1753	287	75	68	35	465
1754	200	117	35	—	352
1755	209	93	64	—	366
1756	213	79	2	4	298
1757	248	206	5	—	459
1758	8	109	16	—	133
1759	226	83	12	—	321
1760	92	97	8	—	197
1761	115	44	—	—	159
1762	138	77	—	—	215
1763	41	38	2	—	81
1764	64	100	—	—	164
1765	210	254	—	—	464
1766	359	179	26	—	564
1767	209	214	7	—	430
1768	357	224	—	—	581
1769	351	124	3	20	498
1770	173	188	1	—	362
1771	162	104	22	—	288
1772	103	203	14	—	320
1773	303	246	40	—	589
1774	342	136	29	—	507
1775*	266	141	9	—	416
	5,428	3,279	570	83	9,360

*To October 1.

tween 1,500 and 2,000, and that about 1,500 annually were servants (*Planters of Colonial Virginia,* p. 41).

   d. 1681.

         15,000 servants in a total population of 70,000 or
80,000. Estimate of Lord Culpeper, in Greene and Harrington,
p. 137.

These are all the statistics which are available to indicate
the numbers of servants in Virginia. Of them, only those under
a and *c* are generally considered reliable. For the eighteenth
century practically no guide is offered by the various censuses
and estimates; nor did the Naval Officers register the arrival
of servants except in a very few cases, apparently almost acci-
dentally. The following quotations, however, are of some use.

   e. 1708.

         ". . . the number of white servants is so incon-
siderable that they scarce deserve notice, so few having been
imported since the beginning of this war." Col. Jenings to the
Board of Trade, *C.S.P. Colonial,* 1708-1709, no. 216.

   f. 1724.

         "These Servants are but an insignificant Number,
when compared with the vast *Shoals* of Negroes. . . ." Hugh
Jones, *Present State of Virginia,* p. 114.

   g. 1730.

         Governor Gooch, giving an account of the popu-
lation to the Board of Trade, says that it is increasing, and
speaks of "the great numbers of negroes and white servants
imported since 1720." *C.S.P. Colonial,* 1730, p. 217.

   h. 1765.

         ". . . the number of Convicts and Indented serv-
ants imported to virginia [is] amazing, besides the numbers of
Dutch and German which is also Considerable." "Journal of a
French Traveller in the Colonies, 1765," *American Historical
Review,* XXVI, 744.

From the same journal may be quoted some more general remarks. "It is Computed that there are at least ten thousand Convicts and passengers, or indented Servants, imported yearly into the Different Colonies, the first are Sent to Virginia and maryland only, and likewise Indented servants; But the Colonies to the Northward of maryland admit no Convicts, but Serv'ts as many as will Come. there has Come to philadel'a alone, 5000 in one year, ¾ of which were from Ireland, great numbers of Dutch and germans; . . ." *Ibid.*, XXVII, 84.

IX. CAROLINA

a. To 1676. Up to this year land was claimed by planters for the importation of about 200 servants. A. S. Salley, ed., *Warrants for Lands in South Carolina,* I, 1-125.

b. 1703. South Carolina census.

Freeman, 1,460; free women, 940; white men servants, 110; white women servants, 90; white children, 1,200; Negroes, 3,000. Greene and Harrington, p. 173.

c. 1708. South Carolina census.

Freemen, 1,360; free women, 900; men servants, 60; women servants, 60; children, 1,700; Negroes, 4,100. *Ibid.*

These are all the statistics available for Carolina. They show why the laws of 1712 and 1716 to encourage the importation of white servants became necessary. The number of references to individual shipments of servants to Carolina is large enough to indicate that a considerable number went there, despite the scantiness of statistics.

Perhaps the best opinion of the importance of white servitude in the continental plantation colonies may be formed by contemplating the following figures of black and white population for the year 1755. That of Maryland is based on a census; the others are estimates, roughly based on numbers of tithables and militia.

Colony	White	Black
Maryland	107,209	42,764
Virginia	173,316	120,156
North Carolina	50,000	30,000
South Carolina	25,000	50,000

Greene and Harrington, pp. 126, 140, 157, 175.

Thus while Maryland had less than half as many Negroes as whites, South Carolina had about twice as many. Even though we cannot distinguish the numbers of servants, the relative importance of white labor becomes fairly clear.

X. GEORGIA AND FLORIDA

a. Georgia.

No good statistics are available for Georgia. A student of the subject decides that during the period of Trust control the ratio of indentured servants to all others was about as one to six. H. B. Fant, in *Georgia Historical Quarterly,* XVI, 3.

b. Florida.

No statistics are available for Florida. After the peace in 1763 the province was thrown open to settlers, headrights were granted, and servants taken in. Most impressive was the venture of Dr. Andrew Turnbull, who brought 1,400 indentured settlers gathered from Mediterranean regions. See W. H. Siebert, "Slavery and White Servitude in East Florida, 1726 to 1776," in the Florida Historical Society *Quarterly,* X (1931-32), 3-23.

XI. BARBADOS

a. 1652.

5,000 freeholders; 5,000 freed servants working for wages; 8,000 servants, mainly Scots and Irish; 20,000 negroes. Estimate in Egerton MSS 2395, f. 625.

b. 1680. Census.

2,193 servants. *C.S.P. Colonial,* 1677-1780, pp. 509-10.

c. 1683-1684.

A statistical account of Barbados, sent to England by the governor.

Free persons, 17,187; servants, 2,381; slaves, 46,602.

During twelve months, 325 freemen came to the island; 385 servants, and 3,995 Negroes. During the same period, 446 free white men left the island, and 307 slaves.

Sloane MSS 2441, ff. 18-20, British Museum.

There are no more statistics concerning servants in Barbados. The heroic measures taken in the last years of the century to encourage the importation of white servants have already been described, but serious depopulation set in nevertheless. In 1684 there were 6,761 white men capable of bearing arms; in 1712 there were only 3,438, though the number of slaves had shrunk only to 41,970. Thereafter, while the number of Negroes climbed steadily throughout the century, the number of white fighting men remained close to 4,000, and the total white population is never again as high as in 1684. See eighteenth-century population tables in the Appendix to Pitman, *Development of the British West Indies*.

XII. THE LEEWARD ISLANDS

The only figures available for servant immigration to these islands are those to be found in the first section of this appendix, listing emigration from England. With them may be compared the following curious statement from Governor Sir Charles Wheler, who was asked in 1670 to state how many people were arriving:

No conjecture can be made of the English, Scotch, and Irish that have come yearly to plant these seven years past, but there have not been six since his arrival, though 40 ships have come and gone, nor has one black or slave been brought these five years. . . . *C.S.P. Colonial,* 1669-1674, no. 680.

This statement was confirmed by Stapleton in 1672 (*ibid.,* No. 896, I.), and yet the impression left from the English figures, and from such sources as the letters of Christopher Jeaffreson is that the immigration of servants must have been fairly steady soon after this time, at least to Antigua (*Young Squire,* I, 207-9).

One set of statistics is worth giving:

List of the Inhabitants of the Leeward Islands
July 18, 1720.

FREE PERSONS				SERVANTS FREE & UNFREE				NEGROES
Men	*Women*	*Boys*	*Girls*	*Men*	*Women*	*Boys*	*Girls*	
2467	2729	2134	2156	731	222	95	73	37477

C.S.P. Colonial, 1720-1721, no. 204, xvi.

XIII. JAMAICA
a. Immigration, June 25, 1671 to March 25, 1679.

5,396 "Christians" and 11,816 slaves. Of the whites, 1,879 were from Barbados or other plantations. C.O. 1/43, No. 37.

This is an annual average of about 700 whites, and from various evidences it may be presumed that about half of these were servants.

b. 1675. Estimates.

From Ireland, by Bristol ships calling there for provisions, have been brought within three or four years, five hundred servants. About 1200 or 1400 men and women come each year from England, "both free and to serve," but at least a quarter of these do not remain. *Journals of the Assembly of Jamaica* (1811), I, Appendix, p. 42.

c. 1679.

"The number of whites is one fifth short of the proportion required by law, viz. one white to ten blacks, which cannot well be made up by servants that come hither for that they make good no more than the deaths and departures of others from the Island." Gov. Lord Carlisle to Sec. Coventry. *C.S.P. Colonial,* 1677-1680, no. 1118.

d. 1730. Census.

2,171 masters and mistresses; 3,009 white men servants; 984 white women servants; 1,484 white children; 74,525 slaves. Pitman, *West Indies,* p. 375.

e. 1739 and 1768.

The historian Long made estimates for the population at these dates, putting the whites in 1739 at 10,080, and in 1768 at 17,949; he stated that about one-third of these were white servants. At the latter date there were 166,914 Negroes. See Pitman, pp. 374-75.

It seems to me quite likely that some of these "servants" were hired overseers rather than indentured workers; hence the census of 1730 distinguishes not "freemen" but rather "masters and mistresses." Long also states that by 1774 the demand for white servants had entirely ceased; in this connection, compare the figures given in section I above, showing 1,146 servants leaving London for Jamaica in 1720-1732, and only 8 in 1774. Apparently a great many went from Ireland also.

CONCLUSIONS

The figures quoted, though adding details, do not modify accepted ideas concerning colonial migration. Four major points may be noted: (1) After about 1689 there was a great falling off in migration from Britain, which lasted until 1768. At the latter date it began to pick up once again, and the greatest English emigration of the colonial period was that from 1770 to 1775.

(2) Beginning in 1728, a vastly increased movement from Ireland began, and by far the greatest number of servants and redemptioners came from that country during the eighteenth century. (3) The German migration, second in volume only to the Irish, began also about 1720, reached its height in the middle of the century, and did not, like the English and Irish, increase during the 1770's. (4) During every period of war there was a marked falling off in migration.

If we exclude the Puritan migrations of the 1630's, it is safe to say that not less than one-half, nor more than two-thirds, of all white immigrants to the colonies were indentured servants or redemptioners or convicts.

During the seventeenth century, the largest movement of servants to the colonies was in the period just before and after the Restoration, but the total number of servants emigrating in one year probably never exceeded 3,500.

During the 1670's there were always between 12,000 and 15,000 servants laboring in the plantations, of whom about 6,000 were in Virginia, 2,000 in Maryland, 2,000 in Barbados, 2,000 in Jamaica, and the rest more or less equally divided between the other southern colonies. About one white person in every ten was under indenture. Thereafter the proportion of servants to the white population declined, though no figures exist by which to measure the rate of decline. After 1750 it again increased, and according to the census of Maryland in 1755 almost one white person in ten is again under indenture, but figures for other colonies do not exist.

The greatest migration of servants to the West Indian colonies, excepting Jamaica, was before 1660, and has left no statistics. After 1670, though servants continued to come, slave labor became relatively far more important, and the emigration of whites from the smaller islands at least equalled the immigration. Considerable numbers of white servants went to Jamaica throughout the first half of the eighteen century.

During the twenty-five years from 1750 to 1775, about 25,000 servants and convicts entered Maryland, mainly from the British Isles. Before 1765 (except perhaps in 1753-55) there were decidedly less than 1,000 a year; after 1765, decidedly more. Immigration to Virginia was not greater, and probably it was less.

During the same period at least twice as many servants and redemptioners entered Pennsylvania, and probably more. Not over a third were Germans; nearly two-thirds were from Ireland.

The number of servants entering New England was negligible after 1645. During the migration of the 1630's there must have been a fair proportion of servants under indenture, but probably considerably less than half.

NOTES

Titles for all works listed in the Bibliographical Note are given in short form. Full bibliographical information is provided for works used only occasionally and, therefore, not discussed in the Bibliographical Note.

PART ONE

CHAPTER I

1. Egerton MSS, 2395, f. 277, British Museum.

2. See C. A. Herrick, *White Servitude in Pennsylvania,* p. 7.

3. Alexander Brown, *Genesis of the United States,* I, 248-49.

4. Nova Britannia, p. 23, in Peter Force, *Tracts,* I.

5. It is computed that up to 1616 there had been 1,650 persons sent to Virginia, of whom nearly 1,000 had died and about 300 returned to England (Brown, II, 782). See W. F. Craven, *Dissolution of the Virginia Company* (New York, 1932), ch. ii.

6. C. M. Andrews, *Colonial Period of American History* (New Haven, 1934), I, 124, 125n; J. C. Ballagh, *White Servitude in Virginia,* p. 21.

7. Susan M. Kingsbury, ed., *Records of the Virginia Company of London,* III, 98-102, cited hereafter as *Virginia Company Records.* See also Craven, ch. iii.

8. Virginia Company Records, III, 314.

9. See below, ch. vii.

10. Virginia Company Records, III, 115, 313, 493-94, 505.

11. Ibid., III, 313.

12. Ibid., III, 221.

13. Ibid., III, 226, 257-58.

14. Historical Manuscripts Commission, *Eighth Report,* Appendix, pt. ii, 39b. The fact was that the company sent far too many emigrants, and encouraged private adventurers to do the same, making inadequate provision for the food and equipment of new arrivals. See Craven, pp. 155-61.

15. Virginia Company Records, I, 351-52, 538; III, 239-40.

16. Craven, pp. 57-64.

17. Virginia Company Records, III, 210-11.

18. Ibid., III, 77. The idea was not new; in the "writing indented" of Sir Humphrey Gilbert in 1582 it was provided that every gentleman bringing five men to the colony at his own charge should have 2,000 acres of land. *Calendar of State Papers Colonial,* Addenda, 1574-1674, no. 16, cited hereafter as *C.S.P. Colonial.*

19. Virginia Company Records, I, 538; II, 350.

20. E. B. Greene and Virginia D. Harrington, *American Population before the Federal Census of 1790* (New York, 1932), p. 144.

21. There are four collections of indentures of sufficient number to make their study conclusive: (1) About 10,000 in the Archives Department of the Council House at Bristol, dating from 1654 to 1684, for which see below, p. 71. (2) Over 700 in the Middlesex Guildhall, 1682-1684; see below, p. 354, n.26. (3) Over 3,000 in the London Guildhall, 1718-1732 and beyond; see below, p. 81. (4) About 2,000 in an entry book of the mayor of Philadelphia, 1771-1773. Only the last is printed, in Pennsylvania German Society, *Publications,* XVI (1907).

22. The facts here briefly stated are discussed, and further particulars given, in chapters x and xi, below.

23. Leo F. Stock, *Proceedings and Debates of the British Parliaments Respecting North America,* I, 291-92 and n. 12, cited hereafter as Stock, *Debates.* The indenture here printed was picked at random from the file of about 700 found at the Middlesex Guildhall. Italicized portions are written in the original by hand. An important point, not always made clear in the contract, was that the stated term of servitude began on the day of the ship's arrival in the colony.

24. "I said, Sir! as you are a Merchant, must needs know the custom of Merchants, that when Servants for Plantations are bound; the Indenture they sign to, is always sent with them to satisfy the Government, and the Persons they are sent to, that thereby they may see when their time is expired, that then they may have their freedom; and for the other Indenture, the party bound takes it in his custody, that by it, when his time is out he may demand his freedom." John Wilmore, *The Case of John Wilmore,* pp. 9-10.

25. John Hammond, *Leah and Rachel* (1656), reprinted in C. C. Hall, ed., *Narratives of Early Maryland,* p. 289.

26. This phrase was generally used, especially in the seventeenth century, and probably because of a dislike of the word "sell" used in connection with the disposal of white men.

27. A. B. Faust, *German Element in the United States,* I, 66; F. R. Diffenderfer, *German Immigration into Pennsylvania,* pt. ii, *The Redemptioners,* p. 174. A redemptioner's agreement is reproduced in Herrick, p. 4. According to an account from the year 1740 it was customary for German redemptioners to pay half their passage on embarking, and to have six weeks after landing to pay the other half. A. D. Candler, ed., *Colonial Records of Georgia,* IV, 672. Hereafter cited as *Georgia Colonial Records.*

28. See, for example, the case of John Harrower, in his "Diary, 1773-1775," *American Historical Review,* VI, 72.

29. Many of the documents concerning this project are in *Selections from the Public Documents of the Province of Nova Scotia,* ed. by Thomas B. Akins, hereafter cited as *Public Documents of Nova Scotia.*

30. Georgia Colonial Records, III, 353.

31. Henry A. M. Smith, "The Orange Quarter and the First French Settlers in South Carolina," *South Carolina Historical and Genealogical Magazine,* XVIII (1917), 101-23. A. H. Hirsch, *Huguenots of Colonial South Carolina,* pp. 12-13. For documents on the 1700 settlement see R. A. Brock, ed., "Documents . . . Relating to the Huguenot Emigration to Virginia," Virginia Historical Society, *Collections,* new ser., V (1886).

32. For de Graffenried, see W. A. Knittle, *Early Eighteenth Century Palatine Emigration,* pp. 99-110. For Pury, see Hirsch, pp. 28-32, and for McCulloch, see W. L. Saunders and Walter Clark, eds., *Colonial Records of North Carolina*, V, xxxii, and William K. Boyd, "Some North Carolina Tracts of the Eighteenth Century," *North Carolina Historical Review*, II (1925), 475-79.

33. *Acts of the Privy Council, Colonial*, IV, 532-34.

34. The information is conveniently collected in Alexander Young, *Chronicles of the First Planters of . . . Massachusetts Bay*. One hundred eighty indentured servants had to be set free to shift for themselves when the Winthrop fleet arrived.

35. J. H. Lefroy, *Memorials of the . . . Bermudas*, I, 165.

36. The books of this company are in the Public Record Office (cited hereafter as P.R.O.), C.O. 124/1 and 124/2, and contain the best material available for a study of "company servitude," but the conclusions to be drawn are essentially the same as those from the Virginia Company's experiments. Some account may be found in A. P. Newton, *Colonizing Activities of the English Puritans*.

37. *Georgia Colonial Records*, II, 275-80, 407. See also H. B. Fant, "The Labor Policy of the Trustees for Establishing the Colony of Georgia," *Georgia Historical Quarterly*, XVI (1932), 1-16.

38. Knittle, ch. vi.

39. *Public Documents of Nova Scotia*, pp. 616-17, 621-22, 677-78. There is also much information on this project in the Board of Trade *Journal*, 1742-1749, pp. 472-73, and *ibid.*, 1750-1753, *passim*.

CHAPTER II

1. Sharpe to John Sharpe, *Archives of Maryland*, VI, 211; Raphael Semmes, *Crime and Punishment in Early Maryland*, p. 278; G. P. Insh, *Scottish Colonial Schemes*, Appendix D; Penn Papers, Official Correspondence, VIII, 25, Historical Society of Pennsylvania. The words of Governor Sharpe and of the president of the Council of Pennsylvania are not to be taken quite at face value, for each was trying to magnify the troubles caused to colonists when their servants were enlisted for service in the British regular army.

2. J. C. Jeaffreson, ed., *A Young Squire of the Seventeenth Century,* I, 257.

3. Egerton MSS, 2395, f. 415 b.

4. *C.S.P. Colonial,* 1722-1723, p. 258.

5. *Journal,* ed. by J. K. Hosmer, II, 228. See a similar complaint by Thomas Lechmere in 1718, quoted in H. J. Ford, *The Scotch-Irish in America* (Princeton, 1915), p. 222. I believe the "servants" of New England were "covenant servants," under contract for a fixed period, paid wages, and rarely bought off servant ships, but nevertheless subject to penalties for breaking the contract. For the typical method of procuring them from Europe, see The Wyllys Papers, Connecticut Historical Society, *Collections,* XXI (1924), 17, 40, 52. See also Albert Matthews, "Hired Man and Help," in Colonial Society of Massachusetts, *Publications,* V (1902), 225-56; and Edmund S. Morgan, "Masters and Servants in Early New England," *More Books: Bulletin of the Boston Public Library,* 6th ser., XVII (1942), 311-28.

6. This point is excellently discussed in L. C. Gray, *History of Agriculture in the Southern United States to 1860,* I, 361-71.

7. *C.S.P. Colonial,* 1675-1676, no. 1022. Dalby Thomas, *An Historical Account of the Rise and Growth of the West-India Collonies,* pp. 14, 21, 28; F. W. Pitman, *Development of the British West Indies,* p. 56 n.

8. George Downing to John Winthrop, Jr., Aug. 26, 1645, Massachusetts Historical Society, *Collections,* 4th ser., VI (1863), 539.

9. ". . . whilst the Richer sort consult their benefitt by serveing themselves cheifly by Slaves." Preamble to "An Act to encourage the bringing in of Christian Servants," C.O. 30/5, f. 44. Yet Jeaffreson's statement quoted above shows that the demand for servants continued in the Leeward Islands.

10. Printed in Insh, Appendix D.

11. *C.S.P. Colonial,* 1675-1676, no. 800. The instructions to the agent are printed in *Interesting Tracts Relating to the Island of Jamaica,* p. 240. A good many similar petitions are brought together in Irish Manuscripts Commission, *Analecta Hibernica,* no. 4 (1932), pp. 265-70.

12. Few of these laws were printed, and they are to be found only in the Public Record Office. References for the laws cited in this paragraph are as follows: Barbados: C.O. 30/2, p. 78; Jamaica: C.O. 139/1, f. 138, renewed in 1673-1674, C.O. 139/3, p. 67; Nevis, Antigua, St. Christopher: C.O. 154/2, pp. 114, 326, 23-24.

13. C.O. 154/2, pp. 340-42.

14. C.O. 30/5, ff. 44-45. Renewed December 19, 1688.

15. C.O. 139/7, pp. 95-97.

16. C.O. 28/3, no. 44. This act was to continue for three years.

17. Some Considerations Humbly Offered to Both Houses of Parliament Concerning the Sugar Colonies (London, 1701), p. 9. For another estimate of £36,000, see *C.S.P. Colonial,* 1699, no. 954 i. Orders to the Treasurer to pay for servants are noted in *C.S.P. Colonial,* 1697-1698, nos. 801, 871.

18. These are described below, pp. 237-38.

19. Montserrat: *Acts . . . 1668 to 1740,* p. 45. Nevis: *Acts,* p. 37. Jamaica: C.O. 324/6, pp. 196-203.

20. C.O. 139/9, f. 89. In 1716 the Council of Jamaica reported that this act had never been put into operation. Pitman, p. 50. There was a good deal of objection to these laws in England, because it was feared that they would encourage kidnapping, and some of them were disallowed. See *C.S.P. Colonial,* 1693-1696, nos. 622, 784, 806; *ibid.,* 1696-1697, no. 381; *ibid.,* 1697-1698, no. 169.

21. See T. D. Jervey, "The White Indented Servants of South Carolina," in *South Carolina Historical Magazine,* XII, 165-66. In 1718 and 1721 it was urged that "deficiency acts" ought to be passed in the colony (*C.S.P. Colonial,* 1719-1720, no. 79; *ibid.,* 1720-1721, p. 425). The only other continental colony to pass an act like these was Massachusetts, which in 1709 offered forty shillings each for male servants; the act to continue for three years (*Acts and Resolves,* I, 634). This may have been suggested by an article attributed to Samuel Sewall, which appeared in the *Boston News Letter* of June 12, 1706, entitled "Computation that the Importation of Negroes is not so profitable as that of White Servants." It is reprinted in *The Historical Magazine, and Notes and Queries,* VIII (1864), 198-99. Whether the act was effective I do not know. When New Jersey imposed a duty on slaves in 1714, Governor Hunter tried to make it appear that the tax was calculated to encourage the importation of white servants (*C.S.P. Colonial,* 1714-1715, no. 35).

22. For an account of these acts and their efficacy, see Pitman, pp. 35-38, 50-55.

23. Tables of population in Pitman, Appendix I. In 1731, despite the general tendency, there were still in Jamaica many Irish, "who come cheap and serve for deficiencys, and their hearts are not with us." *Analecta Hibernica*, no. 4, p. 282, quoting Governor Hunter.

24. See above, p. 343, n. 7.

25. Herrick, *White Servitude in Pennsylvania*, chs. iii, iv, v, reviews exhaustively the causes for the demand for white servants.

26. *Virginia Company Records*, I, 277-78; Board of Trade, *Journal*, 1750-1753, p. 62; *Georgia Colonial Records*, I, 209; II, 115, 117.

27. Board of Trade, *Journal*, 1704-1709, p. 511.

28. Evidence in Ballagh, *White Servitude in Virginia*, p. 41, and P. A. Bruce, *Economic History of Virginia in the Seventeenth Century*, I, 629. There was regularly a fee of 2/6 per passenger to the ship's surgeon.

29. Jonathan Forward chartered a ship to transport 131 servants in 1717 on terms which work out at about £3 each (*Archives of Maryland*, XXV, 426). In the same year it was computed that 500 Palatines could be sent to the Bahamas for £5 each, including clothing, provisions, and medicines (*C.S.P. Colonial*, 1717-1718, no. 76). Jeaffreson and William Bullock both estimated the price of passage as being only half the usual rate for merchants who owned and victualled their own ships. *Young Squire*, II, 102; William Bullock, *Virginia Impartially Examined*, pp. 48-49.

30. Bullock, p. 36.

31. E. Littleton, *Groans of the Plantations*, p. 17. Additional MSS, 11410, p. 532, British Museum; *North Carolina Colonial Records*, I, 987. There is an elaborate estimate of expense in Richard Ligon, *True and Exact History of Barbados*, pp. 113-16.

32. See below, p. 63.

33. The Providence Company once complained that the cost to them of each servant sent to the island was £30, and this despite the fact that the price of passage was only £6, and the equipment for at least one contingent consisted of three canvas suits, three pairs of stockings, three

shirts, and three pairs of shoes per servant (C.O. 1/8, no. 83; C.O. 124/2, pp. 52, 198; C.O. 124/1, f. 86). The Massachusetts Bay Company spent from £16 to £20 on each servant in 1628-1629 (Young, *Chronicles of First Planters,* p. 312).

34. Peter Williamson, *State of the Process, Peter Williamson against William Fordyce, and Others.* I am indebted to Mr. Julian P. Boyd for calling this pamphlet to my attention and allowing me to use a microfilm of it which he had procured. The feeding of twenty-nine servants for one week at the house of Helen Law, in Aberdeen, cost £2.3.6, which was certainly a modest sum.

35. Of many testimonies to this effect, some are collected in *Analecta Hibernica,* no. 4, pp. 265-70. "Scotch-Irish" were much more highly esteemed.

36. This was the ship *Tristram and Jane,* whose account books have been preserved in the High Court of Admiralty Miscellany, H.C.A. 30/635 and 30/636. The average price of the seventy servants sold was 527 pounds of tobacco.

37. See below, p. 66. In 1638 the Providence Company in London insisted that the value of a servant on the island was 150 pounds of tobacco per year of service; the planters on the island set it at only 100 (C.O. 124/2, pp. 343-44).

38. E. I. MacCormac, *White Servitude in Maryland,* p. 42; Ballagh, p. 41; Bruce, II, 51-52.

39. *C.S.P. Colonial,* 1669-1674, no. 277.

40. Charles Leslie, *A New and Exact Account of Jamaica,* p. 16.

41. Stock, *Debates,* IV, 855-56. For the selling price of convicts, see below, pp. 122-23.

42. The Naval Officers' Returns for the port of Annapolis show that 619 ships registered between 1757 and 1775 as coming directly from the British Isles. Of these, 302 carried servants or convicts, and since the officer did not always record a cargo of servants, the actual proportion was probably greater. Of 180 ships from Ireland, only 58 were without servants.

43. John Dick to Hugh Davison (1750), C.O. 217/9, F 160.

44. Evidence on this point is reviewed by Herrick, pp. 201-3. In the

Huntington Library is a "List of Servants belonging to the Inhabitants of Pensilvania, and taken into His Majesty's Service" which gives the amounts of "consideration money" paid for more than 600 servants in the early 1750's, and confirms other evidences. A photostat of this document is in the Historical Society of Pennsylvania.

45. These documents are in the Historical Society of Pennsylvania, "Indentures of Apprentices." John Dick wrote to Hugh Davison, ". . . as to the Currency of Nova Scotia I am quite a Stranger to it but hope you'l take care that I am no Sufferer. the £170 Philadelphia money makes £100 sterling." Dick was at this time sending redemptioners to Halifax for the Board of Trade. For the argument of exploitation, see Herrick, p. 202.

46. For a further discussion of this see below, chs. v-vi.

47. W. C. Ford, ed., *Washington as Employer and Importer of Labor* (Brooklyn, N. Y., 1889), p. 72.

48. Maryland Land Books, Liber 18, p. 74, Land Office, Hall of Records, Annapolis. For the situation in Virginia see Bruce, I, 518-20.

49. It seems to me that Marcus Hansen, *The Atlantic Migration, 1607-1860* (Cambridge, Mass., 1940), ch. ii, greatly overestimates the importance of the headright system, which he considers to have been the principal stimulus to migration during the seventeenth century.

CHAPTER III

1. Gregory King, "Natural and Political Observations and Conclusions upon the State and Condition of England," in *Two Tracts,* ed. by G. E. Barnett (Baltimore, 1936), p. 31. Dorothy Marshall, *The English Poor in the Eighteenth Century,* pp. 26-27. A note in the Minute Book of the Providence Company, June 16, 1631, is interesting as an indication of the effect of fluctuations in the "business cycle" on the servant trade: ". . . it was considered, That it was doubtfull, that the proportion of 60 men by them resolved to be sent to the said Island, would hardly in theis tymes of Imployment be soone enough raised." C.O. 124/2, p. 28.

2. G. L. Beer, *Origins of the British Colonial System*, ch. ii, exaggerates the idea of overpopulation, and should be compared, e.g., with E. A. J. Johnson, *American Economic Thought in the Seventeenth Century* (London, 1932), pp. 49-57. Hansen, *Atlantic Migration*, p. 27, goes to the other extreme, and says that fears of overpopulation had entirely subsided before 1600, a statement which is less supported by evidence than those of Beer.

3. See Eli F. Heckscher, *Mercantilism*, tr. by Mendel Shapiro (London, 1935), II, 158 ff. A good many examples of official opposition to emigration will appear in the following pages, but here it may be noted that there was but one flat prohibition of emigration during the colonial period. This was an order of the Privy Council of Scotland in 1698, threatening all who took away emigrants with prosecution as men stealers (*Tudor and Stuart Proclamations*, S 3167). This cannot have had much permanent effect, but it was a subject of complaint in *Some Considerations Humbly Offered to Both Houses of Parliament Concerning the Sugar Colonies.*

4. *An Enquiry into the Causes of the Late Increase of Robbers* (London, 1751), sec. iv. Fielding was quoting "Mr. Shaw," with whom he did not agree.

5. Carl Van Doren, *Benjamin Franklin* (New York, 1938), p. 393.

6. *Calendar of Home Office Papers*, 1773-1775, no. 585, April 25, 1774.

7. Charles E. Banks, *The Winthrop Fleet of 1630* . . . (Boston, 1930), pp. 21-23.

8. The economic and social circumstances attending the Irish migrations are well discussed in C. K. Bolton, *Scotch Irish Pioneers in Ulster and America*, and C. A. Hanna, *The Scotch-Irish*. There has never been a fully satisfactory economic analysis of the condition of Ireland during the hundred years after the Restoration.

9. Hanna, I, 621, II, 180; *Acts Privy Council, Colonial*, III, 205, ff; John F. Watson, *Annals of Philadelphia*, ed. by W. P. Hazard (Philadelphia, 1898), II, 260, 266.

10. The best treatment of this matter is to be found in two articles by Margaret I. Adam: "The Highland Emigration of 1770," *Scottish Historical Review*, XVI, 280-93, and "The Causes of the Highland Emigrations of 1783-1803," *ibid.*, XVII, 73-89.

11. P.R.O., T. 47/12 (Emigration Lists). Among the female emigrants, one went for "Want of a Man," and another because she "Cannot get a Husband." There are other evidences in letters from Collectors of Customs in T. 1/500 (Treasury In-Letters), but all come to the same thing. For some analysis of the Scottish emigration lists, see A. R. Newsome, ed., "Records of Emigrants from England and Scotland to North Carolina, 1774-1775," *North Carolina Historical Review,* XI (1934), 39-41.

12. January 5, 1774, P.R.O., T. 1/500. These reports from customs offices came in because the government had become alarmed at the magnitude of emigration, and demanded fuller information. For a report to the Board of Trade on this subject in 1771, see *North Carolina Colonial Records,* VIII, 621-22. Acts passed in Georgia and North Carolina extending encouragement to these immigrants were disallowed in England because of the desire to stop the movement. *Acts Privy Council, Colonial,* V, 112-13; *North Carolina Colonial Records,* IX, 251-52. On Highlanders en route to the West Indies as indentured servants see [Janet Schaw], *Journal of a Lady of Quality . . . in the Years 1774 to 1776,* ed. by Charles M. and Evangeline Walker Andrews (New Haven and London, 1923), pp. 33 ff., 54-55, 257-59.

13. There is as yet no very good account of the background of German migration to the colonies. Of the many works on this movement Knittle, *Early Palatine Migration,* and T. J. Wertenbaker, *Founding of American Civilization; the Middle Colonies* (New York, 1938), pp. 259ff, are the most useful summaries.

14. Diffenderfer, *Redemptioners,* p. 144; *C.S.P. Colonial,* 1728-1729, no. 380.

15. Henry Jones Ford, *The Scotch-Irish in America,* p. 222, quoting Thomas Lechmere; Hanna, II, 180.

16. Brown, *Genesis,* I, 238-39, 439; *Virginia Company Records,* I, 391-92.

17. C.O. 124/2, pp. 4, 43.

18. See e.g. Winthrop Papers, Massachusetts Historical Society, *Collections,* 5th ser., I (1871), 213. *Georgia Colonial Records,* I, 110. In the case of Halifax, the Board of Trade ordered "that a book be opened for entering the names of such persons as shall apply to be settled . . . provided they be properly recommended by one or more persons of credit and reputation" (*Journal,* 1750-1753, p. 51). The Providence Company voted to bind out some "able Stronge boyes" to craftsmen in England, in order to prepare them for service in the colony (C.O. 124/2, p. 198).

19. William Eddis, *Letters from America, . . . 1769-1777,* pp. 67-68.

20. Calendar of Home Office Papers, 1773-1775, no. 673. For "printed handbills" in Scotland, see *ibid.,* no. 331. A Scottish emigration pamphlet of 1773 is reprinted in the *North Carolina Historical Review,* III (1926), 591-621. The town clerk of Aberdeen said in 1765 that he had "often observed in the publick News-papers, Advertisements for Servants to indent with different Merchants and Ship-masters at the Sea-ports" Williamson, *State of the Process,* pt. iii, p. 8. For Georgia: *Georgia Colonial Records,* I, 96, 110. For Halifax: *Public Documents of Nova Scotia,* pp. 495-97. Other examples of proposals made in early days to attract servants may be found in Insh, *Scottish Colonial Schemes,* Appendices E and F, and V. T. Harlow, ed., *Colonising Expeditions to the West Indies and Guiana,* pp. 117, 174. A thoroughgoing study of colonial promotion literature ought to be made.

21. North Carolina Colonial Records, IV, 18. For Ochs, Pury, and a controversy between them, see *ibid.,* p. 160.

22. John Dick to the Board of Trade, C.O. 217/11, G 74. For Crellius, see Erna Risch, "Joseph Crellius, Immigrant Broker," *New England Quarterly,* XII, 241-67.

23. A. B. Faust, "Swiss Emigration to the American Colonies in the Eighteenth Century," *American Historical Review,* XXII, 40-41.

24. John Dick to the Board of Trade, C.O. 217/9, F 160.

25. C.O. 124/1, ff. 90 b, 106 b.

26. C.S.P. Colonial, 1697-1698, no. 890.

27. Ibid., 1677-1680, p. 503; Jeaffreson, *Young Squire,* II, 61.

28. Georgia Colonial Records, XXI, 12.

29. Virginia Company Records, III, 266; C.O. 124/2, pp. 93, 324; see A. P. Newton, *Colonizing Activities of the English Puritans,* p. 169 n.

30. John Bruce, ed., *Letters and Papers of the Verney Family to . . . 1639,* Camden Society, LVI (London, 1853), 160-61.

31. South Carolina Historical Collections, V, 124. *Georgia Colonial Rec-*

ords, II, 110. The German servants sent to Georgia are not to be confused with the "salzburgers" who went on the *Charity. Ibid.,* II, 98, 101; XXI, 418-19.

32. C.S.P. Colonial, 1730, no. 302. Board of Trade, *Journal,* 1729-1734, pp. 87, 119, 126, 133.

33. Dick to the Board of Trade, March 6 and May 29, 1750; C.O. 217/9, F 112 and F 140.

34. Williamson, *State of the Process,* pp. 110 ff.

35. Stock, *Debates,* IV, 852. In 1635 a Dutch ship of 400 tons, bound for the Hudson River, lay at Cowes, and it was reported that her officers were engaged in recruiting English emigrants. The Privy Council ordered this stopped. *Acts Privy Council, Colonial,* I, 206.

36. Bullock, *Virginia Impartially Examined,* p. 47.

37. The London Spy (1704 edit.), pp. 54-55.

38. Letters from America, p. 77.

39. Nearly all evidence concerning Newlanders has been drawn from well-known writings of Gottlieb Mittelberger, Christopher Sauer, and Pastor Muhlenberg, and is conveniently collected in Diffenderfer, ch. iv. But Faust, in the *American Historical Review,* XXII, 32 ff., points out that most of them were far more astute, tactful, and unscrupulous than the traditional description suggests. There is much material on their methods in a series of articles by H. A. Ratterman, in *Der Deutsche Pionier,* XIV-XVI, and best of all accounts in English is that by Erna Risch, in *New England Quarterly,* XII, 241-67.

40. Shaftesbury Papers, G.D. 24/48, no. 14, P.R.O. Printed from the State Papers in *South Carolina Historical Collections,* V (1897), 152.

41. I am indebted to Mr. Richard Pares for calling my attention to these papers. They are in the High Court of Admiralty Miscellany, Bundle H.C.A. 30/636. Handwriting and spelling are so extraordinarily bad that I have had to guess at a word now and then, and occasionally to change the spelling into something fairly comprehensible.

CHAPTER IV

1. Virginia Company Records, II, 112-13, 124, 130-31. As a matter of fact, the first evidence of kidnapping we have is in connection with the first cargo of emigrants that were exchanged in the colonies for money; this was the shipment of young women sent by the company to make wives for the settlers. The alleged kidnapper was one Owen Evans; his case is set forth in *Virginia Magazine of History and Biography,* VI (1898-99), 228-30.

2. Bullock, *Virginia Impartially Examined,* p. 14.

3. See *Middlesex County Records,* ed. by J. C. Jeaffreson, index "kidnapping."

4. Bullock, p. 47.

5. The English Rogue: Described in the Life of Meriton Latroon . . . pt. i (1665), pp. 158-60. This part was probably written by Richard Head. It is, of course, fictional, but not therefore inaccurate.

6. Middlesex County Records, III, 181, 182, 255.

7. Tudor and Stuart Proclamations, no. 2613a. The quotation is from a printed copy of the proclamation in the Bodleian Library.

8. Rawlinson MSS, C. 416. 18, Bodleian Library; *Tudor and Stuart Proclamations,* no. 2677; Stock, *Debates,* I, 185-86.

9. The ordinance is entered in the first volume of the registry books. The registers have been partially printed, i.e. the names and destinations of the servants, without dates or terms of indenture, in *Bristol and America: A Record of the First Settlers in the Colonies of North America,* with a preface by N. Dermott Harding. An index can be obtained, separately bound. See also John Latimer, *The Annals of Bristol in the Seventeenth Century* (Bristol, 1900), pp. 254-55.

10. C.S.P. Colonial, 1574-1660, pp. 411, 457, 458. Bruce, *Economic History of Virginia,* I, 612. A similar petition of the year 1655 is noted in *C.S.P. Domestic,* 1655-1656, p. 84.

11. Acts Privy Council, Colonial, I, 296.

12. Ibid., I, 372. The Council told the clerk that "the assertion of the

Parties themselves who were concerned [was] no sufficient Evidence, that they were surprised and embarqued against their Wills." Just what would constitute sufficient evidence is not made plain, and indeed this was at the heart of the whole problem.

13. C.S.P. Colonial, 1661-1668, nos. 321, 770, 769, 798; *Acts Privy Council, Colonial,* I, 384; *C.S.P. Colonial,* Addenda, 1574-1674, no. 351.

14. C.S.P. Colonial, 1661-1668, no. 802. It is hardly necessary to point out that an earlier, and famous, regulation for the registering of emigrants was adopted in order to check the movement to New England, and was not primarily concerned with the servant trade. In 1630 commissions under the Privy Seal were issued for this purpose to local officials, and Edward Thorowgood was made registrar of such passengers for twenty-one years. *43rd Report of the Deputy Keeper of Public Records,* Appendix I, p. 169. For some of the lists thus taken, see J. C. Hotten, ed., *Original Lists of Persons* . . . ; and Samuel G. Drake, *Result of Some Researches among the British Archives* . . . *Relative to the Founders of New England* (Boston, 1860). See also *Tudor and Stuart Proclamations,* nos. 1745, 1773.

15. C.O. 389/2, pp. 11-13.

16. Petitions for redress are in *C.S.P. Colonial,* 1661-1668, nos. 771, 1720; other notes, *ibid.,* Addenda, 1574-1674, no. 382; and *ibid.,* 1675-1676, no. 827. The merchants' petition is in C.O. 389/2, p. 1, and the proceedings of Parliament in Stock, *Debates,* I, 302-4, 357-61, 366, 375, 382, 397, 400-401. Nearly all writers state that the death penalty was prescribed for kidnappers by a law of March 18, 1670, e.g. Ballagh, *White Servitude in Virginia,* p. 39; Bruce, I, 618; Gray, I, 345. This is not so. See Stock, *Debates,* I, 357-61; and George Ives, *A History of Penal Methods; Criminals, Witches, Lunatics* (London, 1914), pp. 117-18.

17. Depositions in C.O. 389/2.

18. A Compendious View of the Late Tumults and Troubles in this Kingdom, by J.W., Esq. (London, 1685), p. 146.

19. This story is taken principally from Wilmore's two pamphlets, which I found in the British Museum: *The Case of John Wilmore Truly and Impartially Related* . . . (1682); *The Legacy of John Wilmer, Citizen and Late Merchant of London* . . . (1692). Further information, which tends to establish Wilmore's account as essentially true, is in *Remarks upon the Tryalls of Edward Fitzharris* . . ., by John Hawles, Barrister of Lincoln's Inn (London, 1689), pp. 5, 16-17, 52; Roger North's *Examen,* . . . (London, 1740), p. 591; and Stock, *Debates,* II, 455. In a printed news letter of September 1, 1681, Wilmore's name is prominently mentioned, and coupled with Shaftesbury's Historical Manuscripts Commission, *Fourteenth Report,* Appendix, pt. iv, 128.

20. *Acts Privy Council, Colonial,* II, 43-44; *C.S.P. Colonial,* 1681-1685, p. 282.

21. Jeaffreson, *Young Squire,* I, 317-18.

22. *Virginia Impartially Examined,* p. 14.

23. Thomas, *Rise and Growth of the West-India Collonies,* p. 40. The same point is illustrated by two letters of the year 1677 about an emigration from Yorkshire to West Jersey, where it is related that a justice of the peace bound over one of the managers of the enterprise "for enticing away servants from their masters," and that the project was a discouragement to those parts "that suffer already ffor want of people." *American Historical Review,* II (1896-97), 472-73.

24. *Acts Privy Council, Colonial,* II, 41-43; Jeaffreson, *Young Squire,* II, 5-6.

25. *Acts Privy Council, Colonial,* II, 43.

26. A file of these forms may be seen at the Middlesex Guildhall, of dates from 1682 to 1684. They are numbered, and were once filed on a piece of string; for an analysis of them see the appendix. If the clerk kept a "fair book" it has disappeared. The servants thus registered came from all parts of England, and it is interesting to find that William Haverland, doubtless the same person as the "spirit" mentioned above (p. 74) appears as the master of many. In the London Guildhall no such files remain from this period, but the mayor's Waiting Book, which was a sort of daybook of his activities, contains memoranda of servants indentured before him.

27. Jeaffreson, *Young Squire,* II, 301; *C.S.P. Colonial,* 1685-1688, nos. 607, 611.

28. Patent Roll, C. 66/3285, no. 13.

29. *C.P.S. Domestic,* 1690-1691, pp. 249, 403; *C.S.P. Colonial,* 1689-1692, nos. 63, 90, 149, 151, 154; 1699, nos. 1177, 1179, 1181. See C. M. Andrews,

Guide to the Materials for American History to 1783 in the Public Record Office, I, 58 n.

30. For a reproduction of an indenture with the accompanying certificate that it is "Registered in the Office for that Purpose appointed by Letters Patents," see Herrick, *White Servitude in Pennsylvania,* opp. p. 146. This one is of the year 1714; there is a precisely similar one of 1698 in the Virginia State Library, and others of various dates as late as 1775 may be seen in the Historical Society of Pennsylvania. All include the formula that the document has been "Registered in the Office for that Purpose, appointed by the Letters Patents." The only evidence of the use of Legg, Guise and Robin's office is in a registry of arrivals in Philadelphia, showing that on January 28, 1687/8, a servant thus indentured appeared. Printed in J. S. Futhey and Gilbert Cope, *History of Chester County, Pennsylvania* . . . , pp. 22-24. For the fee paid to Thompson's office, see *C.S.P. Colonial,* 1689-1692, no. 154.

In vol. LXIV (1910) and following, of the *New England Historical and Genealogical Register,* is printed a "List of emigrants to America from Liverpool," of dates from 1697 to 1707. The transcriber writes concerning it as follows (LXIV, 158): "This list, comprising over 1500 names, is to be found in the back of vols. 5 and 7 of the Records of the Corporation of Liverpool, deposited in the Town Clerk's Office, Leasing Department, Liverpool. . . . The entries are apparently not official, and most of the writing can only be described as scribbling. The writer or writers—the entries seemingly being made by three different scribes—were evidently employed to draw up the indentures. The words 'pd.' and 'delivered' in the margin appear to refer to the indentures, and there is one entry stating that twenty shillings was paid for five indentures." The date, destination, time of service, and often the ship were entered for each servant, but apparently not further terms of the indentures. There are occasional interesting entries like the following: "If I find Jno. Lealand bound to Virg or Maryland I must write to his father a Tapeweaver in Salford." No indication of why these entries were made is given; their writers may have been carrying out a municipal ordinance like that of Bristol, or they may have been acting for a magistrate in furtherance of James II's order of 1686, or they may have been in one of Thompson's branch offices. I have examined the originals of these books, which are still in the same office, and I can find nothing to add to the information given by the former transcriber, nor any further light on the reason for making these registrations.

31. Roger North, *Lives of the Norths* (London, 1826), II, 24ff.

32. Stock, *Debates,* II, 36, 46-50, 390, 453-55, 457; III, 401, 402. *C.S.P. Colonial,* 1716-1717, no. 505. The Act is 4 Geo I, c. 11.

33. The procedure was the same as that followed by the Middlesex justices in 1682-1684, but in this case we have the clerk's "fair book" as well as the file of indentures. The loose certificates, instead of being true indentures, read as follows: "These are to certify, that *Henry Holmes of Wanstead in the County of Essex Vintner Aged Twenty One Years* came before me, one of His Majesty's Justices of Peace, and Voluntarily made Oath, That *he this* Deponant *is* not Married, no Apprentice nor Covenant, or Contracted Servant to any Persons, nor listed Soldier or Sailor in His Majesty's Service, and *is* free and willing to serve *Neale MacNeale of London Chapman* or his Assigns *four* Years in *Jamaica* [here is a large space for inserting special terms] His Majesty's Plantation in America, and that *he is* not perswaded, or enticed so to do, but that it is *his* own Voluntary Act." The document is signed and sworn.

34. *Letters from America,* p. 77.

35. Williamson, *State of the Process,* pt. iii, pp. 5-7. Herrick used this material, apparently from a different source (pp. 150-56). The Town Clerk of Dublin, on the other hand, was able in 1743 to produce books containing the names of all transported servants indentured before the mayor (see below, p. 135). There were printed indenture forms with the arms of the city of Dublin on them (Stock, *Debates,* IV, 857). Many colonies had laws providing that servants brought against their wills should be free; in 1751 the Provincial Court of Maryland liberated eight, but what evidence they presented is not made clear; perhaps their indentures were not properly signed by magistrates in England (September Term, pp. 839-44).

36. See Herrick, pp. 148-56.

37. *C.S.P. Colonial,* 1661-1668, no. 331.

38. *C.S.P. Colonial,* 1661-1668, no. 769. A committee of the Council of Trade and Plantations confirmed this story.

39. *C.S.P. Colonial,* 1669-1674, no. 160.

40. Stock, *Debates,* II, 453-55.

41. *The Negro's and Indians Advocate,* p. 171. This figure has been quoted and requoted by nearly every writer touching this subject, until it has acquired a quite undeserved authority.

42. *William and Mary College Quarterly*, 1st ser., III (1894-95), 198.

43. "The waies of obtaineing these Servants have beene usually by employeing a Sort of men and women who make it their profession to tempt or gaine poore or idle persons to goe to the Plantations and haveing perswaded or deceived them on Shippboard they receive a reward from the persons who employed them." Copy of the Committee's Report, Egerton MSS., 2395, f. 277.

44. Boucher, in *Maryland Historical Magazine*, VIII (1913), 252; Eddis, *Letters from America*, pp. 67-69, 77.

45. James Smith of Aberdeen put some of his servants into jail. In 1638 John Winthrop remarked that merchants, in order to furnish the southern plantations with servants "were forced to send about their stalls, and when they had gotten any, they were forced to keep them as prisoners from running away" (*Journal*, I, 272). A jury of the Suffolk County Court in 1671 brought in a special verdict to the effect that a servant who changed his mind after going on board ship, and wished to be free, but was nevertheless brought to the colonies, should be held liable to pay his passage before freedom should be granted. Colonial Society of Massachusetts, *Publications*, XXIX (1933), 43-44.

PART TWO

CHAPTER V

1. Sir Matthew Hale, *Historia placitorum coronae, or History of the Pleas of the Crown* (London, 1736), I, 13.

2. Arthur L. Cross, "The English Criminal Law and Benefit of Clergy during the Eighteenth and Early Nineteenth Centuries," *American Historical Review,* XXII (1916-17), 544-65.

3. Sir William Blackstone, *Commentaries on the Laws of England* (Philadelphia, 1771-72), I, 137; IV, 394. The statute 22 Car. II, c. 5 permitted judges to transport for seven years "such as steal cloth from the rack or purloin ammunition," and 18 & 19 Car. II, c. 3 allowed the transportation of notorious criminals from the border counties.

4. Emile Campion, *Etude sur la Colonisation par les Transports Anglais, Russes, et Français* (Rennes, 1901), pp. 44-45.

5. *C.S.P. Colonial,* 1574-1660, p. 12.

6. Patent Roll, C. 66/2043, *in dorso.* The date of witnessing is January 21.

7. *Acts Privy Council,* 1615-1616, pp. 23-25.

8. On the following dates: March 19, 1616/17; April 30, 1622; September 2, 1622; March 8, 1625/6; September 20, 1628; February 23, 1632/3. These dates were ascertained from the contemporary manuscript index to the Patent Rolls, in the Legal Search Room of the Public Record Office.

9. *Acts Privy Council,* 1621-1623, p. 294.

10. The evidence is in *Acts Privy Council, passim,* to 1626 (see index under "Convicts"), and thereafter an entry or two may be found in *Acts Privy Council, Colonial,* I. See also *C.S.P. Domestic,* 1619-1623, pp. 111, 213, 552: and *Middlesex County Records,* II, 224, 226. A conditional pardon for sixty-eight Newgate felons in November, 1622, may have doomed them to transportation; see A. E. Smith, "The Transportation of Convicts to the American Colonies in the Seventeenth Century," *American Historical Review*, XXXIX (1934), 238, n. 20, where the relevant clauses of the pardon are transcribed. At the time of writing that article the Privy Council Calendar had not progressed to the year 1622, and I did not know of the quotation given above. In the light of that quotation, it would seem obvious that this batch of convicts, pardoned immediately afterwards, were intended for some special purpose in the kingdom.

11. C.S.P. *Domestic,* 1635, pp. 262, 535; *ibid.,* 1635-1636, p. 437; *ibid.,* 1638-1639, p. 425; *ibid.,* 1639-1640, pp. 183, 349, 486.

12. Stock, *Debates,* I, 175-76, 210-11.

13. Or to St. Lucia, where he had a plantation (A. P. Newton, *Colonizing Activities of the English Puritans,* p. 219).

14. C. 66/2912, no. 3.

15. The two other pardons are on the same roll. During the next few years the Middlesex Sessions Records contain notes of felons who pleaded their transportation pardons in court, but there is a gap in the series of Patent Rolls between 1656 and 1660. *Middlesex County Records,* III, 247, 292, 294, 296.

16. Acts Privy Council, Colonial, I, 310, 314, 315.

17. For a discussion of the accuracy of this figure and of the method of using the Patent Rolls in this connection, see *American Historical Review,* XXXIX, 238, n. 22.

18. Sir Henry C. Maxwell-Lyte, *Historical Notes on the Use of the Great Seal of England* (London, 1926), pp. 92-96, and ch. v. The justices' recommendations for clemency, with all the information contained in them, may thus be found in the Chancery Warrants class (C. 82).

19. In 1703 an act provided that when prisoners had been reprieved for a pardon, and a warrant under the sign manual for preparing such a pardon should be received, they might then be delivered out of custody according to the conditions of the pardon without waiting for the final engrossing and sealing of the document. Stock, *Debates,* III, 12.

20. Fifteen prisoners were given to Captain Joy, for Jamaica, in April, 1662 (*C.S.P. Colonial*, 1661-1668, no. 292), and others to Captains Foster and Longman, for Virginia, in October, 1662 (*ibid.*, no. 377; and see nos. 382 and 294).

21. S.P. 44/14, p. 46. At about the same time, Sir Thomas Modyford was granted £1200 towards the cost of transporting 1,000 persons to Jamaica; this number may have included some convicts. (*Calendar of Treasury Books*, 1660-1667, p. 667).

22. *C.S.P. Domestic*, 1667, p. 250. For the story of Pate's shipment, see *American Historical Review*, XXXIX, 245.

23. *Ibid.*, 245-46.

24. MSS Sessions Records at the Guildhall, London. Some bonds for the transportation of convicts, of dates between 1666 and 1670, found in the Guildhall MSS, appear to me to be worthless. See *ibid.*, 247-48.

25. *C.S.P. Colonial*, 1675-1676, nos. 783, 784, 809; *ibid.*, 1677-1680, no. 280.

26. C.O. 324/4, pp. 30-31, printed in *American Historical Review*, XXXIX, 241.

27. *C.S.P. Colonial*, 1677-1680, nos. 582, 741; *Acts Privy Council, Colonial*, I, 708-9.

28. *C.S.P. Colonial*, 1677-1680, no. 1441; *ibid.*, 1681-1685, nos. 147, 232, 429, 619, 717.

29. Jeaffreson, *Young Squire*, I, 319.

30. *Ibid.*, II, 6-7, 13; *C.S.P. Colonial*, 1681-1685, nos. 800, 802.

31. Jeaffreson, *Young Squire*, II, 42-43.

32. *Ibid.*, II, 44-48, 58-59, 73, 102, 116, 122-28; *C.S.P. Colonial*, 1681-1685, nos. 1046, 1668, 1826; *Acts Privy Council, Colonial*, II, 68-69.

33. Jeaffreson, *Young Squire*, II, 182, 185-87, 191-201, 215-16, 235.

34. See especially II, 44-46.

35. C.O. 139/7, f. 3.

36. *C.S.P. Colonial*, 1669-1674, no. 881.

37. *Acts Privy Council, Colonial,* I, 553; *C.S.P. Colonial,* 1669-1674, nos. 175, 178; *Archives of Maryland,* II, 540-41. In 1678 the king ordered Governor Culpeper of Virginia to admit a cargo of transported Scottish Covenanters (see below, p. 182). A considerable number of writers have taken this order as meaning that the Virginian law was disregarded, and that criminals were forced into the colony (see e.g. Hansen, the *Atlantic Migration,* p. 37). Scottish Presbyterians were not felons, however; the law was not disregarded, and there is no evidence whatever that any criminals were shipped to Virginia or Maryland between 1670 and 1718.

38. *C.S.P. Colonial,* 1696-1697, nos. 535, 657.

39. *C.S.P. Domestic,* 1697, pp. 160, 167.

40. *Ibid.,* p. 202. London Court of Aldermen, Rep. 101, pp. 225-26 (MSS at the Guildhall). *C.S.P. Domestic,* 1697, pp. 210, 221.

41. *C.S.P. Colonial,* 1696-1697, nos. 1134, 1140, 1156, 1157, 1166, 1172, 1190, 1194, 1195.

42. *C.S.P. Colonial,* 1696-1697, nos. 1189, 1205, 1216, 1398; *C.S.P. Domestic,* 1697, p. 322. See also *C.S.P. Colonial,* 1697-1698, no. 1.

43. *C.S.P. Domestic,* 1697, p. 458; *C.S.P. Colonial,* 1697-1698, no. 65.

44. *Middlesex County Records,* ed. Hardy, p. 296, Calendar of Sessions Books, 1689-1709.

45. The collection of printed sessions records from which the following illustrations are taken is in the Bodleian Library. The crimes for which all pardoned felons were convicted may of course be learned from the warrants for their pardons, in the Public Record Office.

46. *A Report of Divers Cases in Pleas of the Crown . . . with Directions for Justices of the Peace and Others,* collected by Sir John Kelyng (London, 1708), p. 4.

47. *The English Rogue,* pt. iv, p. 198.

48. *The German Princess Revived, or the London Jilt, Being a True Account of the Life and Death of Jenney Voss.* (1684). Copy in Bodleian Library. The name Jane Vasse appears in a Newgate pardon of January 13, 1679.

CHAPTER VI

1. 4 Geo. I, c. 11.

2. For other crimes subsequently added to this list, see Stock, *Debates,* IV, xviii-xix. An excellent discussion of "The Criminal Laws and Punishments," with special reference to transportation, is in ch. ii of Eris O'Brien, *The Foundation of Australia* (London, 1936).

3. 6 Geo. I, c. 23. This act also provided that all charges for transporting the felons should be borne by the county, and that the contractor might use whatever means he thought fit for securing and conveying them to the seaport, while anyone rescuing them should be held guilty of felony. In 1721 the Board of Trade ordered printed copies of the convict act sent to colonial governors (*Journal,* 1718-1722, p. 334).

4. A small number were annually pardoned "on condition of transportation for and during the terms of their natural Lives." I can find no evidence of any kept in servitude for this period.

5. Treasury Money Book, T. 53/25, pp. 224, 281. It will be remembered that in 1697 the Lords Justices had agreed to pay £8 apiece for the transportation of convicts in naval vessels (see above, p. 105). They said that it would be better for the government to pay than for convicts to be let loose (*C.S.P. Domestic,* 1697, p. 160). In April, 1716, the Treasury made a contract for the transportation of Scottish rebels which was very similar to the later one with Francis March here described. (See below, p. 197).

6. Calendar of Treasury Papers, 1714-1719, p. 389.

7. These contracts are entered in the Treasury books called "Warrants not Relating to Money" (T. 54), but I have taken their various dates and rates of payment from the warrants for the payment of Forward and his successors, entered in the Treasury Money Books (T. 53). On May 4, 1722, Forward was granted a special bonus of £114 for his pains and losses in transporting convicts to date (T. 53/29, p. 454).

8. Just why these counties were favored with grants from the Treasury, while others had to pay for the transportation of their felons by a county levy, is not clear.

9. Calendar of Treasury Books and Papers, 1739-1741, p. 18. Forward was notified of the change, and told not to meddle (*ibid.*, p. 20), but the reason for his replacement does not appear.

10. The first payment to Stewart was on March 2, 1757 (T. 53/46, p. 110).

11. Wilfrid Oldham, "The Administration of the System of Transportation of British Convicts, 1763-1793" (Typewritten doctoral thesis, 1933, in University of London Library), pp. 78-80.

12. Assizes 23/5 (unpaged), Western Circuit Gaol Book.

13. S.P. 44/232, p. 40. In the Maryland Shipping Returns Sydenham appears frequently as the owner of ships bringing convicts. He was apparently a nephew of Jonathan Forward; in 1749 the latter announced his intention "of declining the Maryland trade, and delivering it up to Messieurs Sydenham and Hodgson (as he has already done the Virginian") (*Maryland Gazette,* Jan. 4, 1749).

14. Maryland Shipping Returns (MSS in Hall of Records, Annapolis, and in library of Maryland Historical Society, Baltimore).

15. Massachusetts Historical Society, *Proceedings,* 1915-1916, pp. 328-29; *Calendar of Home Office Papers,* III, pp. 169, 615. See also *Hertfordshire County Records,* VII, 184, 231, 259, 280, 312.

16. These contracts are transcribed in an entry book of Baltimore County, Maryland, labelled "Convicts" (Hall of Records, Annapolis).

17. See O'Brien, *Foundation of Australia,* pp. 125-28, for a review of these.

18. Assizes 24/24 and 24/25, Western Circuit Order Books.

19. John Howard, *An Account of the Principal Lazarettos in Europe* (Warrington, 1789), pp. 252, 253.

20. Campbell to Evan Nepean, quoted by Oldham, p. 80.

21. *American Historical Review,* XXII, 560.

22. Pardons may be studied in the *Calendar of Home Office Papers.* For the year 1766, e.g., one finds that 116 sentences of death were commuted to transportation for 14 years, 12 to transportation for 7 years, and 19 to transportation for life. Eleven sentences of transportation were cancelled by a free pardon, and 8 of death also (*ibid.,* II, 112-24). These figures refer, of course, to the whole country, and not merely to the Old Bailey convicts. For years previous to 1760 figures for pardons have to be collected from the "Criminal Books" (S.P. 44/81 ff.) which are as yet uncalendared.

23. Oldham, p. 35.

24. The names of the ships may be ascertained from the Treasury Money Books, together with the number of convicts on board and the name of the captain. In the Guildhall, London, are 44 certificates of the arrival of convict ships in the colonies, of dates between 1718 and 1736; these are conclusive evidence for these ships. Maryland Shipping Returns are fairly complete from 1756 to 1775, and exist incompletely from 1742; these give the names of incoming ships, with their captains and owners, and furthermore they usually record the number of convicts on board. The *Maryland Gazette* printed notices of incoming ships and convicts for a few years around 1750 and 1751; and one may learn from the newspaper of arrivals which are not listed in the Shipping Returns. Virginian Shipping Returns (in the Public Record Office) are available for the latter part of the period; they very rarely mention the arrival of convicts, but one may trace the movement of ships in them. By fitting together these various evidences, the facts stated in the text were ascertained. For a more precise description of the Shipping Returns, see the Bibliography.

25. *Journals of the House of Commons*, XXXVII, pp. 310-11; *Letters from America*, p. 66; "Journal of a French Traveller in the Colonies," *American Historical Review*, XXVII, 84.

26. *South Carolina Historical Magazine*, XII, 170-71; Massachusetts Historical Society, *Proceedings*, 1915-1916, pp. 328-29; Historical Manuscripts Commission, *Records of the City of Exeter*, p. 237.

27. See Note at the end of this chapter.

28. See John T. Scharf, *History of Maryland*, I, 371: "The number of convicts imported into Maryland before the revolution of 1776 must have amounted to at least twenty thousand." It should be remarked that the estimate given above does not include Irish felons, of whom there were certainly several thousand transported.

29. *Archives of Maryland*, XXXIII, 345, 349-50.

30. C.O. 5/1387 (Acts of Virginia, unpaged). This law is listed, but not

printed, in Hening's *Statutes,* IV, 106, "repealed by proclamation, 18th Jan. 1723."

31. C.S.P. Colonial, 1722-1723, nos. 613, 616, 629, 637; Board of Trade *Journal,* 1723-1728, pp. 30, 31; *Acts Privy Council, Colonial,* III, 54-55.

32. The act is in *Archives of Maryland,* XXXVIII, 320-22, and the dis-allowance, *ibid.,* XXXV, 212.

33. Ibid., L, 562; VI, 294-95, 328-29, 422. Governor Sharpe wrote: ". . . all the Persons who contract for the Transportation of Felons from Great Britain except Mr Steuart of London have paid the Duty on such as they imported into this Province without murmuring & tho it might be justly said that he is much more affected by the Act than the others because he transports a much greater Number yet I cannot help thinking that he ought to have readily submitted to the payment of so small a Sum when his profitts from trading hither are so exorbitant." Sharpe to Joshua Sharpe, May 27, 1757, *ibid.,* IX, 5.

34. Ibid., XIV, 411-13, 524, 535; *Acts Privy Council, Colonial,* V, 115, 116, 163-64, 363. For the whole subject see Basil Sollers, "Transported Convict Laborers in Maryland during the Colonial Period," *Maryland Historical Magazine,* II, 17-47.

35. Acts Privy Council, Colonial, IV, 20-21; Board of Trade *Journal,* 1742-1749, pp. 215-16, 226-27, 239-40, and also 424; *Pennsylvania Colonial Records,* V, 499. Despite these repeals, Pennsylvania contrived to collect a duty of £5 on imported convicts throughout the colonial period (Herrick, *White Servitude in Pennsylvania,* p. 127).

36. C.S.P. Colonial, 1722-1723, no. 382; *ibid.,* 1730, no. 544. *Acts Privy Council, Colonial,* III, 161-62; Board of Trade *Journal,* 1729-1734, pp. 284, 314.

37. Sharpe to Calvert, October 20, 1755, *Archives of Maryland,* VI, 294.

38. Journals of the House of Commons, XXXVII, 310.

39. T. 1/500 (bundle of Treasury In-Letters). Campbell's account is headed "A State of the Contract for Felons for Six Months after the Death of Mr Stewart."

40. The Maryland Shipping Returns show 493 convicts entering the colony in ships owned by Campbell after April, 1772. Those for which he submitted an account, and no doubt others as well, went to Virginia.

41. Oldham, pp. 149, 225ff. See also Sollers, in *Maryland Historical Magazine*, II, 45.

42. Journals of the Continental Congress (Library of Congress edit., Washington, 1904-37), XXXIV, 494-95, 528. Governor Paca informed the legislature of Maryland in 1783 that the agent in London had sent notice of a plan to transport more convicts, but no action was taken by the assembly (*Archives of Maryland*, XLVIII, 484). For a report of 140 convicts arrived at Fisher's Island, in Long Island Sound, during 1788, see *William and Mary College Quarterly*, 1st ser., VII, 113.

43. Maryland Gazette, Aug. 20, 1752.

44. Virginia Gazette, November 19-26, 1736. In the Baltimore County entry book "Convicts", is a list of felons brought on the ship *Trotman*, in 1770, five of whom are said to have "Freed themselves in London." Duncan Campbell said that many bought themselves off, and were subjected only to banishment (*Journals of the House of Commons*, XXXVII, 310).

45. Sir Walter Besant, *London in the Eighteenth Century* (London, 1902), p. 556. In the Library of Congress MSS is a picturesque, rhyming account of the experiences of a transported convict written by one James Revel.

46. Quoted by Sollers, in *Maryland Historical Magazine*, II, 41n.

47. Calendar of Treasury Papers, 1714-1719, p. 389. The examples given are taken from the certificates of the arrival of ships, filed at the London Guildhall.

48. Archives of Maryland, XIV, 413; *Journals of the House of Commons*, XXXVII, 310-11. About one-quarter of all transported convicts were women.

49. Maryland Gazette, January 3, 1750. The names and statistics of ships, and the names of their captains, come from the Maryland Shipping Returns and the Treasury Money Book entries.

50. Virginia Gazette, May 22-29, 1746.

51. Calendar of Home Office Papers, III, 169.

52. Guildhall MSS certificates of arrival.

53. Historical Manuscripts Commission, *Fourteenth Report*, pt. ix, p. 77 (Trevor MSS); *Calendar of Home Office Papers*, I, no. 198.

54. *Calendar of Home Office Papers*, IV, no. 39.

55. ". . . our subtle Criminals have found out Means hitherto to render [transportation] ineffectual; some have made their escape in the Voyage itself; others, condemn'd to this Punishment, never have been put on board; several have reach'd the Plantations, but been returned by the first Shipping, and Great Numbers have come back before half their time was expir'd." B. Mandeville, *An Enquiry into the Causes of the Frequent Executions at Tyburn* (London, 1725), p. 47. An odd case happened in Maryland: one Evan Jones bought a servant, Jonathan Brinley, in 1719. The servant ran away and went to England, but returned as a convict transported in 1722. Jones demanded that Brinley return to his service, and the Provincial Court ruled that he should do so, and serve out his original time. Provincial Court Records, April, 1722, p. 639 (Hall of Records, Annapolis).

56. *Calendar of Home Office Papers*, IV, no. 39. See Henry Fielding: "this I am confident may be asserted, that pardons have brought many more men to the gallows than they have saved from it." *Causes of the Increase of Robbers*, sec. x.

57. There is a collection of examples from Virginia in Fairfax Harrison, "When the Convicts Came," *Virginia Magazine of History*, XXX, 250-60.

58. *Executive Journals of the Council of Colonial Virginia*, IV, 281-82.

59. Provincial Court, April, 1721, p. 362. The court said: "it is become the Common Complaint of the Honest house Keepers Inhabitants within this province that the peace is not sufficiently Secured to them whilst so many of those people are suffered to goe without security."

60. This time the ruling was mandatory; security of fifteen pounds was to be taken for every imported convict (Provincial Court, April, 1722, p. 639). The dispute came before the Council on Jan. 2, 1724/5, and the Council ruled in favor of the magistrates. See *Archives of Maryland*, XXV, 437; and *Maryland Historical Magazine*, II, 30-32.

61. *Maryland Gazette*, Aug. 21 and Oct. 16, 1751; Provincial Court Record, September, 1751, p. 838.

62. Harrison, in *Virginia Magazine of History*, XXX, 256. Dinwiddie

wrote on Aug. 25, 1755, that he had been ordered to enlist no convicts, and accordingly there were none in the drafts (Dinwiddie Papers, II, 178), but two years later Loudoun said that the Virginia recruits were bad, "most of them being *Convicts,* & many of them bought out of the Ships before they landed." In Stanley M. Pargellis, ed., *Military Affairs in North America, 1748-1765* (New York and London, 1936), p. 319.

63. Maryland Historical Magazine, II, 33, 41.

64. Hening, *Statutes,* V, 546-47; *Archives of Maryland,* L, 623-25. See also Harris and McHenry, *Maryland Reports* (New York, 1812), II, 378.

65. Lancaster County Order Book, 1729-1743, p. 275 (Virginia State Library).

66. Letters from America, p. 69.

67. 6 Geo. III, c. 32, sec. 1.

68. Historical Manuscripts Commission, *Tenth Report,* pt. v, pp. 26, 35, 47, 73, 85, 91-92, 94-95.

69. Stock, *Debates,* III, 518, 532, 534, 536, and xv.

70. Journals of the House of Commons of the Kingdom of Ireland, IV, Appendix, pp. cciii and following.

71. See *Maryland Gazette,* Aug. 1, 1754, where is an account from Dublin of the indenturing of more than twenty convicts before the Lord Mayor, for transportation to America.

CHAPTER VII

1. Quoted from Ribton-Turner, *History of Vagrants and Vagrancy* (London, 1887), pp. 128-29.

2. Ibid., p. 133.

3. Virginia Company Records, II, 526.

4. Many references and quotations are given in Beer, *Origins of the British Colonial System,* ch. ii.

5. 12 Anne, c. 23. For a few records of vagabonds sentenced to transportation see *Middlesex County Records,* ed. by Jeaffreson, II, 225, 305.

6. Ribton-Turner, pp. 143-44; E. M. Leonard, *Early History of English Poor Relief,* pp. 229-30 and note.

7. *Virginia Company Records,* I, 253, 259, 271-72, 287-89.

8. *Ibid.,* I, 520; II, 108; "Decisions of Virginia General Court, 1626-1628," *Virginia Magazine of History,* IV (1896-97), 250; Bruce, *Economic History of Virginia,* II, 41n.

9. Leonard, pp. 229-30. See Edward G. O'Donoghue, *Bridewell Hospital* (London, 1923). Most of the illustrations given above were taken from some manuscript notes containing excerpts from the Bridewell Court Books, furnished to the Virginia State Library by Rev. Mr. O'Donoghue.

10. *Virginia Magazine of History,* XXV (1917), 50.

11. *North Carolina Colonial Records,* II, 371-72.

12. M. Dorothy George, *London Life in the XVIIIth Century,* p. 143; Richard Ligon, *True and Exact History of Barbadoes.*

13. Newgate Calendar and Gaol Delivery Book, MSS at Guildhall, London. For Pate, see *American Historical Review,* XXXIX, 245.

14. Here are two entries from the mayor's "Waiting Book" at the Guildhall: July 4, 1684, five "pilfering boys that lye day & night in the marketts and streets of this City and haveing no freinds or Relacons to take care or provide for them came before his Lordship and of their own free accord bound themselves" for ten years in the plantations to John Haslewood, mariner.

August 18, 1684, "This day John Sewell was bound apprentice to Abraham Wilde, merchant, to serve in Maryland for 7 yeares and discharged out of Bridewell per warrant." Such entries are not plentiful; there are not more than half a dozen for the year 1684.

15. Samuel R. Gardiner, *History of the Commonwealth and Protectorate* (London, New York and Bombay, 1901), III, 117, 244-45; S.P. 25/177, pp. 329-31.

16. Thurloe, *State Papers,* IV, 686. Also *ibid.,* V, 211; IV, 218, 394, 439, 695.

17. S.P. 25/77, p. 283.

18. C.S.P. Venetian, 1655-1656, pp. 184, 309; *C.S.P. Domestic,* 1655-1656, pp. 209-210.

19. Tudor and Stuart Proclamations, no. 3300.

20. 14 Car. II, c. 12. See also Historical Manuscripts Commission, *Seventh Report,* p. 148, for a proposed act of Parliament for the transportation of rogues and building of houses of transportation in which to keep them while awaiting shipment.

21. Acts Privy Council, Colonial, I, 370, 389. *Ibid.,* II, 36, is a list sent up by justices of the peace in Devonshire, following exactly the procedure laid down in 39 Eliz. c. 4.

22. Register of the Privy Council of Scotland, 1616-1619, pp. 289, 445-46; *ibid.,* 1619-1622, pp. 149-51, 219-20; *ibid.,* 1622-1625, pp. 429-31.

23. 18 and 19 Car. II, c. 3; *C.S.P. Domestic,* 1665-1666, p. 205.

24. Thurloe, *State Papers,* III, 497; IV, 41.

25. Register Privy Council of Scotland, 3rd ser., I, 181.

26. Ibid., II, 101.

27. Ibid., II, 111.

28. Ibid., II, 201-2.

29. These are entered *ibid., passim.*

30. Ibid., II, 503; III, 113.

31. Ibid., III, 507, 523; IV, 103.

32. Ibid., II, 263; III, 13, 263, 335, 337; IV, 142-44, 675.

33. C.S.P. East Indies, 1571-1616, no. 432.

34. Ribton-Turner, p. 141; Brown, *Genesis of the United States,* I, 252-54.

35. Virginia Company Records, I, 304; W. A. Bewes, *Church Briefs,* (London, 1896), p. 96; *Notes and Queries,* 7th ser., V, 196; *C.S.P. Domestic,* 1611-1618, p. 584. While awaiting shipment these children were kept in Bridewell, and are entered in the Court Book of that establishment on Feb. 27, 1618/9.

36. Virginia Company Records, I, 270.

37. Journal of the Common Council, XXXI, f. 122 (Guildhall MSS).

38. *Virginia Company Records,* I, 304-6.

39. *Ibid.,* p. 355; *Acts Privy Council, Colonial,* I, 28-29.

40. *Notes and Queries,* 7th ser., V, 196; *Virginia Company Records,* I, 411, 424, 489; II, 136-37.

41. Journal of the Common Council, XXXII. See also *Virginia Company Records,* II, 90.

42. E. D. Neill, *Virginia Carolorum* . . . (Albany, 1886), pp. 46-47.

43. Minutes of the Council for New England, American Antiquarian Society, *Proceedings,* April, 1867, pp. 60, 61, 72, 73, 79, 85, 111.

44. R. P. Stearnes, "The Weld-Peter Mission to England," in Colonial Society of Massachusetts, *Publications,* XXXII (1937), 214-16, 239-41. The statement of account is printed in *New England Historical and Genealogical Register,* XXXVI (1882), 64-70.

45. *Journal,* II, 187-88. See also *ibid.,* p. 96.

CHAPTER VIII

1. The protests of Barbadians are voiced in *A Brief Relation of the Beginning and Ending of the Troubles of the Barbados, with the True Causes Thereof* (London, 1653).

2. Stock, *Debates,* I, 206, 207.

3. *C.S.P. Domestic,* 1650, pp. 333, 334, 340, 346, 397, 419; *ibid.,* 1651, pp. 105, 245.

4. Haselrig to the Council of State, printed in *Original Memoirs Written During the Great Civill war* . . . (Edinburgh, 1806), pp. 339ff. See also *C.S.P. Domestic,* 1650, p. 419.

5. *C.S.P. Domestic,* 1650, pp. 421, 423, 438; *ibid.,* 1651, pp. 105, 245; *ibid.,* 1651-1652, p. 164; *C.S.P. Colonial,* 1574-1660, p. 421.

6. *C.S.P. Domestic,* 1651, pp. 415, 417, 418, 430, 431, 432, 433-34; *ibid.,* 1651-1652, p. 44; *C.S.P. Colonial,* 1574-1660, p. 360.

7. Gardiner, *Commonwealth and Protectorate,* I, 464-65, and note.

8. Tanner MSS (Bodleian Library), 55, f.141; *C.S.P. Domestic,* 1651, p. 458; *ibid.,* 1651-1652, pp. 67, 166, 217; *C.S.P. Colonial,* 1574-1660, pp. 363, 373.

9. C. H. Firth, ed., *Scotland and the Protectorate,* pp. 79-80, 81, 100, 299; *C.S.P. Domestic,* 1654, p. 333.

10. C. E. Banks, in Massachusetts Historical Society, *Proceedings,* LXI, pp. 4-29. Some of these exiles in Boston founded the Scot's Charitable Society in 1657 which is still in existence. Carl Bridenbaugh, *Cities in the Wilderness* (New York, 1938), pp. 81-82.

11. Bruce, *Economic History of Virginia,* I, 609, n. 2.

12. *William and Mary College Quarterly,* 2nd ser., II (1922), 160.

13. Lefroy, ed., *Memorials of the Bermudas,* II, 81.

14. Firth, pp. 153, 246-47.

15. Thurloe, *State Papers,* III, 488, 743; IV, 7, 39.

16. *C.S.P. Domestic,* 1660-1661, pp. 87, 320; *ibid.,* 1661-1662, p. 16; *Calendar of Treasury Books,* 1660-1667, pp. 44-45.

17. *Ibid.,* 1660-1667, pp. 243, 273, 307, 356, 413.

18. Stock, *Debates,* I, 303, 304; Historical Manuscripts Commission, *Twelfth Report,* Appendix, pt. vii (S. H. Le Fleming MSS), p. 35.

19. Thurloe, III, 453-54; IV, 39; VII, 639; Barbados Council Minutes (typescript copy in P.R.O.), under dates Sept. 4, 1655, and Feb. 27, 1655/6; Gardiner, III, 160-62; Thomas Burton, *Diary,* IV, 305.

20. Thurloe, III, 375; *C.S.P. Domestic,* 1655-1656, pp. 43-44; Burton, IV, 255-57.

21. Barbados Council Minutes, June 3, 1656.

22. The debate amounted to a discussion of civil liberty under a dictatorship, and is worth reading. Burton, IV, 255-73, 301-8. The exiles published their story in *England's Slavery or Barbados Merchandize* . . . (London, 1659).

NOTES TO PAGES 161-169

23. A. H. A. Hamilton, *Quarter Sessions from Queen Elizabeth to Queen Anne* (London, 1878), p. 174.

24. *C.S.P. Domestic*, 1655, p. 346.

25. *Ibid.*, pp. 329, 393; *C.S.P. Colonial*, 1574-1660, pp. 329, 393; Thurloe, IV, 360-1.

26. The whole subject has been excellently treated by the Rev. Aubrey Gwynn, S.J. in a series of articles in an *Irish Quarterly Review*, XVIII, 377, 648; XIX, 279, 607; XX, 291, but the plan of the present discussion is somewhat different. See also Father Gwynn's collection of "Documents Relating to the Irish in the West Indies," in *Analecta Hibernica*, no. 4.

27. *Tudor and Stuart Proclamations*, Irish, no. 265; *C.S.P. Domestic*, 1649-1650, p. 96; *Oliver Cromwell's Letters and Speeches*, ed. by Thomas Carlyle, Letters CIV and CV.

28. Robert Dunlop, ed., *Ireland under the Commonwealth*, I, 177, 183, 282; *C.S.P. Domestic*, 1651-1652, p. 374.

29. Dunlop, I, 250-51; II, 310, 373; *C.S.P. Domestic*, 1654, p. 219; Sir William Petty, *The Political Anatomy of Ireland* (London, 1691), ch. iv. See a Jesuit report of 1656, estimating the number of exiles at 60,000, printed in *Analecta Hibernica*, no. 4, p. 230.

30. *C.S.P. Domestic*, 1651-1652, pp. 324, 432; *C.S.P. Colonial*, 1574-1660, p. 387.

31. Dunlop, II, pp. 341, 343, 354-55; *Tudor and Stuart Proclamations*, Irish, no. 520.

32. *C.S.P. Colonial*, 1574-1660, pp. 407, 410; Dunlop, II, 374-75.

33. *Records and Files of the Quarterly Courts of Essex County, Massachusetts*, II, 293-96.

34. *C.S.P. Colonial*, 1574-1660, pp. 401, 409; Dunlop, II, 399-401, 421-22, 432, 434.

35. *Ibid.*, II, 467.

36. *Ibid.*, II, 655-56.

37. *Ibid.*, II, 437, 613, 686-87.

38. Thurloe, IV, 23.

39. Ibid., IV, 40.

40. C.S.P. Colonial, 1574-1660, p. 431; Thurloe, IV, 87, 100.

41. Ibid., IV, 23, 40, 75; V, 121, 150, 348, 474, 558, 570-71; *C.S.P. Colonial,* 1574-1660, pp. 441, 446.

42. Dunlop, II, 436, 477, 549, 555-56; John P. Prendergast, *The Cromwellian Settlement of Ireland* (2nd edit., Dublin, 1875), p. 338.

43. Thurloe, V, 250.

44. Analecta Hibernica, no. 4, pp. 233, 235.

45. Bruce, *Economic History of Virginia,* I, 609.

46. Northumberland County Order Book, 1652-1665, f.30 (Virginia State Library).

47. Lefroy, II, 100, 103, 159-60.

48. Analecta Hibernica, no. 4, pp. 236-38.

49. Ibid., pp. 252ff., especially p. 257.

50. Thurloe, IV, 39. Egerton MSS, 2395, f. 625.

51. Additional MSS, 11411, f. 9.

52. Analecta Hibernica, no. 4, pp. 208-13, 230, 231.

CHAPTER IX

1. 16 Car. II, c. 4.

2. Joseph Besse, *Sufferings of the People Called Quakers,* II, 345.

3. Ibid., II, 62. The certificate is noted also in *C.S.P. Colonial,* 1661-1668, no. 909.

4. Besse, II, 199ff. Fuller account in *A True and Impartial Narration of the Remarkable Providences of the Living God....*

5. C.S.P. Colonial, 1661-1668, nos. 858, 872; *Acts Privy Council, Colonial,* I, 414, 417.

6. *Ibid.,* 393. See Besse, II, 320, 322, 323. An account of transportations under the Conventicle Act is given in William C. Braithwaite, *The Second Period of Quakerism* (London, 1919), pp. 40-51. The elaborate notes on which Braithwaite's account is based were deposited by him in the Friends' Library, Friends' House, London (Braithwaite MSS, Folder 29). These notes were called to my attention by Mr. Douglas Lacey.

7. Besse, II, 323ff.

8. *Another Cry of the Innocent and Oppressed for Justice . . . ,* pp. 25-26; Besse, II, 317-18.

9. Quarter Sessions Book, 1653-1671, ff. 66-67 (Bristol City Archives).

10. Willem Sewel, *History . . . of the Society of Friends* (Lindfield, 1833), II, 268.

11. Acts Privy Council, Colonial, I, 402.

12. C.S.P. Domestic, 1666-1667, p. 343.

13. Register of Privy Council of Scotland, 3rd ser., II, 195.

14. Ibid., II, 307, 470, 500, 503, 534.

15. Stock, *Debates,* I, 448.

16. Register of Privy Council of Scotland, 3rd ser., III, 204, 206, 207, 228-29, 308, 320.

17. Ibid., V, 465; *C.S.P. Domestic,* 1678, pp. 340, 523-24.

18. C.S.P. Domestic, 1678, p. 340.

19. Register of Privy Council of Scotland, 3rd ser., V, 482; VI, 76; *Acts Privy Council, Colonial,* I, 788; *C.S.P. Colonial,* 1677-1680, no. 850.

20. C.S.P. Domestic, 1679-1680, p. 63.

21. There are two accounts of this affair: (1) in a petition of Williamson for redress, in *Register of Privy Council of Scotland,* 3rd ser., VII, 61-62; and (2) in Robert Wodrow, *History of the Sufferings of the Church of Scotland,* II, 476. The former is certified as accurate by two bishops; the latter is less detailed.

22. Register of Privy Council of Scotland, 3rd ser., VI, 257, 306, 330-31, 335, 343, 416.

23. Paterson's own story is in *ibid.*, 3rd ser., VI, 415-17. Wodrow's version is practically the same (III, 130-32). A list of the names of the prisoners is printed in an appendix to W. H. Carslaw, *Exiles of the Covenant* (Paisley, 1908).

24. *Register of Privy Council of Scotland*, 3rd ser., VII, 219.

25. *Ibid.*, VIII, 437, 508 (April and May, 1684).

26. On Lockhart: *Register of Privy Council of Scotland*, 3rd ser., VIII, 235, 516; E. B. O'Callaghan, ed., *Calendar of Historical Manuscripts in the Office of Secretary of State, Albany, N. Y.* (Albany, 1865-66), II, 134.

On Gibson and Malloch: *Register of Privy Council of Scotland*, 3rd ser., VIII, 521-22, 524, 526; IX, 12, 16, 28, 95, 102, 111, 208. The voyage and arrival of Gibson's group is narrated by Wodrow, IV, 10-11. Malloch sailed in August, and on Nov. 13, 1684, entered 74 servants in the secretary's office at Carolina, claiming 3,700 acres of land as headrights (A. S. Salley, ed., *Warrants for Lands in South Carolina*, II, 163). Perhaps not all of the 74 were covenanters; according to Wodrow there were 32 of them on Gibson's ship.

27. Instructions on September 6 empowered commissioners in the south and west to administer the oath of allegiance and banish to the plantations all who refused to take it. *Register of Privy Council of Scotland*, IX, 159.

28. *Ibid.*, X, 19-20. Christopher Jeaffreson, in London, knew on February 19, 1684/5, that four or five hundred men were available in Scotland for anyone who would send a ship for them, but he could not interest Leeward Island merchants in the matter (*Young Squire*, II, 166).

29. *Register of Privy Council of Scotland*, 3rd ser., XI, 114-15, 118, 119, 129. Robert Barclay petitioned for prisoners on July 30 (*ibid.*, 127), and was given 24, but these were transferred to Ewing. See also Sir John Lauder of Fountainhall, *Historical Notices of Scotish Affairs*, pp. 586, 658.

Ewing's shipment: *Register of Privy Council of Scotland*, XI, 136, 145, 148, 149.
Scot: *ibid.*, X, 79, 181; XI, 137, 148, 154-55, 157.
Arbuckles: *ibid.*, XI, 94.
Fearne: *ibid.*, XI, 233, 243, 251, 252, 254.

30. Wodrow, IV, 10; Carslaw, p. 157.

31. Wodrow, IV, 333; Lauder of Fountainhall, p. 664. According to the latter account, Scot's contingent included not only persons "of phanaticall principles," but also some "criminall prisoners given him by the Privy Councill; others, who ware distressed by poverty, debt, and captions, or ware whoores or prodigall wasters."

32. Wodrow, IV, 185-87.

33. Wodrow, IV, 333.

34. Menzies' letters are in *Register of Privy Council of Scotland,* 3rd ser., IV, 648-51, 671-75.

35. Jeaffreson knew on August 5 that "some hundreds" would be transported, and he consulted Secretary Blathwayt about obtaining some for St. Christopher (*Young Squire,* II, 224).

36. S.P. 44/56, pp. 284-85.

37. Printed in J. C. Muddiman, *The Bloody Assizes* (London, 1929), pp. 32-33.

38. C.O. 1/66, nos. 142, 144, 145, 146, 147; C.O. 1/58, nos. 63, 64, 74, 75, 97.

39. C.O. 1/58, nos. 89,i, 90, 102; C.O. 1/59, nos. 7,ii, 43; C.O. 1/66, nos. 149, 151, 152. Blathwayt's letter is in C.O. 153/3, pp. 188-89.

40. C.O. 153/3, p. 188.

41. Barbados: C.O. 1/59, nos. 7,iii,iv, 15,iv,v,vi, 43, 44. Jamaica: C.O. 142/13. (Naval Officers' Returns, unpaged, in which may be found notices of the arrival of the ships and of the number of passengers on board.)

42. Penne to Nepho, Oct. 21, C.O. 1/66, no. 148. Henry Pitman (for whom see below) said that Nepho sold them to Penne, but the documents relating to them continue to use Nepho's name.

43. Six of them may have received a free pardon. See Muddiman, appendix. On May 26, 1686, Nepho wrote to Giles Clerk, Esq., in Lyons Inn, requesting him to make arrangements for eight felons "to make up the like number taken out of the hundred" originally allotted to him. Rawlinson MSS, C. 421, f. 192.

44. *C.S.P. Colonial,* 1685-1688, no. 442.

45. Governor Stede to Sunderland, May 27, 1687, C.O. 1/62, no. 56. Lord Howard of Effingham, governor of Virginia, proposed to Blathwayt in Feb. 1685/86 that "you . . . use your Interest to send over 100 of the Rebells hither." He promised Blathwayt "halfe the produce of them honestly accounted for to you by me" in return for paying half the charge for their passage, and urged "the more Trad[e]smen the better." However, before Effingham's letter was dispatched he learned that "the Rebells serving 10 years . . . are disposed of allready into private hands," so that his proposal was evidently too late. Effingham to Blathwayt, Feb. 6, 1685/86, MS in Blathwayt Papers, Colonial Williamsburg, Inc.

46. This list is alphabetically arranged and printed in Muddiman, appendix.

47. John Coad's relation (see below), and C.O. 1/58, nos. 88, 90.

48. Evidence for the statements in these paragraphs is listed above, p. 377, notes 38, 39, and 41.

49. C.O. 153/3, p. 188.

50. *C.S.P. Colonial,* 1685-1688, no. 517.

51. *Ibid.,* nos. 632, 657. The act is found in C.O. 30/5, ff. 145-53, and is printed in Henry Pitman, *A Relation of the Great Sufferings and Strange Adventures of Henry Pitman . . .* (1689).

52. *C.S.P. Colonial,* 1685-1688, nos. 591, 606, 625, 627, 775, 780. I have not found the text of either act.

53. *C.S.P. Colonial,* 1689-1692, nos. 222, 698, 699, 700. Historical Manuscripts Commission, *Twelfth Report,* Appendix, pt. vii (Le Fleming MSS) p. 314. The pardon is on the Patent Roll C. 66/3339, no. 1, and is dated Feb. 4, 1689.

54. *C.S.P. Colonial,* 1689-1692, no. 968.

55. *C.S.P. Colonial,* 1689-1692, nos. 1184, 1193, 1108, 1158. The repealing act is in C.O. 30/3, ff. 231-33.

56. *C.S.P. Colonial,* 1689-1692, nos. 1041, 1698.

57. Pitman, *Relation.*

58. John Coad, *A Memorandum of the Wonderful Providences of God*

. . . during . . . Monmouth's Rebellion and to the Revolution of 1688.

59. I am indebted to General Sir Reginald and Lady Pinney, of Racedown, Dorset, for an opportunity to use the Pinney family papers. For Azariah Pinney, see also *Archaeologia*, XXXIV, 350-56.

60. *Calendar Treasury Papers*, 1714-1719, p. 196. The terms of the agreement are set forth in T.53/25, p. 251 (Treasury Money Book).

61. *C.S.P. Colonial*, 1716-1717, nos. 128, 129, 144, 145, 215, 223.

62. Historical Manuscripts Commission, *Stuart Papers*, II, 232-33.

63. T.53/25, p. 251.

64. *Executive Journals of Council of Colonial Virginia*, III, 429. For a list of those arriving on the *Elizabeth and Anne*, see W. P. Palmer, ed., *Calendar of Virginia State Papers*, I, 185-87.

65. Scharf, *History of Maryland*, I, 386, 388.

66. *Calendar Treasury Papers*, 1714-1719, p. 238.

67. South Carolina asked for some of the prisoners (*C.S.P. Colonial*, 1716-1717, no. 230). See also E. McCrady, *The History of South Carolina under the Proprietary Government* (New York, 1897), I, 558.

68. Historical Manuscripts Commission, *Stuart Papers*, III, 304-5, and also p. 40. This is an account by Andrew Ramsay, who is first on the list of thirty shipped on the *Hockenhill* (*C.S.P. Colonial*, 1716-1717, no. 312).

69. *Executive Journals of Council of Colonial Virginia*, III, 430-32; *Calendar Virginia State Papers*, I, 187-88.

70. *Ibid.; Archives of Maryland*, XXV, 347-49; XXXIV, 164-65; *C.S.P. Colonial*, 1722-1723, no. 58.

71. Edgar E. Hume, "A Colonial Scottish Jacobite Family," *Virginia Magazine of History*, XXXVIII (1930), 1-27, 97-124, 336.

72. *Maryland Historical Magazine*, I (1906), 346-48.

73. *Calendar Virginia State Papers*, I, 186; *Virginia Magazine of History*, XXXVIII, 336-42, where is an account of the voyage of the *Elizabeth and Anne*.

74. *New Jersey Archives*, 1st ser., XI, 56.

75. Sir Bruce Gordon Seton, Bt., and Jean Gordon Arnot, eds., *The Prisoners of the '45*. This work does not give a very full account of the transportations, but, unless otherwise noted, the following account is from evidence set forth in the first volume.

76. Dates and terms of these contracts from Treasury Money Book, T.53/42, pp. 400-7, 418-19.

77. T.53/42, pp. 406-7, 414-15, 418 (certificates of shipment).

78. T.1/325 (Treasury In-Letters): Samuel Smith's memorial describing the fate of his ships, as a result of which he receives the balance of money due him (T.53/42, pp. 519-20; Mar. 22, 1747/8). Governor Trelawney of Jamaica sent a list of 126 rebels safely landed there (C.O. 137/58, ff. 40-43). For Maryland, see Scharf, I, 435, where those arriving on the *Johnston* are listed. A certificate concerning both ships from the Naval Officer is copied in T.53/42, p. 500.

79. *North Carolina Colonial Records*, IV, 926, 956; V, 1195-96.

80. *Scots Magazine*, IX (1747), 243.

81. "Narrative of Alexander Stewart," *Maryland Historical Magazine*, I (1906), 349-52.

82. *Archives of Maryland*, XXVIII, 394.

PART THREE

CHAPTER X

1. Gottlieb Mittelberger's Journey to Pennsylvania in the Year 1750, trans. by Carl Theo. Eben, p. 18.

2. Knittle, *Early Palatine Emigration,* pp. 61-65.

3. Quotation from *Georgia Colonial Records,* XXII, pt. ii, 106-7 (Robert Trevor to Mr. Martyn, March 3, 1739). For Trevor, see Historical Manuscripts Commission, *Fourteenth Report,* pt. ix, p. iii. For Hope as the merchant referred to by Trevor, see *Georgia Colonial Records,* XXI, 100, 418; IV, 672; Gilbert T. Voigt, "Swiss Notes on South Carolina," *South Carolina Historical Magazine,* XXI (1920), 100; Diffenderfer, *Redemptioners,* p. 243.

4. Georgia Colonial Records, XXII, pt. ii, 106.

5. Board of Trade *Journal,* 1750-1753, p. 247.

6. Dick to the Board of Trade, March 6, 1750; C.O. 217/9, F 112.

7. Owners of ships may be ascertained from Ralph B. Strassburger, *Pennsylvania German Pioneers,* and *Pennsylvania Magazine of History,* XXVIII (1904), espec. p. 89.

8. For the statements in this paragraph, see Appendix A. Galloway's servants came in the brig *Grove,* and were advertised for sale in the *Maryland Gazette,* Feb. 20, 1752; Mar. 22, 1753; Oct. 2, 1753; May 30, 1754.

9. Diary of John Harrower, *American Historical Review,* VI, 73. In 1671 the Suffolk County Court of Massachusetts heard the story of a kidnapped servant, who said that at London the sailors told him he would be released by the customs searchers at Gravesend, but the searchers ignored him. Colonial Society of Massachusetts, *Publications,* XXIX (1933), 18-20.

10. Of the many sources for the tonnages of ships, the Naval Officers' Returns are, of course, most useful. For the Virginia Company's Ships, see *Virginia Company Records,* II, 496.

11. Georgia Colonial Records, II, 357-58.

12. Board of Trade to John Dick, Feb. 1, 1750/1, C.O. 218/3, pp. 331 ff.; Diffenderfer, *Redemptioners,* p. 51.

13. Tonnage from Maryland Naval Officers' Returns; numbers of convicts from Treasury Money Books.

14. Dick to the Board of Trade, Feb. 23, 1750/1; C.O. 217/11, G 69. The law is in Pennsylvania *Statutes at Large,* V, 94-97.

15. See nn. 12 and 14.

16. For example, the Georgia Trustees paid £6.16.6, "for the Charge of inclosing the twenty One Cabins between Decks," and £8.10 "half Charge of the Awning upon Deck." This was for German Protestants (*Georgia Colonial Records,* II, 79). A ship carrying Huguenots to Virginia in 1700 was fitted with "Lodgings or Cabbins for the said passengers for two in an apartment," Virginia Historical Society, *Collections,* new ser., V, 39.

17. John Josselyn, "An Account of Two Voyages to New England [1675]," in Massachusetts Historical Society, *Collections,* 3rd ser., III (1833), 220-21.

18. Georgia Colonial Records, III, 408-9.

19. Contract for the Huguenots, 1700, Virginia Historical Society, *Collections,* new ser., V, 41.

20. C.O. 217/11.

21. Maryland Gazette, July 2, 1752.

22. Pennsylvania Magazine of History, XXXVIII (1914), 79.

23. "Records of Board of Selectmen, 1736-1742," *Report of the Record Commissioners of Boston,* XV, 317-20.

24. American Historical Review, VI, 74.

25. Mittelberger's Journey, p. 20.

26. John Coad, *A Memorandum of the Wonderful Providences of God,* pp. 24-25.

27. Report of Dr. Tho. Graeme and Thomas Bond, *Pennsylvania Colonial Records,* VI, 170-75.

28. *Pennsylvania Magazine of History,* LVI (1932), 12; Diffenderfer, *Redemptioners,* p. 262; James O. Knauss, *Social Conditions among the Pennsylvania Germans in the Eighteenth Century* . . . (Lancaster, Pa., 1922), p. 60.

29. Board of Trade *Journal,* 1742-1749, pp. 393, 397, 398, 402. The *Gentleman's Magazine,* XIX, 185, stated in the same year that the ventilators for the Halifax ships were designed by the Rev. Dr. Hales, and that only one child was lost on the voyage. For a curious design of a ship's ventilator, with a bellows worked by a heavy pendulum which swayed with the ship's motion, see *ibid.,* XXXIII (1763), 340.

30. Board of Trade *Journal,* 1750-1753, pp. 115, 157.

31. Francis Moore, "A Voyage to Georgia, Begun in the Year 1735," in *Georgia Historical Collections,* I (1840), 87.

32. "An Impartial Inquiry Into . . . the Province of Georgia," *ibid.,* I, 155.

33. Charles Leslie, *A New and Exact Account of Jamaica,* pp. 16-17. For seventeenth-century cases of overcrowding and underfeeding, see Bruce, *Economic History of Virginia,* I, 625-27.

34. Virginia, 1619, *Journals of the House of Burgesses,* 1619-1659, p. 13; 1699, Hening, *Statutes,* III, 193. Barbados, 1656, Council Minutes, August 12. Antigua, 1669, C.O. 154/1, f.29. Nevis, 1672, C.O. 154/1, f.98. Pennsylvania, 1684, Herrick, *White Servitude,* p. 291; 1717 and 1727 (Germans), *Pennsylvania Colonial Records,* III, 29, 282-83. New Jersey, 1684, see American Historical Association, *Annual Report for 1903,* I, 484. New York, 1721, *Colonial Laws of New York,* II, 60. Boston, 1707, *Boston Town Records,* Selectmen, 1701-1715, p. 60; 1746, *ibid.,* Selectmen, 1743-1753, p. 149. New Hampshire, 1718, *Laws,* II, 312.

35. Pennsylvania, 1722, *Statutes at Large,* II, 264. Maryland, 1728, Bacon, *Laws,* 1728, c. 3, and 1769, c. 22. New Jersey, 1730, *Laws* (edit. 1776), p. 86.

36. "Register of the Collector of the Port of Oxford, Maryland," MSS in Maryland Historical Society, Baltimore.

37. Herrick, p. 161.

38. See above, p. 211, and *Acts Privy Council, Colonial,* IV, 115-76.

39. Archives of Maryland, XXII, 497; XXVI, 289; XXX, 283 (c.36); LII, 147. These are only a few references; see Scharf, *History of Maryland,* I, 370-71.

40. C.S.P. Colonial, 1730, nos. 317, 501.

41. Herrick, p. 175 and note 24.

42. Bridenbaugh, *Cities in the Wilderness,* p. 391.

43. Archives of Maryland, XXXVIII, 51-52, 70.

44. Hening, *Statutes,* III, 193-95, 212-13, 346, 492.

45. The account books of the servant ship *Tristram and Jane* (1636) are in H.C.A. 30/635 and 30/636. John Harrower, in 1773, was employed to make a "Clean list" of the servants on his ship. It is curious to note that lists in the Maryland Land Books at Annapolis of servants in the early 1670's who were convicts follow the same order of names as that in the collective pardons on the Patent Rolls.

46. See Herrick, p. 118, n. 22. Maryland, Virginia, and the Carolinas passed laws giving remedy to masters whose servants had pretended to skills they did not possess.

47. One of the best descriptions of the arrival of servants is in "A Sorrowful Account of a Transported Felon" (Library of Congress MS, Ac 2780). See also Harrower's diary, *American Historical Review,* VI, 75-77, and Herrick, p. 213.

48. From the "Record of Servants and Apprentices bound before Mayor James Hamilton," as printed in *Pennsylvania Magazine of History,* XXX-XXXII (1906-1908), *passim.*

49. Lancaster County Order Book, 1729-1743, Court of April 13, 1739.

50. Journals of the House of Commons, XXXVII, 310-11.

51. C.O. 139/7, p. 95, and Coad, *Memorandum,* pp. 35-36. The time was reduced to six days in 1703 (C.O. 139/9, f. 89). For a time in the seventeenth century Virginia forbade the sale of servants for 24 hours after the ship's arrival (Bruce, I, 631-32).

52. Mittelberger's Journey, p. 27; Diffenderfer, pp. 240-57; Knauss, pp. 58-67.

53. Erna Risch, "Immigrant Aid Societies," *Pennsylvania Magazine of History,* LX (1936), 19-20.

54. Statutes at Large, VI, 432-40; Risch, "Immigrant Aid Societies," 15-33.

55. Mittelberger's Journey, p. 27. In Chester County Court, Aug. 30, 1737, Mathias Lambert produced a "transcript of his Childrens Age from one of the Churches in Germany where he did formerly belong," proved the child to be 21, and got him discharged from servitude. Chester County, Quarter Sessions Docket, 1733-1742, p. 112. (County Court House, West Chester, Pa.)

CHAPTER XI

1. Journals of House of Burgesses of Virginia, 1619-1659, pp. 1-16.

2. Instead of giving numerous and rather complicated footnote references to colonial statutes I have made a section of the bibliography on the subject; the sources for statements about these laws in the following pages may be found in that place.

3. Journals of the Assembly of Jamaica, I, 34 (Oct. 2, 1678).

4. Figures from Virginia were obtained from court records in the Virginia State Library; those from Maryland from *Archives of Maryland,* LIV.

5. White Servitude in Pennsylvania, pp. 200-201.

6. Herrick, pp. 288, 293, 302. And perhaps in Massachusetts, *Records of the Court of Assistants* (Boston, 1901-28), II, 105, 109.

7. The latter not in Pennsylvania, Herrick, pp. 290, 292 (abstracts of statutes). There are many examples of it in Maryland, e.g. *Archives of Maryland,* LIV, 378-79, 389.

8. D. P. DeVries, *Voyages* (New York, 1853), pp. 53, 183. This author remarked, "The English are a villainous people, and would sell their own fathers for servants in the Islands" (p. 113).

9. *Virginia Magazine of History,* XXV (1917), 228 (1625).

10. There has been some disagreement as to whether he could vote in earliest years; but see A. E. McKinley, *The Suffrage Franchise in the Thirteen Colonies* (Philadelphia, 1905), pp. 110, 137-38, 148, 223, 282, 365-66. J. C. Hurd thought that they had been allowed to vote in Plymouth during the first sixteen years of the colony's history (*The Law of Freedom and Bondage,* I, 255). There was a scandalous example of Jamaican servants voting in 1688 (*Interesting Tracts Relating to the Island of Jamaica,* p. 244).

11. "Whereas Josias Long Servant to Mr Alexander Watts, who was apprehended for being a confederate with his said Master in bringing a servant of Robert Goffe's out of Carolina, which Long petitioned this Court for his release, pretending himself servant to the said Watts & noe confederate, & presenting the said petition to the honorable the Governor his honor being pleased to write under the said petition that if the petition preferred to this Court by the said Long were true he could be responsable to noe person but his master. This Court doe judge that the said Longs allegacons is true, & therefore order that he be released from his restrainte." Northumberland County Order Book, 1666-1678, f. 88 b. Court of April 21, 1673 (Virginia State Library).

12. Jamaica, 1673: *C.S.P. Colonial,* 1669-1674, no. 1055. Barbados, 1685: C.O. 30/5, pp. 19-20.

13. Yet sometimes the courts set injured servants free when their masters were negligent in caring for them, which seems fully as bad as if the master himself had done it. For examples, see below, pp. 247ff.

14. Jamaica: C.O. 139/1, f. 125; C.O. 139/5, ff. 6-9. Barbados: C.O. 30/5, f. 45; C.O. 28/3, no. 44.

15. Ligon, *History of Barbadoes,* p. 43; *C.S.P. Colonial,* 1700, no. 391.

16. Antigua: C.O. 154/1, f. 39. Nevis: *Laws of Nevis,* p. 38. Barbados and Jamaica, as above.

17. Bruce, *Economic History of Virginia,* II, 8-9; *William and Mary College Quarterly,* 1st ser., XI (1902-03), 36. Eighteenth-century laws of the continental colonies generally provided that the servant be given "sufficient" food and clothing, and we cite later the case of a servant in Virginia who successfully maintained before a court that his master had not clothed him "according to law." See below, p. 246.

18. *Tudor and Stuart Proclamations,* no. 2735.

19. *C.S.P. Colonial,* 1661-1668, p. 82.

20. Best evidence for this is in the Bristol Tolzey Book. See also V. T. Harlow, ed., *Colonising Expeditions,* p. 44.

21. *Leah and Rachel,* in *Narratives of Early Maryland,* p. 289.

22. Bruce, II, 41-44; *C.S.P. Colonial,* 1696-1697, no. 1411, where James Blair writes in 1697 that freedom dues were prescribed by a "law" of the country.

23. Chester County, Quarter Sessions Docket, 1742-1759, p. 74.

24. Lancaster County Order Book, 1696-1702, ff. 100b-101.

25. Spotsylvania County Order Book, 1724-1730, f. 40, March, 1724/5 (Virginia State Library).

26. "Notes from the Records of Stafford County, Virginia, Order Books," *Virginia Magazine of History,* XLIV (1936), 204; XLV (1937), 181-82.

27. *Archives of Maryland,* LIV, 515 (Talbot County, January, 1671/2).

28. McCormac, *White Servitude in Maryland,* p. 65; Ligon, *History of Barbadoes,* p. 44; *C.S.P. Colonial,* 1685-1688, no. 1854. This last was written by a man who was something of a nuisance to Governor Stede, and was looking for arguments in a quarrel (*ibid.,* no. 1881).

29. *Letters from America,* p. 70. As for the instructions to governors, they may have been significant at first, but the clause was kept as "common form" for a hundred years, and is not to be taken seriously. See *Acts Privy Council, Colonial,* IV, 473 ff.

30. Spotsylvania County, Minute Book, 1755-1765, p. 96.

31. *Records of Plymouth Colony,* I, 7 (Court Orders). Another case may be seen in *Archives of Maryland,* LIII, 431.

32. Northumberland County Order Book, 1666-1678 (Court of December 9, 1668).

33. Baltimore County, "Court Proceedings," 1757-1759, August session, 1758 (Hall of Records, Annapolis).

34. Chester County, Quarter Sessions Docket, 1723-1733, p. 33.

35. Suffolk County Court, Colonial Society of Massachusetts, *Publications,* XXX, 807.

36. C.O. 1/5, no. 101.

37. Barbados Council Minutes, May 7, 1640, December 2, 1656.

38. Records and Files of the Quarterly Courts of Essex County, Massachusetts, III, 303.

39. Baltimore County, Liber I.S. No. C, p. 208, August Court, 1719 (Hall of Records, Annapolis).

40. Anne Arundel County, Judgments, November Court, 1720 (Hall of Records, Annapolis).

41. Baltimore County Court, March, 1720/1.

42. Ibid., November, 1759.

43. Bruce, II, 11.

44. Archives of Maryland, X, 534 ff., 73-74; XLIX, 166-68, 233-35, 304-14; LIV, 8, 9, 361, 372.

45. Quarter Sessions Docket, 1733-1742, f. 69.

46. Ibid., October 2, 1716.

47. Quarter Sessions Docket, 1742-1759, p. 11 (August 31, 1742).

48. Leah and Rachel, in *Narratives of Early Maryland,* p. 295.

49. C.S.P. Colonial, 1685-1688, no. 1876.

50. Northumberland County Order Book, 1666-1678, f. 74, April 4, 1672.

51. Dedham Town Records, V, 165, 183.

52. Quarter Sessions Dockets, 1723-1733, p. 12.

CHAPTER XII

1. *C.S.P. Colonial,* 1685-1688, no. 1854; Thomas, *West-India Collonies,* p. 27; *The Case of John Wilmore,* p. 3.

2. Richard Frethorne to his parents, Historical Manuscripts Commission, *Seventh Report,* Appendix II, p. 40; *Leah and Rachel,* in *Narratives of Early Maryland,* p. 291.

3. *Archives of Maryland,* LIII, xxxiii; Samuel Smith, *History of New Jersey,* p. 81, quoting a letter from Gawen Laurie to a friend in London, March 26, 1684.

4. *Letters from America,* p. 70; Leslie, *New Account of Jamaica,* p. 320.

5. *Mittelberger's Journey,* p. 117. Many more quotations are brought together in Gray, *History of Agriculture,* II, 505-6.

6. J .C. Ballagh collected some examples from the Middlesex Records (*White Servitude in Virginia,* pp. 76-77n).

7. Hening, *Statutes,* II, 415.

8. Ligon, *History of Barbadoes,* pp. 44-45·

9. *Virginia Company Records,* III, 21.

10. Ligon, p. 44.

11. *Leah and Rachel, Narratives of Early Maryland,* p. 290; George Alsop, *Character of the Province of Maryland,* p. 57; Baltimore County Court, August, 1718, Liber I.S. No. C.

12. Ligon, pp. 31, 37, 43-45·

13. Smith, *History of New Jersey,* p. 181.

14. *Archives of Maryland,* XLIX, 8-10.

15. *The Life of Thomas Hellier* (London, 1678); Jeaffreson, *Young Squire,* I, 257.

16. Lancaster County Order Book, September 11, 1667.

17. Quarter Sessions Docket, 1733-1742, p. 190. For some examples of indentured artisans "commuting" their service, i.e. performing some specific piece of work and then going free instead of working out their full time, see "Brick-making in Goochland [County, Va., 1737/38]," *William and Mary College Quarterly,* 1st ser., V (1896-97), 109-10; and *Archives of Maryland,* IV, 283.

18. Leah and Rachel, in *Narratives of Early Maryland,* p. 291.

19. History of Barbadoes, p. 44.

20. Leslie, *New Account of Jamaica,* p. 320.

21. History of Barbadoes, p. 44.

22. Narrative of a Voyage to Maryland . . . [Maryland Historical Society], Fund Publication, no. 7 (Baltimore, 1874), p. 24.

23. Ligon, pp. 45-46; Hall, *Acts of Barbados,* obsolete acts no. 61; "Petition of Colonel Guy Molesworth," Davis Transcripts, Box 3, Royal Empire Society, London; and see Harlow, *Barbados,* pp. 47-48.

24. William and Mary College Quarterly, 1st ser., XI (1902-03), 34-36 (spelling altered).

25. Virginia Magazine of History, XV (1907-08), 38-43; Hening, *Statutes,* II, 191, 204.

26. Harlow, ed., *Colonising Expeditions,* p. 88.

27. Documents on this subject are collected in *Analecta Hibernica,* no. 4.

28. "Journal of a French Traveller," *American Historical Review,* XXVII, 84; C. H. Van Tyne, *The War of Independence* (Boston, 1929), p. 449.

29. Boucher to William Knox, Under Secretary of State [?] Nov. 27, 1775, *Maryland Historical Magazine,* VIII (1913), 252-53.

30. It is worth repeating here that in no colony, after customs became established, was a prolongation of the period of servitude permitted unless magistrates gave assent and recorded the agreement. Servants could and did protest if improperly held beyond their time, and courts always set them free.

31. Archives of Maryland, I, 72, 107. The offense was "clergyable."

32. A freeman in Baltimore County, in 1719, was put in jail as a runaway. When released the clerk was ordered to make out a pass for him; but he was made to pay jail fees. Baltimore County Court, Liber I.S. No. C, p. 70.

33. Anne Arundel County, Judgments, VII, 239, June Court, 1720.

34. E.g. Anne Arundel Court, November, 1719, Judgments, VI, 567.

35. Quarter Sessions Docket, 1733-1742, p. 44 (May 27, 1735).

36. One servant who had run away and been returned gloomily observed to his master that "hee [the master] Could have his bussiness done as hee plaised for A botle of Drams." The court, receiving testimony of this remark, ordered thirty lashes administered for the scandalous reproach brought on the court by his "abrading speeches." *Archives of Maryland,* LIV, 417 (Talbot County, 1668).

37. Anne Arundel County, Judgments, VI, 311.

38. Barbados Council Minutes, August 1, 1654; June 3, 1656.

39. *C.S.P. Colonial,* 1685-1688, no. 1876; Gray, I, 362; Scharf, *History of Maryland,* II, 38; McCormac, *White Servitude in Maryland,* pp. 52-53; Massachusetts Historical Society, *Collections,* 5th ser., I, 412. Georgians complained in 1739 that their runaways were sheltered in South Carolina (*Georgia Colonial Records,* IV, 171-72, 238, 333; XXV, 508-9). The articles of the New England Confederation provided for mutual delivery of runaway servants on certificate of a magistrate (Winthrop, *Journal,* II, 103).

40. Chester County, Quarter Sessions A, August 30, 1768.

41. The preceding paragraphs are based on colonial statutes and court records. The same conclusions are stated in the works of Ballagh, McCormac, Geiser and Herrick, and it does not seem necessary to present special evidences here.

42. Baltimore County Court, June, 1721, Liber I.S. No. C, p. 499.

43. C.O. 154/2, p. 98; Law of 1675, reenacted in 1682 (*ibid.,* p. 163).

44. In Lancaster County, Virginia, especially in the 1720's, it was common for a servant to appear in court and "voluntarily" agree to serve his master an extra period because of some misdemeanor he had committed. This method was used instead of a process of trial and sentence. I have not found it elsewhere, and indeed this court was very fond of registering agreements for extra service, made for all manner of reasons.

45. All white males, and all Negroes, over sixteen, were counted as tithables, but women servants only if they worked in the fields; hence I do not believe that my estimates of the numbers of white servants can possibly be too high. The account is based on figures in the Lancaster County Court books in the Virginia State Library.

46. Historical Manuscripts Commission, *Seventh Report,* p. 572; Thurloe, *State Papers,* III, 500.

47. *C.S.P. Colonial,* 1699, no. 954 i; Hall, *Acts of Barbados,* p. 149.

48. See *Journals of House of Representatives of Massachusetts,* IV, 49.

49. The story of the recruiting of servants in Pennsylvania is fully set forth in Herrick, *White Servitude in Pennsylvania,* ch. xii.

50. Penn MSS, Assembly and Council, no. 41, Historical Society of Pennsylvania. A court at Havana in 1745 judged a number of Irish servants, taken on board an English ship, to be "cargo" (*Virginia Gazette,* July 4-11, 1745).

51. Hening, *Statutes,* V, 95.

52. Herrick, ch. xii; Penn MSS, Official Correspondence, VIII, 25.

53. *Archives of Maryland,* XXXI, 105-13, 154-56; LII, xxx-xxxi; Pargellis, ed., *Military Affairs in America,* p. 174.

54. This document is in the Huntington Library, and there is a photostat copy at the Historical Society of Pennsylvania.

55. Dinwiddie to Captain John McNeil, December 25, 1756, *Dinwiddie Papers,* II, 571-72.

56. Baltimore County, Court Proceedings, 1757-1759, August and November sessions, 1757. Compensation was awarded for forty-two enlisted servants.

57. *Archives of Maryland,* XLV, 629; Herrick, pp. 251-53; *Pennsylvania Archives,* 1st ser., V, 340; Samuel McKee, *Labor in Colonial New York,* pp. 175-76.

CHAPTER XIII

1. Printed in *The Narrative of General [Robert] Venables,* ed. C. H. Firth (London and New York, 1900), p. 146.

2. *Virginia Magazine of History,* IX (1901-02), 271-72.

3. *A Publication of Guiana's Plantation* (London, 1632), p. 13. See Christopher Jeaffreson, who wrote in 1681 that the West Indies, at their first peopling, had been a "Kinde of Bedlam" (*Young Squire,* I, 259).

4. Charles Davenant, *Discourses on the Publick Revenues, and on the Trade of England* (London, 1698), II, 196.

5. *C.S.P. Colonial,* 1699, no. 473.

6. *Ibid.,* 1685-1688, no. 1876.

7. *Leah and Rachel,* in *Narratives of Early Maryland,* p. 285.

8. Hugh Jones, *The Present State of Virginia,* p. 114.

9. *Georgia Colonial Records,* IV, 117, 267-68, 301, 302; XXV, 508.

10. Examples from the *Maryland Gazette,* and from an article by Allen Walker Read, in *Journal of English and Germanic Philology,* XXXVII, 70-79.

11. William D. Hoyt, Jr., "The White Servants at 'Northampton,' 1772-74," *Maryland Historical Magazine,* XXXIII (1938), 126-33.

12. Bullock, *Virginia Impartially Examined,* pp. 53-54; *Leah and Rachel,* in *Narratives of Early Maryland,* p. 292. Jeaffreson wrote "no goale bird can be so incorrigible, but there is hope of his conformity here" (*Young Squire,* I, 258, and see pp. 207-9). Samuel Smith of New Jersey said "Many that came servants, succeeded better than some that brought estates; the first inured to industry, and the ways of the country, became wealthy, while the others obliged to spend what they had in the difficulties of first improvements" (*History of New Jersey,* p. 103n.).

13. Lancaster County Order Book, 1721-1729, p. 52; and court held November 10, 1725.

14. Letter iii.

15. Long, *History of Jamaica,* I, 263, 249; *Tudor and Stuart Proclama-*

tions, no. 2735. By 1663 Barbados was described as overcrowded (*C.S.P. Colonial,* 1661-1668, no. 565).

16. Ibid., 1669-1674, no. 977.

17. Young Squire, I, 256.

18. Deposition in H.C.A. 30/873.

19. C.S.P. Colonial, 1693-1696, p. 446.

20. Ibid., 1677-1680, pp. 503, 510.

21. Ibid., 1720-1721, no. 148. Back in 1671 a Carolinian said that one English servant was worth two Barbadians, the latter being too much addicted to rum (*ibid.,* 1669-1674, no. 472). Nevertheless, it was worth a good deal to get settlers who had been "seasoned" to the climate.

22. The Case of John Wilmore, p. 3.

23. West-India Collonies, p. 27.

24. Acts Privy Council, Colonial, III, 471; Leslie, *New Account of Jamaica,* p. 320. See Pitman, *Development of the British West Indies.*

25. Yet they often insisted on procuring their own land; see McKee, *Labor in Colonial New York,* pp. 24, 113. In a very instructive paper, the Board of Trade summarized the results of inquiries made in 1697 to determine which colonies offered the best opportunities for disbanded soldiers. After reviewing the West Indian laws offering special inducements, and citing the high wage scales of the continental colonies, especially the middle ones, the Board concluded that Maryland, Virginia, and Jamaica held out the best chances (C.O. 324/6, pp. 196-203).

26. Official Letters of Alexander Spotswood, II, 227. The governor had a low opinion of these folk.

27. T. J. Wertenbaker, *Planters of Colonial Virginia,* pp. 75, 80.

28. Ibid., pp. 81-83, 97-99. For the shortcomings of these registries, see Bruce, *Economic History of Virginia,* I, 518 ff.; and *C.S.P. Colonial,* 1697-1698, p. 390.

29. For the sources of the following paragraphs, see an article by the present author on "The Indentured Servant and Land Speculation in Seventeenth Century Maryland," in *American Historical Review,* XL, 467-72.

30. Georgia Colonial Records, III, 387.

31. McCormac, *White Servitude in Maryland,* p. 61.

32. Van Doren, *Franklin,* p. 7.

33. Helen Hill, *George Mason, Constitutionalist* (Cambridge, Mass., 1938), p. 18.

34. Virginia Impartially Examined, p. 54.

35. R. P. DuTertre, *Histoire Generale des Antilles Habitées par Les Fran-çois* (4 vols., Paris, 1667-1671), II, 455.

36. Letters from America, pp. 66-67.

37. Annals of Philadelphia, II, 267.

BIBLIOGRAPHICAL NOTE

A. DOCUMENTARY MATERIAL, PRINTED AND UNPRINTED, GREAT BRITAIN AND IRELAND

I. COLONIAL OFFICE PAPERS (PUBLIC RECORD OFFICE, LONDON).

These consist of correspondence between the British government and its officials in the colonies, sessional papers from the colonies, acts of colonial legislatures, minute books of the various councils for administering colonial affairs, etc. See C. M. Andrews, *Guide to the materials for American History to 1783, in the Public Record Office of Great Britain,* 2 vols., Washington, 1912-14. Most of these papers up to the year 1733 have been summarized in the *Calendar of State Papers, Colonial Series, American and West Indies,* 1574-1733, 40 vols., London, 1862-1939. Sometimes the summary is adequate; sometimes not, and the earlier volumes are the least satisfactory. The Board of Trade Journal, which is abstracted in the Calendar as far as the year 1704, is thereafter printed as *Journal of the Commissioners for Trade and Plantations,* 1704-1782, 16 vols., London, 1920-37.

Many Colonial Office Papers of dates subsequent to 1733 which are as yet uncalendared are printed in the documentary publications of American states, especially those of New York and North Carolina, which see below. Access to them is also rendered fairly easy by references contained in the Board of Trade Journal.

Of unprinted Colonial Office Papers, the most important for this study are the Shipping Returns, which are reports of Naval Officers in various colonies giving the names, descriptions, owners, captains, cargoes, and routes of ships entering and leaving colonial ports. Those for Maryland are most useful, since they generally mention the presence of convicts or servants on board; there are, however, only two volumes of them in the Public Record Office, as follows: C.O. 5/749, 1689-1702, and C.O. 5/750, 1754-1765. A Shipping Return for the port of Annapolis, 1756-1775, may be found at the Maryland Historical Society, Baltimore, and another for the same port, 1748-1759, is at the Hall of Records, Annapolis, while the latter repository also has Returns for Port Oxford and the Patuxent District of dates 1742-1757. Just why these records should overlap in this way, and why they should be distributed between Maryland and London, is not clear. The Shipping Returns of other colonies do not generally mention passengers on ships; an early return from Jamaica (C. O. 142/13, 1680-1705) was useful in tracing Monmouth Rebels nevertheless, and returns from Virginia in the eighteenth century show the arrival of ships which we know to have taken convicts from London.

The record books of the Providence Company, whose life extended through the 1630's, are numbered C.O. 124/1 and 124/2. The entry book C.O. 389/2 is devoted almost entirely to material on the practice of "spiriting," of date 1671.

II. OTHER DOCUMENTARY MATERIAL IN THE PUBLIC RECORD OFFICE.

The State Papers, Domestic, contain a considerable amount of material on political and convict transportation, especially correspondence concerning pardons for felons. These papers are calendared as follows: *Calendar of State Papers, Domestic,* 1547-1704, 80 vols., London, 1865—; *Calendar of Home Office Papers of the Reign of George III,* 1760-1775, 4 vols., London, 1878-99. Entry books S.P. 44/81 ff. contain records of pardons issued to felons after the act of 1717. The entry book S.P. 44/56 contains letters from Sunderland to Jeffreys about the disposal of Monmouth Rebels.

The Privy Council Register contains the formal reprieves of felons for transportation before 1633. Disallowances of colonial laws were made in Privy Council, and many orders concerning kidnapping are found there. The Register has been printed as follows: *Acts of the Privy Council,* 1542-1604, 32 vols., London, 1890-1907; *Acts of the Privy Council,* 1613-1626, London, 1922—, in progress; *Acts of the Privy Council, Colonial,* 1613-1783, 6 vols., London, 1908-12. It would appear that not all reprieves for convicts were included in the Colonial Calendar, but an inspection of several volumes of the original register of a date later than that of the full printing did not disclose any further convicts transported.

Treasury Papers most important for this subject are the Money Books (T. 53), in which are entered warrants for the payment of money, and documents appertaining thereto. Here are found the lists of felons transported by Jonathan Forward and his successors, from 1718 to 1772, with the amounts paid the contractors, the dates of shipment, etc. The contracts made for transportation are entered in the books of Warrants not Relating to Money (T. 54). Other papers of great importance are the registers of emigrants from Great Britain: T. 47/9-11 referring to England, and T. 47/12 to Scotland. For a further description of these see Andrews, *Guide,* II, p. 224. The bundle T. 1/500 contains many letters concerning emigration of the same period, and a very interesting account of Duncan Campbell's transportation of convicts after the subsidy had ceased in 1772. Calendars are as follows: *Calendar of Treasury Books,* 1660-1705, edited by W. A. Shaw, 19 vols. in 33 parts, London, 1904-38; *Calendar of Treasury Papers,* 1557-1728, edited by H. Redington, 6 vols., London, 1868-89; *Calendar of Treasury Books and Papers,* 1729-1745, edited by W. A. Shaw, 5 vols., London, 1897-1903. The last of these contains notices of convicts transported within the dates covered. The first includes lists of Monmouth Rebels sent by the judges to the Treasury on November 12, 1685. Payments for transporting rebels of 1715 and 1745 are entered in the Money Books.

Chancery Documents. Pardons for convicts transported between 1655 and 1718 are to be found in the Patent Rolls (C. 66). There is no calendar, but a contemporary manuscript index, in the Legal Search Room, acts as a guide. This lists under "Pardonaciones" the majority of relevant enrollments, without any indication of whether or not the pardons are conditional; thus the originals must always be consulted. The Chancery Warrants (C. 82), contain the justices' recommendations for these pardons, with notes of each convict's crime, and of any extenuating circumstances. They are arranged by months, and a warrant for any given pardon may be found by consulting the bundle for the month in which the pardon was dated. On the Patent Rolls may be found the grants to Roger Whitley and his successors of rights to set up offices of registration for servants going to the plantations.

Admiralty Papers. Two bundles of ships' papers among the High Court of Admiralty Miscellany (H.C.A. 30/635 and 636) contain the accounts and letter books of the ships *Tristram and Jane,* and *Abraham,* both of which carried servants to the plantations in 1636.

III. PARLIAMENTARY PROCEEDINGS, ENGLAND.

Stock, L. F., ed. *Proceedings and Debates of the British Parliaments respecting North America,* 1542-1739. 4 vols., Washington, 1924-37.

Burton, Thomas. *Diary of Thomas Burton, Esq. . . . from 1656 to*

1659. 4 vols., London, 1828. This contains an account of the proceedings relative to the petition of Rivers and Foyle, who had been transported to Barbados.

IV. JUDICIAL RECORDS, ENGLAND.

By far the most useful printed records for this subject are contained in the *Middlesex County Records,* II-IV, ed. by J. C. Jeaffreson (1887-92). These are selections from various classes of sessions records, rather than complete editions of proceedings. There is a great deal of material on kidnapping, on Quakers, and on felons after 1655. The *Hertfordshire County Records,* VI-VIII (1930-35), are calendars of the Sessions Books, Sessions Minute Books, and other records, and contain a few records of the transportation of convicts during the eighteenth century. All other published quarter sessions records which I have inspected have yielded no evidences for this study.

During the last of the seventeenth century and the eighteenth, printed sessions reports were regularly issued after the Newgate jail deliveries. A sample title is as follows: *The Proceedings on the Kings Commisions of the Peace and Oyer and Terminer, and Gaol-delivery of Newgate, held for the City of London, and County of Middlesex, at Justice Hall, in the Old-Baily, the 11th and 12th of July 1688. And in the Fourth Year of His Majesties Reign.* Collections of these are in the British Museum and the Bodleian Library; they give some account of the trial of each prisoner, and record his sentence, but they are not of primary importance for the history of transportation.

At the Guildhall, London, are sessions records similar to those edited for Middlesex by Jeaffreson. The Newgate Calendars are also kept here. I have used these records in an attempt to establish the actual transportation of seventeenth-century convicts, but except for occasional definite notices of shipment in isolated cases, found no information.

A quarter sessions record in the Bristol City Archives yielded notice of twelve Quakers sentenced to transportation in 1665, but had not a single vagabond or felon condemned.

Most useful of all judicial records are those of the Western Circuit for the eighteenth century, which are in the Public Record Office (Class: Assizes). The Order Books contain records of transportation, and from 1725 there is a special series for this purpose (Assizes 24/24 ff.) From 1730 a large part of each order is printed, the necessary sections, names of prisoners, etc. being filled in by hand. This constitutes the only collection of evidence concerning the transportation of convicts from the provinces.

V. SCOTLAND AND IRELAND.

Stock, L. F. *Proceedings and Debates of the British Parliaments respecting North America,* has material up to 1739 from the Scottish and Irish Assemblies.

Register of the Privy Council of Scotland, 1545-1625, 14 vols.; 2nd ser., 1625-1660, 8 vols.; 3rd ser., 1661-1689, 14 vols. Edinburgh, 1877-1933.

Firth, C. H., ed. *Scotland and the Protectorate. Letters and Papers relating to the Military Government of Scotland from January 1654 to June 1659.* Edinburgh, 1899.

Dunlop, R., editor. *Ireland under the Commonwealth,* 2 vols., Manchester, 1913.

Gwynn, Rev. Aubrey, S.J., ed. "Documents relating to the Irish in the West Indies," in *Analecta Hibernica* (Irish Manuscripts Commission), no. 4, October, 1932, pp. 139-286.

Journals of the House of Commons of the Kingdom of Ireland, IV, Appendix, pp. cciii and following, contains a long report on the transportation of felons for the seven years before 1743, which is the date of the report.

Thurloe, John. *A Collection of State Papers of J. T. . . . 7* vols., London, 1742. Though not primarily concerned with Scotland and Ireland, these volumes yielded material for this study chiefly in that connection.

VI. MISCELLANEOUS DOCUMENTARY SOURCES, GREAT BRITAIN.

British Museum. Egerton MSS, 2395. A large and mixed collection, dating mainly from the 1650's and early 1660's, and containing many copies of State Papers in the Public Record Office. Additional MSS, 11410 and 11411 are the letter books of Thomas Povey, a merchant trading to the West Indies at the time of the Protectorate and Restoration.

Guildhall, London. Here are found twelve bonds for the transportation of convicts, of dates between 1666 and 1670, and forty-four certificates of the arrival of shipments of felons in various colonies between 1718 and 1736. There are a few original transportation pardons of the seventeenth century, and some letters of the secretaries of state notifying officials of the pardon of felons, *temp.* George II and George III. These documents exhibit, to a limited degree, how the transportation system was supposed to work.

The registration of servants is demonstrated by memoranda in the mayor's "Waiting Book," which I have inspected for the year 1684. Entry books of departing servants' names, and blank forms containing the terms of their indentures of dates from 1718 to 1736 and after have been described in the Appendix.

Guildhall, Middlesex (Parliament Square, London). Here is a file of indentures as registered by the justices of Middlesex in 1683-1685, and described in the Appendix. There may also be seen many bonds executed in the eighteenth century for the transportation of convicts, the contractor giving security of £40 each to convey them safely away. No certificates of the arrival of convicts in the colonies were found here, and no vestige of any eighteenth-century registration of indentured servants has remained.

Bristol. Archives at the Council House. Two volumes of registrations of servants' indentures, 1654-1686. Partly printed in N. Dermott Harding, ed., *Bristol and America: A Record of the First Settlers in the Colonies of North America 1654-1685,* Bristol, n.d.

Royal Empire Society, London. The Davis Transcripts. This is a collection of transcripts made by N. Darnell Davis, from records in the West Indies, mainly Barbados. Many of the originals from which these were taken have now deteriorated so as to be unusable.

At Racedown, Dorset, by the kindness of General Sir Reginald and Lady Pinney, I was able to inspect the Pinney family papers for an account of Azariah Pinney, a Monmouth Rebel.

B. DOCUMENTARY MATERIAL, PRINTED AND UNPRINTED, VARIOUS COLONIES.

I. NOVA SCOTIA.

Atkins, Thomas B., ed. *Selections from the Public Documents of the Province of Nova Scotia.* Halifax, 1869.

"Calendar of Papers relating to Nova Scotia," in *Report on Canadian Archives, 1894,* by Douglas Brymner, Archivist. Ottawa, 1895.

The first of these works contains many documents on the settlement of Halifax, printed *in extenso.* The second is a calendar of documents relating to Nova Scotia, copied from originals now in the Public Record Office, and deposited in the Canadian Archives at Ottawa. I have used this calendar principally as a guide to the correspondence between John Dick and the Board of Trade concerning the transportation of Germans to Halifax in 1750-1753. This correspondence throws much light on the whole trade in German emigrants; it is insufficiently calendared, however, and the original documents, rather than the Ottawa transcripts were used by me in this study.

Nearly all of the most enlightening documents on the recruiting and outfitting of servants in the earliest years are collected in Alexander Young, *Chronicles of the First Planters of the Colony of Massachusetts Bay From 1623 to 1636*, Boston, 1846. The Minutes of the Council for New England are printed in the *Proceedings* of the American Antiquarian Society for April, 1867; they contain a good many references to the procuring of children for apprentices, but in general are by no means as valuable for this study as the minutes of the Virginia or Providence Companies.

The official records of the colony of Massachusetts Bay contain so little on this subject that it is not worth while to list them here. More is found in the *Records of the Colony of New Plymouth in New England*, ed. by Nathaniel B. Shurtleff, 12 vols., 1855-61, especially in vol. I, which prints court orders of dates 1633-1640. Massachusetts Bay, instead of requiring its highest dignitaries to supervise servant cases, naturally disposed of them in the lower courts; hence the *Records of the Suffolk County Court, 1671-1680*, Colonial Society of Massachusetts, *Publications*, XXIX-XXX (1933), and the *Records and Files of the Quarterly Courts of Essex County, Massachusetts*, 8 vols., Salem, 1911-21, will be found rich in servant cases.

The *Reports of the Record Commissioners of the City of Boston*, 39 vols., 1876-1909, print in chronological order the records of the Board of Selectmen, which contain various orders concerning immigration and the registration of servants. Vol. XXIX of these reports, "A Volume of Records Relating to the Early History of Boston containing Miscellaneous Papers," prints fragmentary registries of immigrants from the records of the Impost Office.

A considerable amount of searching among published New England records has failed to disclose any other important sources of information concerning indentured servants.

O'Callaghan, E. B., ed. *Documents Relative to the Colonial History of the State of New York*. 10 vols. and an index volume, Albany, 1856-61.

New Jersey: *Documents Relating to the Colonial History of the State of New Jersey.* 1st ser., 33 vols., Newark, 1880-1928.

IV. PENNSYLVANIA.

There is a short record of persons arriving at the port of Philadelphia, 1682-1686, preserved at the Historical Society of Pennsylvania; it is printed in J. Smith Futhey and Gilbert Cope, *History of Chester County, Pennsylvania* (Philadelphia, 1881). Registrations of the arrival of Germans begin systematically in 1727; these have several times been printed, but the best edition is now titled as follows: Ralph B. Strassburger, *Pennsylvania German Pioneers: A Publication of the Original Lists of Arrivals In the Port of Philadelphia From 1727 to 1808*, ed. by William J. Hinke, 3 vols., published by the Pennsylvania German Society, 1934.

Records of indentures made before the mayor have been preserved from two periods, 1745-55 and 1771-73. The first is preserved in manuscript at the Historical Society of Pennsylvania and printed in the *Pennsylvania Magazine of History and Biography*, XXX-XXXII (1906-08), *passim*. The second is in the library of the American Philosophical Society, and is printed in the *Proceedings* of the Pennsylvania German Society, XVI (1907). At the Historical Society of Pennsylvania is a rough copy of part of this record, which contains some information not found in the fair copy.

Among the Penn MSS at the Historical Society of Pennsylvania are several statistical accounts of immigration, some of which have been quoted in the Appendix.

This Society has a collection of "Indentures of Apprentices" in which may be found redemptionist agreements, sales of servants, and indentures with the certificate of the registry office in England.

Court proceedings are not plentifully printed; indeed the only publications available are as follows: "Record of Upland court; from the 14th of November 1676, to the 14th of June 1681," in *Memoirs* of the Historical Society of Pennsylvania, VII, Philadelphia, 1860; *Record of the Courts of Chester County, Pennsylvania*, 1681-1697, published by the Colonial Society of Pennsylvania, Philadelphia, 1910; *Records of the Courts of Quarter Sessions and Common Pleas of Bucks County, Pennsylvania, 1684-1700*, also published by the Colonial Society of Pennsylvania, Philadelphia, 1943. I have been through the records of the Chester court for the eighteenth century, and have drawn many examples of the treatment of servants from them. They are kept in the county court house at West Chester.

There is a good deal of material which is relevant to this subject in *Minutes of the Provincial Council [of Pennsylvania]*, I-X, Philadelphia, 1852-53 (binder's title: *Colonial Records*).

V. MARYLAND.

The *Archives of Maryland,* published by authority of the state, under the direction of the Maryland Historical Society, Baltimore, 1883, has now reached its fifty-eighth volume, and is for the purposes of this study by far the most useful of all printed colonial material. Special mention ought to be made of the local court records of the seventeenth century, printed in vols. LIII and LIV, and of the series of proceedings of the Provincial Court, making up various volumes of the series, all of them full of records of the crimes and misdoings of servants, and of their treatment in the colony.

None of the printed court proceedings extends into the eighteenth century. I have therefore been through many volumes of records of the courts of Anne Arundel and Baltimore counties, and of the proceedings of the Provincial Court, all of which are now conveniently accessible at the Hall of Records, Annapolis. I have drawn many examples from these volumes, but it must be said that they are not as rewarding as the earlier, printed, records. The clerks began to learn their legal formulas, and with each passing year the weight of verbiage becomes greater, and the amount of historical information less, so that long before the middle of the eighteenth century the records become weary and unprofitable to the layman. The *Proceedings of the Maryland Court of Appeals, 1695-1729*, ed. by Judge Carroll T. Bond, Washington, 1933, contain much material on a suit by Jonathan Forward against his Maryland factors.

The twenty-six volumes of Land Books in the Land Office, Hall of Records, covering the period from 1633 to 1680, contain the names of more than 21,000 immigrants, nearly all servants, who were registered during that period for the purpose of obtaining headrights. They also contain record of servants who took up their land as freedom dues, and I have found them among the most valuable of all documents for a study of servants in the plantations.

The eighteenth century Shipping Returns, some of which are at the Hall of Records and some in the library of the Maryland Historical Society, Baltimore, have already been described in the first section of this Bibliographical Note, as they seem to fall more naturally into the class of Colonial Office Papers even though not now located in London.

They, together with the Land Office Books just mentioned, render statistics for the immigration of servants and convicts into Maryland far more satisfactory than those for any other colony.

VI. VIRGINIA AND BERMUDA.

Brown, Alexander. *The Genesis of the United States.* London, 1890.

Kingsbury, Susan M., ed. *Records of the Virginia Company of London.* 4 vols., Washington, 1906-35.

Lefroy, J. H., ed. *Memorials of the Discovery and early settlement of the Bermudas or Somers Islands, 1518-1685.* 2 vols., London, 1877-99.

McIlwaine, H. R., ed. *Executive Journals of the Council of Colonial Virginia.* 4 vols., Richmond, 1925-30.

McIlwaine, H. R., ed. *Journals of the House of Burgesses of Virginia, 1619-1776.* 13 vols., Richmond, 1905-15.

Palmer, W. P., ed. *Calendar of Virginia State Papers.* . . . Vol. I, Richmond, 1875.

"Documents . . . relating to the Huguenot Emigration to America," Virginia Historical Society, *Collections,* new ser., V (1886).

These are all the printed documents which have yielded much information concerning indentured servants; of them all the second is much the most important, providing as it does the principal sources for the origins of white servitude.

Local court records have not been printed in satisfactory fashion, but many of them are collected either in the original or in photostat copies in the Virginia State Library, Richmond. I have drawn much material from the Order Books of Lancaster and Northumberland counties, and some from those of Spotsylvania County.

The Land Books are in the Land Office at the State Capitol, Richmond. I did not find them nearly so useful as those of Maryland, but they contain registers of headrights.

VII. THE CAROLINAS AND GEORGIA.

Saunders, William L., ed. *The Colonial Records of North Carolina.* 10 vols., Goldsboro and Raleigh, 1886-90.

Salley, A. S., ed. *Warrants for Lands in South Carolina, 1672-1711.* Published by the South Carolina Historical Commission, 3 vols., 1910-15.

Candler, Allen D., ed. *The Colonial Records of the State of Georgia.* 26 vols., Atlanta, 1904-16.

VIII. THE WEST INDIES.

Journals of the Assembly of Jamaica, printed by order of the House of Assembly, 1811-29. Vol. I, 1663/4-1709, has a statistical Appendix which is useful.

Interesting Tracts Relating to the Island of Jamaica, consisting of curious State Papers, Councils of War, Letters, Petitions, Narratives, etc. . . . St. Jago de la Vega, 1800.

Barbados Council Minutes, of dates before 1661, which formerly existed only on the island, may now be seen in a typewritten copy in the Public Record Office.

C. COLONIAL LAWS CONCERNING INDENTURED SERVANTS.

The following is by no means a complete list, but is intended to give the dates and titles of the more important statutes, indicate the sources from which they were taken in the present study, and furnish the basis for a rough comparison between them.

I. NEW ENGLAND.

The lack of statutory law respecting servants in New England is one of the chief reasons for believing that there were few indentured servants there; but it is a reason which ought not to be given undue weight, as it usually is. A law stating that "If any man smite out the eye or tooth of his man-servant or maid servant, or otherwise mayme or much disfigure him, unlesse it be by meere casualtie, he shall let them goe free from his service" (New Hampshire, *Laws,* I, 761-62; *Colonial Laws of Massachusetts,* Boston, 1887, pp. 104-5) was often enacted, but is merely a transcription of the Mosaic law in Exodus, 21: 26, 27. Likewise the injunction that servants who have served diligently and faithfully for seven years should not be sent away empty handed, is biblical (Deuteronomy 15: 12, 13). The Puritans added to the former a clause giving the cruel master "such further recompense as the Court shall allow him." These found their way into the "Duke of York's Laws," and thus were in effect for a time in New York and in the province which later became Pennsylvania.

The chief reference for the Massachusetts laws is, of course, *The Acts and Resolves, Public and Private, of the Province of the Massachusetts Bay.* 21 vols., Boston, 1869-1922.

No general statute concerning servants, but many separate acts, will be found in *Records of Plymouth Colony. Laws 1623-1682.* ed. by David Pulsifer. Boston, 1861.

II. NEW YORK.

1684. "A Bill Concerning Masters servants Slaves Labourers and Apprentices." *The Colonial Laws of New York,* Albany, 1894, I, 157-58.

This is the only important servant law in the colonial period, and is by no means comprehensive in scope. Previous to its enactment, the "Duke of York's Laws," which may be found in the same volume, embodied principally the biblical precepts of the New England laws described above.

III. NEW JERSEY.

1682. Two laws fixed times of service for servants in West and East Jersey. They may be found in *The Grants, Concessions and Original Constitutions of . . . New Jersey.* Philadelphia, printed by William Bradford, n.d., pp. 236, 447.

1713/4. "An Act for regulating of White Servants . . . ," in *Acts of the General Assembly of . . . New Jersey.* Burlington, 1776, p. 21. This law, despite its title, actually deals only with runaways.

IV. PENNSYLVANIA.

1700. "An Act for the better Regulation of Servants in this Province and Territories," in *Statutes at Large,* II, 54-56. This law covers the subjects of runaways and freedom dues, but is not of broad scope. Previously, the "Duke of York's Laws" had been temporarily in force, succeeded shortly after 1682 by other enactments. Herrick, *White Servitude in Pennsylvania,* arranges Pennsylvania servant laws in tabulated form in an Appendix.

V. MARYLAND.

1676. "An Act Relateing to Servants and Slaves," in *Archives of Maryland,* II, 523-28.

1692. "An Act Relating to servants and Slaves," *ibid.,* XIII, 451 Renewals of this act, with slight changes may be found in 1704, 1715, 1719, 1748, *ibid.,* XXVI, 254; XXX, 283; XLVI, 149; and in *Laws of Maryland at large . . . ,* collected by Thomas Bacon, Annapolis, 1765. The latter is unpaged, and reference is made by year and chapter: 1715, ch. 44; 1719, ch. 2; 1748, ch. 19.

Earlier acts were fairly plentiful, but each dealt with only one subject. The first law fixing freedom dues seems to have been in 1640, and is found in *Archives of Maryland*, I, 97. Others are referred to in the footnotes to this study.

VI. VIRGINIA.

1705. "An Act concerning Servants and Slaves," in Hening, *Statutes*, III, 447-62.

1748. "An Act concerning Servants and Slaves," *ibid.*, V, 547-58. This law was repealed by the Privy Council; see *Acts Privy Council, Colonial*, IV, 140, for the reasons.

1753. "An Act for the better government of servants and slaves," in Hening, *Statutes*, VI, 356-369.

There are many earlier laws dealing with specific problems; for some of the more significant concerning time of service and runaway penalties see Hening, *Statutes*, as follows: 1642/3, I, 254-57; 1657/8, I, 440, 471, 483; 1663, II, 187-88, 266; 1666, II, 240.

VII. NORTH CAROLINA.

1715. "An Act Concerning Servants and Slaves."

1741. A new act concerning servants and slaves, repealing the former. The latter may be found in *Laws of the State of North Carolina*, published . . . by James Iredell, Edenton, 1791, pp. 85-95. I have found only the title of the earlier act.

VIII. SOUTH CAROLINA.

1717. "An Act for the better governing and regulating White servants."

1744. A new act for the same purpose, and for repealing the former. Both may be found in *The Statutes at Large of South Carolina*, ed. by Thomas Cooper, III, 14, 621. The earliest act is of the year 1687, and sets the time of service for incoming servants without written indenture, *ibid.*, I, 30.

IX. BARBADOS.

1652. Various acts concerning white servants were approved by the governor in this year, and can be found only in an extremely rare book of which I have used a copy at the British Museum: *Acts and Statutes of the Island of Barbados. Made and Enacted since the Reducement of the same, unto the Authority of the Commonwealth of England*, collected by John Jennings, printed at London, n.d.; Preface dated at Indian Bridge, Barbados, July 9, 1654. Contains 102 acts of the years 1651-1654, compiled from "the Original Record Book of the Acts and Statutes of this Island." These laws are not to be found in the Public Record Office.

1661. "An Act for the good governing of Servants, and ordaining the Rights between Masters and Servants." Printed in *Acts passed in the Island of Barbados, 1643-1672,* carefully revised by Richard Hall, London, 1764, pp. 35-42. This act has been described in the text; it is the first comprehensive statute concerning white servitude, and it remained in force throughout the colonial period.

1703. "An Act for the encouragement of White Servants, and to Ascertain their allowance of Provisions and Clothes." Hall, *Acts,* p. 157. This is the only printed act of this type. Other laws for encouraging the importation of white servants have been taken from the class C.O. 30 in the Public Record Office, and reference has been made to them in footnotes.

X. THE LEEWARD ISLANDS.

1669, Antigua. "An Act Stateing Servants Tymes, Wages, provisions, Apparrells, etc." C.O. 154/1, f. 39. This is the only general act which I have noted from this period. In 1672 Nevis passed a law fixing times of service, freedom dues, and a good many other details; this may be found in C.O. 154/1, f. 98. In 1675 a law of Nevis concerning runaways is in C.O. 154/2, p. 114. Other acts encouraging the importation of servants have been referred to in footnotes in the text.

St. Christopher in 1715/16 passed "An Act for the good governing of Servants . . . ," and replaced this in 1722 with "An Act for the good Government of Servants, for ordering the Rights between Masters and Servants . . . ," etc. This may be found in *Acts of Assembly Passed in the Island of St. Christopher, from 1711 to 1735, inclusive.* London, printed by John Baskett, 1739, pp. 64-69.

In 1740 John Baskett printed a volume of *Acts passed in the Island of Montserrat, from 1668 to 1740;* one of *Acts of Assembly passed in the Island of Nevis;* and one of *Acts of Assembly passed in the Charibee Leeward Islands, From 1690 to 1730.* All of these contain laws about servants; the Nevis volume includes the act of 1681 reducing freedom dues from 800 pounds of sugar, where it had been put in 1675, to 400.

XI. JAMAICA.

1661. The Barbados act (probably as we have it in Jennings, and not as in Hall) is put in force by order of the governor and council. C.O. 139/1, f. 3.

1664. "An Act for the Good Governing of Servants and ordaining the Rights betweene Masters and Servants." This act is copied from the Barbados statute in Hall. C.O. 139/1, ff. 60-63.

This law was frequently reenacted, with minor changes; thus: 1672, C.O. 139/1, f. 123; 1675, C.O. 139/5, f. 19; 1677, C.O. 139/5, f. 6. It took permanent form in

1681. "An Act for Regulating Servants." Printed in *Acts of Assembly Passed in the Island of Jamaica, from 1681, to 1754, inclusive*. London, printed for Curtis Brett & C., 1756. It appears also in a compilation under the same title, published in Jamaica, St. Jago de la Vega, 1769.

The "deficiency" laws, and laws encouraging the importation of white servants, have been sufficiently referred to in the footnotes.

D. PERIODICAL LITERATURE.

Of contemporary periodicals, the only ones extensively used in this study were the *Maryland Gazette,* published at Annapolis (file at the State Library, Annapolis), and the *Virginia Gazette,* published at Williamsburg (file at Virginia State Library). The editors of colonial newspapers filled many columns with items clipped from English papers; these often prove the most illuminating contributions the paper makes to this subject, for many stories of the departure of felons and other emigrants are reproduced.

A list of modern historical journals follows. These are as apt to yield original documentary evidence as anything else; I have been through complete files of those listed.

The American Historical Review.
The Journal of the American Irish Historical Society.
Maryland Historical Magazine.
New England Historical and Genealogical Register.
North Carolina Historical Review.
Pennsylvania Magazine of History and Biography.

South Carolina Historical and Genealogical Magazine.
Tyler's Quarterly Historical and Genealogical Register.
Virginia Magazine of History and Biography.
William and Mary College Quarterly.

An invaluable assistance in using the last three periodicals is the *Virginia Historical Index,* by E. G. Swem, 2 vols., Richmond, 1934-36.

The *Publications* of the Colonial Society of Massachusetts, and the *Collections* and *Proceedings* of the Massachusetts Historical Society were of considerable use in this study. Some guide to the voluminous publications of the latter society is contained in: Massachusetts Historical Society, *Handbook of the Publications and Photostats, 1792-1933,* Boston, 1934.

A few special articles or documents from these and other periodicals are cited in the following sections of this bibliography.

E. OTHER CONTEMPORARY OR NEARLY CONTEMPORARY MATERIAL.

Nearly everyone who travelled in the colonies and wrote about them made some mention of indentured servitude. The following list contains only those works which have been used most often in preparing this study, or which are not commonly included in other bibliographies.

Anonymous. *Some Memoirs of the First Settlement of the Island of Barbados, and other the Carribbees Islands* . . . Barbados, 1741.

———— *A True and Impartial Narrative of the Remarkable Providences of the Living God* . . . *appearing for his oppressed servants called Quakers.* London, 1664.

———— *The Cry of the Innocent and Oppressed for Justice, or a brief Relation of the Late Proceedings against the Prisoners called Quakers.* London, 1664.

———— *Another Cry of the Innocent and Oppressed for Justice* etc. London, 1664.

———— *A Third Cry of the Innocent* etc. London, 1665.

———— *The English Rogue* . . . *Being a Compleat History of the Most Eminent Cheats of Both Sexes.* London, Part I, 1665; Part II, 1668; Part III, 1674; Part IV, 1680. Part I is probably by Richard Head; Part II by Francis Kirkman, and parts III and IV probably also by Kirkman.

Alsop, George. *A Character of the Province of Maryland.* 1666. Maryland Historical Society, *Fund Publication,* no. 15. Baltimore, 1880.

Besse, Joseph. *An Abstract of the Sufferings of the People called Quakers.* 3 vols., London, 1733.

Boucher, Rev. Jonathan. Letters. *Maryland Historical Magazine,* VII-X (1912-15), *passim.*

Bullock, William. *Virginia Impartially Examined* . . . London, 1649.

Coad, John. *A Memorandum of the Wonderful Providences of God to a poor unworthy Creature, during the time of the Duke of Monmouth's Rebellion and to the Revolution of 1688.* London, 1849.

Dinwiddie, Robert. *The Official Records of Robert Dinwiddie . . . 1751-1758.* Virginia Historical Society, *Collections,* new ser., III-IV. Richmond, 1883-84.

Eddis, William. *Letters from America, Historical and Descriptive; Comprising Occurrences from 1769, to 1777, Inclusive.* London, 1792.

Godwyn, Morgan. *The Negro's and Indians Advocate.* London, 1680.

Hammond, John. *Leah and Rachel, or, the Two Fruitful Sisters, Virginia, and Maryland.* London, 1656. Reprinted in *Narratives of Early Maryland,* pp. 277-307.

Harcourt, Robert. *A Relation of a Voyage to Guiana.* London, 1613.

Harlow, V. T., ed. *Colonising Expeditions to the West Indies and Guiana 1623-1667.* London, Hakluyt Society, 1925.

Harrower, John. "Diary, 1773-1776." *American Historical Review,* VI (1900-01), 65-107.

Hotten, John Camden, ed. *The Original Lists of Persons of Quality, Emigrants; Religious Exiles, Political Rebels; Serving Men Sold for a Term of Years; Apprentices; etc. Who Went from Great Britain to the American Plantations, 1600-1700* . . . London, 1874.

Jeaffreson, J. C., ed. *A Young Squire of the Seventeenth Century.* From the papers (A.D. 1676-1686) of Christopher Jeaffreson, of Dullingham House, Cambridgeshire. 2 vols., London, 1878.

[Johnson, Robert]. *Nova Britannia.* London, 1609. (Peter Force, *Tracts,* I, no. 6).

Jones, Hugh. *The Present State of Virginia.* 1724. New York, reprinted for Joseph Sabin, 1865.

"Journal of a French Traveller in the Colonies, 1765." *American Historical Review,* XXVI, XXVII (1920-22), *passim.*

Lauder, Sir John of Fountainhall. *Historical Notices of Scotish Affairs.* 2 vols., Edinburgh, 1848.

Leslie, Charles. *A New and Exact Account of Jamaica.* Edinburgh, 1739.

Ligon, Richard. *A True and Exact History of the Island of Barbadoes.* Second edition, London, 1673.

Littleton, E. *Groans of the Plantations.* London, 1689.

Mittelberger, Gottlieb. *Gottlieb Mittelberger's Journey to Pennsylvania in the year 1750 and return to Germany in the year 1754.* . . . Translated by Carl Theo. Eben. Philadelphia, 1898.

Pitman, Henry. *A Relation of the great sufferings and strange adventures of Henry Pitman, Chirurgeon to the late Duke of Monmouth.* 1689. Reprinted in Edward Arber, ed., *An English Garner.* Birmingham, 1883.

Revel, James. "A Sorrowful Account of a Transported Felon, That Suffered Fourteen Years Transportation at Virginia, in America. In Six Parts. Being, A Short History of James Revel, the unhappy sufferer." (Manuscript in the Library of Congress, Ac. 2780).

Smith, Samuel. *The History of the Colony of Nova-Caesaria, or New-Jersey.* Burlington, New Jersey, 1765.

Spotswood, Alexander. *The Official Letters of Alexander Spotswood . . . 1710-1722.* Virginia Historical Society, *Collections,* new ser., I-II. Richmond, 1882-85.

Thomas, Dalby. *An Historical Account of the Rise and Growth of the West-India Collonies.* London, 1690.

Tudor and Stuart Proclamations. A Bibliography of Royal Proclamations of the Tudor and Stuart Sovereigns. . . . Oxford, 1910. Originally issued as part of the *Bibliotheca Lindesiana,* V and VI.

Williamson, Peter. *State of the Process, Peter Williamson against William Fordyce, and others.* London, 1765. (British Museum).

Wilmore, John. *The Case of John Wilmore Truly and Impartially related: or, A Looking-Glass for all Merchants and Planters That are Concerned in the American Plantations.* London, 1682.

―――― *The Legacy of John Wilmer, Citizen and Late Merchant of London: Humbly offered to the Lords and Commons of England.* London, 1692.

Winthrop, John. *Journal,* ed. by J. K. Hosmer. New York, 1908, 2 vols.

Wodrow, Robert. *The History of the Sufferings of the Church of Scotland from the Restoration to the Revolution.* Edinburgh, 1721. References in the text are to the Glasgow edition, in four volumes, 1829.

F. MODERN WORKS.

All modern works on the colonies discuss white servitude with more or less detail. There are, however, several studies devoted entirely to the

subject in particular colonies. I have relied much on these, and list them
here with some other titles which have been most useful.

Adam, Margaret I. "The Highland Emigration of 1770," *Scottish Historical Review,* XVI (1918-19), 280-93.

———— "The Causes of the Highland Emigrations of 1783-1803," *Scottish Historical Review,* XVII (1919-20), 73-89.

Ballagh, J. C. *White Servitude in the Colony of Virginia.* Baltimore (Johns Hopkins Studies), 1895.

Banks, C. E. "Scotch Prisoners Deported to New England by Cromwell, 1651-1652," Massachusetts Historical Society, *Proceedings,* LXI (1927), 4-29.

Bassett, John Spencer. *Slavery and Servitude in the Colony of North Carolina.* Baltimore (Johns Hopkins Studies), 1896.

Beer, G. L. *The Origins of the British Colonial System.* New York, 1908.

Bolton, C. K. *Scotch Irish Pioneers in Ulster and America.* Boston, 1910.

Bruce, P. A. *Economic History of Virginia in the Seventeenth Century.* 2 vols., New York, 1907 (c. 1895).

Butler, J. D. "British Convicts Shipped to American Colonies," *American Historical Review,* II (1896), 12

Eickhoff, A. *In der Neuen Heimath.* New York, 1884.

Diffenderfer, F. R. *The German Immigration into Pennsylvania through the Port of Philadelphia. 1700 to 1775.* Part II. *The Redemptioners.* Lancaster, 1900.

Faust, A. B. *The German Element in the United States . . .* 2 vols., New York, 1909.

———— "Swiss Emigration to the American Colonies in the Eighteenth Century." *American Historical Review,* XXII (1916-17), 21-44. Documents attached, pp. 98-132.

Geiser, K. F. *Redemptioners and Indentured Servants in the Colony and Commonwealth of Pennsylvania.* New Haven, 1901.

George, M. Dorothy. *London Life in the XVIIIth Century.* London, 1925.

Gray, L. C. *History of Agriculture in the Southern United States to 1860.* Vol. I. Washington, 1933.

Gwynn, Aubrey. Articles under various titles on the transportation of Irish to the West Indies, in *Studies,* XVIII, 377-93; 648-63; XIX, 279-94; 607-23; XX, 291-305.

Hanna, C. A. *The Scotch-Irish, or, The Scot in North Britain, North Ireland, and North America.* 2 vols., New York, 1902.

Harlow, V. T. *History of Barbados, 1625-1685.* Oxford, 1926.

Harrison, Fairfax. "When the Convicts Came," *Virginia Magazine of History,* XXX (1922), 250-60.

Hennighausen, L. P. "The Redemptioners and the German Society of Maryland," Society for the History of the Germans in Maryland, *Second Annual Report,* 1887-1888, pp. 33-54.

Herrick, C. A. *White Servitude in Pennsylvania, Indentured and Redemption Labor in Colony and Commonwealth.* Philadelphia, 1926.

Higham, C. S. S. *The Development of the Leeward Islands under the Restoration.* Cambridge, 1921.

Hirsch, A. H. *The Huguenots of Colonial South Carolina.* Durham, N. C., 1928.

Hurd, J. C. *The Law of Freedom and Bondage in the United States.* 2 vols., Boston, 1858.

Insh, G. P. *Scottish Colonial Schemes, 1620-1686.* Glasgow, 1922.

Jernegan, M. W. *Laboring and Dependent Classes in Colonial America, 1607-1783.* Chicago, 1931.

Jervey, Theo D. "The White Indented Servants of South Carolina," *South Carolina Historical and Genealogical Magazine,* XII (1911), 163-71.

Kilty, John. *The Landholder's Assistant . . .* Baltimore, 1808.

Knittle, W. A. *The Early Eighteenth Century Palatine Emigration.* Philadelphia, 1936.

Leonard, E. M. *The Early History of English Poor Relief.* Cambridge, 1900.

McCormac, E. I. *White Servitude in Maryland, 1634-1820.* Baltimore (Johns Hopkins Studies), 1904.

McCrady, Edward. "Slavery in the Province of South Carolina," American Historical Association, *Annual Report for 1895,* pp. 631-73.

McKee, Samuel, Jr. *Labor in the Colonial New York, 1664-1776.* New York, 1935.

Marshall, Dorothy. *The English Poor in the Eighteenth Century.* London, 1926.

Newton, A. P. *Colonizing Activities of the English Puritans.* New Haven, 1914.

Pitman, F. W. *The Development of the British West Indies, 1700-1763.* New Haven, 1917.

Ribton-Turner, E. *A History of Vagrants and Vagrancy.* London, 1887.

Risch, Erna. "Joseph Crellius, Immigrant Broker," *New England Quarterly,* XII (1939), 241-67.

Scharf, J. T. *History of Maryland.* 3 vols., Baltimore, 1879.

Semmes, Raphael. *Crime and Punishment in Early Maryland.* Baltimore, 1938.

Seton, Sir Bruce Gordon, and Arnot, Jean Gordon, eds. *The Prisoners of the '45.* 3 vols., Edinburgh, 1928.

Siebert, W. H. "Slavery and White Servitude in East Florida, 1726 to 1776," Florida Historical Society, *Quarterly Periodical,* July, 1931, pp. 3-23.

Smith, A. E. "The Transportation of Convicts to the American Colonies in the Seventeenth Century," *American Historical Review,* XXXIX (1933-34), 232-49.

———— "The Indentured Servant and Land Speculation in Seventeenth Century Maryland," *American Historical Review,* XL (1934-35), 460-72.

Sollers, Basil. "Transported Convict Laborers in Maryland during the Colonial Period," *Maryland Historical Magazine,* II (1907), 17-47.

Wertenbaker, T. J. *The Planters of Colonial Virginia.* Princeton University, 1922.

G. MISCELLANEOUS.

Two modern collections of documents have been made which extensively illustrate this subject: Commons, J. R., ed., *A Documentary History of American Industrial Society,* I, Cleveland, 1910; and Abbott, Edith, *Historical Aspects of the Immigration Problem. Select Documents,* Chicago, 1926.

Two recent bibliographies have been especially useful: Meynen, Emil, *Bibliography on German Settlements in Colonial North America . . . ,* Leipzig, 1937 (text in both German and English); and Lancouer, A. H., "Passenger Lists of Ships Coming to North America, 1607-1825," New York Public Library, *Bulletin,* XLI (1937), 389-98.

INDEX

Abdy, Anthony, 150

Abdy, Nicholas, 150

Abdy, Roger, 150

Aberdeen, Scotland: emigrant agents in, 59; magistrates register servants, 81

Abraham, ship, 62–66

Adams, Eleanor, 107

Advertisements: for British emigration, 53–55; for German emigration, 50–51; influence emigration, 57–58; of servants' sale, 221

Africa, ship, 198

Allison, Robert, 242

American Revolution: servants' attitude toward, 263; servants' enlistment in, 283–84

Amity, ship: transports Irish, 167; transports Quakers, 178

Annapolis, Md.: Irish convicts sent to, 135; ships trading to with servants, 346 n. 42

Anne, ship, 198

Anne Arundel county, Md.: court cases, 268; orders security for convicts' good behavior, 130

Anthony, Thomas, 62

Antigua: establishes code of laws for servants, 228; freedom dues in, 238; government pays for servants, 32; rebels of 1715 sent to, 198; regulates clothing for servants, 237; requires one servant to ten Negroes,

31; statistics on immigration to, 309, 310; term of servitude in, 230

Apprentices. *See* Children

Arbuckles, William, 185

Argyle uprising, 184–85

Artisans: encouraged to go to Va., 9; servants trained as, 291–92

Atley, Charles, 107

Baird, James: convict ship of wrecked, 127; transports convicts, 116

Baldwin, Abraham, 124

Baltimore, Lord, 121

Baltimore county, Md.: orders security for convicts' good behavior, 130; riots against recruiting servants, 282

Banishment: as penalty for rogues and vagabonds, 137–38; as penalty in Scotland, 133; for Scottish Covenanters, 376; transportation sentence commuted to, 366

Barbados: accepts convicts, 104; allows servants to sue, 234; British navy recruits servants in, 280; clothing for servants regulated, 237; convicts sent to, 117; courts enforce payment for servants, 31; courts free servants, 248; defines terms of servitude for Monmouth rebels, 194; demand for servants low in, 34; establishes code of laws for servants, 227; food for servants

AMERICAN HISTORY TITLES IN THE NORTON LIBRARY

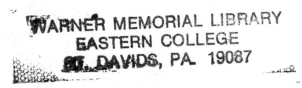